POPULISTS AND PATRICIANS

POPULISTS AND PATRICIANS

Essays in Modern German History

DAVID BLACKBOURN
Birkbeck College, University of London

London
ALLEN & UNWIN
Boston Sydney Wellington

Allen & Unwin, the academic imprint of
Unwin Hyman Ltd
PO Box 18, Park Lane, Hemel Hempstead, Herts HP2 4TE, UK
40 Museum Street, London WC1A 1LU, UK
37/39 Queen Elizabeth Street, London SE1 2QB

Allen & Unwin Inc.,
8 Winchester Place, Winchester, Mass. 01890, USA

Allen & Unwin (Australia) Ltd,
8 Napier Street, North Sydney, NSW 2060, Australia

Allen & Unwin (New Zealand) Ltd in association with the Port Nicholson Press Ltd,
60 Cambridge Terrace, Wellington, New Zealand

First published in 1987

British Library Cataloguing in Publication Data

Blackbourn, David
Populists and patricians : essays in modern German history.
1. Germany – History – 1866–1871
2. Germany – History – 1871–
I. Title
943.08 DD210
ISBN 0–04–943047–5

Library of Congress Cataloging-in-Publication Data

Blackbourn, David, 1949–
Populists and patricians.
Includes index.
1. Germany–Politics and government–19th century.
2. Germany–Politics and government–20th century.
3. Social classes–Germany–History–19th century.
4. Social classes–Germany–History–20th century.
I. Title.
DD204.B53 1987 305.5'0943 87–1416
ISBN 0–04–943047–5 (alk. paper)

Typeset in Garamond by MCL Computerset Ltd, Ely, Cambridgeshire and printed in Great Britain by Biddles Ltd, Guildford and Kings Lynn

For Debbie

Contents

Acknowledgements

It is a pleasure to thank the many individuals and institutions that have helped to make this book possible. I have to thank, first, the following journals and publishers, and the appropriate editors, for permission to reprint material that first appeared elsewhere: *Archiv für Sozialgeschichte*, *European History Quarterly* (formerly *European Studies Review*), *History Today*, Holmes & Meier, the *Journal of Modern History* and the University of Chicago Press, the *London Review of Books*, Macmillan and Crane Russak, Methuen, *Past and Present*.

There are two important general debts I should like to acknowledge. The following essays are based on work done in many libraries and archives in Britain and West Germany, and I should like to express my appreciation for the helpfulness their members of staff have invariably shown me over the years. Most of these essays also began life as papers or lectures, and I am very aware of the contribution made by audiences in Britain, West Germany and the United States in helping to curb my errors and sharpen my ideas.

I am very grateful to Birkbeck College, University of London, for granting a year of sabbatical leave in 1984–5, during which I was able to work on Chapters 10 and 11, and to put together some of the material and arguments in Chapter 7. I should also like to express my appreciation of the financial support provided by the Alexander von Humboldt Foundation, Bonn, during the same period. The Institute for European History in Mainz was my second home in 1984–5, as it has been on previous occasions.

Some of my individual scholarly debts are recorded in the notes that follow each chapter, but I should like here to express particular thanks to a number of people. Geoffrey Crossick and Gerhard Haupt have contributed much to my thinking on the petty bourgeoisie, and Chapter 5 has greatly benefited from their ideas. Nicholas Hope, Hugo Lacher and Kaspar von Greyerz have my thanks for encouraging me, in their different ways, to develop my earlier works on German Catholics in new directions. Together with a number of London colleagues, Dick Bessel tried hard to impose some discipline on the ideas in Chapter 11, and he also commented valuably on a draft of the introduction and Chapters 1–3. I should like, finally, to express my thanks to Geoff Eley. He and I have been discussing many of the questions addressed in this book since the early 1970s, and this collection would be the poorer without the exchange of ideas with him and the stimulus it has provided. The notes that accompany the following essays provide a reminder that historians are all engaged in a collaborative enterprise. My largest debt is the one most difficult to acknowledge directly, for it is owed to the many friends and colleagues who have helped to shape the arguments in this book by their suggestions, discussions or raised eyebrows. They should at least know that I am aware of what is owed to them.

I am grateful to Allen & Unwin and Jane Harris-Matthews for their encouragement and patience. The thanks I owe to my wife Debbie for so many reasons cannot be properly expressed here. This book is dedicated to her.

London, *October 1986*

Introduction

I

This book contains eleven essays, all written since the late 1970s and dealing with various aspects of German history in the nineteenth century and the first third of the twentieth. There is a brief preface to each essay which tries to set it in an immediate context, and notes the place of original publication. In this introduction I want to talk more generally about the contents of the collection, pulling together the common threads of the essays and discussing the broad historiographical background.

The British historian of a foreign country necessarily leads something of a double life. On the one hand he spends a great deal of time in that country and tries to make a contribution to its history on equal terms with native practitioners. Sometimes he will acquire a 'second identity', in the manner of a Richard Cobb;[1] more usually he will enjoy the tension – and it is enjoyable – of being part-insider and part-outsider in the adoptive culture. On the other hand he has the task of interpreting his chosen country to an Anglo-Saxon audience which has no direct access to the primary sources or to most of the secondary literature. Trying to convey the feel and texture of another nation's history is obviously not straightforward. The problems that arise, for example, over when and how to translate certain terms invariably reflect genuine cultural and conceptual differences. When, as in the German case, the native historiography is extremely rich and sophisticated, discharging this obligation becomes even more important. I therefore want to begin by outlining some of the major debates in German historical writing against which the essays in this book should be read.

Until the early 1960s West German historical writing shared much of the confined, conservative character of the Federal Republic during the Adenauer years.[2] The historical 'guild' (*Zunft*) reflected the paternalist and rather complacent mood that existed in Bonn and the provinces alike, and in institutions such as the churches and the schools. The mainstream of historical research and teaching remained heavily indebted to a subject matter and an approach that had their origins in the great founding period of modern German historical scholarship in the middle of the nineteenth century. This meant, first, a central preoccupation with political history understood within the context of state-building and the relations of the great powers. Hence the widely employed phrase *Der Primat der Außenpolitik*, the primacy of foreign policy, to describe this orientation. From Bismarck's Germany to Adenauer's, political history in this narrow sense was commonly designated 'general history'.[3] At the same time, members of the guild – which was still very small in the period – remained generally committed to the classic canon of German historicism, which stressed the need for an intuitive, 'understanding' (*verstehend*) approach to the individual historical actor in order to explain the unique historical event.[4] This conception of historical understanding, unexceptionable in itself, had come to assume a frozen and highly conservative form, manifested in a fixed hostility towards any kind of comparative history, together with a dismissal of economic and social history and of approaches drawn from the social sciences.[5]

Up to the early 1960s, therefore, important questions remained unasked in West German historiography, and more critical voices went largely unheard. Awkward figures had often in the past been rendered marginal by the guild: the advocate of cultural history, Karl Lamprecht, before the First World War; liberal or left-liberal historians such as Johannes Ziekursch, Veit Valentin and Eckart Kehr in the Weimar Republic.[6] This pattern was apparent once again in the 1950s. Take, for example, the cases of Hans Rosenberg and Francis Carsten, both of whom had emigrated from Nazi Germany. In the 1950s both wrote methodologically imaginative books that dealt with the emergence of the modern Prussian state and diverged from the ingrained tendency among conservative historians to identify with Prussian traditions. Each met a hostile response at the hands of reviewers, and was denied a full German reception by the decision not to publish his work in Germany.[7] Gerhard Ritter, often called 'the dean of German historians', was a crucial figure here. In 1931 he had suggested that the 'Bolshevik' Eckart Kehr should follow an academic career in Russia (in fact Kehr died young as an *émigré* in America). Then, in the late 1950s, Ritter hindered a German edition of Rosenberg's book on the Prussian bureaucracy, aristocracy and monarchical autocracy by his 'curtly dismissive opinion'.[8] It was clearly not just in methodological terms that the works of Rosenberg and Carsten were considered offensive. Both raised matters of substance and interpretation that ran against the conventional wisdom, above all in questioning the indulgent view of historic Prussia and its elites that generally prevailed. The criticism Rosenberg and Carsten faced was similar to that which befell historians within West Germany during the 1950s, such as Ludwig Dehio and Otto Büsch, who were also attacked when they offered a critical appraisal of Prussian values and institutions, and thus – if only implicitly – raised the question of the responsibility that these might have borne for the German catastrophe of the twentieth century.[9]

The dominant conservative historians of these years, it should be clearly said, were no apologists for the Third Reich. Indeed, Ritter himself had been imprisoned as a member of the group around Goerdeler that was implicated in the July 1944 plot against Hitler. In approaching the German past, however, they sought to isolate the events of 1933–45 from the history of the preceding years. On this reading, Hitler was a demonic, elemental force. His support was seen as a product of the bewitching power exerted by an outsider, to be explained as a late and bitter fruit of the 'mass politics' first unleashed by the French Revolution.[10] This patrician emphasis on the activist, revolutionary pedigree of National Socialism had an important corollary: it effectively denied any continuity between Bismarck's Germany and Hitler's, between the sober statesmen of the Prussian elite, such as Bismarck himself or Bethmann Hollweg, and the revolutionary gangsters who had seized power in 1933. Such a reading also underlined the absolute distinction between the origins of the First World War and those of the Second. For if Hitler, the special case, had instigated the latter, it was not conceded that the former was a German responsibility. The dominant school of West German historians up to the early 1960s argued, as their predecessors had done more aggressively in the 1920s, that in 1914 the powers had all slithered into war.[11]

These prevailing assumptions were subjected to a historiographical revolution in the 1960s, just as other institutions in the Federal Republic underwent a long-delayed and often intense bout of self-examination. A series of debates broke out which re-opened fundamental questions about the German past, and about the continuity of modern German history. One obvious area of discussion was the nature of National Socialism, as writers such as the political scientist Karl Dietrich Bracher and the historian Hans Mommsen began to develop interpretations concerning the structural features of the Third Reich that went well beyond arguments about Hitler himself or Hitlerism.[12] A further area of revision, less often noted by subsequent commentators, centred on the German revolution of 1918–19. A series of well-documented studies explored the democratic qualities of the ultimately unsuccessful 'council movement' during the revolution, questioning the easy assumption that it had been a mere tool of Bolshevism, and suggesting that the failure of the revolution beyond the formal political level had bequeathed a dangerous legacy to the Weimar Republic.[13] The line of argument here was similar to that put forward in the major work published by Barrington Moore in 1966, *The Social Origins of Dictatorship and Democracy*, which argued persuasively that the absence of revolution, or failed revolution, could have political consequences as explosive as those of successful revolution. Germany and Japan played an important part in Moore's schema, for he suggested that, in part as a prophylactic against revolution from below, they had instead experienced a potentially dangerous 'revolution from above'. On this reading, the final price for the avoidance of revolution from below had been paid in the form of fascism. In each case, he argued, it was the actions of traditional elites, of conservative modernisers in the nineteenth century, which set the historical course leading to twentieth-century fascism. In Japan this role was ascribed to the architects of the Meiji Restoration; in the German case it was filled by the Prussian Junkers, with Bismarck at their head.[14]

Barrington Moore's book was widely discussed among younger German historians and was translated into German in 1969. Long before then, however, many of its arguments had entered German historical debate more directly. They did so as the result of a further and more explosive debate concerned initially with the origins of the First World War. The 'Fischer controversy' has by now itself become an historical episode, the subject of numerous books and articles.[15] In 1961 the Hamburg historian Fritz Fischer published a book, *Griff nach der Weltmacht*, dealing with German aims in the First World War. He argued at length that the German role during the July crisis of 1914 was more aggressive and intransigent than had generally been assumed, and he sought to document the consistency of German expansionist ambitions during the war itself. This in itself would have prompted major debate, particularly since Fischer questioned the distinction between the 'bad Germans' in the High Command and Pan-German League, and 'good Germans' like Chancellor Bethmann Hollweg. It was two further features of the book, however, which established it as a symbolic landmark in postwar West German historiography. First, Fischer explicitly suggested lines of continuity between German aims in the two World Wars. Secondly, he pointed to the role played by economic interests in Wilhelmine Germany and stressed the domestic social and political instability that existed in Germany on the eve of the First World War. These two emphases help to explain the hostility that Fischer and his relatively small group of mainly younger supporters faced, from the then Christian Democratic government as well as from the historical establishment. As had occurred in the earlier rejection of works by Eckart Kehr and Hans Rosenberg, Fischer's book met with hostility on grounds both of interpretation and method. Gerhard Ritter, for example, indignantly denied the legitimacy of comparisons between German foreign policy before 1914 and in the 1930s, between the Imperial Germany created by Bismarck and Hitler's Third Reich. Moreover, those wedded to the pure historicist approach were unsympathetic towards the anonymous forces they believed Fischer had introduced with his talk of economic and social interests. This combination of political and methodological aversion prompted some to suggest that Fischer would be more at home in the German Democratic Republic.

Commenting on the Fischer controversy 'Fifteen Years After', one of his strongest supporters recorded gloomily how little Fischer's interpretation seemed to have influenced the accounts given in best-selling German textbooks.[16] Volker Berghahn illustrated his point by looking at subsequent discussions of the July crisis. Yet it is not in Fischer's treatment of July 1914, or his ambitious contentions about Germany's active preparations for pre-emptive war from 1912, that the essential strength and significance of the book lie. Many who are broadly in sympathy with the thrust of Fischer's thesis would now accept that his arguments on these particular points require qualification. *Griff nach der Weltmacht* was important because it broke a taboo and prompted new questions. At the most general level it gave a stimulus to historians who were impatient with what they believed was the complacency in the Federal Republic towards the German past, and with the historical guild which they reproached for reinforcing this complacency. One result was a zealous crusade against conservative historicism in the name of a critical, emancipatory history. Building on isolated initiatives of the 1950s from historians like Werner Conze, and consciously drawing on approaches that had long been employed outside Germany, an important generation of West German historians launched a long overdue debate about the relations of history with neighbouring social sciences, the nature of 'social history', and the civic function of the discipline.[17] The strongly political and pedagogic element in this intellectual movement certainly derived in part from the moral charge that interpretation of the recent historical past carries in contemporary Germany, and from the seriousness with which these issues are debated. It probably acquired a particularly sharp edge because many of those who carried the debate to their opponents in the 1960s belonged to the generation that had joined the Hitler Youth, manned anti-aircraft guns in 1945 as adolescents, or travelled to the West as young refugees from former German territories.[18] Personal experience helped to forge their critical perspective, rather as it did in the case of a writer like Günter Grass (although most of the historians in question were a little younger). Their arguments formed only one part of a much broader and very vigorous debate that took place in West German society during the 1960s about its own past.

II

The interpretation of modern German history that emerged from the revisionism of the 1960s looked very different from what had preceded it. In the first place the emphasis was now placed very firmly on the way in which German foreign policy was a product of society and politics at home, rather than the other way round. When, in 1965, one of the leading new historians edited a collection of Eckart Kehr's essays from the 1920s, he stood the old Rankean axiom of the guild historians on its head by giving his book the provocative title 'The Primacy of Domestic Policy'.[19] Stress was also placed on the continuity rather than discontinuity of German history from Bismarck to Hitler. Following Fritz Fischer's lead, the economic, social and political structures of Imperial Germany came under the microscope, examined not only for what they might reveal about German responsibility for the First World War, but also for their bearing on the long-term reasons for German susceptibility to fascism in the interwar period. In the space of a few years a number of major historical studies appeared, sharing this broad approach to the recent German past and dealing with central aspects of the Imperial period: the role of the army and bureaucracy in Bismarck's 'Prussia-Germany'; the roots of German imperialism in the 1880s; the flaws and restrictions in German political life under Bismarck and his successors; the domestic function of battleship building and the aggressive foreign policy under Wilhelm II; the winners and losers of the economic policy pursued in Germany between the 1870s and 1914.[20]

These studies played variations on a striking central theme. This was the idea of a peculiar pattern of German history, a *Sonderweg* or special road that set Germany apart from the West in its modern development.[21] The idea, it should be emphasised, was not invented by West German historians of the time. But those who had talked in the past about a German *Sonderweg* had usually been inclined to endow it with a positive value. Thus nineteenth-century, university-educated Germans frequently exalted the particular German combination of political, economic, military and educational institutions. The German blend of monarchy and industrial success, army and university, signified for many the happy triumph of a solution to modern problems superior to that achieved elsewhere. A belief that the 'excesses' of French or British parliamentary democracy had been kept at bay, coupled with complacent assumptions about the importance of 'spiritual' rather than merely 'materialist' values in the new Germany, belonged to the same broad set of views. Where *hubris* of this kind was found, it frequently manifested itself in feelings of superiority *vis-à-vis* England. The historian Treitschke was not alone in his scornful view that the mean-spirited, unheroic English confused soap and civilization. A similar indictment of America became common at the end of the century. Those who admired the raw energy and social flux of the new world power, such as Max Weber, belonged very much to a minority among academic and professional middle-class opinion.[22] The outbreak of war gave a fillip to notions of a positive German *Sonderweg*, expressed in the supposed superiority of the German 'ideas of 1914' over the Western 'ideas of 1789'. Attitudes of this kind retained a powerful hold in the years of the Weimar Republic, not least among historians.[23]

The idea of a positive special German road was still residually present in the thinking of conservative German historians after the Second World War. But the Third Reich and the total defeat of 1945 had naturally done much to discredit it, even among those who preferred anyway to believe that Hitler had been an aberration. The postwar idea of the *Sonderweg* had negative connotations. To the question 'how was the German catastrophe possible?' came the answer: 'because of Germany's fateful divergence from the Western pattern of historical development'. In the 1950s and early 1960s it had been *émigré* and other Anglo-Saxon historians who, understandably perhaps, made most of the running in arguing this case. Some talked of Germany's unique geographical position between East and West; others looked for the key to German peculiarity in the tradition of militarism; yet others turned their attention to intellectual history in an effort to capture the peculiar 'German mind'.[24] Such an influential historian as A. J. P. Taylor could be said to have woven many of these strands together in his writing on modern German history. Elements of all these approaches survive in the Anglo-Saxon literature. Since the 1960s, however, it is the Anglo-Saxon re-educators who have been re-educated. For it has been West German historians who have taken up the running in turning the old, positive idea of the *Sonderweg* on its head.

The emphasis on continuity that was given such a stimulus by the Fischer debate led in the work of German revisionist historians to a restatement of the thesis that German history had diverged disastrously from that of the West. And the terms in which these arguments were now couched showed the debt owed by the so-called critical school of historians to the social and political science models that they championed against the conservative guild. The central proposition concerned the partial modernization of Germany in the nineteenth century, now seen as the fundamental structural flaw that burdened German political development up to the Nazi period.[25] Germany, as everyone agreed, had become a great industrial power in the era of Bismarck and Wilhelm II. But, it was argued, there had been no corresponding transformation of social and political life. The failure of revolution from below in 1848 had been followed by a Bismarckian revolution from above which unified Germany and consolidated the basis for dynamic economic advance, yet left the institutional and political framework of old Prussia intact. Thus the power and prestige of the Hohenzollern dynasty, the Prussian army and the bureaucracy persisted, closely linked with the continuing role played by a group now cast as the villains of modern German history: the landowning Junkers. The survival of the old elite, it was argued, went well beyond the fiscal privileges and agricultural tariff barriers the Junkers were able to win from a political system that favoured them. These material rewards were themselves a sign of the willingness of the German bourgeoisie – unlike, say, its Corn-Law repealing English counterpart – to compromise with the landed elite. In economic terms this meant the much-vaunted 'marriage of iron and rye', whereby conservatively inclined heavy industrialists allied with the Junker estate owners against more liberal, internationally minded capitalists, and against the German consumer. In social terms it meant the self-humbling of a German bourgeoisie that was unhealthily in awe of the strong state and increasingly aped the values of the old elite, as transmitted by the reserve officer corps, a bureaucracy in which the Junkers continued to play a major role, and student corporations which embodied 'Prussian' virtues through practises such as duelling. This process of social self-abasement has generally been referred to as the feudalization of the bourgeoisie.[26]

According to this interpretation it was in the political sphere that Germany paid the largest price for its partial modernization. For the old pre-industrial elite remained entrenched, protected by the 'sham constitutionalism' of the Imperial German political system, the reactionary three-class franchise to the Prussian parliament, and the effective dominance of Prussia within the politics of the Reich. The army, which enjoyed a sheltered position within the constitution, added to the traditional weapons wielded by the old elite; for its availability as a potentially repressive force at home cowed the advocates of reform by presenting a 'permanent threat of *Staatsstreich*', or right-wing *coup d'état*. But it was not the merely repressive features of the Prusso-German political system that received most emphasis from revisionist historians. Imperial Germany, after all, was not Tsarist Russia. Greater attention was paid to the more sophisticated political repertoire allegedly developed by the ruling elite in order to preserve its dominant position. Thus the political parties, for example, were played off against each other by Bismarck, emasculated to the point where they became the vehicles of economic interests. The bourgeoisie was tied to the status quo by the process of feudalization, and through the receipt of titles and honours. More broadly, family, church and school served to inculcate obedience, while the army became the 'school of the nation'. Moreover, the support of potential adherents to the old order, such as the peasantry and petty bourgeoisie of master craftsmen and small shopkeepers, was actively encouraged through a policy of agricultural tariffs and economic 'reinsurance' for the small man.[27] It was also these social groups, so it was maintained, whose apprehensions and resentments about the modern world allowed them to be wooed by a conservative elite that identified convenient scapegoats such as the Jews. The Great Depression of 1873–96 was pinpointed as the seed-time of this popularized politics of the right.[28]

In short, the work of the 1960s and early 1970s suggested an old elite whose stubborn persistence in power was matched by tactical flexibility. More Bonapartist than Bourbon, it looked for – and found – popular allies against liberalism, socialism and other challenges to the existing distribution of power. The figure of Bismarck played an important part in this new interpretation. In the works of historians such as Hans-Ulrich Wehler and Michael Stürmer he was portrayed, not as a statesmanlike conservative, but as a Bonapartist who used foreign policy success to head off reform at home ('social imperialism'), and aimed to dish the liberals by introducing universal manhood suffrage to the new German national parliament, the Reichstag. The subsequent use by Bismarck of imperialist ventures and war scares, and the branding of minorities like the Catholics and Social Democrats as internal 'enemies of the Reich', were brought within the same framework of interpretation.[29] The policies pursued under Wilhelm II did not represent therefore the recklessness of a callow and wilful young ruler, but the continuation of a pattern set by Bismarck himself. The threat of a *coup d'état* continued to be held in reserve. The peasantry and petty bourgeoisie were further encouraged to ally themselves with the Junker landowners, especially after the founding of the Conservative-fostered Agrarian League in 1893. The friend–foe distinction continued to serve Germany's rulers as a means of rallying support behind throne and altar. Above all, it was contended, an aggressive foreign policy remained a means of deflecting domestic criticism.[30] As one leading historian remarked of the decision to build a battle fleet, 'Tirpitz's naval policy was nothing less than an ambitious plan to stabilise the Prusso-German political system and to paralyse the pressure for change.' The role of popular organizations like the Navy League was viewed in the same light.[31]

Arguments of this kind reinforced many of Fritz Fischer's conclusions by providing evidence about the social and political instability of Imperial Germany. On this reading, German 'encirclement' on the eve of the First World War was not only largely self-imposed, but also the result of policies aimed at staving off domestic reform.[32] An aggressive tariff policy had created resentment abroad, especially in Russia. Foreign suspicion was further fuelled by the German gambit of whipping up nationalist sentiment at home as a means of rallying popular support behind the status quo. The anti-English feeling that accompanied the naval policy provided the most obvious example. Moreover, the material burden of high armaments expenditure on both army and navy, coupled with the shortcomings of a tax system that virtually exempted the owners of large landed wealth, produced mounting financial difficulties in the years after 1909. When, all the efforts of the ruling elite notwithstanding, the Social Democrats became the largest single party in the Reichstag in 1912, a dangerously unstable domestic situation ensued. Conservative intransigence, financial strains, and a threatening international situation combined to produce a growing pessimism among both military and civilian members of the elite. It was this background of cumulative domestic crisis, so it was argued, that compelled the 'escape forwards' into war in 1914.[33] For revisionist historians, the costs of Germany's failure to modernize its institutions in line with its economy were therefore deferred once again. Not until 1918 did the price for these evasions begin to be paid, as the privations of war reacted with unsolved social and political problems to bring about the revolutionary downfall of the Empire.

But if most of these historians concentrated on Imperial Germany, the real message of their accounts did not stop in 1918. As Hans-Ulrich Wehler put it, in the general work that more than any other symbolized the new departure, 'the guiding question underlying this book has been to investigate why Hitler's National Socialist regime came to power some dozen years after the end of the monarchy'.[34] For on this reading, the fateful survival of the pre-industrial elite into the formal democracy of Weimar marked a continuing obstacle to real institutional reform. The Kaiser may have gone, but the power of the army, the bureaucracy and the Junkers remained, along with the habits of social deference and obedience to the state that they had encouraged. It was they who did much to destabilize the Weimar Republic, and who ultimately helped Hitler into the saddle. National Socialism, accordingly, was no aberration, but the product of a malign continuity in modern German history that could be traced back at least as far as the founding of Imperial Germany under Bismarck.

III

This approach to modern German history constituted a watershed, a 'paradigm shift' in Wehler's words. It marked, first of all, a major change in the way German historians sought to 'come to terms with the past'.[35] In addition, the revisionists did much to stimulate discussion about the historical discipline, effectively rediscovered the work of previously neglected historians like Kehr and Rosenberg, and gave a fillip to research in fields that were previously more advanced in Britain or France, such as the family and social mobility. The so-called critical school also emerged at a time of major debate over the structure of West German higher education, when the opening of new universities helped to increase the numbers of academic staff and students in history departments more than fourfold between 1960 and 1975.[36] Part of the ferment of these years was seen in the founding of new journals (especially *Geschichte und Gesellschaft*), monograph and textbook series and historical readers that enabled the new arguments to be aired.

By 1976 one American historian had already referred to the existence of a 'new orthodoxy'.[37] This was never strictly true, if the phrase is considered against the background of West German history and historians as a whole. The revisionists were, for one thing, concerned almost exclusively with modern history; their work seldom touched on interpretation of the medieval and early modern periods. Moreover, the bulk of German historical research continued to be unaffected by the debates of these years. This is true of almost all of the work within the strong West German tradition of local and regional history; it is also true of most of the research conducted within the Catholic historical camp, where innovatory tendencies associated with figures such as Max Braubach and Rudolf Morsey followed a quite separate course. The critical school constituted one current among many, as the programmes of the biennial German Historical Conferences demonstrate. Furthermore, developments since the middle of the 1970s suggest a considerable reaction to the new arguments.[38] Thoughtful critics such as Thomas Nipperdey have rightly reminded us about the non-moralizing virtues of the historicist tradition, while warning against the dangers of confining nineteenth-century German history in a straitjacket of interpretation.[39] The conservative sea-change (*Tendenzwende*) in the Federal Republic since the later 1970s has also been accompanied by much acrimonious sniping at figures like Wehler from historians calling for a return to pure political history.[40] At the same time, what appeared as emancipatory in the 1960s seemed to many younger German historians to have reached the limits of its usefulness. The debates at the 1984 German Historical Conference in West Berlin brought into the open a series of differences between the 'middle generation' which had provided the pioneers of the 1960s, and a younger generation. The latter were more sceptical about the application of historical models drawn from American social and political science, and particularly about the lingering attachment to theories of 'modernization' that characterized the main protagonists of the critical school. These younger historians were drawn more to the example of work done by social anthropologists such as Clifford Geertz, to the French *Annales* school, and to British historians such as E. P. Thompson. These, it was believed, often had more to say to historians concerned to explore the broadly cultural sphere in the history of society that had been neglected in the work of the 1960s and early 1970s, particularly in the task of recovering and interpreting the realm of 'experience'. The conviction that history – and especially the history of those at the bottom of society – can and should be written 'from below and from within' has been a driving belief behind the explosion of works in recent years dealing with the history of everyday life, or *Alltagsgeschichte*.[41] The analogues between this historical trend and broader movements of opinion and sentiment among the under-40s in West German society – Green politics, scepticism about 'progress' and Americanization, a new interest in small communities and *Heimat* – are as clear as the links between historical revisionism and wider social and political debates in the 1960s.[42]

My own research on German history began in 1970, and my ideas have developed against a backcloth of the debates described above. Readers will find consideration in this book of arguments put forward by the older conservative school of historians, especially on the supposedly 'revolutionary' roots of National Socialism, and by German historians of political Catholicism. They will also find signs of the interest I share with many of my German (and non-German) contemporaries in a social history from below that does justice both to the cultural sphere, broadly defined, and to the importance of experience, as well as to the questions that so exercised revisionist historians of the 1960s and 1970s.

Above all, however, the following essays form part of the dialogue that continues between the German historians who emerged in the wake of Fritz Fischer, and many of their Anglo-Saxon colleagues in the same field. For if it would be untrue to portray the history written by the former as a 'new orthodoxy' in the Federal Republic itself, its impact on historians of modern Germany working in Britain and North America can hardly be exaggerated. This is true, in part, because of the way these historians have re-established a link with the work of *émigré* scholars in those countries, as well as drawing widely on the canon of American social and political science. It is also partly a result of their own close contacts with individuals and institutions in North America and Britain. The internationalism – or, at any rate, the Atlanticism – of scholars such as Wehler, Berghahn, Puhle, Witt and Kocka has helped to internationalise the study of modern German history. But it is, above all, the quality of their contributions to historical debate that has justly given them such an important position. The interpretation they have offered of Germany's troubled 'passage to modernity' remains cogent and compelling, an advance both on older, quasi-apologist approaches and on much of the work done in the same field by historians in the German Democratic Republic.

I have tried to make clear in two earlier books how much my own approach owes to this body of work, but also where my research has led me to different conclusions.[43] I have become more sceptical over the years about the version of continuity in modern German history that relentlessly catalogues the malign role played by pre-industrial elites and institutions. This is partly because of the way in which the pattern of German history has been judged against a yardstick of 'Western' historical development and found wanting. Such an approach, particularly when it has become implicit and ingrained, has often seemed to offer an idealised picture of the course of British and French history, one that would be rejected by most historians of those countries. It has certainly led to a sometimes startlingly truncated picture of German history itself. We hear much about the Germany of the spiked helmet and too little about top-hatted Germany, much about the feudalization of the German bourgeoisie and too little about the embourgeoisement of German society, much about the power of a pre-industrial elite and too little about the effects of capitalism in structuring German society and politics. Many fields of social-historical enquiry that have attracted British, French or American scholars have remained very thinly cultivated in Germany. They include the history of law, associational life, the professions, philanthropy, and local elites – all, not coincidentally, spheres of life where bourgeois strength was more apparent than bourgeois weakness.[44] I have discussed elsewhere the bearing of these points on the way we regard the 'peculiarities of German history', and some of the main lines of argument are sketched in Chapter 4. For that reason I do not want here to provide a systematic account of my own position in the recently renewed debate over the German *Sonderweg*. Readers should bear this general background in mind, however, when considering the points raised in the remainder of this introduction.

The first of these concerns geography and what we understand when we talk about Germany in this period. It has often been remarked that the revisionists of the 1960s retained much of the framework favoured by their conservative predecessors, but turned the moral judgements upside down. Nowhere is this clearer than in their preoccupation with events at the centre of what is habitually termed 'Prussia–Germany'. This Prussocentric perspective is potentially misleading in a number of ways. The area of central Europe that became Imperial Germany was strikingly heterogeneous. There was not even a standard German time until the coming of the railway, and nineteenth-century travellers frequently remarked on the great social and cultural differences between states and regions. These were not residues of a long-standing provincialism that disappeared in the Imperial melting pot. A sense of identification with the local state actually grew during the phase of state-building that occurred in the nineteenth century. When, after 1871, German-wide standardization took place in matters like communications and currency, it was accompanied by the celebration of diversity in other spheres such as language and 'traditions'. Unification may even have encouraged this trend, giving an extra fillip to the stage Bavarian and other stylised manifestations of local loyalty. We may not want to take this too seriously (although we probably should); but it is impossible to ignore the state-particularist dimension in Imperial German politics. Bismarck's celebrated 'revolution from above' did, after all, create a federal rather than a unitary Reich. Within the new Germany the individual states retained their own parliaments, police forces and powers of taxation. Even as Imperial Germany became *de facto* more unitary in a political and constitutional sense, the imprint of regional and local aspirations on national politics remained crucially important.

It is perhaps unfortunate that in Germany two strong historical traditions have developed in such a way that they reinforce their mutual isolation: one tradition concerned with the central state (which is strongly echoed by revisionist historians), another that occupies itself exclusively with local history. There is good reason why we should seek to integrate what was happening in the regions into our understanding of Germany as a whole. That means taking seriously the individual states such as Bavaria, Saxony, Baden, Thuringia – and Prussia. Prussia was by far the largest and most powerful of the states that composed the Reich, and it enjoyed an undeniable special status. That is fully reflected in many of the essays below. But Prussia itself was a more heterogeneous and contradictory state than we commonly associate with the idea of 'Prussia'. We should not limit our sights to Berlin, or to the Junker heartland east of the Elbe referred to so often by historians. Prussia stretched in the nineteenth century from what is today Kaliningrad in the east to the left bank of the Rhine in the west. It was the home of the great estate owners, but also the motor of German industrialization in the decades before and after unification. It formed the Protestant core of a Protestant-dominated Lesser Germany, but also contained more than half of the Catholics in the Reich (and well over twice as many Catholics as Bavaria). Historic Prussia and what it stood for was important in the new Germany, but not all-important. The view from official Berlin or from East Elbia can lead us to neglect other aspects of Prussia, just as a preoccupation with 'Prussia–Germany' can lead us to neglect other parts of the Reich.

Many of these points no doubt struck me with particular force because I began my research looking not only at a southern state, but at the Catholic minority within it. Catholics made up just over a third of the population in the Empire of 1871 and were distributed in a German variant of the British Celtic Fringe to the west, east and south of the Reich. The neglect of this important minority by exponents of the 'new orthodoxy' has been almost as complete as its neglect by their conservative predecessors in the historical guild. The history of Catholics has been left to the Catholic historians, just as the regional perspective has been left to the regional historians. It has in fact been widely noted in recent years that German Catholics fit very awkwardly into the model propounded by revisionist historians.[46] It is not simply that a number of generalizations come unstuck when applied to Catholics, true though that is (see Chapters 7–9). In a more positive spirit, there are two respects at least in which the experience of German Catholics can give us a better understanding of how Imperial Germany worked. In the first place, Catholics inhabited a political and economic ghetto, which some wished to leave and others to render more secure against the outside world. These tensions within the Catholic Celtic Fringe, and especially the contradictory attitudes towards state authority on the one hand and material progress on the other, have considerable significance for the larger history of Imperial Germany.

Secondly – and ironically – through the Centre Party for which the majority of them voted, German Catholics came to play a pivotal role in shaping the political life of the Reich. Attacked and disdained as a disloyal and backward minority, Catholics took their revenge by making themselves an indispensable part of the political system. That is one reason (although only one) for the depth of anti-Catholic sentiment in Imperial Germany. Neither the representative character of Catholic Germany, nor the importance of the role played in German politics by the Catholic Centre Party, can be easily fitted into the account of Germany given by post-Fischer historians. Both can be seen more clearly when attention is shifted from 'Prussia-Germany' to Germany as a whole.

This point does not apply only to Catholics. There were many other Germanies even within the Protestant Reich, from states with powerful liberal traditions such as Oldenburg and Württemberg, to those like Saxony and Hamburg where the local species of conservatism owed little to the Prussian model. This widening of perspective is particularly helpful in making sense of the popular movements of the right that emerged in Imperial Germany, and are discussed below in Chapters 5, 6 and 10 especially. A large number of these new movements were based in the south and west, or in central Germany. This is true of the Christian Peasant associations that were linked to the Centre Party, and it applies equally to independent agrarian organisations like the Bavarian Peasant League and the Otto Böckel movement, with its main support in Hessen, Saxony and Thuringia. The leading centres of the *Mittelstand* movement of craftsmen and shokeepers were Saxony, Westphalia and Bavaria. The anti-semitic organisations of the late nineteenth century found support in these same areas. If there was a classic region of rural anti-semitism from the Wilhelmine period to the advent of National Socialism it was Hessen; and if one tried to pinpoint where a modern, pseudo-scientific and urban anti-semitism found most resonance, it would arguably be a Saxon city such as Dresden or Leipzig.[47] A similar geographical profile emerges if we look at radical nationalist organisations like the Pan-German and Navy Leagues. Recent studies by Geoff Eley and Roger Chickering have both emphasized the importance for radical nationalism of a broad central belt of Germany stretching from the Rhineland and Palatinate in the west, through Hessen to Thuringia and Saxony.[48] Indeed, this axis from Düsseldorf to Dresden was important generally for the emerging populist politics of the new right.

This is not to deny the existence or the importance of entrenched interests in Prussian East Elbia and in Berlin. The Junkers did enjoy a disproportionate influence at the highest political level and in the local Prussian bureaucracy, where administration was often estate management writ large.[49] They also dominated the Prussian Upper House, while the reactionary three-class franchise gave them a powerful block of seats in the Lower House. The problem for the historian is to establish the connection between this power-base and the new mass politics on the right: with the winning of peasants, craftsmen and ardent nationalists behind the old elite and the status quo. East Elbia was an adequate base for the old conservative politics of paternalism; it was quite inadequate to the new political tasks of making friends and influencing people. Where there were attempts by the old elite to mobilize a mass following on the right in the Imperial period, the terrain over which they fought necessarily lay outside their own narrow Prussian domains. This is clearly true of the organization so often cited as the classic vehicle of Junker political mobilization, the Agrarian League.[50] Had the League remained confined to East Elbia, it would hardly have been necessary in the first place (which was indeed the view taken by more old-fashioned Junkers). It was both necessary and important because it sought to rally support behind the old elite by 'popular' means in areas that were not at all susceptible to direct Junker control. In doing so it had to come to terms with patterns of local politics that could not be simply bent to the East Elbian will. James Hunt and Dan White have shown us what this meant in practice in Württemberg and Hessen respectively.[51] Our map of Germany ought, therefore, to extend beyond one particular – albeit highly important – part of Prussia. This is not a perverse or wilful insistence on regional diversity for its own sake. It is too easy a gambit to argue simply that things were much more complicated at the local level, although in this case it is clearly true. It is at least as important (and no less productive of generalizations) that we recognise the interaction between centre and periphery, between the narrow elite in Berlin and core-Prussia, and the rest of Germany.

That perspective informs many of the essays in this book. It is closely linked at many points with my scepticism about the usefulness of looking at modern German society and politics largely from the top down. To what extent, for example, can family, school and university really be seen as agents of an authoritarian socialization? When we look in any detail at these institutions, it becomes clear that such generalizations are difficult to sustain (see the essays below that deal with Catholics, or with the petty bourgeoisie). The points that need to be made here are comparable to those made about geography.

Not only has empirical work underlined the importance of class, religious, regional and other variables. No less important, we might do well to stop viewing the family or the school as one-way institutions. They were not so much transmission belts, as fields of force within which social and civic struggles were acted out. Similar considerations apply to the army. It is difficult to regard the army as the school of the nation *tout court*, even if it is made easier by the absence of a German work dealing in detail with, say, the effects of conscription in the way that Eugen Weber's *Peasants into Frenchmen* does in the French case.[52] There is certainly considerable evidence in the essays that follow of a marked anti-militarism in Imperial Germany – not only among workers, but among peasants and craftsmen as well, who resented the taxation costs, the loss of family labour entailed by conscription, and (in the case of peasants) the disruption associated with military exercises. We should also remember that conscription worked two ways. The army authorities were sufficiently concerned about the influence of socialist workers in the barracks that they tried to restrict the numbers of proletarian conscripts and banned Social Democratic publications among recruits; while the left-liberal Oskar Muser hoped that military service would heighten the dissatisfaction of young peasants with the supposed conservatism of rural life.[53]

Claims about the formative social and moral influence of the army on the German bourgeoisie also need to be placed in perspective. It is not difficult to think of bourgeois liberals who saw themselves as social imperialists and were committed to the extension of German power and influence overseas, yet were highly critical when it came to those parts of the armed forces that betrayed a Junker ethos.[54] On this point, if on few others, they found themselves in agreement with many middle-class Catholics, who adopted an increasingly '200 per cent German' stance in the Wilhelmine years, yet still had good reason to distrust the Prussian army. The latter had been used repressively against Catholics during the 1870s, and the composition of the officer corps continued to show a crass anti-Catholic discrimination (indeed, a Protestant officer who married a Catholic was expected to convert his bride or resign his commission). For a bourgeois liberal like Max Weber, or a bourgeois Catholic like the Centre leader Adolf Gröber, a sense of German identity was not only not reinforced by the Junker attributes of the army; it defined itself to some extent against those very qualities.[55] In both cases we find a position that has parallels with the dilemma of Social Democrats who wrestled with their celebrated 'double loyalty' as Social Democrats and as Germans. This is something rather different from the 'social militarism' supposedly disseminated through the army and reserve officer corps.

These points raise the question of how we should regard the state in modern Germany. Certainly the importance of the state constitutes a genuine difference between modern German history and that of Britain or the USA. In areas of life ranging from guild traditions to patterns of policing, the historical divergence is clear – although it is not at all so obvious if we compare Germany, in turn, with any Continental European country.[56] If revisionist historians are nevertheless right to argue about the importance of the state, the picture of the state they have presented requires some qualification. It is difficult to escape the conclusion that they have, once again, taken the account offered by an older, more conservative historiography and reversed all the moral signs. In place of the powerful, benign state standing above society we have a mighty and malign state occupying the same position. But the state was neither unchanging nor an entity that stood outside society. The enormous expansion of bureaucracy at all levels in the latter part of the nineteenth century – in education and training, the provision of welfare and social services, the manning of libraries and public utilities – made 'the state' a creature in the process of transforming itself. Its personnel expanded, its role changed. In the first place, the state did not simply embody the entrenched power of a pre-industrial elite. Those who fit this description certainly hung on stubbornly in the inner fastnesses of the foreign service, cavalry and guards regiments, and the Prussian field administration, and they enjoyed an influence out of proportion to their numbers. But their rearguard action, however impressive, has to be set against the growing numbers of factory inspectors, engine drivers, steamship booking clerks, schoolteachers and librarians who increasingly represented the public face of the state, and against the growing numbers of bourgeois consular officials and technical artillery experts from middle-class backgrounds.[57]

Moreover, we have to consider measures as well as men: the functions of the state as well as the social background of its leading servants. Here the familiar distinction between a dynamic German capitalism and a pre-modern German state becomes problematic. It was, after all, the state itself that did much to foster the new economic and social order in Germany, whether directly through railway construction, or indirectly through a wide range of legal, educational and other institutional changes which cut through the dead wood of 'backward' vested interests. The role of the state as the harbinger of a new social order during the *Kulturkampf* of the 1870s (see Chapter 7), and the scepticism of the state bureaucracy in practice when it came to propping up marginal craftsmen and shopkeepers (see Chapter 5), suggest just two examples of this process. This is not, of course, to argue that the German state was the creature of capitalist interests, only to question how far we can really maintain that it embodied the aspirations of a pre-industrial power elite. As I have argued elsewhere, it might make more sense to recognize the reciprocity between a bourgeois economic and social order, and a state that was itself in the process of change.[58] One writer has suggested that the state 'tolerated the bourgeois economy only to the extent that it could be used as a tool of the feudal state order'.[59] It might be wise to complete the proposition by adding that the reverse is also true: that the feudal-state order was tolerated only to the extent that it guaranteed the bourgeois economy.

Partly for this reason, it would also be misleading to view the state in Germany as an institution that helped to perpetuate wide-eyed obedience. As I try to show in a number of the essays below, popular attitudes towards bureaucrats could be antagonistic as well as deferential. It is arguable that perceptions of the state became similarly ambivalent. By the beginning of the twentieth century the state certainly continued to present itself as a model of disinterested authority, claiming to arbitrate in areas of social dispute as a kind of sternly benevolent umpire; but it also levied taxes, conscripted and interfered. The state in its many forms (Reich, federal states, municipalities) was both provider and scourge, employer and policeman. Its actions were perceived with correspondingly mixed feelings by many parts of the population. Certainly we should not underestimate the bull-frog arrogance of the petty official or the respect shown to the *Kommerzienrat*.[60] Nor should we disregard the mystique of the state, which Imperial Germany's rulers worked so hard to foster. But we should remember that there was another side to the story.

IV

The view from the top down can also present a partial picture when it comes to politics. Writing about Wehler's account of Imperial Germany, Thomas Nipperdey has commented that 'political movements and mentalities essentially fall into the role of objects, as the means of the great system of rule and its strategy of survival'.[61] There is much that falls through the historian's net if we proceed in this way. One is the reality of the political parties, which were much less inert than is often implied. German political parties were not simply played off against each other from above; nor were they merely the vehicles of interest groups, even if there is plenty of evidence in the following essays to underline the importance of this factor. We need to pay attention to the organizations and the communities of sentiment that bound the parties, as well as the material interests that helped both to sustain and to divide them. There were numerous sources of authentic division and mutual antipathy between the German political parties, and these deserve to be treated at least as seriously as the sticks and carrots wielded by a manipulative executive.[62] The leading German historians of the Imperial period have actually written curiously little about the character of party politics in the broadest sense.[63] Only in the last decade or so has a more detailed picture emerged, and it seems to confirm the importance of chronic party divisions for the opening and closing of political (and potentially constitutional) options in modern Germany. It also suggests that the origins and ramifications of these divisions were more complex than is often implied.[64] Successive governments from Bismarck onwards were not above encouraging these antipathies on the principle of 'divide and rule', but they were hardly the prime movers.

The political parties provide the historian, in fact, with an essential link between politics at the centre and the periphery. So do the elections they fought. There is now a great deal more work available on German electoral history than was the case twenty years ago, including an excellent recent account in English by Stanley Suval.[65] This work tends to confirm the evidence now accumulating from other sources that points to a marked increase in political involvement in Imperial Germany from about the 1890s. Turn-out at Reichstag elections rose from 50–60 per cent in the first half-dozen contests after unification to 85 per cent in the last elections before the war. A similar pattern can be seen in state and municipal elections, almost certainly encouraged by electoral reform in many places. When non-voting by choice falls to not much more than 5 per cent,[66] this is worthy of attention. Of course, the figures on electoral participation would hardly demonstrate the flowering of a vigorous popular politics if voters were merely being herded to the polls by landlords and priests in larger numbers. In fact, the evidence on uncontested seats, changing patterns of campaigning and voting volatility suggests an erosion of the politics of deference that had taken shape in the 1860s and 1870s. Contrary to arguments that stress the continuity of party blocs from the Bismarckian years to the 1920s, the 1890s seem to have constituted something of a caesura.[67]

It was the same period that saw the emergence of a very wide range of new political organizations that also placed their stamp on the politics of the Wilhelmine era and the years that followed. These included the major organizations of the peasantry and petty bourgeoisie, a number of new anti-semitic political parties, the major radical-nationalist groupings, the Young Liberals, the Evangelical League and the People's Association of German Catholics, the German feminist movement, the German Peace Society, and numerous other single-issue organizations and pressure groups. Some of these organizations can be seen as parallels to the Social Democratic Party. They provided subaltern social groups such as the peasantry, craftsmen and shopkeepers with the possibility of seeking compensation, in a political system that boasted universal manhood suffrage, for material grievances sustained in the market place, or social slights suffered in civil society (in the law courts, or in associations where they felt cold-shouldered). Others, while by no means 'progressive' in their demands, represented an impatient rejection of political deference, whether in the form of tutelage by bishops, bureaucrats or party notables. Many of the single-issue groups were symptomatic of the way in which the definition of what was 'political' became increasingly wide. All of these new movements were aided by the effects of changes in education and communications towards the end of the nineteenth century.

The changes in the established parties and the emergence of new organizations helped to bring about a recasting of the political nation. Many of the essays below are concerned in one form or another with this political ferment in Imperial Germany. They question the usefulness of a largely manipulative model of political mobilization, and argue that we should not see those who were mobilized merely as the pawns of a calculating elite. Commentators have often labelled this approach with the handy phrase 'politics from below'.[68] The label has some value if it draws attention to the view expressed by a number of recent Anglo-Saxon scholars that modern German history should not be viewed solely from the top down. But the shorthand is misleading if it suggests support for the view (whether it be judged laudable or naive) that popular aspirations were decisive and determining. It seems unlikely that anyone would want to resurrect the view once so favoured by conservative historians of a political 'revolt of the masses'. My own purpose is to get away from the lack of differentiation and respect for social and political specifics inherent in such an approach, from whatever ideological corner. Hence the attention paid in many of the essays below to the role played by intermediate political elites, whether village mayors, priests, peasant tribunes who were not themselves peasants, or the professional functionaries and pamphleteers who became so important in many of the new organizations. Among this new political leadership stratum can be found many of the populists who figure in the title of this book. That these populist leaders did not simply 'reflect' the aspirations of their supporters ought to go without saying, and the precise contours of that relationship are examined in many of these essays.

The interaction between populists and patricians, between new politics and old, occupies a central place in these essays. To put it another way, I am concerned with the interplay between politics from above and from below. That has meant, in practice, looking at the way German elites – whether chancellors and ministers, conservative Junkers, or political party leaders – responded to the threat as well as the opportunity presented by the leavening of German political life at the end of the last century. These essays examine some of the changes in the style or quality of politics that were to become so important in the future, such as new forms of campaigning, rhetoric and self-presentation. I have tried to move beyond a manipulative model by exploring the terms on which the political nation was reconstituted as patrician notables learned the common touch. In Chapter 10 (and less explicitly elsewhere) I have taken the frequently invoked term 'demagogy' and asked whether this actually succeeded in securing the allegiance of groups such as the petty bourgeoisie and the nationalist public behind the status quo. What was the effect, for example, when craftsmen and shopkeepers found their rhetoric appropriated but their demands unmet, or when impatient nationalists came to believe that official foreign policy consisted largely of sound and fury? Chapter 6 pursues the relationship between the peasantry and the established political forces in similar fashion, while Chapter 8 looks at one particular – and relatively unfamiliar – case of how anti-semitism could be simultaneously instrumentalized and made 'respectable'. The broad conclusion from these chapters is that elites of varius kinds – by no means only the Junkers – did indeed attempt to secure or sustain mass support by fairly unscrupulous means. But because they were trying to harness popular forces of some vigour, their efforts sometimes caused as many problems as they solved – not least because much of what they offered was merely rhetorical or cosmetic, and frequently recognized as such.

The importance of this for our understanding of the continuities between Imperial and Weimar Germany, implicit in many of these essays, is pointed up in the last two chapters. At the vital level of popular politics, the continuity was not straightforward and linear, but irregular and convulsive. The Nazis benefited ultimately from a cumulative resentment over attempts by patrician politicians – by no means all of them Junker Conservatives – to channel popular sentiment through demagogic political means. It is the failure of old elites to achieve what they intended, as much as their success, which deserves our attention – and also makes the eventual advent of Hitler more explicable.[69] This question of intentions seems to me generally to be one of the areas of pre-1914 German history most in need of further discussion. There has certainly been disagreement over what members of the German elite did intend at crucial junctures. Was the navy seen by men like Tirpitz as a means of rallying support behind the status quo? Does the so-called 'War Council' of 1912 indicate the firm intention to conduct a German pre-emptive strike? Fairly compelling doubts have been aired on both counts, and they certainly have not been registered only by apologist historians.[70] But there remains a more fundamental question about the weight we attribute to the willed intentions of Bismarck, Tirpitz, Bethmann and the managers of the Agrarian League. To what extent, in the end, was what happened the result of what they wanted to happen – the product of what Tim Mason, writing in a different context, has called 'calculated intention'?[71]

It is that other context, the animated debate between so-called 'intentionalists' and 'structuralists' over the interpretation of the Third Reich, which makes the absence of an equivalent discussion over Bismarckian and Wilhelmine Germany a matter of regret.[72] For this is one area where the historiographical vantage point of 1933–45 could be of benefit to historians of the earlier period. Intentionalists argue that Nazi leaders followed an aggressive and finally genocidal policy because that was what they wanted to do. Hitler's own intentions are central to this reading. Structuralists maintain that the most inhuman Nazi policies were the outcome of a cumulative radicalization. It was the way political power was organized in the Third Reich, the manner in which decisions were taken (or avoided), the blurred demarcations of competence within the 'polycracy' that drove the system forward and led ultimately to the pursuit of the most destructive options. On this reading Hitler was not the all-determining fount of sovereign will but a 'weak dictator'. I should say that my own preference is for the account offered by the structuralists – because they venture beyond the self-limiting historicist insistence that history is what the human actors tell you it is, and because their explanations seem more adequate to the complex interplay between individual intentions and collective institutions or deeper social forces.

As one might expect, this is also the general position taken by the revisionist historians of Imperial Germany. They have, after all, been closely associated with a methodological rejection of historicist forms of interpretation, and have frequently invoked a dictum of Jürgen Habermas to the effect that history is not exhausted by 'what human actors mutually intend'.[73] Hence their fruitful application of concepts such as flawed modernization which cannot be derived in any direct way from the words of contemporary participants in events. For all that, it seems to me that – somewhat ironically – revisionist historians of Imperial Germany have in fact attributed too much importance to the intentions of historical actors. To take the most central example, readers have legitimately inferred from Hans-Ulrich Wehler's accounts of Bismarckian Germany that Bismarck was a 'puppet master' – rather than, in Lothar Gall's telling figure, a sorcerer's apprentice (see Chapter 1). Similarly, whether it is the 'Prusso-German' elite in general or the Agrarian League in particular which is under discussion in the revisionist literature, we are given the clear impression that policy turned on their willed intentions. They said what they did and did what they said.

The result has often been a kind of history that is, if I may put it this way, more 'intentionalist' than its authors probably intended, in which results are presented as motives, objective effects as subjective calculations. The reason for this probably lies in the intellectual and moral climate during the Fischer controversy and in subsequent years, when the critical historians understandably reacted against an idealized version of the statesmanlike Bismarck and an elegiac version of the stable Wilhelmine *belle époque*. It perhaps seemed necessary to establish the malign intentions of the Prussian elite in order that it not be allowed to evade responsibility for the German catastrophe. There are advantages, however, if we try to keep motives and responsibilities distinct. One is that we can address ourselves better to what historical actors themselves were unaware of, as opposed to those actions in which they sought to deceive others. The sociologist J. G. Merquior has distinguished usefully between 'the veil and the mask'.[74] My strong feeling is that the emphasis in much influential German historiography on the mask – on conscious dissimulation and manipulation by an elite – needs to be redressed by a greater concern for the veils of misperception through which members of that elite viewed their world. It should be said, in fairness, that Volker Berghahn has made some extremely valuable suggestions along these lines.[75]

A second reason for distinguishing between intention and responsibility is that we could then attend more carefully to unintended consequences. This would mean breaking away from the idea of a manipulative Imperial elite that said what it was doing and proceeded to do it, by considering in the first place how the nature of political and administrative structures helped to shape the outcome of policies in ways not originally envisaged. The structuralist case against the intentionalists over the Third Reich rests heavily on the unsystematic nature of that regime, on the lack of 'rationally' bureaucratic decision-making in Hitler's Germany. There can be no direct comparison with the Second Reich of Bismarck and Wilhelm II; but it has become common to refer to Wilhelmine Germany as a polycracy, and recent work on the pattern of decision-making under the Kaiser suggests interesting parallels (see Chapter 2). Given the surprising paucity of such research, it may well be that further detailed investigation into what went on around the green baize tables and in the interstices of the formal system of government would reinforce this impression.[76] No less important, attention to unintended consequences might also illuminate the interaction of the elite and its leading figures with larger forces in German society. Let me take the example of something that is dealt with in a number of the following essays. Bismarck did not intend the *Kulturkampf* to create the problems of administrative implementation or to assume the stridently progressive overtones that it did (just as the left liberals did not intend the repressiveness with which it was ultimately carried out). Nor did he intend, any more than the left liberals or National Liberals did, that the *Kulturkampf* should cement a powerful political Catholicism in Germany. His large share of responsibility for what transpired is indisputable; but here, as in so many other areas, he conjured up, or went along with, forces that acquired their own momentum. In Chapter 10 I have suggested that we consider the importance of unintended consequences when we approach two other, more central questions: the domestic impasse which Germany's rulers faced in the summer of 1914, and the popular resentments that fuelled the Nazi seizure of power, and which the elites (both traditional and non-traditional) were unable to contain. In neither case were the elite groups in question the innocent historical victims of the 'masses'; but the responsibility of the elites is perhaps most convincingly established if we recognise the complex and sometimes explosive relationship that developed between those whom I have called populists and patricians.

V

The controversy over Fritz Fischer's work, the clash between 'intentionalist' and 'structuralist' interpretations of the Third Reich and recent debates over the *Sonderweg*, remind us of the strong moral charge that writing on German history continues to carry. The growing distance that separates us from the Third Reich does not alter this basic fact; it only changes the perspective from which we view the recent German past. The study of post-1945 German history is now gathering pace, opening up new questions of continuity across the divide that used to be called 'Year Zero'. Meanwhile the Bismarckian and Wilhelmine Empire on which the present essays are centred has been generally recognized as a crucial period for understanding the overall shape of modern German history. That is true, not least, because of the historiographical revolution described above. The essays that follow reflect some aspects of my continuing concern with this period, although they also range considerably beyond the years 1871–1918. Some present variations or elaborations on arguments that are already familiar; others try to break new ground. All represent an attempt to go beyond the advances made in the 1960s and 1970s. They should be read as a contribution to the continuing debate about how we come to terms with the recent German past.

NOTES

1 R. Cobb, *A Second Identity, Essays on France and French History* (Oxford, 1969).

2 The best guide to German historiography is provided by the works of Georg Iggers: *The German Conception of History: The National Tradition of Historical Thought from Herder to the Present* (Middletown, Conn., 1968); *New Directions in European Historiography* (Middletown, Conn., 1975); 'Introduction', in *The Social History of Politics: Critical Perspectives in West German Historical Writing since 1945* (Leamington Spa, 1985), pp. 1–48.

3 H.-U. Wehler, 'Historiography in Germany Today', in J. Habermas (ed.), *Observations on 'The Spiritual Situation of the Age'* (Cambridge, Mass., 1984), p. 222.

4 To prevent confusion it should be noted that the term historicism as used by German (and non-German) historians has a quite opposite meaning from the one given to it by Karl Popper in *The Poverty of Historicism*.

5 Kenneth Barkin has suggested that German historical writing suffered from the same malady as British industrial performance: that of the ageing pioneer. See K. Barkin 'From Uniformity to Pluralism: German Historical Writing since World War I', *German Life and Letters*, vol. 37, no. 2 (1981), p. 234.

6 Iggers, 'Introduction', pp. 9–16.

7 H. Rosenberg, 'Rückblick auf ein Historikerleben zwischen zwei Kulturen', in Rosenberg, *Machteliten und Wirtschaftskonjunkturen* (Göttingen, 1978), pp. 20–21; V. R. Berghahn, 'Francis Carsten: Politics and History in Two Cultures', in Berghahn and M. Kitchen (eds), *Germany in the Age of Total War* (London, 1981), pp. 11–13.

8 Wehler, 'Historiography', pp. 225, 229.

9 Ibid., pp. 229–39.

10 Gerhard Ritter, 'The Fault of Mass Democracy', in J. L. Snell (ed.), *The Nazi Revolution: Germany's Guilt or Germany's Fate?* (New York, 1959); *Carl Goerdeler und die deutsche Widerstandsbewegung* (Stuttgart, 1955). A reflective version of this case was put by the octogenarian Friedrich Meinecke in his postwar essay on *The German Catastrophe*.

11 In addition to the works by Iggers (see note 2 above), see B. Faulenbach, *Ideologie des deutschen Weges. Die deutsche Geschichte in der Historiographie zwischen Kaiserreich und Nationalsozialismus* (Munich, 1980).

12 Significantly, some of the most searching questions about the advent of Nazism had previously been posed by historically-minded political and social scientists, such as Bracher himself, Ernst Fraenkel and Ralf Dahrendorf. Bracher's *Die Auflösung der Weimarer Republik* (*Dissolution of the Weimar Republic*) was first published in Germany in 1955. *The German Dictatorship* (London, 1971) appeared in German in 1969. Hans Mommsen's first major book, *Beamtentum im Dritten Reich* (Stuttgart, 1966), has never been translated. A work that adopts a comparable approach, Martin Broszat's *Der Staat Hitlers* (Munich, 1969) has now been translated as *The Hitler State* (London, 1981).

13 See E. Kolb, *Die Arbeiterräte in der deutschen Innenpolitik 1918/19* (Düsseldorf, 1962); P. von Oertzen, *Betriebsräte in der Novemberrevolution* (Düsseldorf, 1963); R. Rürup, *Probleme der Revolution in Deutschland 1918/19* (Wiesbaden, 1968). For an excellent overview, see Wolfgang J. Mommsen, 'The German Revolution 1918–20: Political Revolution and Social Protest Movement', in R. Bessel and E. J. Feuchtwanger (eds), *Social Change and Political Development in Weimar Germany* (London, 1981), pp. 21–54.

14 B. Moore, *The Social Origins of Dictatorship and Democracy* (London, 1967). An important book whose main thrust was similar appeared at the same time: R. Dahrendorf, *Society and Democracy in Germany* (London, 1968).

15 See J. A. Moses, *The Politics of Illusion* (London, 1975); I. Geiss, *Studien über Geschichte und Geschichtswissenschaft* (Frankfurt/Main, 1972), pp. 108–98; A. Sywottek, 'Die Fischer-Kontroverse', in I. Geiss and B.-J. Wendt (eds), *Deutschland in der Weltpolitik des 19. und 20. Jahrhunderts* (Düsseldorf, 1973), pp. 19–74, as well as the works cited in notes 2 and 3 above.

16 V. R. Berghahn, 'Die Fischerkontroverse – 15 Jahre danach', *Geschichte und Gesellschaft*, vol. 6, no. 3 (1980), pp. 403–19.

17 See the works cited in notes 2 and 3 above.

18 See Wehler, 'Historiography', p. 255 n. 25.

19 E. Kehr, *Der Primat der Innenpolitik*, ed. H.-U. Wehler (Berlin, 1965), subsequently translated as *Economic Interest, Militarism and Foreign Policy* (Berkeley, 1977).

20 These include a number of important collections of essays: H.-U. Wehler (ed.), *Moderne deutsche Sozialgeschichte* (Cologne and Berlin, 1966), H. Böhme (ed.), *Probleme der Reichsgründungszeit* (Cologne and Berlin, 1968), and M. Stürmer (ed.), *Das Kaiserliche Deutschland. Politik und Gesellschaft 1870–1918* (Düsseldorf, 1970). The major monographs include H. Rosenberg, *Grosse Depression und Bismarckzeit* (Berlin, 1967), H.-U. Wehler, *Bismarck und der Imperialismus* (Cologne and Berlin, 1969), D. Stegmann, *Die Erben Bismarcks* (Cologne and Berlin, 1970), P.-C. Witt, *Die Finanzpolitik des deutschen Reiches von 1903–1913* (Lübeck and Hamburg, 1970) and V. R. Berghahn, *Der Tirpitz-Plan* (Düsseldorf, 1971).

21 On the history of the *Sonderweg* concept, see D. Blackbourn and G. Eley, *The Peculiarities of German History* (Oxford, 1984) and the literature quoted there.

22 See, for example, Marianne Weber, *Max Weber, A Biography* (New York, 1975), pp. 279–304, which includes Weber's description of standing on Brooklyn bridge admiring 'the magnificent view of the fortresses of capital' on the southern tip of Manhattan.

23 See especially Faulenbach, *Ideologie*.

24 The geographical/geopolitical argument has recently been restated in D. Calleo, *The German Problem Reconsidered* (Cambridge, 1980). On German militarism, see the pioneering Anglo-Saxon work of Gordon Craig, *The Politics of the Prussian Army 1640–1945* (Oxford, 1955); on the 'German mind', see H. Kohn, *The Mind of Germany* (London, 1961), F. Stern, *The Politics of Cultural Despair* (Berkeley, Calif., 1961) and G. Mosse, *The Crisis of German Ideology* (London, 1966).

25 For the following account, in addition to the works cited in note 20 above, see H.-U. Wehler, *Das Deutsche Kaiserreich 1871–1918* (Göttingen, 1973), now translated as *The German Empire 1871–1918* (Leamington Spa, 1985), Rosenberg, *Machteliten*, and M. Kitchen, *The Political Economy of Germany 1815–1914* (London, 1978).

26 The literature on this receives detailed discussion in Blackbourn and Eley, *Peculiarities*.

27 H.-J. Puhle, *Agrarische Interessenpolitik und preussischer Konservatismus* (Hanover, 1966); H.-J. Puhle, 'Conservatism in Modern German History', *Journal of Con-*

temporary History, vol. 13 (1978), pp. 701–7; and H. A. Winkler, 'Der rückversicherte Mittelstand', in W. Rüegg and O. Neuloh (eds), *Zur soziologischen Theorie und Analyse des 19. Jahrhunderts* (Göttingen, 1971), pp. 163–79.

28 Rosenberg, *Grosse Depression*; S. Volkov, *The Rise of Popular Antimodernism: the Urban Master Artisans 1873–1896* (Princeton, NJ, 1976).

29 Wehler, *Bismarck und der Imperialismus*; M. Stürmer, *Regierung und Reichstag im Bismarckstaat 1871–1880: Cäsarismus oder Parlamentarismus* (Düsseldorf, 1974).

30 I. Geiss, *German Foreign Policy, 1871–1914* (Boston, Mass., 1976).

31 V. R. Berghahn, *Germany and the Approach of War in 1914* (London, 1973), p. 29; and in more detail in *Der Tirpitz-Plan*, pp. 90–173.

32 A succinct summary is P.-C. Witt, 'Innenpolitik und Imperialismus in der Vorgeschichte des 1. Weltkriegs', in K. Holl and G. List (eds), *Liberalismus und imperialistischer Staat* (Göttingen, 1975), pp. 7–34.

33 See, for example, Wehler, *German Empire*, ch. 8: 'The First World War: escape forwards'.

34 Ibid., p. 7.

35 The term is placed in inverted commas because the German original – 'Die Bewältigung der Vergangenheit' – has become a universal shorthand for dealing with the legacy of National Socialism.

36 Wehler, 'Historiography', p. 241.

37 James Sheehan, in a review in the *Journal of Modern History*, vol. 48 (1976), p. 567.

38 See, for example, R. Fletcher, 'Recent Developments in West German Historiography: The Bielefeld School and Its Critics', *German Studies Review*, vol. 7, no. 3 (1984), pp. 451–80.

39 T. Nipperdey, 'Wehlers Kaiserreich: Eine kritische Auseinandersetzung', *Geschichte und Gesellschaft*, vol. 1 (1975), pp. 539–60. See also H.-G. Zmarzlik, 'Das Kaiserreich in neuer Sicht?', *Historische Zeitschrift*, no. 222 (1976), pp. 105–26.

40 A. Hillgruber, 'Politische Geschichte in moderner Sicht', *Historische Zeitschrift*, no. 216 (1973), pp. 529–52; K. Hildebrand, 'Geschichte oder "Gesellschaftsgeschichte"? Die Notwendigkeit einer politischen Geschichtsschreibung von den internationalen Beziehungen', *Historische Zeitschrift*, no. 223 (1976), pp. 328–57.

41 Very little has been written in English on *Alltagsgeschichte*, but see Iggers, 'Introduction', pp. 40–43. The most thoughtful introduction probably remains L. Niethammer, 'Anmerkungen zur Alltagsgeschichte', *Geschichtsdidaktik*, 5 (1980), pp. 231–42.

42 At the West Berlin German Historical Conference of 1984, and in many newspaper articles and reviews, Hans-Ulrich Wehler has attacked the potentially anti-theoretical and sentimental aspects of *Alltagsgeschichte*, especially as practised by the *barfuss* (barefooted) zealots. See 'Neoromantik und Pseudorealismus in der neuen "Alltagsgeschichte",' in Wehler's collection *Preußen ist wieder chic* ... (Frankfurt/Main, 1983), pp. 99–106. For a similar warning, see J. Kocka, 'Theorien in der Geschichtswissenschaft', in P. Leidinger (ed.), *Theoriedebatte und Geschichtsunterricht* (Paderborn, 1982), pp. 7–27.

43 D. Blackbourn, *Class, Religion and Local Politics in Wilhelmine Germany* (London and New Haven, Conn., 1980), and *The Peculiarities of German History* (see note 21 above), the revised version of a book which first appeared in German (1980). Readers are referred to this second book for a full account of the points made in this paragraph.

44 It is worth noting, however, that two major research projects have recently begun at Bielefeld which take 'Bürgerlichkeit' as their central theme. These very welcome new departures both work within a comparative framework that goes well beyond the old German/Anglo-Saxon polarity. A volume of papers from the conference that preceded one of these projects, at the Bielefeld *Zentrum für interdisziplinäre Forschung* (ZiF, or Centre for Interdisciplinary Research), is to be published in early 1987, edited by Jürgen Kocka.

45 W. Schivelbusch, *The Railway Journey* (Oxford, 1980), p. 51.

46 It is pointed out, for example, in Nipperdey, 'Wehlers Kaiserreich', and by James Sheehan in 'Klasse und Partei im Kaiserreich: Einige Gedanken zur Sozialgeschichte der deutschen Politik', in O. Pflanze (ed.), *Innenpolitische Probleme des Bismarck-Reiches*

(Munich and Vienna, 1983), pp. 1–24. This is also a central theme of the important article by Kenneth Barkin and Margaret Anderson, 'The Myth of the Puttkamer Purge and the Reality of the *Kulturkampf*: Some Reflections on the Historiography of Imperial Germany', *Journal of Modern History*, vol. 54 (1982), pp. 647–86, whose arguments are similar in many respects to those put forward in the present collection of essays.

47 See, for example, P. W. Massing, *Rehearsal for Destruction: A Study of Political Anti-Semitism in Imperial Germany* (New York, 1949).

48 G. Eley, *Reshaping the German Right. Radical Nationalism and Political Change after Bismarck* (London and New Haven, 1980); R. Chickering, *We Men Who Feel Most German: A Cultural Study of the Pan-German League, 1886–1914* (London, 1984).

49 In fact, the reality of Junker estate-management on the ground and its links with local social and political power is surprisingly little explored. There is no book that does for Germany what F. M. L. Thompson did for England in *English Landed Society in the Nineteenth Century* (London, 1963). Detailed studies are now underway, however, including an exhaustive examination by William Hagen at the University of California in Davis of one particular Junker *Gut*, or estate.

50 See below, Chapter 6.

51 James C. Hunt, 'The "Egalitarianism" of the Right: The Agrarian League in Southwest Germany, 1893–1914', *Journal of Contemporary History*, vol. 10 (1975), pp. 513–30. D. S. White, *The Splintered Party. National Liberalism in Hessen and the Reich 1867–1918* (Cambridge, Mass., 1976), has much valuable material on agrarian politics. See also below, Chapter 6.

52 E. Weber, *Peasants into Frenchmen. The Modernization of Rural France, 1870–1914* (London, 1977).

53 Chapter 6.

54 See especially Stig Förster, *Der Doppelte Militarismus* (Stuttgart, 1985).

55 On the non-Prussian form of German nationalism among bourgeois Catholics, see Blackbourn, *Class, Religion and Local Politics*, and Chapter 9 below. The outstanding work on Weber and Imperial politics remains Wolfgang J. Mommsen, *Max Weber and German Politics 1890–1920* (Chicago, 1985), first published in German in 1959.

56 One thing that has emerged clearly from the debate over the *Sonderweg* is a general recognition that German history has too often been measured against an Anglo-Saxon yardstick, while too few comparisons have been made with historical developments in other European countries, either East or West. Continental comparisons would certainly help to place German traditions of bureaucracy, policing and standing armies in perspective.

57 Blackbourn and Eley, *Peculiarities*, esp. pp. 239–60, contains more detailed arguments and references. See also J. Caplan, '"The imaginary universality of particular interests": The "tradition" of the civil service in German history', *Social History*, vol. 4 (1979), pp. 299–317.

58 Blackbourn and Eley, *Peculiarities*, pp. 241–51.

59 L. Kofler, *Zur Geschichte der bürgerlichen Gesellschaft* (Neuwied and Berlin, 1966), p. 540.

60 The importance of titles such as *Kommerzienrat* (literally: commercial councillor) and of the honours system more generally receives extended discussion in Blackbourn and Eley, *Peculiarities*, pp. 228–37.

61 Nipperdey, 'Wehlers Kaiserreich', p. 376.

62 Nipperdey makes this point in 'Wehlers Kaiserreich'. I have also tried to make it in a number of previous publications, for example in *Class, Religion and Local Politics*, and *Peculiarities*, pp. 259–85.

63 'Leading', in the sense of those identified with the historiographical revisionism of the 1960s and 1970s. Significantly, one of the most valuable books on political parties in Imperial Germany is still Thomas Nipperdey's *Die Organisation der deutschen Parteien vor 1918* (Düsseldorf, 1961), which is broader than its title suggests.

64 On liberalism, for example, we now have the American works of D. S. White (see note 52 above), J. C. Hunt, *The People's Party in Württemberg and Southern Germany* (Stuttgart, 1975), and J. Sheehan, *German Liberalism in the Nineteenth Century*

(Chicago, 1978). The previously neglected Centre Party has received detailed treatment in R. J. Ross, *Beleaguered Tower: The Dilemma of Political Catholicism in Wilhelmine Germany* (Notre Dame, Ind., 1976), J. K. Zeender, *The German Center Party, 1890–1906* (Philadelphia, Pa., 1976), M. L. Anderson, *Windthorst, A Political Biography* (Oxford, 1981) and W. Loth, *Katholiken im Kaiserreich* (Düsseldorf, 1984), as well as my own work. Work on the SPD continues to multiply, both general histories and a growing number of local studies such as M. Nolan, *Social Democracy and Society. Working-Class Radicalism in Düsseldorf, 1890–1920* (Cambridge, 1981). Conservatism in Imperial Germany remains markedly under-researched, but the forthcoming publication of James Retallack's Oxford D.Phil. (see note 20, Chapter 10) will do much to improve our understanding.

65 S. Suval, *Electoral Politics in Wilhelmine Germany* (Chapel Hill, NC, 1985).

66 8 to 10 per cent of non-voters were accounted for by death, illness, change of residence after registration, or unavoidable absence as a result of work. See ibid., p. 21.

67 For detailed evidence on the points in this and the following paragraph, see Chapter 10, and also my *Class, Religion and Local Politics*.

68 The literature on this point is cited in Chapter 10, note 2. Many other works allude to the question.

69 This does not, of course, add up to anything like a complete explanation of National Socialist success; I am concerned here with only one particular aspect of continuity. As I argue in Chapter 10, Nazi success cannot be explained solely in terms of the popular support they received, even if it cannot be properly explained without it. For a fuller account, see the 'Introduction' to Blackbourn and Eley, *Peculiarities*.

70 The role of the navy in the calculations of Germany's ruling elite in the late 1890s has been convincingly questioned by Geoff Eley, '*Sammlungspolitik*, Social Imperialism and the Navy Law of 1898', now reprinted in G. Eley, *From Unification to Nazism. Reinterpreting the German Past* (London, 1986), pp. 110–53. The Fischerite view of the 'War Council' of 1912 has been taken furthest by John C. G. Röhl, 'Die Generalprobe. Zur Geschichte und Bedeutung des "Kriegsrates" vom 8. Dezember 1912', in D. Stegmann, B.-J. Wendt, P.-C. Witt (eds), *Industrielle Gesellschaft und Politisches System* (Bonn, 1978), pp. 357–73. It is not accepted by many other historians, even those broadly sympathetic to Fischer's views. See Röhl, 'Generalprobe', note 3, for the large literature on the subject.

71 T. Mason, 'Intention and Explanation: A Current Controversy about the Interpretation of National Socialism', in G. Hirschfeld and L. Kettenacker (eds), *Der 'Führerstaat': Mythos und Realität* (Stuttgart, 1981), pp. 23–42.

72 In addition to Mason's excellent essay, see also the measured account of these debates in Ian Kershaw, *The Nazi Dictatorship. Problems and Perspectives of Interpretation* (London, 1985). Both have a full guide to the relevant literature.

73 J. Habermas, *Zur Logik der Sozialwissenschaften. Materialien* (Frankfurt/Main, 1970), p. 116. Hans-Ulrich Wehler and Jürgen Kocka have written frequently on these methodological questions. See, for example, Wehler's *Geschichte als Sozialwissenschaft* (Frankfurt/Main, 1973), and Kocka's *Sozialgeschichte* (Göttingen, 1977).

74 J. G. Merquior, *The Veil and the Mask. Essays on Culture and Ideology* (London, 1979), pp. 1–38.

75 Most accessible to English readers in *Germany and the Approach of War in 1914*.

76 P.-C. Witt's *Die Finanzpolitik* is, amongst other things, an exemplary study in government and administration. A more recent work in English which engages very effectively with decision-making in this period is J. C. Albisetti, *Secondary School Reform in Imperial Germany* (Princeton, NJ, 1985), one of many recent works on German schools and universities that also fills out our view of the social role played by educational institutions.

I

'Great Men'?

1

Bismarck: the Sorcerer's Apprentice

While historical biography retains an ample respectability among British historians, many of their German counterparts – especially among the middle generation – regard the genre coolly, even with suspicion. They see the biographical approach as 'personalistic', at best as an auxiliary tool that can be used to fill in the gaps left unexplained by other kinds of historical analysis. It is a view clearly shared by some British historians of Germany. German historians have not always preached such an austere gospel. There is a German tradition of double-decker biographies of the kind so familiar to historians of Victorian and Edwardian Britain (Oncken on the National Liberal leader Bennigsen, Herzfeld on the radical forty-eighter turned conservative minister Miquel). Many have a particular value for the study of German high politics (and especially party politics) because they contain material subsequently destroyed in wartime. More distinctive is a biographical mode that reflects German regional and denominational diversity: the many biographical collections dealing with local notables (like the *Nassauische Lebensbilder*) or with figures from the Catholic political tradition (like the four-volume *Gestalten aus dem Schwäbischen Katholizismus*). Works of this kind often have a provincial and antiquarian character. But it is not so much these acts of homage to the small fry, but the way in which 'great men' have been chronicled that has probably done most to produce an allergic reaction. The conservative historians who dominated the Weimar Republic's historical 'guild' and held sway down to the early 1960s celebrated Prussia's heroes boldly. Gerhard Ritter wrote lives of Freiherr von Stein and Carl Goerdeler; others lionized Bismarck, a more suitable case for great-man treatment than either the Kaiser (a 'failure') or Hitler (the Austrian 'lance-corporal'). Many Bismarck biographies served much the same function as Bismarck towers and monuments.

Bismarck remains a touchstone of attitudes among historians towards the German past, just as work on Bismarckian Germany remains a major laboratory of methodological innovation. This essay is concerned with both. Of the four books considered below. Hillgruber's sketch is methodologically conservative but entirely free of the apologist tones still often heard in the 1960s. Reiners and Crankshaw represent two opposed traditions, the former taking his cue from earlier Bismarck admirers like A. O. Meyer, the latter from debunkers like Erich Eyck. Gall's book is by far the most substantial and valuable.[1] Although it appeared at the height of the West German *Preußenwelle*, the wave of nostalgia for old Prussia that manifested itself in many books and a major exhibition, it insistently rejects the elegiac tone. It cuts Bismarck down to size, but not by turning the hero into a villain, rather by showing how neither approach is adequate. Gall's book makes a significant contribution to the continuing debate about Imperial Germany and Bismarck's place in it. It has also been successful in making the results of modern historical research available to a general readership. There is a clear demand for historical biography – for accessible works generally – among the West German public. Recent years have shown that if specialists like Gall do not meet it, others certainly will.

This essay is based on a review article first published in the *Archiv für Sozialgeschichte* (1981), pp. 756–60. It was originally intended for a German readership. I have tried to adjust the balance, partly by including material from a review of Crankshaw's biography (in *History Today*, January 1982), partly by broadening some of the general points. I have also moved page citations referring to the books reviewed from text to footnotes, and added a number of explanatory notes and references for the benefit of the non-German reader.

Anglo-Saxons are much given to biography. Nor do they merely chronicle their own, as the field of modern German history amply demonstrates. While Hitler is served by a growing legion of English-speaking biographers, Anglo-Saxon historians – both professional and amateur – have also been responsible for many Bismarck lives. These extend from J. W. Headlam's in the 1890s to the works of Alfred Apsler, George O. Kent and Alan Palmer in the 1970s, with such notable figures as Grant-Robertson, Medlicott and A. J. P. Taylor falling chronologically in between. This list is now joined by Edward Crankshaw, who has already written biographies of Conrad, Khrushchev, Maria Theresa and Tolstoy.

His book is vigorous, generally accurate and abreast of some, at least, of the best modern German research (Böhme and Wehler are in the bibliography, even if Stürmer is not). Crankshaw's account is nevertheless flawed, both over-written and in many respects ill-balanced. It lacks balance, first of all, in the allocation of space. The twenty years of power after 1870 are largely an epilogue to this long book, while the period after Bismarck's dismissal, the years of bitterness and the creation of a legend, are almost disregarded, even though it is these years to which much recent scholarship has fruitfully addressed itself.[2] If the coverage of the Imperial Chancellor in the 1870s and 1880s is sketchy, the treatment of the 1890s spent out of office is plainly inadequate. It is a major distortion to pass over Bismarck's role in those years. He helped to bring down his successor Caprivi (the German Peel *manqué*) by acting as a stalking-horse for the powerful agrarian Conservatives whom Caprivi's 'New Course' had antagonized. He also allowed himself to become the hero and lodestone of the growing radical-nationalist public, as Bismarck monuments, towers and his own memoirs fostered the mystique of the 'strong man'. These developments, as much as Bismarck's direct spoiling actions in the politics of the 1890s, give the last years of his life their long-term significance. Crankshaw rather unconvincingly justifies his neglect of almost everything after 1871 on the grounds that Bismarck began to repeat himself, a failing to which the author himself is quite often susceptible.

The book also lacks proportion in its relentlessly lurid and critical judgments on Bismarck. When we read on page after page how he bullied, cheated, lied, flattered, blackmailed, bamboozled, manipulated, made mischief, tortured, hectored and much more besides, we begin to feel that the currency of criticism has been devalued. This undermines the many valid points Crankshaw has to make about the man – his ruthlessness, arrogance and coarseness. It also presents us with an over-drawn monster, whose power is then also overdrawn. Few historians would now deny that Bismarck bears much responsibility for the tensions which built up in a Germany that was unified late and unevenly; that his balancing act at home and abroad left a dubious legacy of unsolved problems; or that the Bismarckian system had negative effects on the political maturity of Imperial Germany, as contemporary critics such as Hermann Baumgarten and Max Weber observed.[3] Most discussions of the Second Reich turn on issues of this kind. But Crankshaw goes much further in attributing personal responsibility to Bismarck. Not only, we learn, did German society 'stop growing' in the quarter-century after 1865 (a notion which is, to say the least, misleading); but 'he himself had stopped it'. Or again, the Reich was 'not really a Reich' because Bismarck 'refused to breathe life into it'. The balance between life and times, the touchstone of the biography, has been wrongly struck. And in judgments of this kind, which run through the book, one sees also a striving for colour and effect that works against the qualities of psychological penetration and historical synthesis the volume possesses. Imperial Germany was indeed a febrile society, for which Bismarck himself bears a good deal of responsibility; but that is no reason to demonize him. The lack of human and historical proportion, and the striving after effect, ultimately make this an unreliable guide to life or times.

In Germany the biography has been less ubiquitous. This is not to deny the existence of a biographical tradition. One thinks of Srbik's Metternich biography, Gustav Mayer on Engels, or the more literary works of Emil Ludwig. The success of Golo Mann's *Wallenstein* and of Joachim Fest's *Hitler* also suggests that, after a period of crisis, historical biography is once again becoming both popular and respectable. Bismarck, however, has always been an attractive subject for German biographers. The bibliography of Lothar Gall's new study lists twelve such works by German authors, many of them written (like his own) for the general reader. Nevertheless, one postwar survey among German apprentices revealed that the name Bismarck was most commonly held to denote either a battleship or a herring, and there is clearly still room for works that address such a public. One hopes that few of them will be taken in by the two reissued paperback volumes by Ludwig Reiners. First published in the middle of the 1950s, they represent a popularized form of the Borussian or German-national tradition of historical writing.[4] The first volume on Bismarck's rise offers a star-struck portrait of the statesman as a young man. It goes on to paint a larger-than-life picture of Bismarck against a distorted backdrop of the German states betwen 1848 and 1863, the latter dominated by 'doctrinaire' liberals and pygmy politicians lacking statesmanship. As the first volume closes, Bismarck faces the Schleswig-

Holstein question rather like a silent-movie heroine: 'On this reef Bismarck's ship of state was bound finally to founder'.[5] The second volume has a highly indicative title ('Bismarck founds the Reich 1864–1871'). It shows our hero unifying Germany single-handed, overcoming Austrian ill-will, French aggression and liberal paralysis, while generally illustrating the superiority of the man of action over mere dreamers and onlookers. The book would be less than convincing even if the account were factually reliable, which it is not. Reiners tells us that 'no educated person will take every word of Bismarck's at face value'; but he comes close to doing just that. Legends from the *Gedanken und Erinnerungen* are perpetuated and Bismarck's descriptions of many events are taken over almost word-for-word, but without any indication that this is the case. For example, Bismarck himself wrote as follows of the 1848 uprising in Polish Prussia, in terms which Lothar Gall aptly characterizes as 'demagogic exaggeration':[6] the rebels 'overran the inhabitants of a Prussian province with looting and murder, butchery and barbaric mutilations of women and children'. Reiners, on the same episode, refers to insurgents who 'plotted a rebellion and exerted a reign of terror with murder, looting and barbaric mutilations of women and children'.[7] Reiners is not only his master's voice; he resolutely resists the idea that Bismarck ever made an error of judgment or was in any respect morally culpable. He told the occasional lie, of course, but only in the greater interest of the state. Indeed, a curious final chapter to the second volume uses a rag-bag of quotations from Luther, Fichte, George Washington and others in trying to persuade us that lying was not only Bismarck's right but his duty. These unattractive apologetics resemble Crankshaw with all the signs reversed: the great man as hero, rather than villain. Those who are interested in the possibilities of German historical *Belletristik* would do well to pass over these reissued volumes and go straight to someone like Emil Ludwig, where at least the gossip is lively.[8]

It is reassuring to turn from Reiners' ill-conceived melodrama to the more sober, even austere book by Andreas Hillgruber. This is a popular work by an established scholar that does not talk down to its readers and presents a compact, chronologically based account of Bismarck's career. It sustains an admirable degree of narrative tension while supplying much subtle synthesis. The sub-title ('Founder of the European Great Power the German Reich') and the chapter headings correctly indicate that the book is built around changing great power relations; and the choice and arrangement of material show that Hillgruber is concerned to restate his frequently expressed belief in the 'primacy of foreign policy' as a historical determinant.[9] While the domestic side tends to take second place, the author nevertheless refers often to the interdependence of domestic and foreign policy. And on important issues aired in the recent historiography he is clearly at pains to give formal recognition to the work of those whose approach he does not share. This is true of the way he treats the impact of German tariff policy on Russia, and the economic and domestic political background to Bismarck's colonial policy in the 1880s. For all Hillgruber's commitment to the primacy of foreign policy, he presents a more satisfying, less exclusively diplomatic explanation of Bismarck's imperialism in these years than does, say, A. J. P. Taylor.[10] Indeed, Hillgruber avails himself twice of the almost talismanic phrase used by post-Fritz Fischer German historians, 'escape forwards' into war. On the first occasion he is discussing Bismarck's foreign initiatives in 1862, on the second occasion looking ahead to 1914.[11] When the author refers to Bismarck's difficulties after 1871 'with the most varied institutions, groups and persons', it is nevertheless the conflict with the German ambassador in Paris, Harry von Arnim, which he offers by way of illustration. We learn less than we might about others of 'the many conflicts and tensions he himself to a considerable extent conjured up'.[12]

The problem, perhaps, is that the very merits of the book – its ability to harness expert knowledge with cool commonsense and lack of extravagance – are accompanied by a corresponding reserve when it comes to pointing up some of the questions raised by Hillgruber's account. For example, he quotes some telling remarks of Bismarck on the problems of moving with the stream of history ('German unity is not at the moment a ripe fruit', 'fert unda nec regitur'[13]); but he refrains from any comment on the implications of these for the idea of a 'belated nation'. The widely discussed idea of Bismarck's Bonapartism is brushed aside peremptorily, and the author has equally little time for the notion of a 're-founding' of the Reich in 1878–79, when the ending of the *Kulturkampf*, the reintroduction of protective tariffs, the anti-socialist law and the turn away from the liberals formed a cluster of events that many historians have found significant.[14] It is certainly possible to view the 1870s and 1880s as a unity, in which the Reich became *de facto* more of a unitary state as a common currency and weights and measures had their effect, as the interventionist state grew while particularism weakened, and national sentiment (as so often) followed rather than preceded formal unification. Equally certainly, however, Hillgruber offers no convincing response to those who stress the climacteric of the late 1870s, other than the bland proposition that the period 1871–90 witnessed a consolidation of what had been achieved by Bismarck at home and abroad.[15]

This question of periodization can be broadened further. It is possible to argue that the entire period from the 1860s to the beginning of the 1890s constituted a unity – one spanned by Bismarck's years of power in Prussia and the Reich, but only partly of his making. It was defined economically by the impact of the first wave of industrialisation that occurred in the 1850s and 60s, socially by the consolidation of a bourgeois order underpinned by new legal and associational forms, politically by the establishment of a 'Lesser Germany' with parliamentary institutions but no parliamentary government, in which an exclusive 'politics of notables' (*Honoratiorenpolitik*) predominated. From this standpoint it is plausible to see the decade following Bismarck's dismissal in 1890 as a true watershed, although Bismarck's own relationship to the changes of the 1890s was largely symbolic. Germany after Bismarck saw qualitative changes in economy and society (accelerating migration and urbanization, a more 'organized' economy, the swelling of the tertiary sector), the pursuit of world policy abroad and the advent of a truly mass politics at home.[16] Hillgruber touches on the importance of new departures in the 1890s, noting for example the emergence of a new popular nationalism. But he sees the changes essentially through the optic of changing great power relations and the accession of the new Kaiser (one of the four illustrations in the book is the celebrated *Punch* cartoon, 'Dropping the Pilot'). It may well be that Bismarck failed 'to prepare Wilhelm [II] for his duties as ruler, and above all to make him familiar with the activities of the [German]Foreign Office'.[17] But if we are to argue convincingly that politics in post-Bismarckian Germany were really different from those of previous decades, our approach must surely be broader than this. This holds true whether or not we are persuaded by a 'manipulative' view of the manner in which a post-Bismarckian ruling elite used foreign policy for conservative domestic purposes.

Hillgruber's ultimate criteria for discussing the continuities and discontinuities of modern Germany's development are those provided by great power relations. When he opens up a little on the final page and suggests that Bismarck's Reich was time-bound (*zeitverhaftet*), it is Germany's place within the system of international relations he has in mind. Bismarck's Empire was 'bound' by the 'Crimean War situation', which 'opened' in the 1850s and 'closed' in 1945.[18] This perspective from the Peace of Paris to Yalta is a striking note on which to end the book, and it illustrates Hillgruber's desire to draw a line under the postwar German settlement. But many historians will still want to ask about the other respects in which the Bismarckian Reich may have been 'time-bound'. In order to do so they will have to continue exploring the domestic social and political arrangements of the Lesser Germany established in 1871 – and the way that these changed.

Hillgruber's short book transcends the rubric of the series it contributes to, which proclaims rather unpromisingly that 'it has always been individual personalities who have decided the fate of peoples'.[19] Hillgruber is certainly no merchant of men-who-make-history. Nor, most emphatically, is Lothar Gall. His justly acclaimed new biography assiduously dispels myths at many levels. He casts a cool eye on much of the dramatic incident and emotional pathos so artfully contrived in the *Gedanken und Erinnerungen*. Even more important, he sets many of Bismarck's famous maxims into perspective by adopting a severely contextual approach: why did Bismarck say this, for whose benefit, why at this time?[20] Bismarck's errors of judgment are presented equally clearly, such as the letters he wrote to General von Alvensleben in Spring 1859 and to Moritz von Blanckenburg in February 1860, where the optimism with which he depicted Prussia's position *vis-à-vis* Austria lacked any real political, diplomatic or military foundation.[21] Above all, and central to the structure and conception of his book, Gall insists again and again that Bismarck made history, but not in circumstances of his own choosing. We are never allowed to be carried away by the great statesman's political or diplomatic dexterity. This theme is developed in two ways. First, Gall sensitively explores Bismarck's own self-understanding, his attitudes towards History and a stern Protestant deity. He quotes to good effect many of Bismarck's references to the stream of history that carries men along with it. He then shows convincingly how Bismarck, far from following some grand design or *Stufenplan*, sought to move with this current – 'to retard it, to canalize it, to confine it', in Gall's words.[22] To adopt another of Gall's metaphors, Bismarck was prepared to alarm more cautious conservatives like the Gerlach brothers and 'play with fire' in order to preserve the basic conservative and monarchical order in which he believed. At the peak of his effectiveness in the decade before 1871 he was the white revolutionary of Gall's title. Yet it is the great merit of the author's approach that he is also able to show the force of the unintended consequences which flowed from these efforts by Bismarck to 'cling to God's coat-tails as He marched through world history'.[23] We are shown how Bismarck became increasingly pessimistic as he became the victim of forces which, in Gall's careful formulation, he had himself helped to set in motion. Even before the final section of the book dealing with the years after 1871, to which Gall has given the heading 'The Sorcerer's Apprentice', this theme has already been raised in a number of places.[24]

This is, then, an unheroic biography, with a cutting-edge against the cult of Bismarck-worship represented by an A. O. Meyer or a Ludwig Reiners. At the same time Gall couples together the old Bismarck-admirers and the new Bismarck-critics. The latter, he repeatedly suggests, have taken over the same Bismarck-centred interpretation and merely turned the moral judgments upside down.[25] In setting up his stall against these modern historians Gall certainly makes some good points. He shows, for example, how important it is to differentiate between liberal aspirations and bourgeois aspirations, and not to view either as failures in the German case, simply because they did not correspond to an English model of what 'ought' to have happened.[26] If the author's scepticism here is in line with broader historiographical trends, so too are his brief but well taken remarks about the central importance some historians have attached to the so-called 'Great Depression' of 1873–96. Neither in economic nor in social-political terms do these years appear now to have the degree of unity and significance attributed to them in Hans Rosenberg's brilliant but speculative book written twenty years ago.[27] It is also salutary that Gall allows us to take seriously the political parties of Imperial Germany (on whose vicissitudes he is very good), and that he encourages the reader to see the non-'manipulated' element in the rise of interest politics. Indeed, he remarks suggestively that, while Bismarck may have tried to 'mediatize' the parties in the 1880s by appealing directly to material interests, the parties themselves sought to slough off awkward and conflicting organized interests by deflecting them on to the government. In these and other ways Gall usefully redresses the balance by reminding us that not everything came from the top down.

The author is nevertheless a little mischievous sometimes in the glancing debate he conducts with these unnamed, but easily identifiable modern historians.[28] It is true that some may have tended to overemphasize the manipulative element in Bismarckian politics; but they have not put Bismarck personally at centre stage in the same way as the old Bismarck admirers did, and the implied identification between the two groups is questionable. Nor have the modern historians alluded to by Gall been at all unaware of the unintended consequences of Bismarck's actions, even if this is an aspect of their work that might have received greater emphasis.[29] Gall also nods rather too dismissively at some of the key concepts employed in recent historical debate on the Bismarck Reich, such as *Sammlungspolitik* and social imperialism, particularly when his own account skilfully but tacitly puts some of these explanatory approaches to use.[30] Take, for instance, his treatment of Bismarck's difficult years after 1884. Gall brings together a number of themes that have been most systematically explored by the very historians from whom he begs to differ: Bismarck's use of the national issue and of the notation 'enemies of the Reich', the Germanization of Polish Prussia, economic protectionism, the war scare used at the 1887 Reichstag elections. He interweaves these themes with a detailed account of Bismarck's attempt to balance above the different party-political groupings, rightly laying as much emphasis on Bismarck's problems as on his successes. Gall's compound of these themes is recognizably different from the compound created by many recent historians; but it is clearly made up of the same elements. This is most obviously the case over the much-discussed question of Bismarck's 'Bonapartism'. Gall dismisses the concept fairly briskly, as he has done elsewhere, yet he comes close on at least a couple of occasions to describing a Bonapartist form of rule.[31]

Gall's kind of revisionism, as hard-headedly sceptical as it is elegant, carries with it a not altogether unwarranted distrust of what Hans Rosenberg once called 'an excess of theoretical *Programmatik*'.[32] There are times, however, when Gall's own suggestive comments might have grown into something more had they been set in a more overt theoretical framework. (I fear this may sound like the Anglo-Saxon pot calling the Teutonic kettle black.) Let me give two examples. Dealing with the year 1864 and the background to the Schleswig-Holstein question, Gall rehearses the arguments that Prussia and Austria might still at this stage have been able to cement an 'anti-revolutionary' (i.e. anti-French) alliance. The problem here, notes Gall, is that 'in reality forms had long outlived contents, and the actual revolution was not tied to an idea and to external power, but to an irresistibly advancing change in all economic and social relationships'.[33] It is the word-play with 'forms' and 'contents' that is interesting here, one of many instances where Gall makes glancing use of a Hegelian vocabulary. Two years and eighty pages later he has another passage discussing attitudes towards progress in 1866, and observes in passing how the idea 'that political progress and social change went closely together was now called fundamentally into question'.[34] Both of these urbane asides whet the appetite, as in Hillgruber's book, for some explicit discussion of the 'belated nation' in modern German history and the connected theme of Germany's 'uneven development' (what Ernst Bloch called the *Gleichzeitigkeit der Ungleichzeitigen*).[35] It is this explicit engagement with an important central theme that is missing. The allusive (and sometimes elusive) manner in which Gall writes is actually a more striking feature of this book than its empirical density. Hence the fact that Gall is sometimes weak in an area where his shadow-opponents among modern historians are relatively strong: in the concrete depiction of the forces making for economic, social and political change. When Gall takes a long view and talks of the years between 1851 and 1890 as ones that witnessed 'tumultuous, often breathtaking change in virtually all fields',[36] that is almost as close as we come to learning the actual content and substance of these changes. On one occasion, it is true, Gall singles out the industrial economy, the modern city, the bureaucratization of life and the principle of mobility.[37] For the most part, though, we have to make do with countless references to forces, tendencies, currents and transformations. Elsewhere the author shows himself expert at expressing the general through the particular; but in this important respect the general remains very general indeed. When he does offer illustration he commonly presents the busy commercial city in which Bismarck spent his early public career as a symbol of the new world. But this is to throw on Frankfurt in the 1850s a symbolic burden it alone cannot bear.

If it is necessary to raise these questions, it would be unfair not to make it clear that this is, by general consent, the best Bismarck biography we possess. In a curious way the shaping of Gall's book is mimetic of the shape assumed by Bismarck's own career. The early chapters dealing with the fretful and troubled years up to 1848 are rather restless and uneven. When Bismarck was at his best, so, undoubtedly, is Gall. The hand-to-mouth years from the 1870s, as the author characterizes them, find their reflection in chapters that lack the large-scale sweep so evident in the treatment of the middle years. The overall composition of the book is nevertheless thoughtful and successful. It is episodic rather than strictly chronological, but Gall's alertness and reflectiveness lend the book a coherence that more than outweighs what is lost in narrative continuity. Within this permissive framework there are some brilliantly executed set-pieces, like the discussion of the von Roon army reforms in the early 1860s, the *Kulturkampf* of the 1870s (on which Gall has written admirably elsewhere)[38] and the social legislation of the 1880s. There are striking 'stills' of particular years, such as 1856 ('The year of the great reviews and analyses of the future, of the far-reaching memoranda and political drafts') and 1864. And there are themes that are trailed throughout the book. Some are familiar, like the centrality of the Polish issue for Bismarck, which the author rightly emphasizes. Others are less familiar, like Gall's frequent comments on the relationship between Bismarck's private and public lives, and his related observations on Bismarck as 'professional politician' (*Berufspolitiker*).[39] The author is generous, finally, with direct quotation from Bismarck's own writings, including letters. This brings out effectively the sheer gargantuan appetite of the man for both actions and words, his combination of coarse sensuality and moral intensity, mental vigour and abusive irony. One is reminded sometimes of Bismarck's contemporary, Marx, with whom he shared not only an ambivalent relationship with the labour leader Ferdinand Lassalle, but a taste for Shakespeare, Heine and Chamisso.

There are naturally omissions: the treatment of Bismarck's relationship with the press is particularly thin. But there is something to be said for not being compulsively all-embracing; and when one regrets that there is not more on a particular subject, that is often because of the thoughts provoked by what Gall does say – on Bismarck's reading, for example, or on life at his country estates Varzin and Friedrichsruh, and the spa towns like Bad Kissingen and Gastein to which he so often retreated. To lament the absence of texture and telling detail on these points is really, however, to complain that Gall has not written either a traditional 'tombstone' biography or a work of modern social history. His book has other merits. In scale this is biography in the grand old manner. At 812 pages, it may not be impossible to put down but it is certainly not easy to pick up. It does not, however, resemble the traditional life-and-times biography. That, like the nineteenth-century bourgeois novel, is to be lived in rather than merely read. Gall's book departs notably from this model in both tone and composition. It does not set out (like Reiners' volumes) to suspend disbelief; its structure and reflectiveness invite distance rather than identification. Gall may at times be a little Olympian in tone, but he is also very properly self-conscious: 'the biographer' himself appears in these pages, reflecting on the tasks and problems that face him. In this sense the book truly is, as the publishers claim, 'modern'. For this, not least, it should be welcomed by scholars and general readers.

NOTES

1 The review article on Bismarck biographies on which this essay is based considered four volumes: Ludwig Reiners, *Bismarcks Aufstieg 1815–1864* (Munich, 1980) and *Bismarck gründet das Reich 1864–1871* (Munich, 1980); A. Hillgruber, *Otto von Bismarck. Gründer der europäischen Großmacht Deutsches Reich* (Göttingen, Zurich and Frankfurt/Main, 1978); Lothar Gall, *Bismarck. Der weiße Revolutionär* (Frankfurt/Main, Berlin and Vienna, 1980); *Bismarck*, 2 vols, translated by J. A. Underwood (London, 1987). I have added material from the review of a further book: Edward Crankshaw, *Bismarck* (London, 1981).

2 See M. Hank, *Kanzler ohne Amt. Fürst Bismarck nach seiner Entlassung 1890–1898* (Munich, 1977), and W. Stribrny, *Bismarck und die deutsche Politik nach seiner Entlassung (1890–1898)* (Paderborn, 1977). The creation of the Bismarck legend is also treated in many other works that deal with the 1890s, such as J. C. G. Röhl, *Germany without Bismarck* (London, 1967).

3 Baumgarten in his 'Der deutsche Liberalismus. Eine Selbstkritik', first published in the *Preußische Jahrbücher*, vol. 18 (1866), pp. 455–517, 575–628; Weber in many places, including his Freiburg inaugural lecture of 1895, where he argued that the German bourgeoisie especially had been burned by gazing too long at the Bismarckian sun: 'Economic Policy and the National Interest in Imperial Germany', in W. G. Runciman (ed.), *Max Weber: Selections in Translation* (London, 1978), pp. 263–68. See also Weber's 'Parliament and Government in a Reconstructed Germany', in G. Roth and C. Wittich (eds), *Economy and Society* (New York, 1968), pp. 1385–92 ('Bismarck's Legacy').

4 On this, see the works of Georg Iggers cited in the Introduction to this book, note 2.

5 Reiners, *Bismarcks Aufstieg*, p. 449.

6 Gall, *Bismarck*, p. 90 (all references are to the German edition).

7 Reiners, *Bismarcks Aufstieg*, p. 107.

8 E. Ludwig, *Bismarck, Geschichte eines Kämpfers* (Berlin, 1926).

9 The three central chapters of Hillgruber's book bear these headings: 'The Making of the Politician [*Grunderfahrungen des Politikers*]: Revolutionary Threat and Prussia's Power-Political Possibilities (1848–1862)'; 'Bismarck as Prussian Prime Minister (1862–1871): the Founding of the German Empire as a Great Power despite the Burden of the European Balance'; 'Bismarck as Imperial Chancellor (1871–1890): Consolidation and Securing of the European Great-Power Status of the German Empire'. For an article that shows Hillgruber's general commitment to the 'primacy of foreign policy', see A. Hillgruber, 'Politische Geschichte in moderner Sicht', *Historische Zeitschrift*, no. 216 (1973).

10 A. J. P. Taylor, *Germany's First Bid for Colonies* (London, 1938).

11 Hillgruber, pp. 43, 105.

12 Ibid., p. 85.

13 Bismarck himself translated this: 'Man cannot create or control the tide of time, he can only move in the same direction and try to direct it.' Hillgruber, p. 67.

14 See the Introduction for the historiography on these points.

15 Hillgruber, p. 71 f.

16 These points are elaborated in my contribution to D. Blackbourn and G. Eley, *The Peculiarities of German History* (Oxford, 1984). See also Chapter 10 of the present volume.

17 Hillgruber, p. 93.

18 Ibid., pp. 106–7.

19 The 'Persönlichkeit und Geschichte' series of the Musterschmidt Verlag.

20 See Gall, *Bismarck*, pp. 84f, 179f. Gall is good on the constraint exercised by Bismarck's need for patrons in the 1850s.
21 Ibid., pp. 136–37, 194–96.
22 Ibid., p. 392.
23 Ibid., p. 56.
24 See, for example, ibid., pp. 146, 325, 366.
25 For example ibid., pp. 127–30, 351–53, 416f, 455, 488f, 526.
26 For the debate over the German *Sonderweg* and the English 'model', see Chapter 4 of this book, and Blackbourn and Eley, *Peculiarities*.
27 H. Rosenberg, *Grosse Depression und Bismarckzeit* (Berlin, 1967). Rosenberg's imaginative and innovative analysis of eocnomic, social, political and social-psychological changes in these years was never intended as a definitive piece of research, but as a stimulus to further enquiry. In this it has succeeded admirably, and deserves an English translation. The economic reality of the 'Great Depression' has been questioned by Volker Hentschel, *Wirtschaft und Wirtschaftspolitik im wilhelminischen Deutschland* (Stuttgart, 1978). The broader usefulness of the concept is discussed sceptically by Geoff Eley, 'Hans Rosenberg and the Great Depression of 1873–96', in G. Eley, *From Unification to Nazism. Reinterpreting the German Past* (London, 1986), pp. 23–41. See also the Introduction and Chapter 6 in the present volume.
28 As one of them, who clearly did recognize himself, has pointed out: H.-U. Wehler, 'Gall's "Bismarck" – Vorzüge, Grenzen und Rezeption einer Biographie', in H.-U. Wehler, *Preußen ist wieder chic* ... (Frankfurt/Main, 1983), p. 89.
29 See Introduction, pp. 23–4, on this point.
30 Gall, *Bismarck*, pp. 589, 535–53, 614f for examples.
31 Ibid., pp. 583f, 716.
32 H. Rosenberg, *Machteliten und Wirtschaftskonjunkturen* (Göttingen, 1978), p. 20.
33 Gall, *Bismarck*, p. 315.
34 Ibid., p. 393.
35 In *Erbschaft dieser Zeit* (Zurich, 1935). Bloch argued that because different aspects of a society's development move at different historical speeds, at any one time we find an uneven and perhaps explosive juxtaposition of old and new, of what has been part-superseded and what is still taking shape. The idea has entered the thinking of many modern German historians, understandably enough. I try to discuss these ideas in Blackbourn and Eley, *Peculiarities*, pp. 238–41.
36 Gall, *Bismarck*, p. 127.
37 Ibid., p. 129.
38 L. Gall, 'Die partei- und sozialgeschichichtliche Problematik des badischen Kulturkampfes', *Zeitschrift für die Geschichte des Oberrheins*, no. 113 (1965), pp. 151–96. On the general neglect of the *Kulturkampf* in studies of Bismarckian Germany see the Introduction and Chapters 7–9 of the present book.
39 One of Gall's best chapters, 'Zwischen den Fronten', deals with Bismarck in the last years of the 1850s, depicting him as a new type of politician between the monarchical-bureaucratic-absolutist system on the one side, and the party-political-parliamentary system on the other. This is also one of many instances where Gall's severely contextual approach to Bismarckiana is illuminating, for he sets the famous exchange of letters with Leopold von Gerlach in the spring and summer of 1857 against a background of Bismarck's political maneouvres 'between the fronts'. See Gall, *Bismarck* , pp. 174 ff.

2

The Kaiser and his Entourage

In 1948 Erich Eyck published a book in German on the 'personal rule' of the Kaiser. His thesis that Wilhelm II had in fact established such a form of rule met with little general acceptance among historians. They continued to point to the role of the army in Wilhelmine Germany, and to the importance of hidden wire-pullers such as Friedrich von Holstein; or they argued, as did the conservative German historian Werner Frauendienst, that there had actually been a silent parliamentarization in the years before 1914. None of these approaches was without an element of myth (and comforting myth at that), but they give a fair indication of the way the political significance of the Kaiser was played down. A. J. P. Taylor, who believed neither in Holstein as an *éminence grise*, nor in a benign process of parliamentarization, made the same point with characteristic punch. 'Who ruled in Berlin?' he asked, and gave the answer 'No-one'. This view has been reinforced in the last two decades by the work of West German historians whose approach is different again. The important group of revisionist historians who emerged in the wake of Fritz Fischer were more concerned with the structural flaws in the Kaiser's Germany than with the role played by the Emperor himself. When they looked at the dangerous instability of Wilhelmine Germany it was not 'personal rule' that they saw, but rather a 'polycratic chaos' which derived from the army, the bureaucracy, the Junkers and the economic pressure groups pursuing their vested interests. These historians may not, as John Röhl puts it, have turned the Kaiser into an unperson; but they were certainly suspicious of emphasizing the personal at the expense of the structural, while accepting what has often seemed a rather rigid division between the two categories.

The two works considered below are, in turn, explicitly revisionist (John C. G. Röhl and Nicolaus Sombart (eds), *Kaiser Wilhelm II: New Interpretations*, Cambridge, 1982; Isabel V. Hull, *The Entourage of Kaiser Wilhelm II 1888–1918*, Cambridge, 1982). Both reopen questions about personal rule, and place the Kaiser and his entourage at the centre of their accounts of Wilhelmine Germany. This approach has received a good deal of criticism, some of it noted by Röhl in his introduction to the essay collection, some apparent from subsequent reviews. The criticism is not entirely without foundation. The psycho-historical essays on the Kaiser raise doubts familiar from other works of that kind (not least on Hitler), and claims about the political significance of Kaiser and entourage are sometimes pushed too far. Yet the broad charge that the historical enterprise in these books is somehow obscurantist seems to me plainly wrong. For all the German historical preoccupation with politics from the top down, we remain surprisingly ill-informed about many aspects of high politics in this period – both its texture and its pattern. Works that systematically address the German 'governing passion' in the way that John Vincent and A. B. Cooke have addressed its British equivalent in their book of that title, are surely welcome. The two books considered are not narrative histories of Kaiser, court or dynasty: they use the palace perspective to talk about the structure of government, the 'kingship mechanism', the role of courtiers and favourites in a sham-constitutional monarchy, and the public significance of royal rituals. At their best they show not only how the personal and structural can be integrated, but why they need to be.

The following essay first appeared in the *Journal of Modern History*, vol. 56 (1984), pp. 378–82. I have, once again, placed page references to the works cited in the footnotes, added a number of additional notes and expanded the text in several places.

Over 3,000 books and articles were written about Wilhelm II during his reign. Since then German writers, at least, have been strangely reticent. There are notably few biographical works on the Kaiser by academic historians. John Röhl suggests at least two different reasons for this. There is, first, the question of success. The Kaiser's uncle, Edward VII, called him 'the most brilliant failure in history', and the older conservative-nationalist school of German historians clearly found this a stumbling-block. Wilhelm II did not fit into the line of 'great Germans' running through Luther, Frederick the Great, Freiherr von Stein and Bismarck to the (Prussian conservative) heroes of the resistance to Hitler. He was therefore tacitly left aside by such historians, who threw the burden of justifying the essential stability and decency of the Second Reich (and hence its difference from the Third Reich) on to Bismarck and Bethmann.[1] A different problem emerged in the 1960s with the change in German historiography that Fritz Fischer helped to initiate, and the group variously known as the 'critical school' or the 'Kehrites' continued.[2] For these historians, concern with the role played by individual personalities in Germany's approach to war in 1914 seemed tainted by association. It had been used too often by conservative apologists, especially by those (such as Gerhard Ritter) who deflected questions about German responsibility with answers about Bethmann's good intentions. Suspicion of 'personalist' history as intrinsically conservative and historicist has informed the writing of prominent German historians such as Hans-Ulrich Wehler in the last twenty years.[3] While research on Wilhelmine Germany has multiplied extraordinarily, the Kaiser and his place in the political system have continued to be neglected.

Röhl justly notes that investigating socio-political structures is by no means incompatible with a concern over the role played by the individual historical actor. Nor should the latter be labelled an obscurantist concern. Röhl's introduction to the volume of essays on Wilhelm II makes a spirited and elegant case for trying to bring together the personal and the structural in considering the Kaiser's Germany, and he lays out the three main areas with which the essays deal: Wilhelm's personality, his symbolic role in German society, and his influence on policy-making. On the first of these, we undoubtedly learn much about the Kaiser's upbringing and subsequent ambivalence towards England (his mother was Queen Victoria's eldest daughter), his sexual proclivities and narcissism, his peripatetic life and choice of friends and courtiers. Isabel Hull contributes an original and measured essay on the Liebenberg Circle, those intimates (above all Philipp Eulenburg) who spoke to the 'soft' and aesthetic rather than the 'hard' and manly side of Wilhelm. Röhl's own character sketch displays both detective zeal for new sources and a sense of proportion in using them. The result is as damning an indictment of the Kaiser's instability and 'caesaromania' as we possess: his love of uniforms and dressing up, his cruel jokes, horse-play and scatological outbursts, his obsessive pursuit of fixed ideas like the navy and the persecution of 'subversives' in the 1890s, his rage against the party-political leaders whom he variously referred to as monkeys, pigs and dogs, and against anyone he believed had 'betrayed' him. While he clearly impressed many (in Germany, but also in Britain) with his charm and energy, his 'glow-worm character' (Holstein) persuaded many others that he was 'not quite normal'. The doubters ranged from Lord Salisbury, the influential courtier Lord Esher and Sir Edward Grey to Philipp Eulenburg, the King of Saxony and Chancellor Hohenlohe.

The Anglo-German dimension is also central to a number of less successful approaches to the Kaiser in this volume. Lamar Cecil has a potentially good subject in 'History as Family Chronicle', but his genial narrative has more to say about character than context. He succumbs often to the tendency he notes in the Kaiser, of identifying problems with personalities. Thomas A. Kohut strikes a more immodest note in the claims he makes for his essay on the psychological roots of Germany's policy towards Britain. His often thoughtful insights into Wilhelm's relations with his parents simply do not warrant the broader and reductionist conclusions he feels entitled to draw. Who could really accept, for example, that with the death of Friedrich III after a 99-day reign in 1888, 'the dream of a liberalization of Germany, of partnership between Germany and England, seemed certain to die with him'?[4] The exaggerated contemporary hopes that were placed on the liberal crown prince may well be a useful reflection of the desperation with which many viewed the sclerotic and unstable German political system by the late 1880s. But that is no reason to consign to oblivion the various liberal openings and 'missed opportunities' of the following years (Caprivi's New Course, the Bülow Bloc), however unrealistic we may ultimately feel them to have been. Nor is it a reason to telescope the complex development of the Anglo-German antagonism, which has been examined in such detail by another contributor to this volume.[5] Kohut's essay, uneasily poised between the jaunty and the ingenuous, bristles with the first-person singular, often stated as a credo ('I believe that Wilhelm II exhibited many of the familiar symptoms of the narcissistically disturbed individual'; 'I believe' – and who could dissent – 'that Wilhelm's parents played a crucial role in shaping his personality').[6] I believe that psychology has rather more to offer history than this.[7] Meanwhile, Jonathan Steinberg's less insistent essay has much to tell us about Wilhelm's relations with the English, as well as offering perhaps the most sympathetic picture of the Kaiser in this volume.

We generally learn more from this book about the Kaiser than about his symbolic place in German society. Only two contributors tackle this problem and both are disappointing. Elisabeth Fehrenbach published an excellent book in 1969 on changing ideas of the Kaiser-figure between 1871 and 1918.[8] Here we have that book reduced to something over ten pages of text, accompanied by four pages of outstanding illustrations (the standard of the illustrations is high throughout). Fehrenbach touches on some important issues: the Bonapartism argument, as applied to Bismarck and Wilhelm II,[9] the historical ambiguity of the 'Kaiser idea' in Germany, Wilhelm as the representative of both a glowing past and a bustling future. But the text is too studded with quotations and the essay, sadly, only whets the appetite for something less allusive. Nicolaus Sombart, by contrast, sweeps through these pages like a whirlwind. He quickly blows away the 'traditional diplomatic-political' approach to German history, the 'fashionable socio-economic approach' and the literary-cultural approach.[10] He proposes to combine them in an approach which he calls cultural-sociological, but might equally be called anthropological-psychological – or almost anything. The result is a baffling mixture of *aperçu* and cliche, insight and silliness, invigoratingly energetic thought and deadly rebarbative prose. German history has finally found its Norman Mailer.

What remains regrettable is that space could not have been found in this volume to address systematically some of the many problems that arise out of the emblematic role of the Kaiser: the way that others viewed him. In the light of work by George Mosse and Arno Mayer, could we not have had something focused on the significance of ceremonial?[11] To what extent, in fact, is it possible to speak of an 'invention of tradition', in the way that British historians have used the term?[12] Fehrenbach certainly has some interesting observations on the way tradition was 'put on show' in these years, referring to the cult of the Hohenzollern dynasty, the Hermann monument and the national monument of 'Wilhelm the Great' on the Kyffhäuser, the restoration of castles and imperial palaces, and the medieval romance and Crusader imagery consciously invoked during the Kaiser's journey to Palestine.[13] It might have been useful to explore the obstacles in the way of a German 'invention' of monarchical tradition as successful as the British cult of monarchy. These obstacles certainly included the rival Bismarckian mystique of the same years, often contrasted by more radical German nationalists with the 'Byzantinism' of court and Kaiser (it was, for example, Bismarck who was most strongly associated with the national festival of Sedan Day).[14] It should also be remembered that the Wittelsbachs and others were also busy inventing traditions of their own in these years, while a third of the Kaiser's subjects owed loyalty to a Catholic Church that showed itself increasingly adept at the organisation of large-scale pilgrimages, festive inaugurations and the like.[15] These points are relevant to a further set of questions. One magnificent illustration shows top-hatted chimneysweeps and white-suited bakers marching in line at Wilhelm's silver jubilee procession of 1913. How far can the arguments of Wehler and others be sustained, that the educational system socialized Germans into a peculiarly abject reverence for authority in general and Imperial authority in particular? And, if so, how did this differ from class to class, region to region, Protestant to Catholic? No one expects definitive answers to such questions; but we might expect some attention paid to them, the more so as research is beginning to indicate that they are not unanswerable.[16]

Where this book is extremely successful is in the analysis it offers of decision-making and its channels. Röhl argues convincingly that the old debate about the Kaiser's 'personal rule' has been conducted in unhelpful terms. Criteria for a personal rule have been so rigid and demanding that they have obscured the full range of Wilhelm's power and influence.[17] The contributors to this volume therefore take personal rule seriously, but interpret it flexibly. The Kaiser's own preferences certainly did much to determine which policies were pursued; they also defined the range of possible options, for Wilhelm's implicit veto automatically ruled out certain decisions in advance. Wilhelm also exercized his power of appointment to considerable effect, over chancellors, ministers and ambassadors, as well as personnel within his own entourage. These appointments, not the wild utterances on foreign affairs, formed the basis of what Bülow called 'personal rule in the good sense'. A number of these essays provide excellent new material and analysis on decision-making, *Personalpolitik* and channels of influence, both formal and informal: Isabel Hull on the Liebenberg Circle, Wilhelm Deist (outstandingly) on the military and naval entourage, and Kathy Lerman on Wilhelm's relationship with Bülow. What emerges particularly from these studies is the way in which the multiplication of direct access to the Kaiser lamed the government machine. Wilhelm was neither able nor willing to impart cohesion to decision-making; and the result – as Röhl notes – is that 'personal rule' was not the opposite of so-called 'polycratic chaos', but was rather one of the reasons for it. The account that emerges here is strikingly similar to recent accounts of a later German leader who followed fixed ideas obsessively, surrounded himself with a fawning entourage and burked the hard decisions if he could. The conflicts and chaos that flowed from the Kaiser's personal rule, in the way it is presented here, seem quite close to the 'institutional Darwinism' under the 'weak dictator' Hitler as they have been presented by historians like David Schoenbaum, Hans Mommsen and Martin Broszat.[18]

These essays carry conviction because they argue the case for personal influence, rather than merely injecting the 'personal factor' arbitrarily into the equation. The personal here is treated as a system in itself. It is not gratuitously invoked, but neither is it a mere residual category, used to explain what cannot be explained by 'structures'. The same is true of Paul Kennedy's essay on Wilhelm's place in the making of German foreign policy, which is acute and judicious in bringing together the personal and structural levels of analysis. Terence Cole, by contrast, provides a more traditional form of political narrative. He does, however, establish a dissenting line within this volume in suggesting Bülow as a liberal hero *manqué*. He argues that with the fall of the Kaiser's favourite chancellor ('my Bismarck'), 'the politics of realism and responsibility had been overwhelmed by the politics of posture and greed'.[19] Most of us would need a good deal of convincing on this. The evidence of Hull and Lerman seems to confirm rather, that – as Lerman puts it – 'Bülow's approach was calculating, manipulative and insincere, and reinforced dangerous illusions in Wilhelm'.[20]

We move in high company in this set of essays. The short index lists six Eulenburgs, four Moltkes, three Hohenlohes, two Dohnas, and one Princess Auguste Victoria of Schleswig-Holstein-Sonderburg-Augustenburg (who became the Kaiserin). There is little about successive chancellors (except Bülow), or state secretaries and ministers like Miquel and Tirpitz with whom recent historians have rightly been much concerned, not to mention (and these authors hardly ever do) party leaders and interest-group fixers. The collection nevertheless vindicates Röhl's claim that the history of high politics need not be synonymous with uncritical narrative history. Isabel Hull's monograph on the Kaiser and his entourage underlines the point still more strongly, if it needs underlining. Her admirably researched and beautifully written study shares the best features of the Röhl–Sombart collection, and also something of its shape. After a general consideration of Kaiser and court, the book traces the 1890s and the establishment of personal rule through the career of Philipp Eulenburg. The central sections are concerned with the Bülow years, culminating with the Moltke–Harden–Eulenburg trials and the *Daily Telegraph* Affair, which together broke the Kaiser's trust in Bülow and ultimately discredited not only Eulenburg, but the civilian entourage in general. The final chapters therefore deal with the growing influence of the military entourage, which meant increasingly the chief of general staff rather than the chiefs of the military and naval cabinets. Within this overall design, Hull shows a deft talent for characterization. Her account of the peripatetic *Reisekaiser* and his court is excellent; so is the depiction of the military milieu. This well-canvassed subject is treated with great liveliness and finesse, even if it is difficult to accept Hull's concluding remark that the entourage perfected 'the well-nigh untrammelled power' of the army.[21] The discussion of caste rigidity is exemplary in demonstrating what is often lazily asserted, and the account of 'compensatory bellicosity' after 1905–6 is particularly outstanding. There is excellent material throughout on the unspoken assumptions of the entourage: attitudes towards women (dismissive), the equating of Social Democracy with 'anarchism', ingrained anti-Catholicism, and an equally ingrained racism (whose variants Hull carefully differentiates). At the institutional level, the author shows a keen understanding of the limits and tolerances within which members of the entourage operated. She shows how those who came to share the misgivings about the Kaiser harboured by the bureaucracy and foreign office faced the choice of resignation, transfer out of court service, or silence (broken by a number of them, not very heroically, after 1918). Perhaps the most curious omission is any mention of money. There is much to be said against writing history as muckraking *à la* Charles Beard;[22] but it would have been helpful to be given some indication of what the entourage cost, especially set against government budgets.

Epigrammatic verve and the sheer intelligence of the book carry the reader over some problems of interpretation and presentation. There is a tendency, especially in the conclusion, to inflate unnecessarily what is already an impressive case. Thus: 'the structure of semi-autocratic monarchy itself defined the basic contours of political and social life in the Reich',[23] which can be accepted only with a number of qualifications. As far as presentation is concerned, there is an awkward chapter on Fürstenberg, Ballin and Krupp as 'other civilians' in the entourage, while – more seriously – the period of 1909–14 is treated very briskly (this is even more true of the essay collection). True, Hull gives us a lucid set-piece on the idea of preventive war in these years, but Bethmann Hollweg remains even more of a shadowy grey figure than he deserves to be, and the Zabern affair of 1913 surely warrants some discussion.[24] Hull is generally at her best when the Kaiser himself was least unhappy, in the 'halcyon years' of Bülow's chancellorship; and the book (like the Kaiser) loses some of its balance after 1908–9. In taking her account up to 1918 the author is nevertheless able to follow through to a conclusion some of the historical ironies noted earlier in the book. In the war it was the conservative civilians who most strongly supported the Kaiser's personal power, not the military with whom this posture had been associated prewar. And the more vacillating members of the military entourage (like von Plessen, the general adjutant) who sought to shield Wilhelm only played into the hands of the hard men in the High Command. There is a faintly elegiac air to the closing scenes, but Hull is certainly not soft on the unwilled but disastrous consequences which flowed from the civilians' earlier sins of omission and commission. As she observes, 'attempts to make Wilhelm's life both successful *and* easier could not work'.[25] Those who liked the Kaiser least often served him best, and *vice versa*: it was Philipp Eulenburg who unwittingly laid the basis for later military dictatorship and nationalist adventurism.

Hull's feeling for the irony of unintended consequences is a major strength of this impressive study. It also prompts a general concluding observation. Recent German historians have properly made much of the argument that history is not exhausted by cataloguing the intentions of historical actors. This is one of their major charges against 'personalist' and historicist kinds of history; and indeed historical causality is a more difficult business than the straightforward reconstructers of intentions would allow. Yet some (not all) critics of historicism, in looking at pre-1914 Germany, have argued backwards from historical effects to individual intentions so relentlessly that Wilhelmine domestic and foreign policy seem to consist largely of the malignly willed machinations of a small clique working themselves out. In the terms of the present debate, one might almost say that here are 'personalists' in 'structuralist' clothing. The irony is that Isabel Hull and other contributors to the essay collection are really the reverse: structuralists dressed up as personalists. For all its formal preoccupation with a narrow group of individuals and their designs, the work considered here often attends more subtly to the dialectic of unintended historical consequences than does the work of some post-Fischer German historians. The cunning of reason has no doubt taken a hand in transforming such sturdy Anglo-Saxon revisionists into unwitting Hegelians.

NOTES

This essay first appeared in a different form in the *Journal of Modern History*, vol. 56 (1984), pp. 378–82.

1 See my Introduction for the historiographical background, and the literature cited there.

2 The term 'Kehrites' was first used by Wolfgang J. Mommsen to describe those historians whose critical perspective on the Second Reich owed a debt to the maverick left-liberal historian of the Weimar Republic, Eckart Kehr. The appropriateness of the label has been acrimoniously disputed. *Pace* Roger Fletcher (see Introduction, note 38), I am not aware of ever having used the term. There are certainly other issues more generally worthy of debate.

3 H.-U. Wehler, *The German Empire 1871–1918* (Leamington Spa, 1985), p. 274, characterizes an earlier book by John Röhl (*Germany without Bismarck*, London 1967) in the following terms: 'purely personalistic approach which minimizes structural conditions and thus totally misses the importance of non-individual processes'. This is both unkind and unfair.

4 J. C. G. Röhl and N. Sombart (eds), *Kaiser Wilhelm II: New Interpretations* (Cambridge, 1982), p. 67.

5 Paul Kennedy, *The Rise of the Anglo-German Antagonism 1860–1914* (London, 1980).

6 Röhl and Sombart, *Kaiser Wilhelm*, pp. 66, 69. See also pp. 68, 78, 83 for almost identical formulations.

7 American historians such as Peter Gay and Peter Loewenberg have been more cautious in the way they have tried to fuse psychology and history. Generally speaking, the evidence of many decades (as well as the more recent boom in 'psycho-history') suggests that psychology has been most helpful as a historical tool when it has been used to explore collective behaviour, such as that of occupational and religious groups, or classes. Just as George Lefebvre's work on the 'great fear' among the French peasantry in 1789 stimulated some outstanding new lines of enquiry on the revolution, so the category of 'moral panic' applied by Theodor Geiger to the behaviour of the German petty bourgeoisie in the late 1920s and early 1930s has remained important for our understanding of Nazism. The attempt to establish the susceptibility of the petty bourgeoisie to fascism because of the particular nature of its family life, social milieu and economic situation is not without its problems (see Chapter 5 below). But this sort of approach to collective social-psychological phenomena is certainly more useful than further probings into Hitler's disturbed upbringing. Similarly, the use of the psychological approach in the Röhl–Sombart volume seems most helpful where it looks at the function of courtiers and the 'kingship mechanism', or considers popular perceptions of the Kaiser.

8 E. Fehrenbach, *Wandlungen des deutschen Kaisergedankens 1871–1918* (Munich, 1969).

9 The Bonapartism concept is discussed in the Introduction, and in Chapters 10 and 11 below. For literature on the subject, see Chapter 11, note 13.

10 Röhl and Sombart, *Kaiser Wilhelm*, p. 288.

11 G. L. Mosse, *The Nationalization of the Masses. Political Symbolism and Mass Movements in Germany from the Napoleonic Wars through the Third Reich* (New York, 1975); Arno J. Mayer, *The Persistence of the Old Regime. Europe to the Great War* (London and New York, 1981). An outstanding German contribution to the related subject of monuments is T. Nipperdey, 'Nationalidee und Nationaldenkmal in Deutschland im 19. Jahrhundert', in T. Nipperdey, *Gesellschaft, Kultur, Theorie* (Göttingen, 1976), pp. 133–73. See also below, Chapter 11.

12 See E. Hobsbawm and T. Ranger (eds), *The Invention of Tradition* (Cambridge, 1983), especially the chapters by Hobsbawm, and by David Cannadine on the British monarchy.

13 Röhl and Sombart, *Kaiser Wilhelm*, p. 276.

14 See Chapter 10.

15 Werner K. Blessing deals very well with both in his study of Bavaria: *Staat und Kirche in der Gesellschaft. Institutionelle Autorität und mentaler Wandel in Bayern während des 19. Jahrhunderts* (Göttingen, 1982). I have also written about the increasing 'organization' of piety in Catholic Germany. See especially Chapter 7, and the works by Jonathan Sperber and Gottfried Korff cited there.

16 Many of the essays in the present volume try to consider class, regional and denominational variables in attitudes towards Imperial authority. So does the work of Werner Blessing (see note 15). Two excellent recent works on radical nationalism offer a differentiated picture of attitudes among the educated. See G. Eley, *Reshaping the German Right. Radical Nationalism and Political Change after Bismarck* (London and New Haven, 1980); and R. Chickering, *We Men Who Feel Most German: A Cultural Study of the Pan-German League, 1886–1914* (London, 1984).

17 Röhl and Sombart, *Kaiser Wilhelm*, pp. 13–14.

18 See the Introduction, and the works cited in footnotes 12, 71 and 72 there. David Schoenbaum first popularised the phrase 'institutional Darwinism' in his book *Hitler's Social Revolution* (London, 1966).

19 Röhl and Sombart, *Kaiser Wilhelm*, p. 266.

20 Ibid., p. 241.

21 I. V. Hull, *The Entourage of Kaiser Wilhelm II 1888–1918* (Cambridge, 1982), p. 304.

22 The reference is to the American Progressive historian Charles Beard, and I have in mind works like *An Economic Interpretation of the Constitution* (1913), an '*exposé*' of the economic interests of the Founding Fathers. There are clearly historical circumstances where it is useful to have the private facts behind the public rhetoric. Beard was moreover, a pioneer tackling a subject long neglected – as was, a little later, Eckart Kehr, whose major

study of the building of the German battle fleet first published in 1930 had something in common with Beard's work (Kehr's book is now available in English as *Battleship Building and Party Politics in Germany 1894–1901. A Cross-Section of the Political, Social and Ideological Preconditions of German Imperialism* (Chicago and London, 1975). This kind of muckraking history is open to the criticism, however, that it presents a narrow and sometimes conspiratorial version of the 'economic interpretation of history'.

23 Hull, *Entourage*, p. 293.

24 This was the occasion when the Prussian army ran amok in a small Alsatian garrison town. The Kaiser characteristically listened only to military advice and set his face against public concessions to ruffled local feelings or the outraged parliamentarians of the Reichstag. Bethmann Hollweg (like the liberal-minded governor of Alsace) was left in the lurch politically by this intransigence. For an excellent account, see David Schoenbaum, *Zabern 1913. Consensus Politics in Imperial Germany* (London, 1982).

25 Hull, *Entourage*, p. 107.

3

The Big Show: Syberberg's Hitler

The ambitious pursuit of great legendary themes has been a characteristic of the renaissance in the West German cinema. Werner Herzog addressed two potent European legends in his films *The Enigma of Kaspar Hauser* and *Aguirre, Wrath of God*. Wim Wenders has consistently explored the mythic idea of 'America', as it was imbibed by his own postwar generation, in works that include *Alice in the Cities*, *Kings of the Road* and *The American Friend*. Hans-Jürgen Syberberg is perhaps less well known to non-German audiences. His films have been concerned with a series of powerfully expressive figures from the recent German past: Wagner, Ludwig II of Bavaria, and the adventure writer (and favourite of Hitler) Karl May. The work considered below, *Hitler: A Film from Germany*, is to Syberberg what *Fitzcarraldo* is to Herzog and *Paris, Texas* to Wenders. It represents a bringing together of earlier themes in a work that combines an intensely personal statement with a valid claim to more universal significance.

The discussion of the 'great man' theme therefore takes a different form in the following chapter. Syberberg's *Hitler* is quite unlike the biographies or documentary films with which historians generally concern themselves. It is not a chronologically ordered, literal or realistic work. Just as Syberberg criticizes historians and social scientists for their alleged failure of imagination faced with the Third Reich, they in turn might jib at many aspects of his richly extravagant creation. But his film has something to say to students of modern German history as well as to Germanists and *cinéastes*. In scale and intensity it recalls the time when, in Thomas Mann's words, 'to be the spiritual battlefield of European antagonisms – that is what it meant to be German'. In his insistence on the 'Hitler within us' Syberberg wants to make a point about German collective responsibility. He also has a less local message (this is a film 'from Germany') that offers events in Germany as a larger metaphor of our times. This is a salutary insistence on the non-uniqueness of the German experience. With their 'run-of-the-mill rationality' (Syberberg), historians naturally tend to make this point in other ways – those, at any rate, who choose to. Most obviously, they place Nazism within a larger framework of the economic, social, political and cultural determinants of fascism. Syberberg's method of coming to terms with the past nevertheless warrants intellectual as well as moral and artistic respect. Not surprisingly he has much that is valuable to say about the intellectual and cultural pedigree of Nazism, particularly in relation to the German Romantic tradition. And he approaches this well-worn, even threadbare subject from an unfamiliar angle. He has also found a way of depicting something that writers on the Third Reich from Hannah Arendt to more recent historians of 'everyday life' have grappled with: the juxtaposition of the routine and the demonic, what Arendt herself called 'the banality of evil'. Syberberg's introduction to the book of the film uses this phrase; he then asks in turn that we also take seriously the 'evil of banality' – the philistine kitsch and sentimentality which were the debased forms of German Romanticism, and provided such fertile soil for Hitler. There is a contemporary point here, as in all efforts to explain the German past. The film makes a powerful plea that Germans should redeem their lost cultural legacy, reclaim concepts such as *Heimat* (homeland) that were despoiled and discredited by the Nazis. Here Syberberg was some years in advance of a more general tendency in West German society – witness the television series *Heimat*, first shown in Germany in the autumn of 1984.

This essay first appeared in the *London Review of Books*, vol. 5, no. 4, 3–16 March, 1983, under the title 'The Big Show'. I have retained the title, for it has a major bearing on the format of the film as well as indicating the important general theme of 'theatrical' Nazism. This subject is considered at greater length in Chapter 11. I have also made no basic alteration to the style or content of the original essay, although the text has been tightened up in some places and explanatory notes have been added.

While Syberberg was making this film,[1] over three thousand West German schoolchildren were asked to write an essay on the subject 'What I have heard about Adolf Hitler'. The wording was deliberate. The idea was to trawl the everyday fragments and commonplaces gleaned by the children from friends and neighbours. The results prompted widespread hand-wringing in the serious press. Hitler's birth was variously placed between the sixteenth century and 1933, his nationality given as Swiss, Dutch and Italian, his politics as Communist and Christian Democratic. Alongside sharp and telling detail ('No more bicycle thefts') came involuntary testimony to thoughts that had been put out of mind: the Jews had 'had their ears boxed'; some had been killed ('many hundreds', 'several thousand'), but they had asked for it, and anyway the Germans were not the only ones.[2] Unacknowledged guilt perhaps explains why Hellmut Diwald's reassuringly apologetic *Geschichte der Deutschen* was a recent best-seller.[3] It certainly reinforces the moral imperative behind this film and explains some of Syberberg's lyrical intensity. It is as if Germany has hurt him into poetry, as it did Heinrich Heine, quoted at the beginning and end of the film.[4] Syberberg wants to confront Germans with their collective responsibility for Hitler, conceiving his art as a 'work of mourning' (*Trauerarbeit*). As Susan Sontag observes in her introduction to this book of the film, he is close to the position of Alexander and Margarethe Mitscherlich, who argued in *The Inability to Mourn* that the Germans remain the victims of a collective melancholia, the result of a refusal to accept and work through the grief of their own recent history.[5]

This is normally dubbed coming to terms with the past – *Die Bewältigung der Vergangenheit*. It is anything but straightforward and brings its own snares. The Third Reich is chic. In addition to the recent 'Hitler boom' we have works which peddle sex in the concentration camps and orgies in the bunker.[6] Syberberg is not alone in his contempt for this. Less obviously pernicious, but arguably no more helpful, is a long-standing form of ritual German self-abasement which ends by implying the opposite of what it states: *qui s'accuse, s'excuse*. Hans-Magnus

Enzensberger has written eloquently on this.[7] At a higher level of moral and academic ambition, tough-minded analysis of the Third Reich and its origins readily generates its own blind spots, unconsciously or otherwise. Isolating 'bad' Germans exonerates the 'good'. Talk about capitalism can mean silence on Hitler's popular support, talk about the revolt of the masses can mean silence about capitalism. Interpretations centred on nihilism, totalitarianism or simply on Hitlerism have all found their critics. And so on. No generally accepted synthesis of interpretation is in sight, and recent acrimonious debates among German historians demonstrate how quickly charges of apologism and 'trivialization' can be touched off.[8]

History and civics can never be innocent, as Syberberg would agree. But what does he offer in his turn? He has certainly courted universal hostility with this gigantic and provocative dream-poem. Syberberg has deployed the aesthetics of excess to come to terms with the excesses of the Third Reich, and the result is easy to dislike. His seven-hour extravaganza is hyperbolic, repetitious, wilful, verbose: it offers a wearying cornucopia of styles, images, allusions and quotations. Sontag rightly notes Syberberg's reluctance to give anything up, his desire to suck everything out of his subject and leave it empty. It is an ambition he indulges deliberately and confidently; and that certainly lends his work a unity that, given its length, is remarkable. Syberberg nevertheless risks exhausting his public along with his theme. The publishers talk of a 'monumental discourse and a necessary act of reflection on Hitler and the Third Reich'; the unkind will see incontinent rumination. Syberberg is the thinking man's Ken Russell. Yet his rich and ambiguous images do penetrate the mind rather than simply blasting the surface of it. It is surely the difficulty of reducing the work to an obvious content that so recommends it to Sontag. Syberberg resists programmatic readings of the kind she attacked in *Against Interpretation*.[9] What he demands is criticism that takes both the form and the content of the work seriously.

Syberberg eschews a naturalistic or documentary style of presentation. His 'facts' are woven into images from which they are inseparable: they would not be much help in passing an exam in history or civics. Syberberg shows an Olympian disdain for predecessors such as Erwin Leiser and Joachim Fest who have addressed the same subject through a documentary mode.[10] It is implied (quite unfairly) that they are merely part of the grubby Hitler industry – 'our Disneyland'. Instead we are offered a film spectacle in which the Third Reich itself is conceived as the 'big show', presented in a variety of dramatic modes from the circus to the death dance. There is no attempt at surface realism. Syberberg's Hitler is protean, constantly reworked and recycled through the film, reappearing from different angles and in different forms. We see the private Hitler through the long monologue of his valet, the public Hitler through speeches by Goebbels and members of the Führer's entourage – these played non-naturalistically by actors. This is intercut with news broadcasts, with backdrop projections of buildings, paintings and other films, and with an array of symbolic props. The major *dramatis personae* of the Third Reich appear as puppets. Fictitious characters like Hitler's film projectionist ('SS-man Ellerkamp') and the Ice Cosmologist (A Dr Strangelove figure set in a Caspar David Friedrich icescape) add to the richness of the texture while reinforcing the central idea that what we are seeing is no more than a film about a 'film'.[11] Hitler, muses Ellerkamp, was 'the greatest film-maker of all time'.[12] Two principal narrators, Harry Baer and Andre Heller, bind these elements together. They introduce, reflect, soliloquise and bear witness.

In Fest's case the book preceded the film; here the film preceded the book. More important, however, is the different way the balance has been struck in the two films between distance and identification on the part of the audience. Fest's naturalistic biography/biopic of Hitler invites unwitting identification, even while its authorial voice/voice-over exhorts moral distance. We can hardly avoid a tacit complicity as we follow the unfolding life – Fest called his film *Hitler: A Career*. This is the naturalist mode, life imitating *Buddenbrooks*. Speculation about Hitler's illegitimate origins and dog-stroking interludes with Eva Braun at Berchtesgaden offer a variant on the family chronicle. Syberberg compels a quite different mixture of distance and identification. At one level he wants to disabuse us entirely of the idea that we are seeing 'how it actually happened' in some finite, Rankean sense.[13] Grand Guignol and the piling up of surreal signs and symbols work very clearly in this direction. And we understand his point that mythic extravagance is appropriate to the extravagance of Nazi myth. Parallels with some of Heinrich Mann's black comedies, with the use of fable and grotesquerie in *The Tin Drum*, with Gabriel Marcia Marquez, come to mind. Syberberg uses Brechtian techniques of alienation (placards, back-projection, narrative monologue) to achieve the same distancing effect.

But he does not only wish to hold up the myth at a distance and ask us to reflect on it, although he certainly achieves that. He also wants his audience to step inside the myth and participate. Syberberg records in his introductory notes: 'I sought an aesthetic scandal: combining Brechtian doctrines of epic theatre with Richard Wagner's musical aesthetics, cinematically conjoining the epic system as anti-Aristotelian cinema with the laws of a new myth'. The second part of this slightly opaque programme is as important as the first. Where Brecht went wrong (Syberberg is seldom modest) was in harnessing the possibilities of epic theatre to mere political didacticism. For Syberberg we can exorcise irrational myths only with irrationalism itself. The malevolence of German history can be dispelled only by recovering its sources and trying to turn their potency to benign ends. Like any good white magician Syberberg insists that rationalist denials of evil can only end in specious evasion.

Hence his bold use of Wagner, not so much to point a historical lesson as to invade the senses. We are encouraged to let ourselves become intoxicated by the music, rather as we might turn to the hair of the dog (Wagnerholics will doubtless appreciate the point). Similarly, the motif of the child used throughout the film is partly a symbol of culpable historical innocence; it is also an injunction that we must 'ultimately bring ourselves to a dreadfully simple, almost childish naivety, if that is still possible, on the basis of our memories of ourselves'. If the film seems dream-like, that is perhaps because one of Syberberg's intentions was to present it as a nightmare – but one from which, once we have admitted and felt its terrors, we can be released.

There are obvious objections to this therapeutic cult of the irrational, and Syberberg anticipates some of them – the risk involved in portraying 'the beauty of evil', for instance, and the danger of 'heroizing' his black magicians. He is careful to extol and to use the tools of irony as a way round these problems. But he suggests that irony and scepticism have their limits. With passionate seriousness he stresses the importance of courage (the word is another hostage to fortune), challenging viewers and readers to put their hands in the fire as he has done, to grapple with the evil of Nazism by grappling with a personal Faust. Hence the constant reminders about 'our Hitler', 'the Hitler within us'. This can be chilling and effective, but there is also another problem here. One of the reasons why Thomas Mann used the 'harmless and simple soul' Serenus Zeitblom as the narrator of *Doctor Faustus* was to avoid the danger of creating 'a new German myth, flattering the Germans with their own "demonism"'.[14] Syberberg might be thought to have fallen into this trap, like those many immediate postwar writers who (over)emphasized the 'demonic' quality of National Socialism.[15] This is only the most extreme manifestation of a more general problem: that of exaggerating the fateful uniqueness of the 'German mind'. Ostensibly at least, Syberberg seems to reinforce a misleading stereotype of the Third Reich when he ties it to the symbols of German cultural peculiarity. We have passed this way before. A string of guides have issued us with their confident directions about the straight road that runs from Luther to Hitler, via Romanticism, Wagner, Nietzsche and German Expressionism.[16] The case against the 'German mind', its errors and omissions, represents one of the most common mega-explanations of the German catastrophe. We are familiar with the indictment: the rejection of the Enlightenment and Western rationalism, the tormented relationship to nature, the cultivation of inwardness (*Innerlichkeit*), the preference for 'spiritual' music over the 'prosaic' novel of the British and French, the yearning for the organic rather than the mechanical society. The list of supposedly fateful German peculiarities could be endlessly catalogued, and often has been. The problems with this loose kind of Nazi pedigree-hunting are also familiar. It is not only that

German singularity is exaggerated. Figures are also ripped out of context and intellectual movements conflated; scant regard is paid to problems of the reception of ideas; and what does not fit in is left out (German preoccupation with the technical and mechanical, to take only one example).[17]

In fact, Syberberg offers an advance on this sterility in two respects. In the first place, he most effectively conjures up the vulgarized Romanticism which arguably provided the deeper cultural roots of National Socialism. He does so by depicting the individuals and artefacts that symbolise this debased culture of kitsch: the adventure writer Karl May (a favourite of Hitler's), or the journal *Die Gartenlaube* ('The Arbour'), which served up its readers a saccharine mixture of sentimentalized nature, popular science, conventional morality and nationalism.[18] Syberberg evokes, through its detritus, a philistine bourgeois and petty-bourgeois milieu with its painful combination of cloying provincialism and latently brutal intolerance.[19] Embodied in a Hitler, a Himmler or an Eichmann we have what Hannah Arendt called 'the banality of evil'.[20] That, not the brooding genius of Wagner or the Superman, is the real problem of the German mind. And it raises both moral and artistic questions. How do we bring the narrow world of the *Spiesser* – the philistine – into the same picture as the terror and the six million? How hold simultaneously in our minds the triviality and the world-historical flatulence of Nazism? As German historians turn in growing numbers to look at the 'everyday life' of the Third Reich, their critics insist that we should focus on the big facts, the central evil. That is understandable, but misses the point: we need to see the conjunction of the evil and the banal. That is one of Syberberg's major achievements, in the scenes such as the conversations between Himmler and his masseur and astrologer, or in the cut from Hitler's complaints about his socks falling down to musings on the cosmos.

Second, and potentially at odds with this, Syberberg has done much to rescue German Romanticism from the tyranny of hindsight. Whatever one's judgment on his advocacy of therapeutic irrationalism, he is surely right to try and redeem Novalis, the Grimms and so many others from the pedigree-hunters: 'Give everything to Hitler and Goebbels? And is Caspar David Friedrich right-wing and a fascist?' In a moving lament during the final part of the film, Andre Heller indicts Hitler and National Socialism for soiling such figures through guilt by association, as well as corrupting concepts like *Heimat*. He completes the charge with an attack on the soulless cities, fast food and road movies (Wim Wenders is presumably the target here) for which Hitler and total defeat paved the way in West Germany. We are uncomfortably reminded (and are surely meant to be) of Hitler's own attacks on arid materialism and the concrete jungle. But we are also reminded that hostility to Mammon and the machine is, at the least, politically ambiguous – even in Germany. Like technocracy and the cult of the machine, arguments for a return to nature can be filled with very different political contents. There is no straight line that runs from the German Romantics and advocates of 'inwardness' to the Third Reich, just as (to take an opposite example) there is nothing unambiguously 'progressive' about the political legacy of Blake and Ruskin. When it comes to the 'influence' of such figures, it is later generations who play the active role. In Britain men like Blake and Ruskin have been plausibly located within a progressive political and cultural tradition, even if it is the Conservative Party that has appropriated *Jerusalem* ; in Germany these filiations have been much weaker. Perhaps the utopian writings of Mühsam and Toller, like those of Ernst Bloch, should have taught us to see these things differently.[21] Certainly the advent of Green politics in the Federal Republic drives the lesson home in a new way, however we may view the choice (if it is a choice) between fast-food civilization and the 'Greening' of Germany.[22]

For all his grasp of cultural mentalities and nuance, Syberberg is the epitome of the Unpolitical German. This is not the only respect in which (as Susan Sontag notes) he inhabits the same cultural and intellectual world as Thomas Mann – or, at least, the same world as that of the earlier Thomas Mann who wrote his celebrated 'Reflections of an Unpolitical Man' during the First World War.[23] We see this clearly in the way Syberberg uses, and fails to use, the allusive possibilities of those puppets with which he litters his sets. When German literary critics hear the word 'puppet', they reach for their Kleist. *On the Marionette Theatre* offers a symbol of fallen man aspiring to a grace and completeness embodied in the puppet. The power of Kleist's story resonates through subsequent literature: it can be seen in the dolls and acrobats of Rilke's *Duino Elegies*, and it is the same story which fires Adrian Leverkühn in Mann's *Doctor Faustus*. Indirectly, through the Faust legend, and ironically, through Syberberg's graceless and tarnished Nazi puppets, this metaphor has a place in the present work. But there is another important associative layer which Syberberg disregards. When German historians hear the word 'puppet', they reach for their Marx. Marxist discourse has enriched our political understanding by deploying the vocabulary of drama, the stage and roles: more specifically, it has given us Hitler as the puppet of German capitalism.[24] Syberberg openly rejects the idea that this can tell us anything. It is admittedly difficult to feel enthusiastic about the woodenly manipulative 'agent' theories of the Third International. But other Marxist approaches have done much to illuminate the rituals and forms, as well as the functions, of German fascism, deepening our understanding of what Walter Benjamin called the fascist 'aestheticization of politics'.[25] If this is one stage Syberberg chooses to leave bare, that can hardly be because he finds it impossible to represent artistically. He does, after all, have a narrator talk us through Max Weber's three pure types of domination.

Syberberg addresses the role-playing of Hitler and his entourage through Freud, but not through Marx. His puppets are correspondingly less expressive. Syberberg is altogether shakier on the drama of politics than on the drama of the soul. The *Sieg Heils* that punctuate the film are a rather hackneyed shorthand for mass politics; and in the depiction of Hitler as the man with the staring eyes ('Two glowing eye-stars, fulminating') inventiveness yields to a flat and misleading image of the Führer as snake-charmer.

Syberberg has made a film for Germany. As the title announces, however, it is also a film from Germany, for the rest of us. It is true that the portrayal of Hitler's universal legacy in the modern world suffers from Syberberg's compulsion to include everything (not only the two Germanies, but South Africa and the USSR, Hollywood and property speculators). But the central moral vision nevertheless has force and integrity. And the film does turn the trick of showing Hitler's Germany as a metaphor of our times. If Paris was (in Walter Benjamin's words, once again) 'the capital of the nineteenth century', Germany here is the 'tragic land' of the twentieth. Since 1945, of course, both Federal Republic and Democratic Republic have come to stand as exemplars in a rather different sense – as models for capitalist economic miracle and socialist economic miracle respectively. Brought up in one German state and resident in the other, Syberberg has harsh words on the legacy of Hitler in each. No one could reasonably fail to disagree with much of what he has to say. But if coming to terms with the German past means coming to terms with the German present, then it is worthwhile also trying to come to terms with Syberberg's *Hitler*.

NOTES

1 Hans-Jürgen Syberberg, *Hitler: A Film from Germany*, translated by Joachim Neugroschel, with an introduction by Susan Sontag (Manchester, 1982). The book contains screenplay and stills and an introduction by the director. It was first published in West Germany in 1978.

2 Dieter Boßmann (ed.), *'Was ich über Adolf Hitler gehört habe . . . ' Folgen eines Tabus: Auszüge aus Schüler-Aufsätzen von heute* (Frankfurt/Main, 1977).

3 H. Diwald, *Geschichte der Deutschen* (Frankfurt/Main, 1978).

4 The famous lines quoted are from Heine's *Nachtgedanken* (Night Thoughts) of 1843:
Denk ich an Deutschland in der Nacht,
Dann bin ich um den Schlaf gebracht.
(I think of Germany in the night
And then sleep leaves me)

5 A. and M. Mitscherlich, *Die Unfähigkeit zu trauern. Grundlagen kollektiven Verhaltens* (Munich, 1968).

6 I had in mind the so-called *Hitlerwelle* which disturbed so many West German historians in the late 1970s and early 1980s.

7 H. M. Enzensberger, *Deutschland, Deutschland unter anderm: Äusserungen zur Politik* (Frankfurt/Main, 1968), p. 10.

8 The best guides to the historiography of National Socialism and the Third Reich are P. Ayçoberry, *The Nazi Question. An Essay on the Interpretation of National Socialism (1922–1975)* (New York, 1981), and I. Kershaw, *The Nazi Dictatorship. Problems and Perspectives of Interpretation* (London, 1985).
9 S. Sontag, *Against Interpretation* (New York, 1961).
10 Fest's film is discussed below. Erwin Leiser, a German *émigré* to Sweden, released his film *Mein Kampf* in Gothenburg in 1960. It won the Golden Award for best documentary at the 1960 International Film Festival in San Francisco. In 1961 Leiser released a further documentary in Switzerland, *Eichmann and the Third Reich*.
11 On Caspar David Friedrich and other German painters of the period, see the excellent work by William Vaughan, *German Romantic Painting* (London, 1980), which also has a select bibliography.
12 Viewers of *Heimat* will recall the part played in the plot by the films of the German army.
13 Leopold von Ranke's phrase *wie es eigentlich gewesen* – 'as it actually happened' – was the great dictum of German 'scientific' history. See the works of Georg Iggers, cited in the Introduction (note 2) on the historiographical background.
14 Quoted in N. Hamilton, *The Brothers Mann* (London, 1978), pp. 325–26.
15 Such as Friedrich Meinecke in *The German Catastrophe* (Cambridge, Mass., 1950).
16 Two classic early examples are Rohan O'Butler, *The Roots of National Socialism* (London, 1941) and William M. McGovern, *From Luther to Hitler. The History of Nazi–Fascist Philosophy* (London, 1946). The approach is perhaps most familiar from the popular bestseller by William Shirer, *The Rise and Fall of the Third Reich* (New York, 1960). A work such as Hans Kohn's *The Mind of Germany. The Education of a Nation* (London, 1961) is much superior in scholarly terms, but still presents a strikingly teleological account.
17 I have discussed the issue of German cultural exceptionalism in more detail in my contribution to D. Blackbourn and G. Eley, *The Peculiarities of German History* (Oxford, 1984), esp. pp. 211–21.
18 For a brief account of the *Gartenlaube*, see the pioneering study by Ernest K. Bramsted, *Aristocracy and Middle-Classes in Germany. Social Types in German Literature* (Chicago, 1964), pp. 203–9.
19 This theme is imaginatively dealt with by Hermann Glaser, *The Cultural Roots of National Socialism* (London, 1978). Glaser uses a wide range of unfamiliar sources – school textbooks, sentimental paintings, evidence from domestic interiors, cigarette coupon catalogues – to build up his convincing picture of this milieu. His bibliography even lists a work on the history of German garden gnomes. The original German title of the book was *Spiesserideologie*, the *Spiesser* being a combination of the philistine and the petty-bourgeois.
20 Hannah Arendt's point was that 'the trouble with Eichmann was precisely that so many were like him, and that the many were neither perverted nor sadistic, that they were, and still are, terribly and terrifyingly normal'. See *Eichmann in Jerusalem. A Report on the Banality of Evil* (London, 1963), p. 253.
21 An English translation of Bloch's great work *Das Prinzip Hoffnung – The Principle of Hope* (Oxford, 1986) – has just appeared.
22 There are, of course, those who see the Green/Alternative movement as dangerously akin to what they believe Nazism to have been: an 'extremist', anti-'system' movement that entices youth with its promise of vaguely specified and unrealisable revolutionary change. These charges tend to come from the right (the left has different and, to my mind, more plausible criticisms) and seem to misunderstand both Nazis and Greens. The two are different in almost every significant respect – social composition, leadership structure, programme, tone. This is not to deny the crass intransigence sometimes displayed by the fundamentalist wing (the 'Fundis') of the Greens.
23 Thomas Mann, *Betrachtungen eines Unpolitischen* (Berlin, 1918), which has recently appeared in an American translation. See also F. Stern, 'The Political Consequences of the Unpolitical German', in F. Stern, *The Failure of Illiberalism* (Chicago, 1975), pp. 3–25.
24 See Chapter 11.
25 W. Benjamin, *Das Kunstwerk im Zeitalter seiner technischen Reproduzierbarkeit* (Frankfurt/Main, 1963), pp. 48, 51. Benjamin argued that fascism aestheticized politics, communism responded by politicizing art.

II

Awkward Classes

4

The Discreet Charm of the German Bourgeoisie

I

The German bourgeoisie has had a bad press. For years historians criticized its seduction by militarism or cultural despair, its lack of civic engagement and political maturity. The broadest indictment came from those scholars who, from the 1960s, helped to refashion our understanding of the recent German past. They pointed to the alleged failure of the German bourgeoisie to assert itself as its counterparts in France and Britain had done. Instead, they argued, it was bought off by material rewards and compromised with the old elite in social and political terms. Hence a central point in attempts to explain the fateful course of modern German history was the 'feudalization' and political abdication of the bourgeoisie.

In the course of the 1970s I became increasingly sceptical about arguments of this kind. My views were first expounded systematically in a book co-authored with Geoff Eley and published in German (*Mythen deutscher Geschichtsschreibung*, Frankfurt/Main, Berlin and Vienna, 1980). The main lines of the argument were presented to an English audience for the first time in the present essay, which appeared originally as a review article in *European Studies Review*, vol. 11 (1981), pp. 243–55. It is reprinted here with minor changes, although I have taken the opportunity to follow up a number of points in the footnotes. The German publication of 1980 has since appeared in a revised and extended English edition as *The Peculiarities of German History: Bourgeois Society and Politics in Nineteenth-Century Germany* (Oxford, 1984). The Introduction to that book reviews the historical debate which the original German edition helped to spark off.

The historiographical cross-currents in the last five years have been extremely interesting. On the one hand, research on nineteenth-century Europe continues to underline the staying-power of old elites everywhere: the economic power of landowners and the social cachet of landowning, the importance of aristocracies as patrons and arbiters of taste, the survival of privilege within mass political systems. Martin Wiener's *English Culture and the Decline of the Industrial Spirit* (Cambridge, 1981) raised many of these issues in the English case. Arno J. Mayer's *The Persistence of the Old Regime* (London, 1981) used evidence from a wide range of European countries (including the UK) to argue these points on a general basis.

Work of this kind has had the effect of making the 'feudalized' German bourgeoisie seem less peculiar after all. It can be argued, though, that Wiener, Mayer and others have made too much of certain cultural symbols and have pushed their general arguments too far – just as earlier historians did in talking about the survival of pre-industrial elites and value-systems in Germany. For there is certainly evidence that points in the opposite direction: to a far-reaching *embourgeoisement* in nineteenth-century Germany, as elsewhere in Europe.

Recent research makes this plain, as German historians have turned to fields once cultivated more intensively by their British and French colleagues. These include a number of the areas noted in the following essay: the rule of law and changes in the legal structure, the development of associational life, the growth of philanthropy, and the importance for all of these of the way in which social and political elites functioned at the local level. This research seems likely to uncover a pattern of bourgeois dominance all the more convincing because it does not rest on the old idea of a 'bourgeois revolution' or a mythical 'rising middle class'. It is striking how much attention is now being devoted by historians in the Federal Republic to the German *Bürgertum* and to *Bürgerlichkeit*. (One major research project on this theme, at Bielefeld, is mentioned in the introduction.) This seems to reflect a recognition of two former blind spots: social historians often ignored elite groups, while those concerned with elites frequently ignored the bourgeoisie. The next decade seems set to witness a new bourgeois era, at least in historiographical terms.

Gordon Craig begins his new history of Germany with an arresting question: 'Is it a mistake to begin with Bismarck?' He continues with characteristic assurance to suggest that it is not, and a finely differentiated picture of the Iron Chancellor dominates the early chapters. Bismarck returns again briefly at the end of the book, placed alongside Hitler in a sideways glance at the roots of the German catastrophe. It is clear, though, that the juxtaposition reflects the needs of artistic symmetry more than it does the author's belief in the essential continuity of recent German history. When Craig addresses himself (on a rare occasion) to this question, we are told that 'those German historians of the modern school who argue that Hitler is part of a continuum that includes Bismarck, William II, and Stresemann are wrong . . . Adolf Hitler was *sui generis*, a force without a real historical past . . . ' At one level this is difficult to disagree with. Indeed, Hans Rosenberg, in one of the waspish reviews reprinted in the present collection, observes impatiently that 'everybody knows that Bismarck was no Hitler'. The question, of course, is whether the problem is most usefully approached in these terms. Rosenberg, whose seminal influence is evident in so many of the books under review here, would argue that it is not. Continuity is too important to be left to the narrative historians.

It is hardly surprising that the question of continuity in German history will not go away. The awful reality of the Third Reich continues to cast its shadows, and both of the present books which deal directly with the subject feature swastikas on their covers, an unnecessary reminder of the very special responses which the period triggers among both the lay public and professional historians. As far as the latter are concerned, Craig notes that many of the most gifted young German historians of the early 1930s were themselves forcibly uprooted to America, among them Hajo Holborn, Felix Gilbert and Hans Kohn. Hans Rosenberg might be added to the distinguished list. Even for historians without this direct experience, the combination of moral and intellectual problems remains very real for those involved in the writing of modern German history. This is true of German historians seeking to 'come to terms with the past'; and it is true in a different but no less complicated sense of those non-German historians who attempt to assume what Richard Cobb has called a 'second identity' in order to write about the subject. Hans Rosenberg tells us that when he published *Bureaucracy, Aristocracy, and Autocracy* in 1958, it was prompted by the question of National Socialism's deeper roots. That question remains very much on the agenda.[1]

When Peter Stachura writes of the enduring problem of 'why Germany should have been the first highly industrialized and advanced country to witness the advent to power of an avowedly totalitarian party', he alludes indirectly to the inevitable corollary of the debate over continuity: the problem of German 'peculiarity'. All national histories are peculiar, but it often seems that some are more peculiar than others.[2] In what precisely is this peculiarity said to reside in the German case? Historians have offered many answers to this question since 1945. Some noted Germany's unique position in Europe, fatefully trapped between East and West. Others, less impressed by the logic of geographical determinism, looked for the essence of continuity in the malign role played by the Prussian army and military values, or in the fatal flaws of the 'German mind'. Both approaches have enjoyed considerable academic and popular respectability, and residual elements of both can be detected in some of these volumes. Neither, however, is nowadays proposed with the assurance which was once the case. The identification of militarist 'bad Germans' can, all too evidently, serve the apologist's purpose of distracting attention away from deeper and more pervasive flaws in German society and politics. The same is true, more involuntarily and in a rather different sense, of Nazi pedigree-hunting in the realm of ideas, with its marked unwillingness to specify, or even to recognize as a problem, who was influenced by what ideas and to what effect. It is probably true to say in general that our present understanding of German historical peculiarity, while incorporating valuable elements of the approaches already noted, has moved on to more sociological and structural terrain.

It has now become customary to locate the 'failure of Western-style liberal democracy to take root in Germany' in a fateful discrepancy between economic development on the one hand, and social values and political life on the other.[3] In this view, Germany simply did not have a bourgeois revolution of the normal, that is the English, kind. Indeed, Ralf Dahrendorf, whose importance is indicated by these works, wrote a vastly influential book which acquired its cutting edge by posing the question 'why wasn't Germany England?'[4] Much that the German bourgeoisie wanted in material terms was provided not by its own efforts but by the state, 'from above'. Moreover, industrial and commercial capital never won a struggle against the great landed estates, but compromised instead.[5] This was notably the case, so it has been argued, during the Great Depression of 1873–96, when both heavy industry and the estate-owning Junkers were protected by a move away from laissez-faire and the reintroduction of protective tariffs. The 'marriage of iron and rye' allegedly continued to hold good as a defensive partnership down to 1914, despite periodic friction.[6]

Perhaps the crucial point about such arguments is the further contention that this 'mis-development' was accompanied by a bourgeois compromise with the Junkers and their allies at the social level. Thus the German bourgeoisie, already weakened by the 'failed bourgeois revolution' of 1848 and the achievement of unification from above by Bismarck, gave a clear sign of its capitulation to the continuing role of 'pre-industrial social, political and economic leadership elites' in the new Reich.[7] And in subsequent years, rather than assert its *own* values, the German bourgeoisie instead aped the values of the old elite: the reactionary values of the landowners, officer corps and Prussian bureaucracy. They underwent, in short, a process which has commonly been dubbed the feudalization of the bourgeoisie.[8] This was, in the end, to prove politically disastrous from a liberal or democratic perspective. For the traditional elite was enabled to survive and keep its hands on the levers of power through to 1914 and beyond. This, for Rosenberg, was one of the 'peculiarities of recent German history' compared with '"western" developments'.[9] Only the Third Reich, to the advent of which they had made such a significant contribution, and the total defeat of 1945, finally dislodged this stubborn pre-industrial elite from its anachronistic but commanding heights. Only then did the German bourgeoisie – at least in the West – really come into its own, casting political life and social values after its own image.

Two things are striking about these views. The first is the emphasis which has been placed on what did not happen rather than on what did. *Wie es eigentlich gewesen* – how it actually happened – was Ranke's celebrated dictum on the way in which history should be written. *Wie es eigentlich nicht gewesen* would perhaps be more appropriate to describe the way in which much current writing catalogues German history's sins of omission. The second point is the central role – or rather non-role – which is ascribed to the bourgeoisie in this lamentable set of developments. Bourgeoisies are supposed to rise, but the German one is commonly depicted as moving disastrously through the modern period in the opposite direction. Retreating into mere money-making or into the private world of sensibility, apeing its betters and revering the martial virtues, supine and star-struck, the German bourgeoisie appears to be a class which sold its liberal birthright, and one which bears a heavy responsibility (in this indirect sense) for the 'authoritarian trend in modern Germany' and ultimately for the rise of Hitler.[10] It is with arguments of this kind that the present review article is principally concerned.[11]

II

It might be useful in the first place to note how normative assumptions are at work here about the 'proper' historical role played by the bourgeoisie. On this reading the joint-stock company and the telegraph are supposed to bring self-consciously bourgeois values and institutions in their wake. If they do not, something must therefore have gone wrong. The 'West' in general and England in particular provide a yardstick against which developments in Germany are measured and found wanting, as in Steinberg's comment that the students of the Weimar Republic, like the professional elite of imperial Germany, had 'little understanding of Western-style individualism and pluralism'.[12] This approach can undoubtedly be illuminating, as Dahrendorf has shown and as Barrington Moore demonstrated with his brilliantly idiosyncratic *Social Origins of Dictatorship and Democracy*,[13] a book which is rather unfairly and mechanically criticized by Schissler. It is also true, however, that if ideal-types of this kind are to be used, they should at least – as Diefendorf argues in his thoughtful introduction – be made explicit. In fact, one might perhaps question whether self-conscious bourgeoisies of the classic kind ever really behaved as they are supposed to have done. Work done by historians of seventeenth-century England and late eighteenth-century France has certainly raised serious doubts on this score.[14] Indeed the subject of German peculiarity calls to mind the oddly parallel debate on 'The Peculiarities of the English' between, on the one side, E. P. Thompson, and on the other, Tom Nairn and Perry Anderson, in which the latter attribute so many of the failings of British public and political life to England's historically 'supine bourgeoisie'.[15] This review article is certainly no place to grapple with such broad questions about the classic historical role of the bourgeoisie; but a consideration of the German case from a rather different angle may be a useful exercise.[16]

A key charge against the German bourgeoisie alleges a willingness to exchange its political birthright for economic opportunities and social prestige. Diefendorf offers a notably subtle variation on this in his account of businessmen in Aachen, Crefeld and Cologne, where he shows convincingly how they were gradually and voluntarily tied to the machinery of authority by successive French and Prussian governments through their role in semi-private, semi-public organs of self-administration like the chambers of commerce and commercial courts. This augments most usefully the work of historians like Wolfram Fischer and Reinhart Koselleck.[17] A less differentiated account is given by

Pierenkemper, who demonstrates how Westphalian entrepreneurs were far more concerned with business interest groups than they were with national, state or even local politics, and rehearses familiar arguments about the 'feudalization' of the bourgeoisie. Craig makes a rare foray into economic territory to suggest similar points, and Rosenberg illustrates the same problem from a different angle by showing how the bourgeoisie bought its way into land from the end of the eighteenth century.

These points are well taken. But it may be asked whether this bourgeois tendency to take the money and run, to seek an *ersatz* for its forfeit of *real* social and political muscle, is the whole story. The very notion of such 'discrepancies' between the economic, social and political spheres (Rosenberg's 'great triad') needs careful examination. There is, of course, nothing inherently implausible about these 'non-identities': it is certainly quite possible for economic power, social prestige and political authority to be differently located in a given society over a considerable stretch of time. This is the essence of Weber's distinction between class, status and power: it is also central to much of Marx's writing.[18] In fact perhaps only vulgar Marxists and vulgar anti-Marxists cling to the view that 'superstructure' should be a perfect reflection of 'base'. We cannot be anything but grateful for the way in which historians like Rosenberg have built these 'non-identities' into their historical accounts. The problem now, however, is that arguments of this kind run the risk of becoming frozen and hardened by habitual repetition. The relationships among the economic, social and political spheres threaten to become as rigidly dissociated as they have been rigidly associated in the base/superstructure model. As a result, the impact of dynamic economic change on both civil society on the one hand and public and political life on the other has been undervalued, yielding an unnecessarily attenuated picture of bourgeois society in nineteenth-century Germany.

Arguments about the feudalization of the German bourgeoisie provide an example of this. Surrounded by the seemingly damning evidence of these authors, we should perhaps remember Weber's comment: 'The entailed estate of the parvenu is one of the characteristic products of capitalism in an old country with aristocratic traditions and a military monarchy. In the German East the same thing now takes place which has been going on in England for centuries.[19] Certainly English radicals like Cobden, with their bitter denunciations of a 'feudalized' bourgeoisie, would have assented.[20] And Pierenkemper reminds us that a similar pattern can be detected in France.[21] What we have here, in fact, is the intermingling of old and new elements of a new ruling class, the latter naturally adopting as a symbol of its wealth and power what its previous superiors had established as the prevailing standards of luxury or conspicuous consumption. In Germany the bourgeoisie marked its arrival by purchasing Junker estates, just as it rejected the simplicity of Biedermeier in its more spacious homes and opted for chairs with embossed leather covers depicting hunting scenes. Moreover, just as David Hansemann saw the bourgeois purchase of Junker estates as a sign of newly-emergent bourgeois strength,[22] so can the process of ennoblement be seen as a measure of bourgeois success. Certainly bourgeois ennoblement and titles should not be viewed as a mere capitulation.[23] Not only were there bourgeois like Theodor Fontane (justly a favourite of Craig's) who accepted honours with an open contempt for the underlying principles. It was also true, as Rosenberg himself shows, that those with longer-established titles were *obliged* to share their former social prestige with 'ennobled or non-noble plutocrats, baptised or unbaptised textile Jews'.[24] A sense of social flux was ubiquitous. It was expressed with cynical clarity by the young Junker Leo Poggenpuhl, in one of the Fontane novels not quoted by Craig: 'Who *doesn't* have a name these days? And what does a name really *mean*? Pears Soap, Blookers Cocoa, malt extract from Johannes Hoff. Knights and heroes simply can't live up to that.'[25] The new elite which was formed in Germany in the nineteenth century continued to have an important aristocratic component, as in Britain, but one should be wary of assuming that the bourgeoisie simply succumbed to the aristocratic embrace.[26] What matters is the terms on which this symbiosis of old and new took place. This is not easy to determine. But at least we should not confuse the form with the substance: much of its behaviour illustrated the buoyancy as much as the capitulation of the German bourgeoisie.

This rather coarse-grained buoyancy had tended, at least by the last third of the nineteenth century, to give ground to bourgeois anxiety. In the process the bourgeoisie undoubtedly grew closer to the aristocracy in the face of growing fears about social tension and the rising labour movement, while simultaneously registering a more marked tendency to cultural despair. Yet as Sheehan says of the latter, 'there was nothing especially new or uniquely German' about it; it has been, rather, 'a persistent and pervasive part of bourgeois culture'.[27] This is true of bourgeois anxieties more generally, which indeed had always existed as the reverse side of the coin of vulgar bourgeois optimism, casting a shadow over achievements like the new urban civilization and extended communications. Here too there seems little reason to suppose the bourgeois fears of crime and the working class, any more than family snobbery, agonizing about the shortage of servants and a patronizing tone towards the petty bourgeoisie, need explaining as part of a residual or revived 'feudal' mentality. They, too, were a 'pervasive part' of a bourgeois culture which, in Germany as elsewhere, was itself pervasive.

III

It might in fact be more accurate to talk of the embourgeoisement of German society rather than the feudalization of the German bourgeoisie. This took many forms, but one of the most important was the securing and consolidation of the rule of law as the necessary foundation of a bourgeois society. At one level this was marked by the progressive erosion of the corporate state (*Ständestaat*), which obstructed the realization of formal equality before the law, although both Schissler and Reif remind us that this was a protracted and uneven process.[28] At a second and no less important level it was characterized by a framework of civil and penal codes which guaranteed principles such as the inalienability and free disposability of property. The civil code which came into effect in 1900 was the culmination of this trend: in the words of one authority, it 'codified the ideals of bourgeois society in the nineteenth century'.[29]

The rule of law in these various forms provided a framework for the unfolding of bourgeois energies and values in ways which are not easy to pin-point with precision. The very fact that bourgeois hegemony was exercised through civil society makes it (and made it) less easy to identify than the prescriptions and proscriptions of the corporate state. We can, however, isolate some strands. There seems little doubt, for example, that inherited status or *Stand* began to give way to wealth and merit as criteria of social worth, just as at a more material level the criteria of the cash nexus – property and competition – eclipsed ideas of the primacy of social harmony or the just price. Both Schissler's book and Rosenberg's classic essay on 'Die Pseudodemokratisierung der Rittergutsbesitzerklasse' provide valuable material on these changes. Similarly, the growing self-consciousness of professional groups like surveyors, accountants, architects and school-teachers accompanied these changes, as a society which placed a growing emphasis on access to and disposability of property, on material calculation and on the discipline of the timetable, came to value their expertise accordingly. Diefendorf and Pierenkemper, who deal with their respective groups of businessmen as 'occupational groups' rather than as part of a class, have disappointingly little to say about these underlying assumptions of a bourgeois society in the process of formation. Reif, however, in his sensitive study of the Westphalian aristocracy, offers some valuable insights. Certainly it is true that a recognition of new standards of 'achievement' and 'efficiency' can be found in some unlikely quarters. Even the Catholic Church, to which the aristocrats of Reif's study remained so committed, seems to have bowed to the logic of new social values: by the end of the nineteenth century it had begun to move saints' days from work-days to week-ends, so that Catholic wage and salary earners should not remain idle when they could be contributing to gross national product.[30]

Values of this kind, like the rule of law, were pervasive and came to seem natural. They were effective not least because they were deemed to be self-evident by 'public opinion', itself a notable product of emerging bourgeois civil society. The characteristic institution here was the voluntary association, which in a sense replaced the former compulsions of the corporate state as a vehicle for moulding and improving values.[31] In the late eighteenth and early nineteenth centuries the classic instance of associational life was the reading club, where the propertied and educated bourgeoisie mingled with sections of the bureaucracy and aristocracy.[32] By the middle years of the nineteenth century, however, associations were incomparably broader in their scope and goals, embracing business, sociable, philanthropic, educational and moral objectives. They ranged from the trade association to the choral society, from the Schiller association to the carnival (*Fastnacht*) association, from the educational association to the society for the protection of animals. Such associations not only reflected the growing strength and density of social, personal and family ties among the propertied and educated bourgeoisie; they also constituted a public sphere which was in fact dominated by the natural social power and self-consciously civilized values of a bourgeoisie which was starting to see itself as a 'general' or 'universal' class. The associations expressed bourgeois aspirations to social leadership. In them the underlying economic, social and moral principles of bourgeois life were publicly acted out as a universal model for both the petty bourgeoisie and working class.[33]

There were many other ways in which the bourgeoisie set the tone of German society from the middle decades of the nineteenth century, for all the 'aristocratic and military values of the Empire' insisted on by Steinberg and other authors.[34] In the sphere of patronage, for example, the bourgeoisie stepped into the role vacated by former princely or aristocratic support. The public park and gallery, financed by bourgeois civic notables, rivalled the princely or aristocratic park and gallery, while other public places of entertainment or edification – the public museum, concert hall, zoo – were still more distinctive creations of nineteenth-century bourgeois energy. In a similar sense, writers now threw themselves on the mercy of the bourgeois reading public rather than being dependent on private patronage, just as the *Gymnasium* (like the English public school) came to supersede the aristocratic private tutor.[35] The development of the spa resorts and great hotels as bourgeois rivals to the aristocratic hunting party or week-end gathering falls into the same category;[36] so does the rise of famous public restaurants like Wilkens Keller in Hamburg. Bourgeois dominance in civil society extended to areas, in fact, to which historians have perhaps paid too little attention, such as taste and dress. A gentlemen's outfitters such as the Golderne Hundertzehn in Berlin, like the restaurant or voluntary association, was the manifestation of a new form of public life in which the bourgeoisie by and large set the tone. The top hat and frock coat, trousers and boots, were the badges of bourgeois respectability, in contradistinction both to the breeches and stovings formerly worn by the aristocracy and to the peasants' *Tracht* and workers' fustian. Indeed, the very fact that this was not a required form of dress, like that prescribed by the corporate state, was significant. In this sense fashion itself was a bourgeois invention.[37]

It was, of course, a purely formal notion that all members of the public could don top hat and frock coat and dine at Wilkens Keller. Access to the free professions was similarly limited in practice to those with the means and education to enter them, which usually meant members of the propertied and educated bourgeoisie. The same groups dominated the voluntary associations for the same reasons. This gap between rhetoric and reality – the same gap which explains how the chambers of commerce 'always claimed to speak for the public' – obviously needs to be recognized.[38] Equally clearly, it was precisely discrepancies of this kind which made up so much of the reality of bourgeois society in nineteenth-century Germany. It is arguably they, as much as aristocratic dominance or feudal values, which explain many of the conflicts and contradictions of that society.

IV

How can all this be related to the political sphere? For surely there the German bourgeoisie *did* unequivocally compromise its birthright? One way of approaching this problem is to re-define it: to question whether one can in fact talk plausibly of a bourgeoisie anywhere which seized power and re-cast the state and politics after its own image. It might be argued that the bourgeoisie characteristically became the dominant class in nineteenth-century European countries (although only exceptionally the ruling class, let alone the sole ruling class) other than through heroic means and open action. Its real power was anchored in the capitalist economic system and in civil society, in the sphere of property relations, the rule of law, associational life, certain dominant values. It is these, perhaps, which truly deserve the label 'bourgeois revolution'. Yet we clearly cannot leave the matter there. For although bourgeois revolution should not be equated with the overt transfer of power to the bourgeoisie, nor can bourgeois politics in the nineteenth century be reduced simply to the primacy of share prices and the advent of the public zoo. Bourgeois politics clearly *was* informed by a forceful idea, even a rhetoric, of 'open action' – of politics as a stage, political action as drama.[39] This was especially true of those sections of the bourgeoisie which were broadly liberal in persuasion. And while France might be thought of as the locus classicus of this aspect of bourgeois aspirations (not least because of Marx's contemporary writings, which are saturated with metaphors like stage, drama and role), it was also true in England and Germany – indeed, perhaps particularly true in Germany, where the relatively late development of the bourgeoisie paradoxically served in certain ways to accentuate both its social buoyancy and its political self-awareness.

In addition to the silent bourgeois revolution in the areas noted above, there was also, therefore, a more specifically public and political set of bourgeois desiderata. These included the freedoms of assembly, association, speech and petition, the legal accountability of the bureaucracy, and the possibility of a public life on a national scale with a parliamentary stage at its centre. Much of this shopping list had essentially been obtained by the 1870s. Yet these two sets of achievements – the stealthier ones in the spheres of economy and society, the more open ones at the political level – were by no means equal. The former were durable and extensive, the latter fragile and limited. The former tended to unite the bourgeoisie, the latter to divide it. The former enabled the bourgeoisie to puts its claim to represent a general interest, the latter provided a forum where such claims could be challenged. The former was a sphere where state institutions reflected the strength of the bourgeoisie, the latter was a sphere where the bourgeoisie accepted the need for strong state institutions.[40] The bourgeois revolution in Germany was thus most secure where it was least visible. It was least secure where it was most visible, which was in the sphere of politics itself – on that open political stage which exposed the divisions, the limitations and the weaknesses of the bourgeoisie as a 'general class'.

It was relatively easy for different sections of the bourgeoisie to agree on matters like property rights, the rule of law and the importance of charity. These were unspoken assumptions of bourgeois life. Voluntary associations, reflecting the local social power and patronage of the bourgeoisie as well as its political, regional and confessional diversity, were apt symbols of where its true strength lay.[41] But when the bourgeoisie acted on a larger political stage its divisions became more visible and more troublesome. This was evident in the splintering of groups at Frankfurt in 1848; it could be observed in regional parliaments through the 1850s and 1860s; and it became still more obvious after 1871. The chief victim of this discord was undoubtedly bourgeois liberalism, about which Sheehan has written with so much balance and insight in his major new study. After 1871 National Liberalism especially was faced with bourgeois critics on the left, who questioned the value of its liberalism, and bourgeois critics on the right, who questioned the quality of its nationalism. It also provoked massive opposition from Catholics because of its enthusiastic support for the Kulturkampf and similar measures. The splintering of the bourgeois-liberal camp was by no means unique to Germany. Nor was the anti-liberal political outcome of attacks on the Church: comparable situations existed in Belgium and Switzerland. The point is that in Germany, as elsewhere, the underlying unity of the bourgeoisie as a class was not matched by an equivalent unity on more openly political issues.

The bourgeoisie was also more vulnerable at the political level in its relations with subordinate classes. As Schissler points out, the interest of the propertied bourgeoisie was in parliamentarization, not democratization.[42] The distinctive form of bourgeois notable politics which crystallized in the decades after the middle of the century was exclusive in substance, style and personnel: its practitioners, in parliamentary institutions and loose political associations, claimed to stand above mere interests. As we have seen, of course, the gap which existed between universal claims and limited realities was not present only at the political level. But it was perhaps most visible here, and it also came to excite particular hostility – not least because various other forms of economic and social anti-bourgeois hostility were 'displaced' on to the political level. This was most obviously true of the German working class, who by voting SPD found a means of expression largely denied them in the workshop, in their social relations and in the courts. Universal suffrage to the Reichstag was a more tangible weapon than universal access to equal justice. But similar considerations applied to the peasantry and petty bourgeoisie. They too, thwarted at the points of production and distribution by an economic system of which they saw themselves as victims, frequently contemptuous of the law and of associations dominated by their 'betters', carried their resentments into the political arena. The aggregate effect of these vulgar interlopers on to the political stage, together with the impact of shrill middle-class mavericks in the nationalist associations, was to fracture the mould in which political life had set in the middle of the century. That mode of politics had been based on main railway lines, the growth of the city press and the organization of the notables. The upthrust of opposition to it at the end of the century was based on local and suburban railway lines, the growth of the local and suburban press and the organization of the masses.[43]

Several things are worth noting here. First, the enlargement of the political nation – and the *importance*, rather than the lack of it, which political conflict assumed in imperial Germany – reinforced the power-brokers of bourgeois economic interests in their desire to retreat off the political stage, away from public scrutiny.[44] This process, as Charles Maier has recently reminded us, was to become still more marked after the First World War.[45]

Secondly, the problems of bourgeois liberalism were particularly exposed by this popular challenge. As Sheehan shows, liberals had always tended (with their especially marked 'universal' pretensions) to think of the lower orders as slacking independence, and thus as a potential prey to reactionaries, revolutionaries and of course to sectional egotism. Peter

Heinrich Merkens objected in 1832 even to an extension of the franchise for the Cologne chamber of commerce, which would supposedly compromise the deliberations of 'the most *excellent* merchants and wholesalers' by admitting petty restaurateurs, artisans and fruit peddlers. David Hansemann, a prominent liberal in 1848, similarly described popular sovereignty as a 'pernicious theory'.[46] Indeed, he not only welcomed, but sat on the commission which introduced, the Prussian three-class franchise – that much-cited 'bulwark of the aristocratic authoritarian state in Prussia'.[47] Divided and organizationally complacent, bourgeois liberalism saw many of its worst fears realized as it became the most palpable victim of the vigorous mass politics at the end of the century, wedged between the SPD on the left and a rejuvenated and popularized right.[48]

The efforts of the Prussian Junkers to gain a new lease of political life at liberal expense were in some ways prefigured by the earlier attempts of Westphalian aristocrats to place themselves at the head of the discontented Catholic peasantry and petty bourgeoisie.[49] And Rosenberg argues that Conservative–Junker demagogy, in turn, helped to open the way for an even more successful application of the 'big lie' by the Nazis.[50] There is much truth in this. But perhaps the point of overriding importance is not that the Junkers were prepared to act in this way, but that all the non-socialist parties were to some extent obliged to. Popular ferment posed a threat as well as an opportunity. In varying degree the National Liberals, left liberals and Centre party performed comparable acrobatics in seeking to head off and harness peasant discontent, and in addressing the petty bourgeoisie with the dubious rhetoric of 'Mittelstandspolitik'. There was a similar stridency in the way in which the non-socialist parties sought to retain their working-class constituencies. The continuing growth of the SPD was the yardstick against which all these efforts should be considered. More generally, it was the very success of a dynamic capitalism and the consolidation of a bourgeois civil society which caused so many grievances to be displaced on to the political level. It is arguably this, and the general re-casting of the political system as a result, rather than the malign role played specifically by the Junkers and the 'pre-industrial elite', which explains much of the unstable and febrile nature of Germany on the eve of 1914. It is in this context of political instability and demagogy that we should view the later success of the Nazis.[51]

Finally, it is against this background that we should judge the 'failure' of reform in 'Prussia-Germany' – the 'possibilities and missed opportunities for a change in the structure of dominance in Prussian society'.[52] It is as well to remember, perhaps, that the German political system before 1914 was not inflexibly authoritarian. From the 1880s especially there was a broad trend towards the confirmation of civic and political freedoms, and successive 'tough' measures directed against such rights failed.[53] The same period saw the growing importance of the Reichstag, indicated by its growing authority *vis-à-vis* the federal Bundesrat, the mounting volume of Reichstag business (especially in committee) and the increasing political importance of the major party figures. But of course major obstacles remained both to a constitutional monarchy and to a more 'liberal' political climate. They included the power of the Kaiser, the non-responsibility of the Chancellor to the Reichstag, the three-class franchise in Prussia and the continuing use of legal and administrative means for repressive ends. It is understandable that historians continue to talk of missed opportunities.

But the lack of a powerful reformist drive should not really surprise us. The non-socialist parties were chronically divided, and this is true even if one considers only the non-conservative bourgeois parties. The Catholic Centre and the liberals were quite prepared to have the law used as a repressive weapon against the supporters of the other, the former in the name of public morality, the latter in the name of progress. And similar divisions weakened the possibility of a reform coalition in the Reichstag and helped to abort successive attempts to alter the Prussian Landtag franchise. These cleavages were reinforced, once again, by the problems which all the parties had in dealing with a popular electorate: it was this, for example, as much as governmental and Junker intransigence, which ultimately scuttled the Prussian electoral reform of 1910.[54]

When we talk about the failure of reform, we should therefore be clear what sort of reform we are talking about. The essential class interests of the bourgeoisie – property relations, the rule of law and basic civic rights – were amply guaranteed in imperial Germany, while at the political level real differences were faithfully mirrored. Between SPD demands and Junker resistance, the bourgeois parties which might have been expected to offer a reformist challenge were in fact at loggerheads, each filling the idea of political and constitutional reform with its own content. And all faced a threat, although they defined it and met it rather differently, 'from below'. As I have tried to suggest, the closing decades before 1914 were a period when the set-piece drama of politics was not only constrained from above by the impresarios of the Old Gang, but was also rudely interrupted by voices offstage demanding to be heard. The demagogic process whereby these demands were met and contained, as much as the failure of reform *tout court*, was to be of crucial importance for German history in the twentieth century.

NOTES

This essay first appeared as a review article based on the following books: Gordon A. Craig, *Germany 1866–1945* (Oxford, 1978); Jeffry M. Diefendorf, *Businessmen and Politics in the Rhineland, 1789–1834* (Princeton, NJ, 1980); Toni Pierenkemper, *Die westfälischen*

Schwerindustriellen 1852–1913 (Göttingen, 1979); Heinz Reif, *Westfälischer Adel 1770–1860* (Göttingen, 1979); Hans Rosenberg, *Machteliten und Wirtschaftskonjunkturen* (Göttingen, 1978); Hanna Schissler, *Preussische Agrargesellschaft im Wandel* (Göttingen, 1978); James J. Sheehan, *German Liberalism in the Nineteenth Century* (Chicago, 1978); Peter D. Stachura (ed.), *The Shaping of the Nazi State* (London, 1978); Michael Steinberg, *Sabers and Brown Shirts: The German Students' Path to National Socialism, 1918–1935* (Chicago, 1978).

1 H. Rosenberg, *Bureaucracy, Aristocracy, and Autocracy. The Prussian Experience 1660–1815* (Cambridge, Mass., 1958).
2 See D. Blackbourn and G. Eley, *The Peculiarities of German History: Bourgeois Society and Politics in Nineteenth-Century Germany* (Oxford, 1984).
3 Diefendorf, *Businessmen*, p. 6.
4 R. Dahrendorf, *Society and Democracy in Germany* (London, 1968).
5 Schissler, *Preussische Agrargesellschaft*, pp. 190–5; Pierenkemper, *Schwerindustriellen*, p. 38.
6 This argument is put forward in the books originally reviewed as follows: Rosenberg, *Machteliten*, pp. 91–5, 165–66, 195–97; Craig, *Germany*, p. 85 ff; Sheehan, *Liberalism*, p. 181 ff. For a general account in English, see M. Kitchen, *The Political Economy of Germany 1815–1914* (London, 1978).
7 Rosenberg, *Machteliten*, p. 70.
8 See Diefendorf, *Businessmen*, pp. 9–10; Pierenkemper, *Schwerindustriellen*, pp. 38–9; Craig, *Germany*, pp. 99–100, 160, 210.
9 Rosenberg, *Machteliten*, p. 83.
10 Steinberg, *Sabers*, p.5.
11 The works listed at the beginning of these notes deal with many aspects of modern German history, and it is not possible to address their individual strengths and weaknesses comprehensively. I have not dealt systematically with Craig's important general history (which has received very thoughtful reviews elsewhere), while the works by Stachura and Steinberg fall largely outside the chronological limits of the present essay, even if the Third Reich is strongly present in so much of what the other authors write about the earlier period. In general the books in question indicate the depth and breadth of research on modern German history. This is demonstrated in the case of the Third Reich by the contributors to Stachura's book, while Craig's bibliography (especially for the period before 1914) also reflects the vigour of recent work. The very different but equally ambitious works of synthesis by Schissler and Sheehan are similarly indebted to a solid substratum of primary research, as both authors generously acknowledge. Of the monographs, Reif's wide-ranging and imaginative study of the Westphalian aristocracy warrants special mention. Methodologically alert and thoughtful, it nevertheless avoids that 'excess' of theoretical relentlessness about which Rosenberg warns (p. 21), something that is often the result of a surfeit of polemics. Outstanding works like Reif's run the risk of falling into the interstices of polemical debates; they deserve not to.
12 Steinberg, *Sabers*, p. 9.
13 B. Moore, *The Social Origins of Dictatorship and Democracy* (London, 1967).
14 On England, see L. Stone, *The Causes of the English Revolution* (London, 1972); J. Morrill, *The Revolt of the Provinces* (London, 1980); and J. H. Hexter, 'The Myth of the Middle Class in Tudor England', as well as several of the other essays in Hexter's *Reappraisals in History* (London, 1961). For an attempt to go beyond the revisionists, see M. Fulbrook, 'The English Revolution and the revisionist revolt', *Social History*, vol. 7, no. 3 (1982), pp. 249–64. On France, see A. Cobban, *The Social Interpretation of the French Revolution* (Cambridge, 1964); F. Furet and D. Richet, *La Révolution française*, 2 vols (Paris, 1965–66); and F. Furet, *Interpreting the French Revolution* (Cambridge, 1981).
15 The phrase 'supine bourgeoisie' is in P. Anderson, 'Origins of the Present Crisis', *New Left Review*, no. 23, p. 43. T. Nairn, 'The British Political Elite', ibid., compares England with 'other countries with an old and unified bourgeois culture' (p. 22). Clearly the grass is always greener on the other side. See also E. P. Thompson, 'The Peculiarities of the English', now reprinted in Thompson's *The Poverty of Theory* (London, 1978), pp. 35–91.

16 I have attempted to address these larger questions in Blackbourn and Eley, *Peculiarities*, esp. pp. 159–75.
17 W. Fischer, *Der Staat und die Anfänge der Industrialisierung in Baden 1800–1850* (Berlin, 1962); W. Fischer, *Unternehmerschaft, Selbstverwaltung und Staat. Die Handelskammern in der deutschen Wirtschafts- und Staatsverfassung des 19. Jahrhunderts* (Berlin, 1964); W. Fischer *Wirtschaft und Gesellschaft im Zeitalter der Industrialisierung* (Göttingen, 1972). R. Koselleck, *Preussen zwischen Reform und Revolution* (Stuttgart, 1967).
18 I have tried to develop these arguments in Blackbourn and Eley, *Peculiarities*, pp. 238–41.
19 Max Weber, 'Capitalism and Rural Society in Germany', in H. H. Gerth, and C. Wright Mills (eds), *From Max Weber* (London, 1974), p. 383.
20 Compare Cobden's bitter remark in the 1860s that 'feudalism is every day more and more in the ascendant in political and social life . . . Manufacturers and merchants as a rule seem only to desire riches that they may be enabled to prostrate themselves at the feet of feudalism', cited in A. Briggs, 'The Language of "Class" in Early Nineteenth-Century England', in Briggs and J. Saville (eds), *Essays in Labour History* (London, 1960), p. 72, note 4.
21 Pierenkemper, *Schwerindustriellen*, p. 8.
22 Diefendorf, *Businessmen*, p. 343.
23 I would now emphasize more strongly the distinction between purported 'feudalization', and attitudes towards the state. The great majority of bourgeois Germans in this period did not aspire to the nobility or a landed estate; they aspired to the title of *Kommerzienrat* ('councillor of commerce') and the equivalents for lawyers, doctors and architects. These were usually granted automatically after twenty years of service in the appropriate business or profession – provided, significantly, that the applicant was guilty neither of a criminal conviction nor of Social Democratic sympathies. Aspirations of this kind, like membership of the reserve officer corps, are often implicitly conflated with the purchase of an estate or a patent of nobility. It is probably better to keep them separate in our minds, and to remember that the latter cases (however we evaluate their significance) constituted only a very small minority.
24 Rosenberg, *Machteliten*, p. 83.
25 Theodor Fontane, *Die Poggenpuhls*. The novel was drafted in 1891–2. It was corrected after a long illness and serialized in 1895, before appearance in book form in 1896. Like the novels immediately before and after it, *Frau Jenny Treibel* and *Der Stechlin*, it has much to say about the economic and social change that occurred in Imperial Germany.
26 Dolores Augustine-Perez is currently completing a dissertation at the Free University Berlin on social identity, social relationships and the family among the wealthy industrial, banking and commercial circles of Imperial Germany. Even for this elevated group she has registered serious doubts about the 'feudalization' thesis. See her paper 'Wealthy Businessmen in Imperial Germany', presented to the 10th UEA Research Seminar on Modern German Social History, dealing with Elites and Ruling Classes, 11–12 July 1986.
27 Sheehan, *Liberalism*, p. 254.
28 Schissler, *Preussische Agrargesellschaft*, pp. 57–9; Reif, *Westfälischer Adel*, p. 177.
29 F. Wieacker, cited in D. Blasius, 'Bürgerliches Recht und bürgerliche Identität' in H. Berding *et al.* (eds), *Vom Staat des Ancien Regime zum modernen Parteienstaat* (Munich, 1978), p. 222.
30 J. Rost, *Die wirtschaftliche und kulturelle Lage der deutschen Katholiken* (Cologne, 1911), p. 211. It should be added that this process began with the Catholic Enlightenment of the late eighteenth century, but the general point still stands. Further details on the self-consciously 'modern' viewpoint of many bourgeois Catholics at the end of the nineteenth century can be found in Chapter 9. New standards and values also found expression in the machinery of state. There is a trenchant discussion of the need to demystify 'the state' in German history in Jane Caplan, '"The imaginary universality of particular interests": the "tradition" of the civil service in German history', *Social History*, vol. 4, no. 2 (1979), pp. 299–317. The same author has contributed one of the best articles to the Stachura collection, on a related theme.
31 Sheehan, *Liberalism*, pp. 32–3.
32 Diefendorf, *Businessmen*, pp. 34–6.

33 And in a sense for the aristocracy as well, although to some extent the protean nature of voluntary associations enabled the aristocracy to use them in certain circumstances as a means of re-establishing – albeit on a different basis – some of the exclusivity it had been guaranteed under the corporate state. For an excellent discussion of this, see Reif, *Westfälischer Adel*, pp. 398–431. It is, of course, true that the working class and to a lesser extent the petty bourgeoisie were also to appropriate the associational form for their own purposes.

An outstanding contribution to the study of associational life is T. Nipperdey, 'Verein als soziale Struktur in Deutschland im späten 18. und frühen 19. Jahrhundert', in T. Nipperdey, *Gesellschaft, Kultur, Theorie* (Göttingen, 1976), pp. 174–205. Historians of Germany are now beginning to research this important subject with the same interest already shown by their British and French colleagues.

34 Steinberg, *Sabers*, p. 21.

35 Reif, once again, has much of value to say on this. See *Westfälischer Adel*, esp. p. 336 ff. I have tried to strengthen these points in Blackbourn and Eley, *Peculiarities*, pp. 199–205. My emphasis is exactly opposite to that found in Arno J. Mayer's *Persistence of the Old Regime*.

36 The mingling of nobility, gentry, merchant patricians, academics, clergy, officials, artists and educated women at an eighteenth-century spa town has recently been very well described in Reinhold Kuhnert, *Urbanität auf dem Lande. Badereisen nach Pyrmont im 18. Jahrhundert* (Göttingen, 1984). It would be interesting to have a study of how spa society evolved in the following century.

37 Since writing these lines I have found further material on this subject. See Blackbourn and Eley, *Peculiarities*, pp. 201–3, 227–8, and the references given there. Much of the work in this sphere has been done by *Volkskundler* (ethnologists), rather than by historians.

38 Diefendorf, *Businessmen*, p. 332.

39 For a contemporary usage of the stage-drama metaphor, with strong Hegelian overtones of the 'world theatre', see the remarks of Gustav Rümelin cited in Craig, p. 35. See chapter 11 for a related discussion.

40 This rather lapidary observation might have been further developed into a more sustained discussion of the state. I have tried to do this subsequently in Blackbourn and Eley, *Peculiarities*, pp. 238–60.

41 Both Diefendorf and Sheehan are illuminating on the way in which bourgeois domination was articulated at *local* level by bourgeois notables (*Honoratioren*).

42 Schissler, *Preussische Agrargesellschaft*, p. 194.

43 See Chapter 10.

44 My emphasis here is rather different from that of many German historians, who have stressed the impotence of parliamentary institutions and the sterility of party-political life, partly as a result of their having supposedly become the tools of interest-groups. Pierenkemper's approach is of this kind. See also Chapter 11.

45 Charles S. Maier, *Recasting Bourgeois Europe* (Princeton, NJ, 1975). This pioneering study, which also deals with France and Italy, reminds us that the process was by no means confined to Germany.

46 Diefendorf, *Businessmen*, pp. 298 ff, 344.

47 Rosenberg, *Machteliten*, p. 96.

48 Sheehan deals with this magisterially, presenting a mass of rich biographical and local electoral detail with great clarity.

49 Reif, *Westfälischer* Adel, pp. 198–9, 212, 418 ff.

50 Rosenberg, *Machteligen*, pp. 97–8.

51 Again, this theme is developed in following chapters, and especially in Chapter 10.

52 Schissler, *Preussische Agrargesellschaft*, p. 191.

53 Thus, for example, the 'Revolution Bill' (*Umsturzvorlage*), the Lex von der Recke and the 'Penitentiary Bill' (*Zuchthausvorlage*).

54 Elaboration on these points and supporting evidence in Blackbourn and Eley, *Peculiarities*, pp. 276–85.

5

Between Resignation and Volatility: the German Petty Bourgeoisie in the Nineteenth Century

The last decade has seen a marked increase of interest in that most heterogeneous and awkward of social groups, the lower middle class. Attention has been directed in part to the increasing numbers of white-collar employees and minor public officials in European societies from the end of the nineteenth century. Historians have considered them as an important manifestation of the expanding tertiary sector and of the growing functions of the state in Europe; they have drawn attention to their importance in pioneering new forms of family and recreational life; and they have tried to examine the significance of this hybrid, intermediate social group for the new mass politics (on both left and right) of the period. A parallel growth of interest is apparent when it comes to the other half of the lower middle class: the 'traditional' petty bourgeoisie of craftsmen, shopkeepers and small businessmen. 'The petty bourgeoisie is currently enjoying a boom', wrote Gerhard Haupt in 1979, and the market remains buoyant. The interest in small-scale producers and retailers also has various dimensions, the most obvious of which is political. It has long been a commonplace that craftsmen and shopkeepers, along with other parts of the lower middle class and of the peasantry, provided the mass base of European fascism. Recent revisionists have done little to undermine this view. But research is beginning to uncover a more complex overall picture of the petty bourgeoisie as a vital 'swing group' whose political behaviour – whether in 1848, the decades before the First World War, or the interwar years – was more volatile and divided than used to be assumed.

If petty-bourgeois politics seem less a simple one-way street and more a twisted road than was once believed, that is true above all because our understanding of the economic and social position of the class has been undergoing an important change. Research on the continuing importance of small-scale production and retailing within a developing European capitalism, on the function performed by the petty bourgeoisie as both economic safety-valve and social buffer, and on the ambiguous and changing relationships between craftsmen and shopkeepers and the classes above and below – all of this has given us a new appreciation of the role played by this most fluid and contradictory of classes. It becomes increasingly difficult to recognize the once-familiar description of a 'pre-industrial' class that succumbed to 'anti-modernist' resentments as it was ground between the wheels of the large concern and organized labour.

The following article discusses these issues in the German case, where the debate about the long-term origins of National Socialism gives the subject a particular interest. It originally appeared under the same title as a chapter in G. Crossick and H.-G. Haupt (eds), *Shopkeepers and Master Artisans in Nineteenth-Century Europe* (London, 1984), pp. 35–61, a book that grew out of the valuable series of round tables on the history of the European petty bourgeoisie held in Bremen and Paris since 1978. The article has been chosen for inclusion in the present collection because it represents the broadest approach to a set of problems I have tried to tackle on a number of occasions. It subsumes many of the main arguments from two articles with more specific concerns, an earlier one on the *Mittelstand* in Imperial Germany (published in *Social History*, no. 4, 1977, pp. 409–33), and one written at about the same time on the German petty bourgeoisie and the state (published in *Le Mouvement Social*, no. 127, 1984, pp. 3–28). I also attempted, in the present piece, to address some of the detailed economic questions later dealt with in 'Economic crisis and the petite bourgeoisie in Europe during the nineteenth and twentieth centuries' (published in *Social History*, vol. 10, 1985, pp. 95–104).

The petty bourgeoisie is less of an 'unknown class' in some countries than in others.[1] There is certainly no absence of work on German craftsmen and shopkeepers in the nineteenth century. In the case of craftsmen this is partly explained by a long tradition of writing on the guilds. The nineteenth-century public debate over the abolition of the guilds, and then over the partial reintroduction of corporate organizations, ensured a high degree of visibility for craftsmen, as well as ready-made sources for the historian. Argument about corporate organizations for shopkeepers at the end of the century, although less important, had something of the same effect. Both groups have therefore come down to us with a collective identity more pronounced than that of their counterparts in countries where organizations of this kind were weaker or non-existent. German economic historians in recent years have cut across the grain of these corporate identities by writing about the contribution of 'small businesses' to economic growth. But this has still served to keep our attention on the place of craftsmen and shopkeepers. The growing volume of work on pressure groups in the later nineteenth century has worked in the same direction. The petty bourgeoisie has taken its place alongside heavy industry and commerce, estate owners and peasants, as one among many noisy interest groups.

There is another and more obvious reason why the German petty bourgeoisie has attracted attention. In the twentieth century craftsmen and shopkeepers were prominent both as members and as electoral supporters of the Nazi Party. Their importance for the advent of German fascism is generally acknowledged. There has been predictable interest in tracing back the pattern of craftsman and shopkeeper politics into the last century. This concern with continuity has spawned work dealing, among other things, with the impact of economic change, status anxiety and the crystallization of an 'anti-modern' petty-bourgeois politics. Perhaps the most striking thing about this literature is the language in which so much of it has been couched. Argument on the petty bourgeoisie has frequently been submerged in argument about the *Mittelstand*. As a category, the *Mittelstand* – literally 'middle estate' – is both elastic and imprecise.[2] The peasantry has sometimes been counted as part of it, others have wanted to include the so-called 'new *Mittelstand*' of lesser officials and white-collar workers. But this imprecision is not the central difficulty for our present purposes, for craftsmen and shopkeepers are normally regarded as the essential core of the *Mittelstand*. The debate about the *Mittelstand* has often therefore been a debate about the petty bourgeoisie with a different label. The real problem is the label itself and its connotations. The term *Mittelstand* carries a powerful ideological charge. It would be difficult and even impoverishing to try to discuss the petty bourgeoisie in nineteenth-century Germany without recognizing the frequency with which contemporaries clothed their arguments in these terms. But there was a gap between rhetoric and reality, and this essay will partly be concerned with this gap.

The term *Mittelstand* has strong corporatist overtones. It implies that the collectivity in question should be regarded as a unity – indeed, as a traditional unity, as a *Stand* or estate, not a class. It is no accident that many contemporaries preferred the term *Mittelstand* to the term *Kleinbürgertum* (the direct equivalent of petty bourgeoisie). The latter, with its Marxist provenance and associations, suggested a divided class doomed to polarization in a two-class society. Indeed Social Democrats generally thought and wrote about the petty bourgeoisie in just this way. The term *Mittelstand*, by contrast, was used by conservatives to suggest that the petty bourgeoisie was a buffer against the polarization of society. Situated in the middle, it supposedly cut across the lines of class conflict, captured neither by the recklessness of *laissez-faire* capitalism nor by the 'class hatred' of the worker. The political corollary was the presumed conservatism of the *Mittelstand*. This view, it should be said, did not have currency throughout the century. In the first half of the century craftsmen and shopkeepers were often suspected of radicalism, and their role in 1848 was difficult to ignore. Yet thoughtful conservatives began to argue as early as the 1850s that these groups, like the peasantry, had ultimately come round to loyalty. And in the second half of the century a picture of traditional craftsmen and shopkeepers came increasingly to reassure them. They were 'the best and strongest bulwark against the red flood, and whoever fights for the *Mittelstand* fights at the same time against revolution'.[3]

Such a view is not surprising. What is interesting is the way many historians have, from a rather different perspective, taken these claims at face value. They have sought reasons for the persistence of the old regime in Prussia-Germany through a period of rapid industrialization and social upheaval. And they have found one explanation in the capacity of the ruling elite to shore up its position against liberal reformers and the socialist challenge by turning to the petty bourgeoisie for support. The Great Depression of 1873 to 1896 has been particularly noted as a period when petty-bourgeois resentments and uncertainty were exploited by conservative forces. This is held to have worked partly through a policy of 'social protectionism', which enlisted the petty bourgeoisie behind the *status quo* by reintroducing neo-corporate chambers and guilds, and by a broadly protectionist policy of *Mittelstandspolitik*. This 'reinsurance of the *Mittelstand*' has been presented as a trade-off between petty bourgeoisie and state, from which each gained by agreeing to support the other. More generally it has been argued that a conservative ruling elite harnessed petty-bourgeois anxieties in winning them over to an aggressive foreign policy and a 'throne and altar' policy at home.[4]

This is a re-statement of an old case with all the moral signs reversed: the conservative dream as liberal nightmare. Arguments of this kind have been directly or indirectly challenged by recent writing, but this broad interpretation continues to have a hold in the secondary literature. In the essay which follows I hope to present a rather different picture, of a petty bourgeoisie whose place in nineteenth-century Germany was more ambiguous. It is particularly important to try to break down the categories of 'craftsmen' and 'shopkeeper', for only by doing so can we recover the truly Janus-faced qualities of the petty bourgeoisie. The second section accordingly deals with the material fortunes of small producers and retailers, emphasizing the important divisions within the ranks of each. The third section takes this point further, considering the ambiguous social relations of a petty bourgeoisie which stretched across the class lines between bourgeoisie and working class. I try finally to probe the way in which these ambiguities found political expression.

Craftsmen and shopkeepers are often bracketed together as the common victims of economic giantism. This is misleading in several ways, not least in suggesting an absolute identity between the two. I shall deal with each in turn, bringing out dissimilarities as well as the obvious similarities. The fate of nineteenth-century craftsmen can usefully be considered in terms of the debate between 'optimists' and 'pessimists'. The pessimist case traditionally stressed the parallel decline of the guild system and artisanal fortunes. The role of the guilds was progressively sliced away in the German states, starting before the nineteenth century but quickening in tempo then, culminating for most in the 1860s with the passage of liberal commercial codes. This stage-by-stage dismantling of guild controls over prices, craft entry, production levels and labour force was confirmed by the North German Confederation and carried over into the new Reich.[5] There is now general agreement, however, that this approach lays too much stress on formal government regulations.[6] It is now more common to emphasize the direct impact of market forces, especially the effects of factory competition and industrial concentration. Craftsmen, argue the pessimists, were at a disadvantage in competing for labour and capital, while suffering from rapid changes in taste and demand prompted by the new industrial civilization. Whole groups like potters, farriers and basket-makers were laid waste, and others (like metal-workers) made insecure through specialization and vulnerability to market changes.[7]

This seemingly plausible case has been subjected to some telling counter-arguments. Optimists have, in the first place, questioned the thesis of decline by blackening the picture of what preceded it. They have little time for the golden age (*Goldener Boden*) of German craftsmen. In the nineteenth century things were not what they were; but they never had been, at least since 1600. The guilds had been steadily declining, tarnished within by abuses, threatened without by non-guild competition and the aspirations of the absolutist state, which sought to clip the wings of all autonomous corporate institutions.[8] It is difficult to resist the basic truth of this. It is also true that the real economy of craftsmen around 1800 was often as parlous as the state of many guilds. If the number of assistants is taken as an index of prosperity, it is a telling fact that no German state could boast a ratio of men to masters which exceeded 1:1. In many trades, and in the south more generally, this was very much lower.[9] Optimists generally stress the plight of craftsmen in pre-industrial Germany, noting the decline of real incomes in the decades before mid-century, as growing population led to overcrowded crafts. Many studies have pointed to the hand-to-mouth existence and poverty of masters, concentrated in over-stocked branches of immediate consumption (food, clothing, furniture) in the pre-1850 era of agricultural subsistence, periodic slump and sluggish demand. Thus it is lack of industrialization which is held to explain straitened circumstances in the pre-railway age.[10] Optimists stress the improvement following industrialization, which increased purchasing power, stimulated growth branches and widened the possibilities for auxiliary and service roles.[11] Moreover – so the argument runs – new forms of co-operative and savings bank credit became available, stimulating capital investment in the small workshop. The growing use of the electric motor at the end of the century is the conventional symbol of this.[12] Typical of such arguments is Adolf Noll's study of two contrasting Westphalian regions, where he argues that craftsmen in the more industrialized Arnsberg markedly outstripped their fellows in less-developed Münster between 1875 and 1907. Not only were Arnsberg concerns larger and more capitalized as a result of 'pruning'; they also weathered the depression better, suffering less in the downturn and recovering more quickly with the upturn.[13] In short, craftsmen benefited overall from industrialization: the Great Depression cleaned out the weakest one-man concerns, while still removing far fewer independent producers from the economy than industrial growth had added since 1850.

This is a bold reversal of the pessimist case. Instead of the degraded craftsman we are offered the embryonic small businessman, bristling with Schumpeterian initiative. In place of the languishing traditional craftsman, we are asked to look at the plumber and hairdresser, and at the building or metal-working entrepreneur who successfully modernized his concern.[14] This is helpful in giving a measure – almost a metaphor – of the distance between 1800 and 1900. But the roseate picture of resourceful adaptation (a favourite word) also has its omissions. Optimists are generally not very forthcoming on the way that a developing capitalism generated old problems in new form, replacing the old agriculture-based boom and slump with cycles of a new kind, as well as accelerating concentration. It is certainly true that industrialization leavened the crowding of craftsmen in the simplest branches of consumer goods, widening the market for (say) ceramics; yet later concentration in turn posed a serious threat to craftsmen in this branch. There were others like soap-makers, dyers and tanners for whom the market worked unevenly, both giving and taking away.[15]

There is, in addition, the problem of what exactly is being investigated. Is it craftsmen or small businessmen employing up to five people, and is it all of these or only the more successful? Aggregate statistics on small businesses can disguise what was happening to craftsmen proper. Nor is this the only difficulty with macro-economic data: there has been a tendency to iron out regional and sectoral differences as well as cyclical fluctuations. Ironically, optimists run the risk of presenting a mirror-image of generalized pessimist accounts. The latter saw industrialization as a juggernaut destroying the old craft world; the former see it as a vehicle for advancement. What can easily fall through the net in both cases is the continuity, in different forms, of differentiation and competition among craftsmen, and the importance of their *de facto* dependence on distributors of various kinds.[16]

It is clear that mature capitalism often reinforced long-standing disparities of wealth and income between different crafts. At the end of the century, as at the beginning, butchers, bakers and glaziers were amongst the highest-earners and most stable, while tailors, shoemakers and carpenters were amongst the poorest and most precarious.[17] This leads to a further point. In 1895 more than a third of all master craftsmen were tailors, shoemakers or carpenters, and they were commonly one-man businesses – there were only seven assistants to every ten shoemakers at that time, nine to every ten tailors.[18] Moreover, half of all masters were rural, at the end of the century as at the beginning. They also had a smaller average number of assistants than their urban counterparts. These were clearly not the budding entrepreneurs of optimist accounts; yet they seem to have survived the 'healthy' shake-out of the Great Depression, signalled by the rising average number of employees in small concerns. How do we explain these contradictory tendencies? It seems likely that the aggregate statistics of growing small businesses mask a more complex double process, of concentration on the one hand and semiproletarianization on the other. A prominent revisionist, Wolfram Fischer, himself suggests that the growing size of concerns in construction may be explained by concentration among a narrow group of masons and locksmiths who were effectively small contractors.[19] In other crafts, too, a minority of craftsmen turned themselves into genuine entrepreneurs. These were the masters who so often decided the fate of craftsmens' producer co-operatives by refusing to join them.[20] Below them were masters working with family labour and maybe one assistant. They lived a 'proletaroid'[21] existence, threatened on the occasion of a downturn in business with the prospect of joining the truly proletarianized *Alleinmeister*. The latter owned little capital, rented back rooms and cellars at a time of rising rents, competed chronically with each other, were usually backward technically. They were hardly independent. This internal differentiation at the close of the nineteenth century was structurally as well as conjuncturally similar to the pattern of shake-out and crisis, concentration coupled with proletarianization, which can be observed in the 1830s and 1840s.

The small number of entrepreneurial success stories,[22] and the larger number of precariously independent middling craftsmen, therefore have to be set against the marginal craftsmen, above all those working alone. A local survey of 1890 showed that up to 87 per cent of craftsmen in the clothing branches worked alone. In 1895 the figure was over 50 per cent for all trades; in Berlin it was almost 60 per cent.[23] These were the shoemakers who sewed on the soles of factory shoes, the tailors who worked in the sweated out-trade, the masons who hired themselves out to the newly-risen contractor, the carpenters like the one in Heilbronn described by Theodor Heuss who made cupboards for a furniture store.[24] The successes emphasized by the optimists extracted a price. It was paid not only by the craftsmen who were squeezed out of production altogether, but by many of those who remained nominally independent.

De facto dependence of this kind had, of course, existed in the early nineteenth century and before, in tailoring and furniture-making for example. But its extent increased as the relative importance and autonomy of craft production within the capitalist economy as a whole diminished. In 1800 small commodity production still employed ten times as much of the labour force as industry and mining together.[25] In 1875 almost two-thirds of all those engaged in manufacturing production were employed in concerns with fewer than five employees. By 1907 this figure stood at one-third.[26] Figures for craft production specifically suggest a slightly lower figure still. Evidence on small workshops' share of the total capital stock tell broadly the same story, although one study suggests a stabilization around the 10 per cent mark after the middle of the 1890s.[27] Overall, craftsmen were *relatively* dwarfed by larger concerns, and increasingly so. They were correspondingly locked into processes of production and distribution over which their own control was slight. This was not only true of the pauperized tailors and shoemakers, who constituted a genuine reserve army of labour which could be employed or laid off as cycle or season dictated. Other craftsmen were effectively built into larger concerns: coopers tied to large breweries, painters to shipbuilders, smiths and wheelwrights to coach-builders.[28] Sometimes these independent workshops were directly integrated into a larger production process, although Reich statistics (which measured technical units, not plant or geographical units) would give no indication of this.[29] Similarly, artisans who turned to repairs, and those *Kunsthandwerker* who specialized in the limited production of high-quality goods, testified in their different ways to the fact that petty commodity production had, by the end of the nineteenth century, become a marginal activity.

The position of shopkeepers was different in some respects. In the early decades of the century they were, simply, an inconsiderable group by comparison with craftsmen. There were only 33 small retailers to every 10,000 inhabitants of the old Prussian provinces in 1837 (there were perhaps ten times as many craftsmen).[30] The density was naturally higher in the market towns and cities, but the overall numbers remained low, except in major trading cities like Hamburg and Cologne. Non-subsistence consumer needs, still very limited, were largely met by pedlars or by markets and fairs. For items of regular use, direct trade between artisan and customer was the norm. In fact, as the roles of craftsman and shopkeeper started to become distinct, a conflict of interest emerged. In the great mid-century debates over 'freedom of trade', shopkeepers often sided with liberal reformers, hoping to benefit from the final demise of the guilds.[31] Sources of friction remained after that time. At the end of the century, bakers complained that milk sellers, greengrocers and even schnapps sellers were encroaching on their preserves;[32] while conflicts arose when craftsmen competed with shopkeepers in the repairs sector.

Above all, industrialization provided an overall stimulus to the expansion of small retail outlets which outweighed its effects on craftsmen. As a contemporary noted, the factory was 'the ally of the retail trade'.[33] At the same time, declining self-sufficiency, urbanization, new forms of transportation and increased purchasing power reinforced the growing retail market. The number of shopkeeping outlets per head of population grew at an accelerating rate. Between the 1860s and the 1890s the ratio of customers to retailers halved. Between 1895 and 1907 the number of shops increased again by 42 per cent while the population rose by less than 8 per cent. By 1907 there were almost 800,000 retail outlets employing fewer than five people.[34] Shopkeepers have nevertheless been seen as the victims – like craftsmen, but at a later date – of large-scale competition. On the one hand they faced the rise of chain and department stores. The latter were slower to develop than in France, but by the 1890s they were 'springing up like mushrooms'[35] and by the next decade numbered over 200 in Germany. There was also competition from mail-order outlets, which made wide use of advertising in the expanding local and popular press. The extension of railway branch lines not only speeded the movement of goods from large firms into the countryside and small towns; it also brought automatic vending machines, sited on station platforms. On the other side stood the competition of the working-class consumer co-operatives. These also developed more slowly than in other countries, notably Britain. But by the First World War they could point to a membership of 2 million and an annual turnover of 750 million marks.[36] Finally, shopkeepers continued to compete with the activities of hawkers and pedlars, even if their importance was gradually eclipsed by the growing army of travelling salesmen – the 'itinerants in patent-leather shoes'[37] as one critic called them.

The impact of department stores, chain stores and co-operatives in the large towns, and of mail-order business in the countryside, was considerable for some retail branches. But they accounted for only a small percentage of total retail turnover before 1914. The central problems of small shopkeepers were rather different. In small-scale distribution, as in petty commodity production, the statistical appearance of large numbers of independents disguised enormous discrepancies of wealth, income and security. A minority of concerns in central city areas and the wealthier suburbs, like solidly established businesses in the market towns, enjoyed a material standard which bordered on the bourgeois. Those with high-priced stock like jewellers clearly fell into this category, as did shops selling many kinds of factory-made goods like leatherware and furniture. Drapery businesses were also commonly located towards the upper end of small retailing. Haberdashers, ironmongers and colonial goods traders tended to occupy a middling position.[38] There was undoubtedly a good deal of movement within and between branches as shopkeepers sought to better themselves. The overall expansion of the market allowed considerable scope for those like the ambitious grocer described by Karl Scheffler, who expanded an old family concern, rented out the floors above the shop to raise capital, undercut, advertised and installed plate-glass windows, until he had turned his corner shop into a substantial store.[39]

The majority of shops, however, fell into a different category. Even in the first half of the century insecure, under-capitalized small concerns had existed in branches like second-hand clothes, perishables and 'mixed goods', merging into stallholding and itinerant selling.[40] Greengroceries, mixed goods and – later – tobacco remained the commercially precarious branches. They were the overcrowded, semi-proletarian equivalents of the impoverished tailor or shoemaker. Overall, more than half of all retail outlets were one-man concerns at the end of the century. In many cases they were actually one-woman concerns, run by a widow or by the wife of a craftsman or factory worker as an extra source of income. In Bremen a third of all shops were part-time in 1907, a proportion which had risen steeply from the previous decade. A third were run by women. Other full-time but single-handed concerns were run by craftsmen squeezed out of production into distribution, by blacklisted or unemployed factory workers, even by former miners, denied advancement within the manual hierarchy, who sank their savings into a business which relied on the custom of former colleagues.[41] Small publicans often shared a similar background. Declining levels of commercial expertise, along with low incomes and high rates of bankruptcy and business turnover, testify to the insecure and insubstantial character of such concerns. In Bremen a third of all retailing concerns listed in trade directories did not survive longer than six years.[42]

All shopkeepers, moreover, shared problems which threatened to compromise their notional independence. Shortage of capital was perhaps the key. Overheads like insurance rose through the century, even for those who owned their own premises and were free from rising rents. The need to extend credit to customers, universal in poorer areas, compounded the problem; so did the slower turnover of stock compared with large concerns. Banks geared to the *Mittelstand* certainly increased their activity in the last decades of the century, but against that shopkeepers' purchasing co-operatives signally failed to alleviate credit problems. In the grocery branch, where co-operatives of this sort made particularly good sense, only three had been set up in Bavaria by 1906. No more than one in twenty shopkeepers belonged to a co-operative organization, compared with perhaps one in four peasants involved at least in a credit co-operative.[43] The reasons for this failure, like the comparable failure of craftsmen, lay in individualism and trade jealousy, but also in the great internal differentiation within shopkeeping. Even the relatively homogeneous retail chemists were described by their historian as 'in so many ways and so frequently disunited'.[44] A common result was dependence on wholesalers and deliverers for credit, a relationship which could effectively turn the independent small shopkeeper into an agent of large-scale commercial capital. By the beginning of the twentieth century it was not so much the competition of department store and consumer co-operative which threatened German shopkeepers, but the tendencies towards incorporation by capital on the one hand, and towards proletarianization on the other. In that respect the problems of shopkeepers and craftsmen converged as the pace of capitalist development quickened.

In its social relations, as in its economic location, the petty bourgeoisie was a hybrid. Craftsmen and shopkeepers had the use of their own labour in common with the working class; they had the ownership of their own means of production, however meagre, in common with the bourgeoisie. They also shared some of the values of each. The petty bourgeoisie as a whole therefore occupied a no-man's-land between the class lines.[45] This awkward location is open to different interpretations. Many petty bourgeois undoubtedly singled out this 'neither/nor' status as a special virtue. Guild masters had seen themselves neither as *fainéant* patricians, nor as feckless paupers. Within the moral economy of the guild world they claimed to stand for a *juste milieu*: owners of small property (neither too much, nor none at all); honourably independent (neither dominating, nor dominated); exemplars of 'fair' competition (neither exploiting, nor exploited). The idea of a fair clientele for every master (the *Nahrungsprinzip*) embodied these claims. The intensely moral and wide-ranging values of the guild system left a powerful imprint on many craftsmen, which survived the demise of the guilds.[46] Indeed elements of a similar outlook were taken over by shopkeepers in the nineteenth century, with their condemnation of 'unfair' competition.

This is a reminder that such a view of the world was not just a 'traditional' survival; it continued to be generated by economic developments. These confirmed the propensity of some petty bourgeois to define themselves against those both above and below, stressing the unique value of their own contribution to a society which was being torn in two directions. It was precisely this which was seized upon by the conservative apostles of the *Mittelstand*, who cast the petty bourgeoisie as a buffer against the polarization of society. But it is in the nature of buffers to absorb shock, and it is worth exploring the price which members of the petty bourgeoisie paid for acting in this capacity. When the problem is posed in this way it is also easier to take into account the divided nature of the class. For we have seen how the material basis of many craftsmen and shopkeepers undermined the conservative rhetoric of 'independence'. Not only were craftsmen and shopkeepers stretched out socially between bourgeoisie and working class. Many, as a result of economic cycle or changing family circumstances, moved in a single lifetime between the fronts. This complex pattern will be explored in the present section.

Occupational and social mobility offer one means of addressing the issue. The upward gaze of craftsmen and shopkeepers has often been commented on: the petty bourgeoisie has been seen as a ladder opening up access to the bourgeois world proper.[47] How far is this true in the German case? The opportunities for artisan masters or shopkeeepers to turn their businesses into large-scale concerns were decidedly limited, especially after the middle of the century. Yet Germany's relatively well-developed educational system provided potential opportunities at least for inter-generational upward mobility. From the early nineteenth century onwards we can note the aspirations of craftsmen to send at least one son to the classical Gymnasium, of the shopkeeper's desire that his son be trained to enter commerce or the professions.[48] The available work on social mobility provides no clear answers on the plausibility of these aspirations. Lack of capital to sustain secondary and – even more – higher education was an obvious barrier. Reinforcing this was the rudimentary educational level of most petty-bourgeois parents, together with the normal absence of books, maps, educational picture-books from the home, or the visit to cultural events, which had become a feature of the upbringing of bourgeois children.[49] These questions have been explored by a recent study of Schleswig-Holstein, which suggests that the self-recruiting of a narrow educated bourgeois elite set in as early as the 1840s.[50] But there is other evidence of the same period, from Cologne and Minden for example, which suggests greater use of a Gymnasium education by petty-bourgeois children. Certainly children from this background seem to have made considerable use of non-classical secondary schools (*Realgymnasien, Realschulen, Oberrealschulen*).[51] As far as post-secondary education is concerned, indications from the first half of the nineteenth century hardly suggest an invasion of petty-bourgeois progeny – but this, of course, was a period when the bourgeoisie itself was still carving out a social place. Only one master artisan's son and one shopkeeper's son were counted among the 110 students from Cologne at Heidelberg between 1840 and 1860.[52] Figures from Berlin University from the 1830s to the 1870s also suggest a growth in the share of students from commercial and landowning backgrounds at the expense of the petty bourgeoisie. Only at the end of our period, in the decades before the First World War, does there seem to have been a significant increase in the number of students from petty-bourgeois families.[53]

Further detailed studies will be necessary before these statistics can be reliably interpreted. What the evidence does suggest is that upward mobility out of the petty bourgeoisie commonly proceeded crab-wise, by means of sideways movement of children into the new lower middle class. Craftsmens' and shopkeepers' sons entered the rapidly expanding ranks of the lesser public and private bureaucracies. They became petty officials in transport utilities, welfare institutions, schools and libraries and various policing agencies; or they took one of a wide range of posts spawned by an increasingly organized capitalism.[54] Daughters also found jobs of this kind, with some expectation of marrying into the world of clean collar and cuffs, regular salary and pension.[55] Mobility of this kind, however, was double-edged. 'Placing' one's children might also entail a recognition that the petty-bourgeois milieu itself offered fewer opportunities for independence and respectability. By the end of the century it was commonplace for craft chambers to report on the reluctance of male children to apprentice themselves to a master.[56] An example brings home the emotional charge that this could carry. Walter Hofmann rejected pressure to follow his father's engraving trade, entering the lower reaches of public bureaucracy instead: he would not stay within the 'narrowness, darkness and Cinderella social life' of the craftsman.[57] The father, for his part, was eventually reconciled to a similar move in the case of his daughter:

> He decided on a step which even half a decade before would have been regarded as monstrous in the old artisan and *Mittelstand* circles: he sent his daughter to a language and commercial course, to prepare her for an office career! Just a few years on and the father, once so ardently bent on handing over his 'fine little business' to his son, would see occupational salvation for his children and grandchildren in an official's post – not because it was 'the best', but because it was the 'most secure'.[58]

For all the contrived autobiographical pathos, the account illuminates the mood of resignation in petty-bourgeois circles in the second half of the nineteenth century. The reports of official and semi-official bodies confirm a sense of declining social status and narrowing horizons. The scope for children to rise in society was not inconsistent with a feeling among craftsmen (an ageing group) and shopkeepers themselves that they were becoming more marginal members of society.

One recent work actually talks of a 'de-classed class'.[59] Certainly there is some support for this. Take for example the changing meaning of the term *Mittelstand*. Up to 1850 it had still frequently referred to the embryonic bourgeoisie as well as the petty bourgeoisie: both could consider themselves the healthy and productive middle of society.[60] Needless to say, there were always very significant income differentials separating even the house-owning and wealthy master dyer, goldsmith or butcher from the average merchant or manufacturer; and these differences were growing in the years before mid-century.[61] The more self-conscious bourgeois were very aware of this. The steamship and insurance magnate Peter Merkens was disdainful that voters to the Cologne Chamber of Commerce should include craftsmen, fruit sellers and small restaurateurs. He complained to the Prussian authorities that under French occupation the membership of the chamber had been determined only by 'the most *excellent* merchants and wholesalers'.[62] But there were few like Merkens in the early nineteenth-century bourgeoisie; and in a town like Bochum, substantial craftsmen and shopkeepers still enjoyed a prominent social position well into the 1850s.[63] The broader meaning of the word *Mittelstand* until that time implied the potential social closeness of at least the better-off petty bourgeoisie to merchants and factory owners. The localist cast of mind in much of the bourgeoisie itself reinforced this, by giving both groups 'outside' enemies in common.

After mid-century, however, *Mittelstand* came significantly to be applied only to the petty bourgeoisie. As the economic and professional bourgeoisie drew socially closer to landowners and officials, so on the other side the line between greater and lesser bourgeoisie became sharper. One measure of this divide was the declining number of *Mittelstand* families which employed a domestic servant, at a time when this was standard in bourgeois households.[64] There are also signs that the petty bourgeoisie began to play a less active role in voluntary associations. It is certainly revealing to find a staunchly status-conscious master bookbinder, on giving up honorary posts in the Giessen veterans' association, fire brigade, historical association and trade association, arguing that these 'cost money and bring nothing in'.[65] Active membership in bodies of this kind had customarily been a hallmark of petty-bourgeois civic pride. Butchers illustrate this marginalized social position. Theirs was and remained one of the richest trades; they were, along with bakers, notably effective in sustaining co-operative self-help organizations;[66] and they also seem to have been more than averagely successful dynasts. In the 1840s the 'sausage brigade' was a recognizable element in the 'brigade' of Cologne property speculators;[67] in Mainz the 'silver sausages' had been equally prominent socially, jealously guarding their reputation for dispensing money freely during carnival.[68] Yet even butchers appear to have sensed a decline in social worth in the course of the century, perhaps connected with them ceasing, on the one hand, to buy their meat direct from the peasant, and their surrender on the other hand of self-regulatory slaughtering powers to public authorities.[69]

This picture should not be overdrawn. Wealthier craftsmen and shopkeepers did retain a place in municipal affairs. And in villages and small towns they would often enjoy considerable social prestige, acting as a kind of surrogate bourgeoisie and taking key roles in local religious, philanthropic, recreational and political life.[70] Some of the many expressions of resentment emanating from the petty bourgeoisie were perhaps examples of what the liberal politician Eugen Richter called 'Klagen ohne Leiden' – social hypochondria. But the resentment was often well-founded, and the expression of it was significant in itself. It also reveals the contours of a petty-bourgeois hostility towards the bourgeoisie. This rather defensive set of sentiments stressed local rootedness against bourgeois 'outsiders', with their growing regional, national and even international links; it juxtaposed petty-bourgeois frugality with bourgeois conspicuous consumption on servants, villas and philanthropy; and it contrasted the solid virtues of the petty bourgeoisie with the speculative propensities of the capitalist and the over-educated nonsense of the professional.[71] Extravagant construction schemes and artistic licence were likely to arouse particular fury, for the petty bourgeoisie shared the early moralism of the bourgeoisie with little of the latter's insouciance.

No doubt many of these attitudes betrayed thwarted aspirations; but they were no less real. As a result, when craftsmen or shopkeepers did bridge the gap with this more expansive bourgeois world, directly or through their children, they necessarily had to deny some of their own values. Joining the 'movers and doers', as Mack Walker has called them,[72] meant deserting the ideal of rootedness. Engaging in financial speculation – as the petty bourgeoisie very conspicuously did in 1846–7 and 1873[73] – contravened the dictates of prudence and rectitude. Seeking credit or social advancement from a bourgeois patron meant repudiating one's own sturdy independence. Sending a son into pharmacy or librarianship entailed questioning the worth of one's own 'fine little business'. In these circumstances the finely struck balance of envy and resentment not only separated some petty-bourgeois from others; it could co-exist within one individual. It is evidence of this kind which has led some to talk of the self-hate of the petty bourgeoisie.

This contradictory and burdensome pattern of attraction and repulsion also manifested itself in petty-bourgeois relations downwards, with the working class. Here it has usually been the line of division between the classes which has attracted attention. There are good reasons for this, for the second half of the nineteenth century saw an increase in areas of potential conflict. There was, first, a sharpening of class relations at the place of work. These had never taken the idyllic form sometimes claimed. Yet the period from the 1840s to the 1870s was characterized by important changes. In the craft workshop the decline of the living-in system for apprentices and (especially) journeymen, the advent of larger concerns and the development of journeymen's organizations into trade unions signalled a 'break between masters and men'.[74] Trade unions were often notably strong in craft-based trades, partly because smaller masters were particularly vulnerable to disputes. The formation of masters' counter-organizations only underlines the sharpening of class conflict in the workshop.[75] In retailing there was also a growth of employees' organizations, and the setting up of courts of arbitration to deal with disputes over hours, wages and conditions testified to growing awareness of distinct class roles in the shop.[76]

Craftsmen and shopkeepers complained that patriarchal authority had been eroded. There was similar opposition to government technical education and work-release schemes which were alleged to rob the small employer of crucial labour.[77] Measures of this kind were also seen, like social insurance and welfare provision, as an unwarranted addition to the small man's overheads and a subsidy to the undeserving. Such reactions continued, in a re-worked idiom, the arguments of 1848, when the petty bourgeoisie attacked public relief for pauperized workers. As one petition had put it: 'The humanity shown to the workers exceeds common sense, only the artisan, the productive *Mittelstand*, has been deserted.'[78] In 1848 these expressions of petty-bourgeois rancour were accompanied by fears of the mob and the dangerous classes; by the 1890s they were associated with fears about the tyranny of the trade unions and consumer co-operatives. In rapidly growing areas like the Ruhr, where the petty bourgeoisie already resented the municipal tax burden which financed new roads and schools, this antagonism could be bitter. It was shown in the pressure shopkeepers brought to bear on customers who used the co-operatives, on householders who rented them shop-space and on newspapers which accepted their advertisements.[79] Here the class line between petty bourgeoisie and working class was clear enough.

But this is not the whole story. In the first place, the material circumstances of substantial numbers of the petty bourgeoisie raises the question of how representative these sentiments were. How widespread were complaints about taxes among the 91 per cent of master craftsmen in Bochum who were not assessed for the business tax in 1884?[80] What relevance did worsening relations between masters and men have for the majority of artisans and shopkeepers who worked alone, or with family labour? How does it modify our view of *Mittelstand* hostility to consumer co-operatives when we learn that the Lübeck co-operative drew 21 per cent of its members from this group at the turn of the century, the Breslau co-operative 27 per cent?[81] There were many areas of life which the petty bourgeoisie, and not only the most indigent, shared with workers. The use of their own labour is an obvious example: master craftsmen often worked longer hours than factory workers, while shopkeepers frequently worked as long as or longer than their assistants, commonly over twelve hours a day, sometimes more than fifteen.[82] Here, as in the working class, a sudden change in family circumstances could have a major impact on the margin of subsistence. There were also many social links between the classes – occupational mobility upwards and downwards, as well as intermarriage.[83] This is not surprising when we consider the degree of residential proximity (except in the mushrooming industrial conurbations), and the fact that so many smaller tradesmen and tradeswomen sold from the front of their homes or from stalls. Their children, serving proletarian customers, running errands and playing with workers' children, were likely to grow up more familiar with working-class street life than with a more genteel domestic regime based on a bourgeois model.[84] The sizeable number of shopkeepers who rented out rooms to workers,[85] and those who extended credit during strikes,[86] also demonstrate the closeness of part, at least, of the petty bourgeoisie to the working class. The relationship of shopkeeper to working-class customer or tenant might have been one of social superiority; but (like that of rural craftsman or shopkeeper to the peasant) it was also one on which his livelihood depended.

None of these social ties between petty bourgeoisie and working class imply a necessarily close and positive relationship. The gap between objective class position and perceived class consciousness is a commonplace in writing on the petty bourgeoisie. It is likely that fears of proletarianization led many craftsmen and shopkeepers to exaggerate the remaining 'small differences' – home-owning, the absence of unemployment (although not under-employment), or outward badges of respectability. The presence of a tenant who was a skilled worker earning more than his landlord for shorter hours would not automatically prompt a sense of kinship. Nor, perhaps, would the mutual dependence of landlord–tenant relations generally. And those tradesmen who lifted themselves out of street selling might be correspondingly keen to deny the world they had left behind. It may even be possible to hypothesize about the origins, at this end of the petty-bourgeois spectrum, of a further form of self-hate induced by proximity to, but resentment of, the working class – a mirror-image of feelings towards the bourgeoisie.

It is necessary to exercise great caution, however, in making such judgements, for it is very difficult to penetrate such structures of feeling. Statistical evidence on occupational and family mobility does not disclose intentions and reactions. What seems clear is the range of divisions within the petty bourgeoisie, and even the divided self of the individual craftsman or shopkeeper. The double-edged and ambiguous social relations of the class were a product of its role as a buffer. Just as, in economic terms, it functioned partly as a reserve army of labour within the capitalist system, so its social existence took some of the edge off the class divisions of a burgeoning bourgeois society. It took urban workers and rural refugees into its ranks, while offering some of its members the prospect of direct or vicarious advancement into the bourgeoisie. As a transitional zone, its members' values were made up of contradictory elements. And as the petty bourgeoisie shaded off into the classes above and below, so the mix of these elements produced differing compounds which nevertheless retained traces of the common elements.

Craftsmen and shopkeepers often paid a heavy price for membership of this contradictory class. The family was a particular arena of conflict. Self-exploitation of family labour was the basis of all concerns which employed no outside help and of many which did. This raised problems, too, when the requirements of the family business conflicted with social aspirations for the children. It was also through the family that respectability was expressed – without servants, and on a tight budget.[87] Finally, the values of fairness, thrift and self-reliance were sufficiently at odds with prevailing conditions of production and distribution that they probably account for some of that commonly noted 'overcompensation' in the domestic sphere, which took the form of moral rigidity and patriarchal authoritarianism.[88]

It is, of course, a commonplace that the petty bourgeoisie looked inwards, to the private sphere, rather than outwards towards public and political life. As we shall see, this is not quite accurate. It might be more helpful to suggest that the habitual petty-bourgeois view of public affairs was one of private affairs writ large – a moralistic approach, in which the state was pictured as a stern but fair paterfamilias. This raises a broader question: to what extent was the *Mittelstand* movement, the political mouthpiece of the German petty bourgeoisie, a pawn in the hands of the ruling elite? It is to this question I want to turn now, and to the related issue of how representative the *Mittelstand* movement was of the petty bourgeoisie as a whole.

The evidence of craftsman and shopkeeper conservatism seems impressive. In 1848, it is true, they played an important part in the revolution, forming a link between the parliamentary notables and the popular revolt. This role, above all locally, is beyond dispute.[89] Yet even here the 'restorationist' demands of craftsmen in particular have often been emphasized. Petitions to the Frankfurt parliament and debates in the parallel craft congress displayed a massive nostalgia, coupled with arguments that craftsmen formed a peculiarly state-preserving stratum.[90] Similar claims were made by artisan spokesmen during the debates over freedom of trade in mid-century, and with notable sharpness in the Great Depression which followed.

In the last quarter of the century this case was increasingly put by autonomous petty-bourgeois organizations. To some extent at least, the petty bourgeoisie became a class 'for itself' as well as 'in itself'. The social marginalization of the class had, as a political corollary, a retreat above all from bourgeois liberalism, tainted by harmfully *laissez-faire* policies.[91] Craftsmen from the 1870s and shopkeepers from the 1890s created their own special-interest organizations and defence leagues, separate from the old trade associations. Some of these organizations were trade- or craft-specific; others were more general, and local, regional or even national in scope. Characteristic of their message was the argument of the *Westfälischer Handwerkerfreund* that 'a strong broad middle stratum is indispensable for the social structure'.[92] Retailers' organizations made similar points. One petition to the Prussian government claimed that the state had a duty to protect the 'loyal classes', while the founding conference of a national organization of defence leagues argued that preserving shopkeepers would 'protect the fatherland' from 'revolutionaries'.[93] These were the stock claims of the *Mittelstand* umbrella movement. Accompanying these arguments were familiar calls for protection: for tax reforms to favour the small man, changes in the tender system to help the artisanal producer, department store taxes.[94] The demands were often highly detailed. One south German government was asked to alter the beer tax in favour of small brewers, not to sell land on which it was rumoured a department store was to be built, and to remove vending machines from station platforms because they constituted unfair competition.[95] At the same time craftsmen called for the reintroduction of a guild system which would return control over apprentices to those with a formal master's qualification.

These aspirations were undoubtedly taken up and flattered by the parties of the right and centre-right. In the 1890s the Conservatives explicitly referred in their revised Tivoli programme to the 'state-preserving' qualities of the *Mittelstand*. Similar policies and sentiments were prominent in the Agrarian League, the Conservatives' mass organization, while the policies of the National Liberal and Centre parties underwent a comparable change of emphasis in the crucial decade of the 1890s.[96] At a time when the newly-legalized SPD was making electoral headway, and the last downturn of the recession had caused exceptionally bitter industrial disputes, the parties of the right were receptive to arguments about the loyalty of the petty bourgeoisie. The government also showed its interest. Measures to support small producers and retailers were part of a broader governmental retreat from the economically liberal policies of the 1860s and 1870s. Voluntary guilds were established as legal corporations in 1881 and their powers extended by subsequent amendments. Reich legislation of 1897 then allowed for the setting up of compulsory guilds, while establishing craft chambers as semi-public bodies. In 1908 masters were given tighter control over the supervision of apprentices.[97] Boetticher expressed the official mind when he hoped that 'the handicraft estate will continue to be, as it has been until now, a protection for the crown and fatherland'.[98] Legislation was also enacted at various levels to meet shopkeepers' complaints. The Hesse government justified extra taxation of consumer co-operatives on the grounds of 'the present difficult situation of small shopkeepers and the interest of the state in preserving the greatest possible number of independent *Mittelstand* existences'.[99]

All of this suggests that there was – as historians have argued – a trade-off between state and petty bourgeoisie in this period, whereby each pledged itself to support the other. The broader illiberal context of government policy underlines the point; and it is reinforced by the statements of *Mittelstand* organizations on morality, the family, religion and (above all) the threat of Social Democracy. Here, apparently, was a class intoxicated with 'statolatry' and wedded to the conservative order.[100]

Even if we take the *Mittelstand* organizations as representative, however, ambiguities appear when we look at the nature of their arguments. These were intensely moralistic and their central concept was fairness ('*unfair* competition'). Hence the appeal to the state to intervene and restore (as it was imagined) conditions in which public life would resemble an idealized version of private family life. But this same moralism and attachment to fairness provided a basis for questioning established authority. At the very least the outward conduct of the state and its patterns of public spending and display were judged in these terms. That is what links the petty-bourgeois attacks on civil lists and the tyranny of officials in 1848, with similar condemnations of public authority in later years – the attacks on postal services which favoured big business, on state slaughterhouses where 'young gentlemen' wasted the time of the honest butcher.[101] The social conservatism within the petty bourgeoisie was coupled with a resentful and vengeful political radicalism whose precise form was unpredictable. Hostility was likely to come to a head over issues where 'scandal' was involved;[102] but a sense of grievance towards the arrogant or olympian official was ubiquitous.

Resentment of this kind was not mere paranoia. Craftsmen and retailers were right to sense that, for all the lip-service paid to preserving the *Mittelstand*, this was actually a more marginal concern of governments at the end of the century than it had been at the beginning. The shrill representations of petty-bourgeois organizations were often received with a sense of weariness,[103] and there was certainly less to the imposing edifice of *Mittelstandspolitik* than meets the eye. Taxes on department stores, for example, were largely ineffectual.[104] Even right-wing politicians admitted their scepticism privately.[105] Measures against consumer co-operatives also had a much smaller effect than shopkeepers hoped for, and the same was true of changes in the tender system supposedly beneficial to craftsmen. The Prussian War Minister argued that they produced poor-quality work and missed their delivery dates. Tenders were often invited in publications which no craftsman read.[106] Above all, the new guilds of 1897 lacked muscle, and even the legislation of 1908 fell short of establishing the masters' desired control over apprentices.[107] As disgruntled craft spokesmen pointed out, the fact that the Reich government did not include a category of 'Handwerk' in its occupational censuses was in itself indicative. In fact the needs of Germany's increasingly sophisticated economy, coupled with the state's own labour and revenue requirements, gave governments as great an interest in pruning the petty bourgeoisie as in preserving it. Much of *Mittelstandspolitik* remained cosmetic.

Only within certain limits was the state prepared to 'preserve the *Mittelstand*'. Perhaps we should therefore question the tidy symmetry whereby the *Mittelstand* was prepared to preserve the state. It would certainly be misleading to think in terms of an automatic petty-bourgeois deference to established authority. Their organizations were angry and frustrated at the end of our period: they felt their worth went unrecognized, and their functionaries were suspicious of being patronized by authority. Petitions betrayed alternate wariness and truculence.[108] There were even expressions of anti-militarism and doubts expressed about imperialism, which was thought to be a distraction of money and energy from domestic concerns.[109] It is true that the height of the direct action they took was probably the setting free of mice in 'Jewish' department stores.[110] Shopkeepers were generally unwilling even to use the boycott weapon because of its associations with the SPD.[111] Yet the rhetoric and style of the petty-bourgeois organizations were not conventionally conservative and deferential. In some ways they were less legalistic than the SPD, and it is worth noting how demagogic *Mittelstand* leaders brandished their libel actions and brushes with authority as badges of honour. We are reminded of the German peasant and anti-semitic organizations of the same period, and also of the affinities with the earlier revolutionary volatility of the petty bourgeoisie itself. These groups were not, as one historian has it, simply 'waiting to be organised'.[112]

Similar points apply to relations with the right-wing parties. This was partly a matter of hard policies. Some of the measures demanded by large industrialists on different parts of the right, or by large agrarians in the Conservative Party, were clearly inimical to the interests even of the more substantial petty bourgeoisie.[113] Tariffs provide an example.[114] The most obvious breach of this kind came in 1909 when a section of the *Mittelstand* movement deserted the right over financial reform and sided with the liberal Hansabund.[115] But there was perennial *Mittelstand* suspicion that it was the pawn of the right. This was, indeed, a major cause of disunity and splintering within the movement. The re-grouping of many of these organizations in 1911 under the aegis of the Conservatives, and their entry into the Cartel of Productive Estates, by no means signalled the unproblematic co-optation of the *Mittelstand* by the old right.[116] Policy differences and petty-bourgeois suspicion remained; and political appetites fed on the eating. The right had become adept at addressing petty-bourgeois grievances, but they had not invented them, nor could they completely control them.[117]

The prickliness of *Mittelstand* organizations needs to be stressed. It is nevertheless true that the very moralism of their politics implied that a fair solution to their grievances could ultimately be found within the existing order. Hence their identification of real enemies on the left and symbolic enemies on the right like 'mobile' or 'Jewish' capital. Similarly, attacks on particular laws were not attacks on lawful authority as such, nor attacks on particular officials attacks on official authority as such. Hostility to the government did not mean hostility to the idea of the state. The *Mittelstand* movement could often be *plus royaliste que le roi*, attacking authority in its own name for 'leniency'. This was clearly the case when it came to softness with the SPD, but also manifested itself over many moral and cultural issues.[118]

If this is true of the *Mittelstand* movement, the question remains: how representative was it of the petty bourgeoisie as a whole? We have seen that many craftsmen and shopkeepers eked out a living in ways which belied the idea of sturdy independence; they personified the process of proletarianization rather than forming a bulwark against it. And it is certainly true that official *Mittelstand* politics largely spoke for the more substantial petty bourgeoisie. The revived guild system was predictably supported by those masters for whom control over apprentices and journeymen still meant something. In 1887 all but one of the 156 members of the Hamburg bakers' guild employed non-family labour in their businesses. This pattern was general.[119] Among shopkeepers the picture was more confused. Some retailing organizations were dominated by substantial shopkeepers, like the Rhineland-Westphalia group centred on *Der Detaillist*, which also had major Bavarian supporters. Wealthy drapers were prominent here, while the *Bund der Kaufleute* was founded by the more secure owners of specialty shops.[120] The local defence leagues, on the other hand, had roots in the small shopkeeping world. But it was grocers, not the sellers of mixed and perishable goods, who were decisive.[121] It is significant that the Bremen discount savings union *Brema* specifically excluded small stallholders. And it is clear from the attention paid to department stores rather than, say, the problem of hawkers, that they viewed the question of unfair competition through the eyes of the substantial shopkeeper. The hostility of organizations like this to the granting of credit to customers betrays a similar provenance.[122] Corporate bodies set up under the aegis of the state similarly discriminated against marginal retailers through property qualifications which denied most shopkeepers the right to vote for their own corporate representatives.[123]

The lack of identity between formal *Mittelstand* movement and petty bourgeoisie makes it difficult to generalize about political attitudes. We should not be tempted, of course, to reduce political sentiments simply to the size and health of a concern. Marginal craftsmen and shopkeepers did not necessarily reject the views of the craft chamber or *Der Detaillist*. Struggling masters might have looked back to the mythical golden age, insecure retailers might have believed that Jewish department stores and socialist co-operatives were destroying their fragile independence. But it is more likely that their feelings, like their position, diverged from the *Mittelstand* model lauded by the right. Shopkeepers in working-class areas often lived within the subculture of the labour movement; so did many of the small publicans who played such an important part in the SPD.[124] This was still more true of craftsmen, who were prominent in the SPD from its earliest years.[125] Rapid changes in the capitalist economy did not dislodge all craftsmen from political liberalism; and it certainly did not dislodge them all to the right. The Kassel craft chamber noted how 'indifference and despondency' led to 'open support for the revolutionary movement'.[126] Governments and the political right argued, of course, that the small producer had to be saved from socialism. Given the failures of *Mittelstandspolitik*, however, it might be more useful to see the craftsman as a potential proletarian, not the proletarian as a prodigal craftsman. While producer co-operatives languished,[127] trade unions, consumer co-operatives and the SPD made headway among small masters in the clothing, footwear, construction and other trades.[128] The SPD could also offer an attractive political home for more established masters, even those within the ambience of the 'traditional' guilds. In 1912 the master joiners of Schramberg formed a voluntary guild and elected the local SPD parliamentary candidate as *Obermeister*.[129] Perhaps it is not surprising that many formally independent craftsmen should have looked to the labour movement, given its growth and *élan* when set against their own *de facto* dependence on capital and the uneven development of the *Mittelstand* movement. The number of small men who were members and leaders of the SPD has often been seen as evidence for the embourgeoisement of the labour movement.[130] It might also be regarded as evidence for the radicalization of the petty bourgeoisie.

There is a familiar picture of German craftsmen and shopkeepers as traditional groups, traumatized in the nineteenth century by modern industrialization. 'Pessimist' writers helped to establish this picture; more subtle brush-strokes have been added by historians concerned with the development of an anti-modernist outlook, and with the reactionary political potential of the petty bourgeoisie. The *Mittelstand* has become fixed in much writing as a dangerously backward entity, one of the reasons why German history went wrong. This is the inverted image of what contemporary conservatives said – or hoped. I have tried to show that it is misleading, at least in the way it is usually presented.

The real petty bourgeoisie, as distinct from that construct called the *Mittelstand*, was not a cohesive group threatened by industrialization. Some craftsmen and rather more shopkeepers benefited from an unfolding capitalism; some were victims; some had both experiences in turn. This element of fluidity is important. For material transformation continued to generate and to renew a hybrid class awkwardly situated between bourgeoisie and proletariat. The petty bourgeoisie had ambiguous material ties and social relations both upwards and downwards. These were manifested in patterns of social mobility, values and personal contacts as well as in the market place. Some craftsmen and shopkeepers were closer to the bourgeoisie, others to the working class. Many were torn between attraction and repulsion towards both. Class divisions ran through the petty bourgeoisie, and often through the individual petty-bourgeois family or individual. I have suggested that we might look here for the roots of that often-cited but seldom investigated self-hate of the class.

What, then, of politics? I have tried to show how that part of the petty bourgeoisie which was closest to the working class did not always, necessarily, turn its back on the labour movement. Indeed, if we are to take SPD reformism seriously, we must take account of the petty-bourgeois presence in the party. This is not a story which ended in 1914.

Parts of the petty bourgeoisie continued to be attracted to the SPD, while struggling 'proletaroid' groups may even, in the crisis of the late 1920s, have turned in desperation to communism. It should perhaps be added that the left also harboured an ingrained (and not entirely unjustified) suspicion of the petty bourgeoisie, which certainly contributed to the Nazis' success in mopping up so many oscillating and distracted petty-bourgeois voters. This should remind us of the convulsiveness of petty-bourgeois politics. It remained the unstable 'swing group' it had been in 1848. Even if we look at the (unrepresentative) *Mittelstand* organizations, we can see how their politics were prickly and unpredictable. They did not automatically defer to authority and the right-wing parties. Their very moralism – which this essay has tried to examine – made them, at best, awkward partners for conservatism. This story did not end in 1914 either. Indeed, the demagogy by which the right sought to harness the petty bourgeoisie to its own purposes had dangerous long-term implications. It raised expectations rather than satisfying them, like the superficially imposing structure of *Mittelstandspolitik*. The effects of war, inflation, the Weimar 'system', and economic rationalization followed by crisis in the 1920s served only to heighten petty-bourgeois uncertainty and unpredictability. After 1928 the old parties of the right and centre-right felt the furious revenge of a class which they had for too long taken for granted. This helped temporarily to swell the regional and special interest parties. But petty-bourgeois rancour and moralism were largely subsumed in the end by the Nazis, appealing deftly to an awkward class which had rejected the old politics of the right, yet found no secure anchorage on the left.

NOTES

The following abbreviations have been used:

AfS	*Archiv für Sozialgeschichte*
GG	*Geschichte und Gesellschaft*
HStA	Hauptstaatsarchiv
HZ	*Historische Zeitschrift*
JMH	*Journal of Modern History*
JSH	*Journal of Social History*
MS	*Le Mouvement social*
SH	*Social History*

1 H.-G. Haupt, 'La petite bourgeoisie, une classe inconnue', *MS*, no. 108, 1979, pp. 11–20.

2 On attempts to define the Mittelstand, see G. Schmoller, *Was verstehen wir unter dem Mittelstande?*, Göttingen, 1897, and J. Wernicke, *Kapitalismus und Mittelstandspolitik*, Jena, 1907, pp. 320ff.

3 The National Liberal Schröder-Kassel, cited in H. A. Winkler, 'Der rückversicherte Mittelstand. Die Interessenverbände von Handwerk und Kleinhandel im deutschen Kaiserreich', in W. Rüegg and O. Neuloh (eds), *Zur soziologischen Theorie und Analyse des 19. Jahrhunderts*, Göttingen, 1971, p. 173.

4 See esp. H. Rosenberg, *Große Depression und Bismarckzeit*, Berlin, 1967; Winkler, 'Rückversicherte Mittelstand'; H. A. Winkler, *Pluralismus oder Protektionismus*,

Wiesbaden, 1972; H.-U. Wehler, *Bismarck und der Imperialismus*, Cologne and Berlin, 1969, 473, 480–1; H.-U. Wehler, *Das deutsche Kaiserreich*, Göttingen, 1973, p. 102.

5 See the articles by Koselleck, Wolfram Fischer and Zorn, which summarize their own and others' work, in W. Conze (ed.), *Staat und Gesellschaft im deutschen Vormärz*, Stuttgart, 1970. Local studies: A. Popp, *Die Einführung der Gewerbefreiheit in Bayern*, Leipzig, 1928; U. Branding, *Die Einführung der Gewerbefreiheit in Bremen und ihre Folgen*, Bremen, 1951.

6 F.-W. Henning, 'Die Einführung der Gewerbefreiheit und ihre Auswirkungen auf das Handwerk in Deutschland', in W. Abel (ed.), *Handwerksgeschichte in neuer Sicht*, Göttingen, 1978, pp. 147–77.

7 This position underlay most of the studies commissioned by the *Verein für Sozialpolitik* in the 1890s and published in its *Schriften* 62–70, Leipzig, 1895–7.

8 J. Bergmann, 'Das "Alte Handwerk", im Übergang. Zum Wandel von Struktur und Funktion des Handwerks im Berliner Wirtschaftsraum in vor- und frühindustrieller Zeit', in O. Büsch, *Untersuchungen zur Geschichte der Frühen Industrialisierung vornehmlich im Wirtschaftsraum Berlin-Brandenburg*, Berlin, 1971, pp. 224–69.

9 K. H. Kaufhold, 'Umfang und Gliederung des deutschen Handwerks um 1800', in Abel, *op. cit.*, pp. 57–60. Kaufhold has calculated the average number of assistants per master throughout Germany as 0.54:1.

10 This is true of many of the essays in Abel, op. cit., and of K. Aßmann and G. Stavenhagen, *Handwerkereinkommen am Vorabend der industriellen Revolution*, Göttingen, 1969.

11 K.-H. Schmidt, 'Bestimmungsgründe und Formen des Unternehmenswachstums im Handwerk seit der Mitte des 19. Jahrhunderts', in Abel, op. cit., 241–84. Wilhelm Abel has stimulated much of this work, but Wolfram Fischer has also played an important role. See his collected articles in *Wirtschaft und Gesellschaft im Zeitalter der Industrialisierung*, Göttingen, 1972, esp. pp. 285–357.

12 W. Fischer, 'Die Rolle des Kleingewerbes im wirtschaftlichen Wachstumsprozess in Deutschland 1850–1914', in F. Lütge (ed.), *Wirtschaftliche und soziale Probleme der Gewerblichen Entwicklung im 15.–16. und 19. Jahrhundert*, Stuttgart, 1968, pp. 131–41 (reprinted in *Wirtschaft und Gesellschaft*, pp. 338–48).

13 A. Noll, *'Sozio-ökonomischer Strukturwandel in der zweiten Phase der Industrialisierung*, Göttingen, 1975.

14 Fischer, 'Die Rolle des Kleingewerbes', pp. 132–3, 137–9.

15 For a differentiated discussion, see S. Volkov, *The Rise of Popular Antimodernism in Germany. The Urban Master Artisans, 1873–1896*, Princeton, 1978, pp. 32–60.

16 There are some penetrating remarks about the problem of distribution rather than production in P. Ayçoberry, 'Probleme der Sozialschichtung in Köln im Zeitalter der Frühindustrialisierung', in W. Fischer (ed.), *Wirtschafts- und Sozialgeschichtliche Probleme der frühen Industrialisierung*, Berlin, 1968, esp. pp. 519–24.

17 On the early part of the century: Kaufhold, op cit., pp. 41–3; D. Saalfeld, 'Handwerkseinkommen in Deutschland vom ausgehenden 18. bis zur Mitte des 19. Jahrhunderts', in Abel, op. cit., pp. 81–2. On the later nineteenth century: Noll, op. cit., pp. 68–9; Volkov, op. cit., pp. 84–94.

18 Wernicke, op. cit., calculated from table, p. 138.

19 Fischer, 'Die Rolle des Kleingewerbes', p. 138.

20 See D. Blackbourn, 'The *Mittelstand* in German society and politics, 1871–1914', *SH*, 4, 1977, pp. 417–18.

21 On 'proletaroid' masters: Ayçoberry, op. cit., pp. 522–4. The concept was used in the important work of Theodor Geiger on the late Weimar Republic: *Die soziale Schichtung des deutschen Volkes*, Stuttgart, 1932.

22 For a concise and differentiated summary of the evidence on this: J. Kocka, *Unternehmer in der deutschen Industrialisierung*, Göttingen, 1975, pp. 47–50.

23 Volkov, op. cit., p. 92.

24 T. Heuss, *Preludes to Life: Early Memoirs*, London, 1955, p. 87.

25 Kaufhold, op. cit., pp. 37–40.

26 Fischer, 'Die Rolle des Kleingewerbes', p. 136.

27 Noll, op. cit., 118–20; K.-H. Schmidt, 'Die Rolle des Kleingewerbes in regionalen Wachstumsprozessen in der zweiten Hälfte des 19. Jahrhunderts', in I. Bog *et al.* (eds), *Wirtschaftliche und soziale Strukturen im säkularen Wandel: Festschrift für Wilhelm Abel*, Hanover, 1974, III, pp. 720ff.
28 Schmidt, op. cit., pp. 726, 738; Wernicke, op. cit., p. 143.
29 Fischer, 'Die Rolle des Kleingewerbes', p. 134.
30 R. Gellately, *The Politics of Economic Despair. Shopkeepers and German Politics 1890–1914*, London and Beverly Hills, 1974, p. 30.
31 Branding, op. cit., pp. 31–2.
32 P. Arnold, *Das Münchener Bäckergewerbe*, Stuttgart, 1895, p. 50.
33 Wilhelm Roscher, cited in Gellately, op. cit., p. 13.
34 Ibid., pp. 29–33.
35 H. Crüger, *Vortrag über gewerbliches Genossenschaftswesen, Warenbazare und Grosswarenhäuser* . . . , Stuttgart, 1899, p. 13.
36 Gellately, op. cit., pp. 37–50.
37 The Württemberg Centre deputy Karl Walter, cited in Blackbourn, op. cit., p. 424. On travelling salesmen (there were over 70,000 by the end of the century) see F. Weyer, *Der reisende Kaufmann*, Cologne, 1948.
38 H.-G. Haupt, 'Der Bremer Kleinhandel zwischen 1890 und 1914. Binnenstruktur, Einfluss und Politik', in W. U. Drechsel *et al.* (eds), *Geschäfte. Teil 1: Der Bremer Kleinhandel um 1900*, Bremen, 1982, esp. pp. 12–21. The articles by Achim Saur and Charlotte Niermann in the same volume also contain valuable material.
39 K. Scheffler, *Der junge Tobias. Eine Jugend und ihre Umwelt*, Leipzig, 1927, pp. 112–13.
40 P. Ayçoberry, 'Der Strukturwandel im Kölner Mittelstand 1820–1850', *GG*, 1, 1975, pp. 87–8.
41 Blackbourn, op. cit., pp. 416, 421–2; contributions by Haupt, Saur, Niermann to Drechsel, op. cit.; Gellately, op. cit., pp. 34–6; D. Crew, 'Definitions of modernity: social mobility in a German town, 1880–1901', *JSH*, VII, 1973, pp. 56–7.
42 H.-G. Haupt, 'Kleinhändler und Arbeiter in Bremen zwischen 1890 und 1914', *AfS*, XXII, 1982, pp. 108–10.
43 J. Wein, *Die Verbandsbildung im Einzelhandel*, Berlin, 1968, pp. 62–3, 164; Gellately, op. cit., pp. 64–5.
44 J. Thiessen, *Die deutschen Drogisten*, Berlin, 1929, p. 133.
45 See the introductin by H.-G. Haupt to Haupt (ed.), *'Bourgeois und Volk zugleich'? Zur Geschichte des Kleinbürgertums im 19. und 20. Jahrhundert*, Frankfurt/M, 1978, p. 9–32.
46 Bergmann, op. cit., pp. 225–61; Mack Walker, *German Home Towns, Community, State, and General Estate 1648–1871*, Ithaca, 1971, esp. pp. 73–107. R. Stadelmann and W. Fischer, *Die Bildungswelt des deutschen Handwerkers um 1800. Studien zur Soziologie des Kleinbürgers im Zeitalter Goethes*, Berlin, 1955. For a contemporary account of the guild system as a 'moral partition' against outside forces and sentiments, see W. Jung, *Der Gewerbsmann und die gewerblichen Verhältnisse Württembergs*, Ulm, 1845, p. 30.
47 See, for example, Arno J. Mayer, 'The lower middle class as historical problem', *JMH*, 1975, esp. pp. 424, 432.
48 Ayçoberry, 'Probleme der Sozialschichtung', pp. 524–7.
49 Stadelmann and Fischer, op. cit.; J. Schlumbohm, '"Traditional" collectivity and "modern" individuality: some questions and suggestions for the historical study of socialisation. The example of the German lower and upper bourgeoisies around 1800', *SH*, 5, 1980, pp. 71–103. On the low levels of formal education among masters in the nineteenth century, Volkov, op. cit., p. 25.
50 R. S. Elkar, *Junges Deutschland in polemischem Zeitalter. Das schleswig-holsteinische Bildungsbürgertum in der ersten Hälfte des 19. Jahrhunderts*, Düsseldorf, 1979, esp. pp. 81–151.
51 J. Kocka, *Die Angestellten in der deutschen Geschichte 1850–1980*, Göttingen, 1981, p. 108, and the further literature cited in note 30.
52 Ayçoberry, 'Probleme der Sozialschichtung', p. 523.

53 C. E. McClelland, *State, Society, and University in Germany 1700–1914*, Cambridge, 1980, pp. 199, 244.

54 R. Engelsing, *Sozial- und Wirtschaftsgeschichte Deutschlands*, Göttingen, 1976, p. 146. Further details in the same author's *Zur Sozialgeschichte deutscher Mittel- und Unterschichten*, Göttingen, 1973, and in Kocka, *Die Angestellten*, chs. 1–4.

55 U. Nienhaus, 'Von Töchtern und Schwestern. Zur vergessenen Geschichte der weiblichen Angestellten im deutschen Kaiserreich', in J. Kocka (ed.), *Angestellte im europäischen Vergleich*, Göttingen, 1981, pp. 309–33. See also Blackbourn, op. cit., pp. 423–4; and Haupt, 'Kleinhändler und Arbeiter', pp. 118–19.

56 See the report of the Frankfurt/Oder Craft Chamber for 1900–4, cited Wernicke, op. cit., pp. 175–84.

57 W. Hofmann, *Mit Grabstichel und Feder. Geschichte einer Jugend*, Stuttgart and Tübingen, 1948, p. 206.

58 Ibid., p. 400.

59 A. Leppert-Fögen, *Die deklassierte Klasse. Studien zur Geschichte und Ideologie des Kleinbürgertums*, Frankfurt/M, 1974.

60 On the evolution of the term's meaning, H. A. Winkler, *Mittelstand, Demokratie und Nationalsozialismus*, Cologne, 1972, ch. 1.

61 Aßmann and Stavenhagen, op. cit., pp. 4–72.

62 J. M. Diefendorf, *Businessmen and Politics in the Rhineland, 1789–1834*, Princeton, 1980, p. 299.

63 D. Crew, *Town in the Ruhr. A Social History of Bochum 1860–1914*, New York, 1979, p. 112ff.

64 Engelsing, *Zur Sozialgeschichte*, pp. 240, 253.

65 P. Adam, *Lebenserinnerungen eines alten Kunstbuchbinders*, Stuttgart, 1951, p. 95.

66 Blackbourn, op. cit., p. 417.

67 Ayçoberry, 'Probleme der Sozialschichtung', pp. 517–18.

68 B. Gottron, *Erlebtes und Erlauschtes aus dem Mainzer Metzgergewerbe im 19. Jahrhundert*, Mainz, 1928, pp. 3–9.

69 Ibid., esp. pp. 52ff.

70 Examples in D. Blackbourn, *Class, Religion and Local Politics in Wilhelmine Germany*, London and New Haven, 1980.

71 Walker, op. cit., and Volkov, op. cit., both contain much material illustrating these attitudes.

72 Walker, op. cit., pp. 119–33.

73 On the 1840s, see J. Bergmann, 'Ökonomische Voraussetzungen der Revolution von 1848', in H.-U. Wehler (ed.), *200 Jahre amerikanische Revolution und moderne Revolutionsforschung: Geschichte und Gesellschaft, Sonderheft 2*, Göttingen, 1976, pp. 277–8. On the boom prior to the 1873 crash, Rosenberg, op. cit., pp. 63ff; M. Kitchen, *The Political Economy of Germany 1815–1914*, London, 1978, pp. 133–8.

74 Volkov, op. cit., pp. 95–122.

75 K. Saul, *Staat, Industrie, Arbeiterbewegung im Kaiserreich*, Düsseldorf, 1974, pp. 61, 84, 99. On counter-organizations, see *25 Jahre Deutscher Handwerks-und Gewerbekammertag 1900–1925*, Hanover, 1925, pp. 156–8; Branding, op. cit., pp. 92–4.

76 Gellately, op. cit., pp. 50–7.

77 See the complaints aired at the AGM of the Rottenburg *Gewerbeverein*, reported in the *Neckarbote*, 1 March 1904. Generally, Noll, op. cit., pp. 124–66, 381–6.

78 Cited in W. Buzengeiger, *Die Zusammenhänge zwischen den wirtschaftlichen Verhältnissen und der politischen Entwicklung in Württemberg um die Mitte des 19. Jahrhunderts*, Munich, 1949, p. 49. See also Blackbourn, *Class, Religion and Local Politics*, pp. 64–73.

79 See G. Huck, 'Arbeiterkonsumverein und Verbraucherorganisation', in J. Reulecke and W. Weber (eds), *Fabrik, Familie, Feierabend*, Wuppertal, 1978, esp. pp. 239–40; and, in the same volume, Reulecke, 'Von der Dorfschule zum Schulsystem', esp. pp. 256–7.

80 Crew, *Town in the Ruhr*, p. 114.

81 F. Naumann, *Demokratie und Kaisertum*, Berlin, 1904, pp. 79–80. The figure in Stuttgart was about 15 per cent by 1914: E. Hasselmann, *Und trug hundertfältige Frucht*, Stuttgart, 1964, p. 66.

82 Haupt, 'Kleinhändler und Arbeiter', pp. 101–4.

83 Ibid., pp. 111–19; J. Kocka, 'The study of social mobility and the formation of the working class in the 19th century', *MS*, 111, 1980, pp. 97–117. As Kocka notes, however, the East German historian Hartmut Zwahr, in a detailed investigation of Leipzig, has suggested a sharpening class division between petty bourgeoisie and working class in the years 1830–70: Zwahr, *Zur Konstituierung des Proletariats als Klasse*, Berlin, 1978.

84 For an imaginative attempt to reconstruct street-life as part of the pattern of socialization at the end of the eighteenth century, see Schlumbohm, op. cit.

85 Haupt, 'Kleinhändler und Arbeiter', 128–9.

86 Crew, *Town in the Ruhr*, pp. 131–45, esp. pp. 135, 142–3.

87 There is interesting evidence on the tensions within petty-bourgeois families in K. Schlegel, 'Domestic servants in Hamburg before 1914'. MA dissertation, University of East Anglia, 1980. An article based on this work is to appear in *History Workshop Journal*.

88 Leppert-Fögen, op. cit., ch. 3: 'Zur Sozialpsychologie des Kleinbürgertums'.

89 There are references to many local studies in D. Langewiesche, 'Republik, Konstitutionelle Monarchie und "Soziale Frage". Grundprobleme der deutschen Revolution von 1848/49', *HZ*, 230, 1980, pp. 529–48. Langewiesche's own monograph on Württemberg is extremely valuable: *Liberalismus und Demokratie zwischen Revolution und Reichsgründung*, Düsseldorf, 1974.

90 Walker, op. cit., pp. 362–5, 390ff; Langewiesche, *Liberalismus*, op. cit., pp. 41–55, 141ff, 212–19; T. S. Hamerow, *Restoration, Revolution, Reaction*, Princeton, 1958, pp. 140–55.

91 Rosenberg, op. cit., pp. 62–78, 118ff; Volkov, op. cit., 172–91; H. Sedatis, *Liberalismus und Handwerk in Süddeutschland. Wirtschafts- und Gesellschaftskonzeptionen des Liberalismus und die Krise des Handwerks im 19. Jahrhundert*, Stuttgart, 1979; Leppert-Fögen, op. cit., pp. 161–83.

92 Cited in Winkler, 'Rückversicherte Mittelstand', op. cit., p. 207.

93 Gellately, op. cit., pp. 90–1, 129.

94 The full range of demands for state intervention is suggested by Wernicke's rather indigestible compendium, *Kapitalismus und Mittelstandspolitik*, Jena, 1907.

95 Blackbourn, *Class, Religion and Local Politics*, esp. pp. 149–51.

96 On the Conservatives and *Bund der Landwirte*, H.-J. Puhle, *Agrarische Interessenpolitik und preussischer Konservatismus im wilhelminischen Reich 1893–1914*, Hanover, 1966; on the Centre, Blackbourn, *Class, Religion and Local Politics*, pp. 53–7, 92–9, 141–64. On programmes: F. Salomon, *Die deutschen Parteiprogramme*, Leipzig and Berlin, 1907, vol. 3, pp. 73, 83–4.

97 Winkler, 'Rückversicherte Mittelstand', for details.

98 Volkov, op. cit., p. 277.

99 B. Adelung, *Der 34. hessische Landtag 1908–11*, n.p., 1911, p. 93.

100 On 'statolatry' and the petty bourgeoisie, see N. Poulantzas, *Fascism and Dictatorship*, London, 1974, p. 241; and *Classes in Contemporary Capitalism*, London, 1975, pp. 291ff.

101 Blackbourn, *Class, Religion and Local Politics*, esp. pp. 158–64; Gottron, op. cit., p. 51.

102 The role of 'scandal' deserves greater attention: it had a central place in petty-bourgeois politics, providing suitable symbols of 'injustice' and 'unfairness'. Construction scandals, especially, were to the petty bourgeoisie what commodity and stock-exchange scandals were to the peasantry – particularly when they could be tied to 'Jewish' capital. For some pointers, see Blackbourn, *Class, Religion and Local Politics*, pp. 158–60; and G. Zang (ed.), *Provinzialisierung einer Region: Zur Entstehung der bürgerlichen Gesellschaft in der Provinz*, Stuttgart, 1978, esp. the articles by Bellmann and Zang.

103 Cf. the response of the Württemberg government to a petition from the *Centralvereinigung deutscher Vereine für Handel und Gewerbe*, concerning state officials' consumer co-operatives and the damage they allegedly did to the shopkeeper. The analysis of the *Centralvereinigung* was dismissed as 'superficial' and its recommendations not acted on. (HStA Stuttgart, E 130 II, Bü 486, Nr. 84.) The south

German and Hanseatic governments were also opposed to a strong pro-guild line in 1897. See, for example, *25 Jahre Deutscher Handwerks- und Gewerbekammertag*, pp. 24–5.

104 Crüger, op. cit., 14; J. Wernicke, *Der Mittelstand und seine wirtschaftliche Lage*, Leipzig, 1909, p. 44.

105 G. Tietz, *Hermann Tietz*, Stuttgart, 1955, p. 46, cites a good example.

106 *25 Jahre Deutscher Handwerks- und Gewerbekammertag*, pp. 121–5.

107 On the cynicism with which craftsmen reacted to the 1897 legislation, see Blackbourn, '*Mittlestand*', pp. 418–19 and note 62.

108 Volkov, op. cit., pp. 241, 278, 332–3, shows how craftsmen's aspirations were first raised, then dashed, by government actions. This pattern of appetites which fed on the eating is an important component of the history of the petty bourgeoisie in Imperial Germany. The dialectic of raised and shattered hopes would repay further attention.

109 See Gellately, op. cit., pp. 92, 96; E. Böhm, *Überseehandel und Flottenbau*, Düsseldorf, 1972, pp. 183–263; G. Eley, 'Defining social imperialism: use and abuse of an idea', *SH*, 3, 1976, p. 278.

110 On violence against the Tietz stores: Tietz, op. cit., p. 45.

111 Gellately, op. cit., p. 67–8.

112 V. R. Berghahn, *Germany and the Approach of War in 1914*, London, 1973, p. 151: 'Here was a potential group of voters which responded to the emotional propaganda of the conservative élites and was waiting to be organised. And organised they became.'

113 Winkler, 'Rückversicherte Mittelstand', p. 175; Gellately, op. cit., pp. 158–61, 165ff.

114 For the negative effect of tariffs on butchers, millers and bakers, see Wernicke, *Kapitalismus*, p. 162 and Blackbourn, '*Mittelstand*', p. 414.

115 On the desertion of the Conservatives by the *Deutsche Mittelstandsvereinigung*, Winkler, 'Rückversicherte Mittelstand', p. 169; S. Mielke, *Der Hansa-Bund für Gewerbe, Handel und Industrie*, Göttingen, 1976, pp. 30ff, 45–51. Support for the Conservative-backed successor varied from region to region, but was strongest (like the new guilds) in the east: D. Stegmann, *Die Erben Bismarcks. Parteien und Verbände in der Spätphase des wilhelminischen Imperialismus*, Cologne, 1970, p. 254.

116 Details of the Cartel in Stegmann, op. cit., p. 342ff.

117 I have tried to show in *Class, Religion and Local Politics* how this pattern of *incomplete* absorption of demands by the right helped to generate an unstable form of demagogic politics.

118 Wilhelm Keil noted in his memoirs how there was an alliance on such issues in the Stuttgart city council between SPD and progressive governmental figures like von Gauss, against the 'wine-growers and petite bourgeoisie': W. Keil, *Erlebnisse eines Sozialdemokraten*, Stuttgart, 1947–8, I, p. 158. See also R. J. V. Lenman, 'Politics and culture: the state and the avant-garde in Munich 1886–1914', in R. J. Evans (ed.), *Society and Politics in Wilhelmine Germany*, London, 1978, pp. 90–111.

119 Volkov, op. cit., pp. 257–9.

120 Gellately, op. cit., pp. 119–20, 144–5.

121 Ibid., pp. 121ff.

122 See the articles by Haupt and Saur in Drechsel, op. cit. A Centre Party functionary expressed the view of the more established shopkeepers when he referred to the fringe of small retailers as 'an evil', and as 'unhealthy parasitism'. See Blackbourn, '*Mittelstand*', p. 422.

123 Gellately, op. cit., pp. 106–7.

124 The Munich SPD in 1906 had 369 members (5.5 per cent) who were publicans or drink retailers: R. Michels, *Political Parties*, New York, 1968, p. 269.

125 Some examples, from the Palatinate, Nuremberg and Brunswick, in W. Guttsman, *The German Social Democratic Party 1875–1933*, London, 1981, pp. 35, 56, 255.

126 Wernicke, *Kapitalismus*, p. 159.

127 Blackbourn, '*Mittelstand*', pp. 416–18.

128 Volkov, op. cit., pp. 229–37. Eugen Sinner ('La politique de la social-démocratie allemande vis-à-vis de l'artisanat à la fin du XIXe siècle', *MS*, pp. 114, 105–23) suggests that the SPD lacked sympathy with the 'backward-looking' demands of the craftsmen. While there is considerable evidence for this, it should also be noted that – in parts of

Germany, at least – the party made explicit attempts to woo the small masters for the socialist cause. Examples in Blackbourn, *Class, Religion and Local Politics*, pp. 171–5, 185–6.

129 *Deutsches Volksblatt*, 26 October 1912. Carl Severing also reported in his memoirs how the customs and emblems of former guild organizations were taken over by carpenters and masons into the trade union movement: *Mein Lebensweg*, Cologne, 1951, I, p. 29.

130 Many of the foremost SPD leaders had this background: Wilhelm Liebknecht, August Bebel, Philipp Scheidemann, Friedrich Ebert, Carl Severing, Wilhelm Keil, Paul Löbe. Nearly a quarter of SPD Reichstag deputies between 1893 and 1914 had a petty-bourgeois occupation. Of these forty-one, nearly a half were practising craftsmen – shoemakers, printers, cabinet-makers, carpenters, cigar-makers, P. Molt, *Der Reichstag vor der improvisierten Revolution*, Cologne/Opladen, 1963, p. 212.

6

Peasants and Politics in Germany, 1871–1914

Much has been written about the different patterns of historical development in Britain and Germany during the nineteenth and early twentieth centuries. One real and important difference was the size of the agrarian sector. By the First World War less than 10 per cent of the economically active British population was engaged in agriculture, forestry and fishing; in Germany the figure was four times as great. The total numbers employed in German agriculture actually rose by more than two million (to 10.7 million) between 1871 and 1913, even though this did constitute a steadily declining share of the overall labour force. In the German case, moreover, there were relatively few tenant farmers. Most were peasant proprietors, of whom those large and middle peasants owning between 5 and 100 hectares (12½ to 250 acres) increased their share of the total cultivated area in this period.

Some have seen the German peasantry (like the petty bourgeoisie) as a 'traditional' residue that was economically backward, resisted social change, and succumbed to the political overtures of a reactionary landed elite. The years from 1871 to 1914 are regarded by those who argue in this way as a crucial period in which the mobilization of anti-modern peasants on a 'proto-fascist' basis helped to establish one of the most malign continuities in modern German history. These years are undeniably important; but there are other ways of approaching the subject of the peasantry in Imperial Germany. Rural Germany felt the effects of new means of communication, high levels of rural migration (within the countryside, as well as from countryside to town), growing levels of production for the market, and changing habits of peasant consumption. To these should be added the impact of agencies like the school and the army. This is not to argue that the German peasantry underwent some kind of painless 'modernization'. But it is important to grasp the full extent of changes in rural society and in popular attitudes if we are to appreciate the political role of the peasantry in Imperial Germany. For in this respect too it was a less inert class than is often suggested. That is the main subject of the following article. It looks at various forms of peasant mobilization in the period, examines the new political leaders who emerged to put themselves at the head of peasant discontents and aspirations, and considers the complex interaction between these new movements and established political forces. The result is to suggest a different kind of continuity between Imperial and late-Weimar Germany, and to offer a revised reading of how and why so many German peasants came to support National Socialism.

The article first appeared under the same title in *European History Quarterly*, vol. 14 (1984), pp. 47–75, and is reprinted here unchanged. Although the bulk of the article was first drafted in the early summer of 1979 for presentation to a conference in July of that year, the final section of it discusses some of the changes in historical approach to the German peasantry that were already apparent by 1984. It is clear that our understanding of German large landowners is also being revised, although it is likely that we shall gain a more rounded picture of such an important group as the Junkers only as more detailed local research accumulates. For the moment, the relationship between peasants and large landowners, and many other themes dealt with below, are considered in two very valuable essay collections published too recently to be considered in the present article: Robert G. Moeller (ed.), *Peasants and Lords in Modern Germany: Recent Studies in Agricultural History* (London, 1986); and Richard J. Evans and W. R. Lee (eds), *The German Peasantry: Conflict and Community in Rural Society from the Eighteenth to the Twentieth Centuries* (London, 1986).

> The school, the army and the railway, these are three powerfully dissolving and levelling forces, and who knows how soon it will be before people read my popular tales as if they were Red Indian stories, telling of things and ways of thinking which no longer exist. (Letter of the *Heimat* writer Berthold Auerbach, 1873)

> The peasant on the land does not have all these [educational opportunities]. The plough and the shovel are his pen, with which he writes his diary on the tilled earth. If the railway lines rush past the end of his fields, and the four corners of the earth meet above his head in the telephone wires, he remains tied to the soil, held within his small circle. (Georg Heim, the Bavarian 'Peasant Doctor')

I

It is the unchanging rather than the changing nature of rural political consciousness to which observers have frequently drawn attention. This is something, indeed, on which politicians and historians of both left and right have often been able to agree. As late as 1956, one West German Christian Democrat argued that it was the traditional qualities of the peasantry which made it 'nothing short of a prerequisite for the stability of political conditions', while Heinrich Lübke cited the peasantry as the 'buttress of the whole social, political and economic order'.[1] From a rather different perspective, those on the left have scorned the conservatism and provincialism of rural life. Theodor Adorno argued in a radio broadcast of 1966 that 'debarbarization' on the land remained a top educational priority, that the level of consciousness there remained well below that achieved by the 'bourgeois cultural liberalism of the nineteenth century'.[2] The agreement of substance from opposite premises mirrors perfectly the agreement of a century earlier between Wilhelm Riehl and Karl Marx, the one praising the conservative good sense of the German rural population, the other cursing the idiocy of rural life.

Both Riehl and Marx, however, were talking about change – about the forging of new social relations. And historians, while they may pepper their texts with telling words like atavism and traditionalism, have seldom tried to argue that rural consciousness remains or did remain static during these hundred years. At the very least it has been necessary to consider the impact on rural society and politics of outside changes, as Germany moved from being a predominantly rural and agricultural society in the middle of the last century to a predominantly urban and industrial/commercial one in the twentieth. A change of this magnitude, with all its concomitants in the changing pace and texture of life, not only helped alter the image of rural society held by urban historians and politicians; it also altered the image of urban historians and politicians held by rural society. The period directly under consideration in this paper is central to both of these changing sets of perspectives. For the years 1871 to 1914 saw massive changes. Imperial Germany moved decisively from an *Agrarstaat* to an *Industriestaat*. It moved from being a largely rural and small-town country, shaken up but not fully stirred by the railway, to a country where the centre of gravity of population lay in the cities and swollen regional and market towns. It was transformed, equally significantly, from a stage where collective organizations on the land were rudimentary and election turn-outs low, to a stage where collective organizations – political, co-operative, educational, recreational – were dense, and election turn-outs high. It is clearly of some importance to know what happened on the ground to the nature of politics during such a period of ferment.

We have, simplifying a little, two main explanatory models. The first is typified by Heinz Haushofer's book on German agriculture, which seeks to deal with social and political changes among the rural population, as well as with technical developments in agriculture itself.[3] Here we have a happy story of modernization, a succession of agronomists, pedigree pigs and 'rural leaders' like Raiffeisen. Haushofer's approach has been rightly criticized by Hans Rosenberg.[4] It tends to degenerate into simply one damn improvement after another; it is organized around diplomatic and political turning-points like 1848, 1871 and 1914, even though these are inappropriate to the historical time of agricultural developments and rural social relations; and its treatment of social and political issues themselves is strikingly ingenuous – Haushofer, for example, invites our suspicion by insisting too much that the leaders of the *Bund der Landwirte* (Agrarian League) were 'in no way demagogues'.[5] In short, we have a history of the rural population with the class relations left out, where technical modernization and co-operative organization go on apace, and everything is for the best in the best of all possible worlds. This blandly untheoretical version of 'modernization' on the land can be found in other works dealing with agriculture, and it is characteristic also of many works concerned with the achievements of particular *Bauernführer*.[6]

The major alternative reading of the problem can be traced back, in part, as far as Lujo Brentano, certainly back to figures writing in the 1940s, like Alexander Gerschenkron.[7] It has been most influentially suggested, however, by Hans Rosenberg, developed by Hans-Jürgen Puhle, and adopted by numerous historians in recent years in a more or less explicit fashion.[8] This view of changing rural relations turns the Haushofer approach on its head. Here, the primary determinants are not arbitrarily-chosen political events, but economic cycles – above all, the Great Depression. Within this framework, moreover, it is not Haushofer's 'prominent figures' like Thaer or Liebig, and well-meaning 'rural leaders' like Raiffeisen and Wangenheim, but the Prussian Junkers as a class, to whom our attention is directed. Threatened economically, so it has been argued, by the agricultural crisis and the changing nature of the world market, the Junkers clung desperately to their remaining social power, while organizing politically to secure their position. They succeeded, at one level, in obtaining high grain tariffs, together with various economic and fiscal privileges from government. At a further level – and one more directly important for the concerns of this paper – they succeeded in both encouraging and exploiting social forces unleashed by the Great Depression. Thus, the argument runs, they were able not only to exploit the uncertainties and anxieties of the petty bourgeoisie, but above all to harness the resentments of the peasantry against the 'urban' enemy – the liberals who allegedly threatened property with their Manchester capitalism, and the socialists who supposedly threatened it with their 'state of the future'. The Junkers, in short, were able to gain a new lease of life by manipulating rural discontent and mobilizing the peasantry and other parts of the rural population behind their own banner. The main agency whereby this was achieved was the Agrarian League.

This reading of changing rural politics deserves to be taken rather more seriously than the first. The work of Rosenberg and Puhle is a necessary starting-point for further consideration of rural politics in Imperial Germany. It is, nevertheless, a starting-point, not a terminus. Both authors had completed their major works on this problem by the mid-1960s, and Rosenberg explicitly intended his contribution as a stimulus to further research, rather than as a hard-and-fast result of such research. In subsequent years a growing body of monograph literature on economic, social and political aspects of the problem, together with changing directions in German historiography as a whole, have suggested ways in which we might move on. Here I want to suggest three points at which this interpretation of the changing nature of rural politics might be reconsidered. First, we should try to overcome the Prusso-centric approach which tends to exaggerate the relative importance both of the Junkers and of the Agrarian League: rural social relations and political mobilization in Bavaria, Hessen and Württemberg, as well as in non-'core'-Prussian regions like Schleswig-Holstein, deserve more consideration. Secondly, the actual material conditions and social values of the rural population itself need to be brought out more (in all their material, regional and confessional diversity), otherwise the risk is run that they will be relegated in the mind of the historian simply to the position of the electoral fodder of manipulative, and particularly Junker, leaders. Thirdly, and closely connected, the recasting of rural politics in the Kaiserreich, about the existence of which there can be little dispute, should be seen as a process, not an event. It proceeded out of the interaction between, on the one hand, aggrieved and demanding rural populations and, on the other, social and political elites of different political colours, who saw themselves required to head off and somehow absorb these pressures.

In the light of these remarks, the intentions of this article are, first, to look at the rural population of Germany under the impact of major economic change, and changes in the fabric of rural social life, 1871–1914; secondly, to consider the political articulation of the pressures and antagonisms occasioned by these changes; thirdly, to demonstrate the threat posed in this way to the traditional dominance of notables (*Honoratioren*) of various political parties; and fourthly, to suggest that the peasantry, having in a crucial period from the late 1880s to the mid-1890s helped to throw up a new kind of maverick political leader, was re-absorbed into the changed political parties on a new basis. This was part of a new interpenetration of 'high politics' and 'parish-pump politics'. The politicians' view of rural society changed; and so did rural society's view of the politicians.

II

The economic changes which affected German rural society after the 1870s have often been depicted as a threat to the Junkers and an opportunity for the peasantry. The depression of grain prices as a result of new supplies on the world market and the international transportation revolution was, supposedly, a direct challenge to the large estate-owning Junkers. But it allegedly opened up new possibilities for the peasant: to purchase his feedstuffs more cheaply, and to take advantage of the lower price of bread to sell more of his animal, dairy and vegetable produce to the growing urban market. Thus the introduction of grain tariffs has been seen as a great missed opportunity, when Germany 'failed' to develop on Dutch or Danish lines of agricultural specialization by peasant producers.[9] These tariffs have, accordingly, been ascribed a central importance in the German agrarian movement, and been regarded principally as a Junker device foisted on the peasantry. In line with this interpretation, the struggle of the East Elbian estate owners against the Caprivi trade treaties in the 1890s, and the closely-connected foundation of the Agrarian League, are viewed as the dominant motifs of rural political organization.

This article is not the appropriate place to consider in detail the economic arguments on tariffs.[10] Two important points should be made on this problem, however. First, prevailing interpretations overestimate the importance of grain tariffs by placing them at the centre of agrarian discontent. Secondly, by doing this, they underestimate the autonomous grievances of a peasantry which was subject in the last three decades of the nineteenth century to a number of adverse economic pressures. The net effect of these two tendencies is to minimize the extent to which rural, peasant areas were spontaneously coming alive, in the 1890s especially. The sources of peasant grievance were many, but they formed part of a common problem: in the last decades of the nineteenth century, agricultural production was locked ever more firmly into a market economy whose operations lay outside the control of the primary producer. With the countryside exposed to the competition of overseas supplies, and price levels fixed on the major and distant exchanges, the peasant as well as the estate owner found his income threatened as the price of peasant grains like oats, spelt and barley was depressed. Peasant producers of other commodities found themselves similarly threatened by 'outside' forces: cattle breeders by foreign cattle and meat imports; hop growers by refrigeration, which put them at a tactical disadvantage *vis-à-vis* brewers; dairy producers by the spectre of chemically-produced margarine. Nor did the threat from outside agencies stop there. Arguably more important to the peasant producer than uncertain or depressed prices was the problem of rising costs. These, too, were perceived (reasonably in the circumstances) as the product of outside forces – whether directly, in the form of higher taxes and insurance contributions, and the price-fixing machinations of the fertilizer rings, or indirectly, as industrialization and construction projects stimulated a flight from the land which greatly increased rural labour costs.[11]

When these developments are considered together with the mounting problem of peasant indebtedness, the authentic roots of peasant grievances become plain. The reaction to these threats was mixed. To some extent the peasantry began to fight back, particularly through the medium of co-operatives – first credit co-operatives and organizations specializing in the marketing of particular fruit, vegetable or dairy produce. This was to reach a high-point in the organizations of the dairy producers, who were actually able in the years after 1895 to effect a price increase for milk which benefited themselves at the expense of the middlemen's margins.[12] The great expansion of dairy, as of other co-operatives, however, came in the period from the 1890s onwards, from which date roughly a thousand new agricultural co-operatives a year were formed up to 1914. In 1890 the number of dairy co-operatives still stood at 639; by 1910 it had reached 3,382.[13] In the 1880s and the early 1890s, however, the main thrust of peasant grievances did not channel itself into organizations of this kind. Rather, it manifested itself as a prickly but organizationally invertebrate rejection of outside manipulation. In a pattern familiar from earlier periods, certain events served as symbols to trigger a more threatening response. A sudden fall in prices, new government pedigree regulations, official complacency in the face of an epidemic of foot-and-mouth disease, or the threat of higher taxation to finance army increases: these, by the 1890s, had become the potential spark-points of an inchoate revolt in the countryside. This was to direct itself against governments and bureaucracies; but, as we shall see, it was also to prove awkward to established notables of all political parties.

Peasant discontent in these years was undoubtedly fuelled by a growing *perception* of exploitation, manipulation and the disparity in living standards between town and country. This heightened perception was the result of the penetration of former rural social and ideological self-sufficiency by outside influences, parallel to the penetration of economic self-sufficiency (subsistence production, practice of ancillary crafts) by outside market forces. What were these influences? In the quotation from Berthold Auerbach which heads this paper, the school, the army and the railway are suggested as the crucial solvents of 'traditional' rural values and perceptions.[14] These are precisely the agencies of change which Eugen Weber argues helped to turn 'Peasants into Frenchmen' between 1870 and 1914.[15] They seem likely also to have had a significant (if often double-edged) effect on the consciousness of the rural population in Germany. The German primary school systems never, of course, had either the unitary character or the centralizing mission of their French counterpart, but the state governments of imperial Germany did, on the whole, attempt to extend both the length of primary education and to enforce school attendance – something which was particularly problematical in rural areas. The establishment of agricultural continuation schools, greater in number and wider in their catchment area than the agricultural 'winter schools', also formed part of official attempts to 'rationalize' the practice of agricultural production.[16] The growing staff of pedagogues in such institutions took their place alongside the expanding number of agricultural inspectors, state slaughter-house officials and veterinary surgeons. These outside agencies are likely to have had most effect on successive generations of peasants' sons, and the same is true of conscription. Whether or not military service made young peasants dissatisfied with rural life, as the left liberal Oskar Muser hoped,[17] it does seem to have had some effect in pointing up the contrast between rural standards of living and those of a more affluent world beyond the parish pump.[18]

The growth of the railways had a similar effect. Long regarded by conservatives as a dangerous solvent of comfortably unchanging rural values, the railways began to penetrate the village and small town in the last decades of the nineteenth century. If the years preceding unification had been the era of main-line building, the period which followed was marked by a crucial if less spectacular consolidation through the construction of local branch lines. This not only locked the countryside more closely into the market economy: it also facilitated movement out of and into the village. The railway carried the occupants of the village to new jobs in the town, like the two hundred commuters (*Einpendler*) who, in 1900, travelled daily into the growing Swabian market town of Ebingen from the rural hinterland.[19] The railways similarly carried peasants and their families into the towns on occasional Sunday outings, as well as on more hallowed enterprises like pilgrimages and the annual excursion of the Brown Cow Insurance Society. Like the letters (and remittances) of relatives who had emigrated to North America,[20] like the periodic return of peasants' sons and daughters from the town, and like the activities of the growing number of travelling salesmen and motorized delivery vans from the city,[21] the railway acted as a leaven in changing rural perceptions.

This is not by any means to say that rural Germany was painlessly 'modernized' by the school, military service and new means of communication. For all the evidence of greater mobility and changing styles of dress and housing in these years,[22] it would be misleading to talk blandly of a transition from 'peasants into Germans', without making it clear that the impact of these outside agencies was, at the very least, a contradictory one. In a number of respects, new forces of this kind served to change the style, rather than the substance, of peasant life: pilgrimages were undertaken by railway rather than on foot; gypsies were attacked in letters to the new local newspaper, rather than physically (although there was no lack of physical attacks on groups like the gypsies in these years). Often, moreover, the penetration of these new influences – like the penetration of new economic market forces – only served to heighten well-established rural grievances and to give a sharper focus to their expression. The school, the army and the railway were, understandably, not always regarded in rural communities as a benign innovation. The school threatened to carry off a crucial part of the labour-force which made up the family economy; and it might, so it was feared, unduly raise the expectations of the young: 'Wenn es heimkommt das Fräulein/Will es nicht mehr wissen vom Säulein.'[23] The army, similarly, carried off the young at vital periods of the summer; and it was also widely feared that army manoeuvres spread epidemics like foot-and-mouth disease. The railway, the means by which competitive produce was carried into local markets, was regarded with equal ambivalence. The schoolteacher, the army officer on manoeuvres and the railway official were, moreover, like the travelling salesman, 'outsiders'. Like the outsiders against whom rural communities had customarily vented their displeasure – the landlord's agent, the tax collector, the hawker – they were castigated as aliens whose parasitical living was gained at the expense of the productive peasant and his family.

Increasingly, in the last decades of the nineteenth century, it was figures of this kind who were added to the familiar figures of the Jewish money-lender and the distant financial manipulator as the prime objects of peasant hostility. They stood as representatives for the distant manipulation of the town, itself the symbol of wealth, political power, administrative caprice and moral self-indulgence. The penetration of new forces into the countryside therefore tended to sharpen rather than blunt sentiments of this kind; for it multiplied the points of intersection with the outside world at which rural communities felt themselves to be exploited.

III

By the later 1880s, radical rural distemper of this kind could not be adequately accommodated either within the official, semi-governmental institutions which claimed to represent the corporate interests of agriculture, or within the pattern of established party politics. Peasant dissatisfaction with governments and officialdom was plain. It expressed itself through indifference to elections, as well as through a more active antagonism towards officials like the 'veterinary surgeon with the top hat and kid gloves' who was scornfully dismissed for his impracticality by one German peasant in the south-west.[24] Certainly, by 1890, the official channels of the agricultural associations (*Landwirtschaftliche Vereine*) did more to arouse than to dampen such resentments. The associations were too closely identified with a distant, olympian government. In Bavaria, for example, the association was 'essentially a bureaucratic mechanism for effecting legislative decrees and technical improvements at the local level', whose meetings alienated the bulk of the rural population with their soporific use of 'Latin names and complicated chemical formulae'.[25] In neighbouring Würtemberg, the official agricultural association similarly antagonized the rural population with 'long, learned articles which no peasant will read'.[26] In all the German states, moreover, the associations tended to be identified not only with arrogant officialdom, but with local landowning and other notables. Social conflict therefore came to the surface over many issues. In the Schleswig-Holstein agricultural *Generalverein*, for instance, the larger landowners paid more attention in educational matters to the question of higher education and agricultural academies, whereas the peasantry was more concerned with agricultural continuation schools. Similarly, over the ostensibly less contentious issue of breeding policy, the larger landowners showed a keen interest in military and race horses, while the peasantry were more concerned with working animals.[27] This was a line of division which seems to have extended to other states. Rural notables tended to set the tone when conflicts of this nature arose, and it is hardly surprising that in 1890 the regional Pinneberg association of the Schleswig-Holstein *Generalverein* had only one-third of local agricultural producers affiliated to it, the other two-thirds being predominantly peasants with smaller concerns.[28] Similarly, in Bavaria, the official agricultural association had only 56,467 members in 1888. Even as a paper membership, this represented only a small percentage of the state's peasant producers.[29]

The political dimensions and implications of this rural alienation were confused, and varied throughout different parts of the Reich. It had least resonance, probably, in the Junker heartland east of the Elbe – in East and West Prussia, Brandenburg, Pomerania, Posnania and Silesia. There, as is well known, the independent peasantry was less important than elsewhere, smaller in number and more marginal to agricultural production as a whole. The social dominance of the Junkers was reinforced by powerful legal sanctions; and the three-class franchise of the Prussian chamber of deputies allowed minimal scope for such peasant-proprietor discontent as did exist.[30] This was not uniformly the case in other parts of Prussia: in the provinces of Saxony and Hessen, in Schleswig-Holstein, and in Westphalia and the Rhineland in the west. Nor was it the case in the southern German states. In all of these areas which did not make up the political and administrative bloc of East Elbia, the period up to the middle of the 1890s witnessed, to a greater or lesser degree, a serious disruption, and in places a decomposition, of the old notable politics – a process which ran in parallel with the alienation of the peasantry from governments and semi-official agricultural associations.

Rural disaffection became more volatile in the late 1880s and the early 1890s in response to a number of short-term grievances: a turn-down of agricultural prices; foot-and-mouth outbreaks and a severe feedstuff shortage in the south (both of which raised, in sharpened form, the problem of obtaining cheap credit to buy new stock); the Caprivi trade treaties; and the preparations for the 'big' military bill (which threatened increased taxation). The ensuing discontent helped to fracture the old mould of the political parties. The modest advance of the Social Democratic Party (SPD) was a straw in the wind. As early as the 1880s there had been sporadic indications in states like Hanover, Hessen, Schleswig-Holstein and Saxony of a rural protest vote for the SPD which could not be accounted for entirely by agricultural labourers and rural factory workers.[31] In 1890, at its Halle conference, the SPD issued the slogan 'out into the countryside', and in the subsequent three years engaged in intensive rural agitation, through pamphlets and word-of-mouth contacts. In the Reichstag elections of 1893, capitalizing on the high level of rural discontent, the SPD was able to register marked improvements in its performance in rural seats. This was particularly so where the party was able to tap material grievances which were conjoined with other discontents – anti-Centre feeling in Bavaria, Guelph particularism in Hanover, anti-Prussian feeling in Schleswig-Holstein. The extent of SPD electoral inroads should certainly not be exaggerated: the majority of its rural supporters were not independent peasants, and the party itself was aware of the shortcomings of its approach to this class. The Prussian Prime Minister, Botho Eulenburg, was nevertheless moved to express his concern about SPD political penetration 'particularly in the countryside'.[32]

A more telling sign of discontent was the support given to independent peasant movements: Otto Böckel's anti-semitic organization in Central Germany, Hermann Ahlwardt's political crusade in Prussia, and the Bavarian Peasant League (BBB).[33] These proved severely disruptive of the hold on the rural population enjoyed by the established parties. Böckel won the Marburg constituency from the Conservatives in 1887, extended his influence into the Grand Duchy of Hessen in the following years and set up his Central German Peasants Association in 1890. By the time of the 1893 Reichstag elections, Böckel's organization had robbed the National Liberals of a number of seats in Hessen and entered the Reichstag as one contingent among the 16 anti-semitic deputies from the central belt of Germany who had obtained a total of 263,900 votes (1890: 47,500). This success was accompanied by the capture of four seats in the Hessen lower house. Ahlwardt's political success gave evidence of a similar political ferment. Adopted by the anti-semites for the Prussian seat of Arnswalde-Friedberg, he took the seat from the Conservatives in a December 1892 by-election, following a rabid campaign which achieved rather greater resonance than the Social Democratic Sunday campaigning processions through the Brandenburg countryside. The BBB erupted similarly into Centre strongholds in Bavaria, addressing itself to anti-Centre feeling in general as well as to particular discontent over the trade treaties and the Caprivi military bill. In the Reichstag and Bavarian Landtag elections of 1893 it was able to make significant inroads into the Centre rural vote.

These incursions into the traditional rural bastions of the main political parties were significant in a number of respects for their effect on the nature and style of rural politics. First, they shook up rural political life by helping to destroy the idea that certain seats were simply not contested. Böckel's Marburg victory was in a constituency which had formerly been virtually uncontested, and Ahlwardt's victory in Brandenburg was similar. In Bavaria, too, the BBB took the Centre on in its strongholds, in a frontal assault on that party's much-vaunted 'safe seats' (*Stammsitze*). Whatever the capacity of these various movements to build upon their beginnings, or to retain what they had won, their very entry into these safe seats was in itself of high significance. It served a similar function, at the political level, to that served by the SPD in the town of Sprenge in the Bielefeld area, where patriotic notables mobilized the local peasants in order to counter the SPD challenge, first trying to drown them out with a brass band, then repulsing the comrades by main force.[34] However much such actions may have been glossed by the conservative notables concerned (and by the press) as a 'traditional' response, they nevertheless marked in reality a new departure. Passive unspoken loyalty was no longer enough, and could not be tacitly relied upon. And the political significance of the independent peasant movements was more pointed still.

Secondly, the movements mentioned tapped a fundamentally populist, anti-elitist current within the peasantry. Böckel adopted the radical-nationalist colours of 1848 and the slogan 'against the Junkers and Jews'. His programme called, *inter alia*, for the abolition of the three-class franchise and a progressive income tax.[35] The BBB fought the 1893 elections on the slogan of 'no aristocrats, no priests, no doctors and no professors, only peasants for the representation of peasant interests'.[36] Its demands also included the abolition of the *Reichsratskammer*, the publication of the proceedings of all public bodies, full freedom of speech, the press and assembly, and a democratic franchise.[37] Both movements, of course, rode the issue of anti-semitism very hard; in both cases (as in the more obviously wayward example of Ahlwardt) the Jew was portrayed as the archetype of the outside manipulator and exploiter, in whose supposedly malign activities those in 'high places' were somehow complicit. The Jew, in fact, was the most tangible symbol of all those who were allegedly deaf or hostile to the discontents of the peasant. As such, the Jew was only part of the anti-elitist demonology developed by the radical agrarian movements, alongside the official, the banker, the effete urban writer, the lawyer and the traditional notable.

Thirdly, and in line with this powerful populist thrust, the Central German Peasants' Association and the BBB illustrate the emergence of a new kind of political leader in imperial Germany. In this respect, the rural experience had much in common with the broader experience of the SPD, the *Mittelstand* movement and the very many less obvious agitational organizations which mushroomed precisely in the period of the 1890s, and directed their fire against the aloofness of governments and traditional parties alike. These new rural leaders are to be seen, that is to say, in the context of a general political leavening in Imperial Germany which witnessed the emergence of 'the homeopaths, the anti-inoculationists, the pro-cremationists, the agrarians and the publicans', as one south German government sourly (but by no means exhaustively) catalogued them.[38] Two particular types of new rural leader may, in fact, be discerned. The first was the self-conscious representative of the parish pump, the man who claimed the sanction of the peasant community because of his *active* allegiance to local interests. The classic figure here was Philipp Köhler, Böckel's ally and later successor in the Central German (later Hessen) Peasants' Association. Köhler was *Dorfkönig* in his native Langsdorf:

mayor, jury foreman, civil registrar, postmaster and founding director of the savings and loan bank. He was at the same time, however, a man who played on the fact that he was himself an agriculturalist.[39] It is noteworthy that many of the important local activists and leaders in the BBB boasted a similar parish-pump pedigree as village mayors.[40] Leaders of this kind were novel in the sense that their role indicated the growing importance of the way in which local, parochial interests and perceptions– *as such* – were coming to be articulated within the imperial political system. The second type of leader was novel in a different way. These were men who can best be described as political mavericks, who owed their support to articulating the grievances of rural communities against official and notables not from within, but from without. They came not from below the level of officials and notables, but from outside. Like various figures within the *Mittelstand* movement whom they resembled, such as Theodor Fritsch, these political leaders lived, in a Weberian sense, from rather than for politics. Ahlwardt was perhaps the model here, a former headmaster sacked for embezzlement, whose political career was *sui generis*. Böckel, the archivist and folklorist turned professional anti-semite and peasant tribune, shared Ahlwardt's rootlessness and waywardness, and came out of the same mould. A number of the most prominent leaders of the BBB shared a similar maverick quality, belonging neither to the Bavarian bureaucratic establishment nor to the rival establishment-in-waiting of the local Centre Party – figures like the writer and ex-priest Ratzinger, the brewer Lutz, the newspaper editors Sigl and Schwab.[41] As a political type, such figures neither belonged properly to the traditional political elite of notables, nor did they spring directly from the self-consciously parochial ambience of local concerns. Rather, they enjoyed something of the position occupied earlier in the nineteenth century by those other 'outsiders' and anti-establishment defenders of the rural population: the bandits and peasant advocates.[42] Indeed, Sigl and Wieland in Bavaria, like Ahlwardt, could establish their credentials by pointing to libel suits and terms of imprisonment.[43]

The peasant dissatisfaction which sustained the rapid initial growth of organizations like the ones noted above posed problems for all the bourgeois political parties. The major victims of this volatile temper among the rural population were, however, the National Liberals, tarred with the brush of an unfeeling governmentalism and often loftily contemptuous of local rural aspirations. Treitschke captured the spirit of urban, and urbane, National Liberal notables when he spoke witheringly of the genre of *Heimat* literature, with its fictional portrayal of endless peasant 'louts and boors'.[44] The olympian presumption of the National Liberal standpoint, exemplified in the south German states, was the object of Willy Hellpach's condemnation of the National Liberal clique in Baden for its 'Liberal–Badense infallibility-arrogance' (*Unfehlbarkeitsdünkel*).[45] In states like Baden and Bavaria, where anti-notable and anti-urban rural sentiment coincided with the resentment of rural Catholic populations at the arrogance with which they were treated from outside, the National Liberals were already on the run electorally in the 1880s or earlier. The 1890s saw the culmination of this rural-Catholic backlash. In that decade, though, the National Liberals also faced a growing challenge in Protestant rural areas from the disaffection which fuelled movements such as Böckel's. Between 1887 and 1893 the National Liberals throughout the Reich lost half of their Reichstag seats and between 8 and 9 per cent of their popular vote. Some of this can be attributed to SPD gains in states like Saxony; but much of it was also accounted for by the loss of rural support in states such as Hessen, Württemberg and the Palatinate region of Bavaria. The same process was under way at state level, where the late 1880s and the 1890s saw the final dislodging of the National Liberals from previously powerful or even dominant positions in a number of state parliaments.[46] Once again, rural defections were a prominent cause of this.

What was happening was not just a reaction on the land against National Liberal parties which seemed identified with the overweening and parasitical institutions of the state. There was also a loss of political control by local notables and 'natural leaders'. In Württemberg, for example, Gottlob Egelhaaf noted the rising populist tenor of the rural and small-town electorate in the last decades of the nineteenth century, which made it impossible for the National Liberals to put up a candidate like Prince Hermann von Hohenlohe-Langenburg in 1887 because of 'the agitation against "the gentlemen"', a phenomenon which drove many notables out of political activity within the party because of the vulgar politicking which was now expected of them.[47] A similar pattern was evident in other states.[48] Where local notables took too much for granted, moreover, they could be disagreeably surprised. In the small Hessian village of Lindheim, for example, the local National Liberal elite consisted of the largest local tenant-farmer, the owner of the local castle, the pastor, the publican and a few of the wealthier farmers. In the mayoral elections of 1888 this natural order was subverted when the notable candidate was defeated by a 'red' opponent, supported by the rural poor and particularly by a neighbouring village which had felt itself treated in a 'stepmotherly' fashion by the former notable incumbent. The impact which this fracturing of customary deference had on the village can be seen in Lindheim in the divisions and bitterness it provoked in the elections to the church council, and in splitting the village choral society and agricultural loan bank. Even families, the most powerful links in the chain of local deference relations, were divided.[49] It is perhaps no accident that this incident occurred in Hessen; for it was here, perhaps above all, that the arrival on the political scene of vulgar interlopers made it clear to National Liberal notables that in the future they would have to compete and fight in four- or five-cornered election contests, with Conservatives, Left Liberals, Social Democrats and anti-semites.

In circumstances of this kind, political success with an aggrieved peasantry was likely to be greatest for those who robustly played the anti-governmental, anti-notable populist card. This was by no means unprecedented before the arrival of Böckel, the BBB and other maverick agrarians in rural politics. In states with a large number of small and medium peasants, like Oldenburg, Hessen and Württemberg, left liberals had gained electoral success on just such a platform.[50] Peasant sentiments of this kind may also help to explain the general liberal success amongst the peasantry of western Schleswig-Holstein. Regional Catholic parties had also been successful with a similar appeal in states like Baden (the *Katholische Volkspartei*) and Bavaria (the *Patriotenpartei*), where rural opposition to a distant liberal-bureaucratic regime over economic matters reinforced discontent over educational and religious policies which were felt as outside impositions from Karlsruhe or Munich.[51] In addition, in the early 1890s the infant Centre Party in Württemberg seems to have benefited from anti-governmental and anti-notable resentment of this sort (at a time of chronic economic crisis) in much the same way as the local left-liberal *Volkspartei*.[52]

Yet both left liberals and the Centre were themselves vulnerable to this kind of agrarian and parochial rancour. Friedrich Payer, a prominent left liberal in later years, lost a rural state by-election in 1890, when his agrarian opponent crudely but successfully depicted him as a city lawyer in league with the Jewish moneylenders against the honest peasant.[53] In the same state of Württemberg, a relative stronghold of left liberalism, the party found itself generally under attack in the early 1890s for the support it had given to the Caprivi trade treaties: a good deal of 'trimming' on the free trade issue was, in fact, thought prudent by the party's candidates at this time.[54] The Centre Party came under similar fire, as the agrarian *fronde* of the early 1890s demonstrated. Local pressures induced a large number of Centre deputies to vote against or at least abstain on the Caprivi treaties which the party was officially committed to supporting.[55] And the fear of rural secessions was heightened by the successful entry of the BBB into Bavarian politics. It is significant, too, that the Reichstag elections of 1893 witnessed not only a marked agrarian disaffection among rural Catholic voters, but also a powerful wave of anti-aristocratic feeling, derived partly from hostility to the Caprivi military bill with which aristocratic conservatives within the Centre were closely identified. In 1893 this rebelliousness in Catholic rural areas was not just articulated through the BBB; it was a potent sentiment within the ranks of those who still, for the moment, remained loyal to the Centre at the polls.[56]

The rural discontent in the first half of the 1890s, with its commingling of anti-semitism, anti-militarism, anti-urbanism and anti-elitism, cemented by a stubborn parochialism, was a source of some concern to established political leaders. Perspicacious National Liberal notables realized that they had failed to keep in touch with the aspirations of their 'natural' supporters.[57] Centre Party leaders were similarly gloomy: Ernst Lieber, writing to a Bavarian colleague in the summer of 1894, thought that at no time since the *Kulturkampf* had the disintegration of the party been so close.[58] The Conservatives, too, were alarmed. The victory of Ahlwardt in 1892, and the challenging appeal of the tenant-farmer Ruprecht-Ransern at the same time, marked an implicit challenge to the usual Conservative ways of managing politics. Otto von Manteuffel, speaking six months later about the Tivoli conference of December 1892 which wrote an anti-semitic plank into the Conservative platform, gave a cynical assessment of the party's vulnerability: 'We could not avoid the Jewish question unless we wanted to leave the demagogic anti-semites the full wind of a movement with which they would just have sailed right by us.'[59] A less conventional Conservative, Adolf Stöcker, referred to the Tivoli conference in terms which summed up the challenge to all the established parties from rural discontent: 'It was not a party conference in black tails and white gloves but in street clothes. This was the Conservative Party in the era of general and equal suffrage.'[60]

IV

From the middle of the 1890s, the inchoate but radical agrarian challenge seemed to dissipate itself with surprising speed. The popular support for Böckel's movement fell away markedly, as did that of the BBB. Ahlwardt's protean career ended in political failure and social isolation. The SPD made negligible inroads into a potential peasant constituency in the years prior to 1914. The established parties apparently closed the gap which had opened between themselves and a disgruntled rural population. The success of the Agrarian League is the outstanding symbol of this. How and why was this so? There are certain explanations which might be described as contingent: the permanent internecine squabbles of the autonomous agrarian movements; the inconsequential rural activities of the SPD, following the defeat of von Vollmar and his supporters in 1894–95;[61] and the upturn in agricultural prices after 1896. Governments, moreover, began to pay more attention to peasant grievances; and peasant producers received many material advantages from the operation of the protectionist system, which was extended further and more widely from the 1890s.[62]

There was, however, no well-oiled mechanism of 'challenge-and-response' about the manner in which the established parties addressed themselves to the threat. The years following the revolution of 1918, after all, witnessed the actual (as opposed to merely threatened) secession of the Bavarian Centre Party, the formation of regional splinter parties of a rural and petty-bourgeois stamp, and the inability of the established parties (with the major exception of the Centre) to hang on to their rural supporters in the years between 1928 and 1933. The come-back of the old parties after the mid-1890s should ultimately be seen, in this perspective, as a provisional achievement. It was an achievement none the less, and one which was carried through by appropriating many of the material demands, and much of the political style, of vulgar rural interlopers like Böckel, Köhler, Sigl and Ratzinger. We are therefore faced, in this period, with a transformation of rural politics, in the broadest sense, at two different levels. The first, and easier to pin down, was at the level of high politics and the political parties. Accompanying this, however, was a second, equally important but much more elusive change in the nature of rural politics itself. This concluding section will try to deal briefly with both.

The transformation of German Conservatism has already been excellently described by Hans-Jürgen Puhle in a pioneering work. While it tends to magnify the singular role of the Junkers, and to play down accordingly the degree of autonomous peasant rebelliousness, his work has nevertheless provided a convincing picture of the way in which 'agrarian radicalism overran Conservatism'.[63] Putting together Puhle's arguments with those sketched in this paper, one could say that the maverick political figure described above was successfully institutionalized within the Conservatives' Agrarian League in the person of functionaries like Hahn, Oertel and Kaufhold.[64] Puhle and others – most notably, now, Dan S. White – have also shown the way in which National Liberalism, where it survived as a significant political force in the countryside, did so by adopting an agrarian posture similar to that of the Agrarian League. Indeed, in areas like Hessen and the Palatinate, local National Liberalism was actually dependent for its electoral success on the organizational backbone provided by the League.[65] Even Left Liberalism, where it had – like the National Liberals – rural constituencies at risk, tended to bend with the agrarian wind. The pro-tariff revolt of six Württemberg Landtag deputies in 1901, which became something of a national *cause célèbre*, had many parallels in that state.[66] In Hessen, the left liberal leader Adolf Korell came round similarly to a defence of agricultural protection.[67] Nor did the echoes of the independent peasant movements of the 1890s end there. Left Liberal parties, particularly in southern Germany, where they had historically used anti-governmental and anti-elitist appeals, also availed themselves of populist slogans which were likely to find favour with the peasantry. The leading newspaper of the Württemberg left liberals, for example, made political capital at the expense of state officials by quoting with approval the hallowed saw of rural Swabians: 'Wer nix isch, und wer nix kah/Goht zur Post und Eisebah!'[68]

Generally, however, bourgeois liberalism (in contrast to France) found it difficult to accommodate itself to such sentiments. Alongside the Conservatives' Agrarian League it was, above all, the Centre which most successfully took on board agrarian material demands and parish-pump nostrums. From the crisis of the mid-1890s, it is possible to follow the pro-agrarian trajectory of the Centre Party up to its support for the tariffs of 1902 and beyond. As early as 1896, a Centre agent on the Lower Rhine complained to Lieber that too little was being done by the party to resist agrarian pressure. In the Rhineland he singled out Karl Bachem as a man too ready to compromise with agricultural demands:

> The Centre has conceded too much to the partially-justified complaints of the peasants and aristocratic trouble-makers, that too little has been done in recent years for agriculture. The impression has been created that certain gentlemen in the Centre, of whom Herr Deputy Bachem is one, believe that they can win back the peasantry through unheard-of concessions in the margarine question.[69]

It was not just over the margarine question, however, but over grain tariffs and meat import quotas, as well as other agrarian issues, that the Centre made 'unheard-of concessions'. Moreover, as disgruntled Centre notables like von Hertling observed, the tendency for the party to become a vehicle for peasant interests was accompanied by a populist rhetoric which men like himself found uncomfortable.[70] This was particularly marked in Bavaria, where Centre deputies were notoriously closer in style to the local BBB than to the party leadership in Berlin;[71] but it was also broadly true in other regional Centre parties, where local politicians of the party assumed a recklessly anti-governmental, anti-urban, anti-elitist and (often) anti-semitic stance which differed only in degree from that of Ratzinger or Böckel.[72] And in the Centre too, as in the Agrarian League, the role of the maverick political leader, as well as the appeal to the parish-pump, was institutionalized within the political practice of the party. In this context, figures like the 'peasant doctor' Georg Heim, and functionaries of the Christian Peasant Associations like Martin Fassbender, perhaps deserve renewed attention.

At this level, then, a new attention was being paid to peasant aspirations by the parties of the right and centre. The rural community became an object of political interest. This occurred, in fact, at the same time as the rural community also became an object of scholarly interest (among academic economists, and among folklorists like Hallgarten and Torney), and of literary interest (in the highly stylized works of *Heimat* authors like Timm Kröger and Clara Viebig). This article has tried to argue that the peasant should not be seen in this just as the dupe of the Junker and priest; that the role of the peasantry itself in the recasting of rural politics should be recognized. Yet it would, of course, be wrong to say that peasant aspirations and grievances were simply 'taken up' benignly and represented by the Agrarian League and Centre Party. The grievances and aspirations of rural communities were refracted through the prism of conservative politics. There is no doubt that in the process they were distorted and caricatured, just as they were distorted and caricatured by scholars and writers who had their own reasons for creating a mythically potent peasant 'tradition'. There is equally little doubt that – *pace* Haushofer – the practice of the Agrarian League *was* demagogic, as was that of the Centre. Whatever the degree of deception practised on the peasantry over tariff and fiscal arrangements, it is certainly the case that Conservative and Centre Party demagogues encouraged the peasantry to attack symbolic but empty targets, like the Jew or the stock exchange, rather than the structural basis of their exploitation. More demagogically still, perhaps, these parties took up and opportunistically encouraged parochial resentments which they then used as a stick with which to beat their own social and political enemies – the liberals and socialists. The *process* whereby this happened has not yet been properly investigated; but its broadly demagogic contours are fairly plain.[73]

The conclusion cannot be left there, however, for the other side of this coin is the very real change in the nature of rural politics on the ground. This should clearly not be exaggerated. In Prussia, local notables still wielded enormous power of a traditional kind. The old lines of authority were still recognized when it came to the election of figures like Kanitz or Schwerin-Löwitz, as they were in the case of Prussian aristocrats like Limburg-Stirum or Mirbach, who still regarded the 'modern' form of Agrarian League political management and agitation as 'alien and unaristocratic'.[74] In Catholic areas too the clergy still used the confessional-box and the sermon to persuade rural Catholics what their political obligations were.[75] The degree of electoral discipline which could result from vigorous clerical intervention was sometimes very striking.[76] More generally, in Catholic as in Protestant rural areas, deference and traditional loyalties remained strong. The stasis which they could produce in local politics is illustrated by a mayoral election in the Upper Swabian village of Hochdorf in 1912. Both candidates were the sons of former mayors; and both of them received exactly the same number of votes.[77] A slightly different example of the same thing can be found in the Schleswig-Holstein Landtag election of 1908, where one contest was between the sociologist Ferdinand Tönnies, standing as a left liberal, and his National Liberal brother.[78] One should not exaggerate the changes which had occurred in rural politics in the decades before 1914.

There nevertheless were changes. At a very obvious level, the number of peasants involved in some form of political, co-operative, educational or recreational organization had increased enormously. The Agrarian League had 330,000 members by 1914, while the numbers organized in the Christian Peasant Associations under the aegis of the Centre exceeded this. By 1913 there were 158,000 members (in over 3,000 local groups) of the Bavarian association, 80,000 in Baden, 58,000 in the Rhineland, 31,000 in Westphalia.[79] In the cases both of the League and the Peasant Associations, membership brought new possibilities with it: legal advice, reduced insurance premiums, co-operative activities. In Bavaria, the turnover of Georg Heim's Central Co-operative increased tenfold between 1899 and 1904, while the circulation of one Peasant Association newspaper, *Der Fränkische Bauer*, rose from 14,500 in 1902 to over 34,000 by 1907.[80] Like the symbolic struggles between country and town which have come to be known as the 'milk war', the 'meat war' and the '*Thomasmehl* war', these developments signified the presence of a new backbone in what had formerly been the invertebrate peasant reaction to outside exploitation.

The tenor of rural politics had also been changed in other ways by the forces described earlier in this article, and by the experience of the 1890s. Rural resentment had always expressed itself in one way or another against 'outsiders'. Now such resentment and its articulation had become the stuff of which local politics was fashioned. When the peasantry of Blasheim, near Bielefeld, was angered by new pedigree regulations for bulls, they manifested their discontent by attending local SPD meetings in 1903, and gave a considerable number of votes to the candidate of that party in the Bielefeld-Wiedenbrück constituency.[81] When parties put up candidates who were considered 'outsiders' – especially lawyers – electoral revolts ensued. The Agrarian League and the Centre were generally adept at manipulating this kind of sentiment; but they had not brought it into being, and they could not entirely control it. In Hessen, Böckel's old organization was absorbed into the League in 1904, but according to Philipp Köhler it degenerated into serving the 'interests of the leaseholders and gentleman farmers'. Renewed and partially successful anti-semitic protest in 1907 was the result.[82] The chequered history of (frequently successful) 'double candidacies' in Centre Party constituencies testifies to a similar continuing potential for volatility among rural Catholics. Taken together, these developments indicate that notable politics of the old, comfortable kind had been eroded. Higher election turn-outs, more intensive electioneering and a much greater degree of competition in rural elections at every level had changed the fabric of rural politics.

V

The paper on which this article is based was written in the first half of 1979. Even in the period since then there have been signs that our perspectives on the German peasantry are continuing to change. A growing body of work is appearing on the economic rationality of peasant producers in the market.[83] This revised idea of the peasant – it is tempting to call it a rehabilitation – has been reinforced in a different way by the continuing development of folklorism or historical ethnology (*Volkskunde*) in West Germany.[84] As *Volkskunde* has stepped out of the shadow cast by its abuse under the Nazis, the ethnological study of German peasant societies has started to resemble in certain ways the approach to the peasantry which has long been practised in France. The resulting picture has been more detailed and more sympathetic. And as social historians have taken note of this, their own attitudes to the peasant have become a little less lofty. The idiocy of rural life now seems less idiotic than it once did. Part of this changing perspective can be observed in the increasing number of works in Germany which try to deal with the so-called 'history of everyday life' (*Alltagsgeschichte*).[85] Where these writers have concerned themselves with rural society, they have usually – like the ethnologists – cast off much of the baggage of disdain which many previous writers brought to their task. Finally, the advent of Green politics in the Federal Republic provides a broader political context in which these changes can be placed. It should be stressed that the works in question cannot, by any means, be characterized simply as 'Green'. Nevertheless, the overall ecological thrust of the Green movement, like its renewed respect for certain benign aspects of peasant values, has run parallel to a scholarly tendency to rescue rural life from its urban and urbane detractors. Scepticism is called for on the significance and value we attach to this would-be Greening of Germany. But it is clear, at least, that new political as well as scholarly preoccupations are prompting new questions. Put simply, we are required to consider very seriously some of our assumptions about the famous transition from 'Gemeinschaft' to 'Gesellschaft'.

There is certainly plenty of scope here for an unwanted sentimentality, as recent work has sometimes demonstrated.[86] Celebrating the timelessness of rural virtue rather than the timelessness of rural vice is not very helpful. But much of this work has also focused our attention on something rather different: the pattern of rural change. Recent research has depicted the ambiguous process of peasant adaptation to the market, or to changes in apparently timeless rural values. That is the connection with the present article. I have been particularly concerned with the changing place of the peasant in German politics between 1871 and 1914. To talk of a change in this period is not, in itself, especially novel. Historians like Gerschenkron, Rosenberg and Puhle have argued that the Great Depression allowed the Junker Conservatives, above all through the Agrarian League, to harness peasant discontent for their own purposes. With one eye on 1933 and the advent of National Socialism, they have seen these Conservative efforts as 'proto-fascist'.[87] The present article has tried to suggest ways in which we might move on by revising these arguments. By breaking away from a Prusso-centric preoccupation with Junker wiles, we might see more clearly the changing place of the peasant in Imperial German politics. The peasant was subject as well as object of these changes. More than that: the re-casting of rural politics, 'below' as well as 'above', was itself a process, not a completed event whereby the success of the Agrarian League fixed a pattern of politics down to 1933. The continuity between pre-1914 Germany and 1933 is real enough. But it was not a straightforward linear continuity, whose unfolding can be deduced from the pre-war exploits of the Agrarian League. The convulsions and the incomplete success which attended the efforts by conservative elites to harness the peasantry help to explain the continuing volatility of the peasantry into the Weimar Republic. By its political conduct after 1928, the German peasantry revenged itself on the 'Old Gang' at least as much as it responded to their bidding. One purpose of this article has been to suggest why this might have been so.

NOTES

This article is based on a paper prepared in the early summer of 1979 for the Third SSRC Research Seminar in Modern German History, on Rural Society, held at the University of East Anglia on 13–14 July 1979. I am grateful to have had that opportunity to bring various ideas together. I have made only minor alterations to the text, although the final section is new. I should like to thank Robert Moeller for his critical comments on a draft of the whole article.

1 W. Wehland, 'Werthaltungen und Ideologien im Entwicklungsprozess der deutschen Landwirtschaft', *Sociologia Ruralis*, 12 (1972), p. 411.

2 Printed in *Stichworte. Kritische Modelle 2* (Frankfurt/Main 1970), p. 91. For a radical critique of such attitudes, see H. Brüggemann et al, eds., *Uber den Mangel an politischer Kultur in Deutschland* (Berlin 1978), pp. 95–6. See also the final section of this article.

3 H. Haushofer, *Die deutsche Landwirtschaft im technischen Zeitalter* (Stuttgart 1963).

4 H. Rosenberg, *Probleme der deutschen Sozialgeschichte* (Frankfurt/Main 1969), pp. 109–23.

5 Haushofer, op. cit., p. 213.

6 For example, F. Jacobs, *Von Schorlemer zur Grünen Front* (Düsseldorf 1957); and *Deutsche Bauernführer* (Dusseldorf 1958).

7 A. Gerschenkron, *Bread and Democracy in Germany* (Berkeley, Calif., 1943). On Brentano see J. J. Sheehan, *The Career of Lujo Brentano* (Chicago, 1966); and on contemporary liberal critics like Brentano in general, K. D. Barkin, *The Debate over German Industrialization 1890–1902* (Chicago, 1970).

8 For Rosenberg's work see especially *Grosse Depression und Bismarckzeit* (Berlin 1967) and the essays collected in *Probleme* (note 4). Some of his most important essays have recently been reprinted in *Machteliten und Wirtschaftskonjunkturen* (Göttingen 1978). Puhle's major work is *Agrarische Interessenpolitik und Preussischer Konservatismus*

(Hanover 1966). Puhle has re-stated his case in 'Der Bund der Landwirte im wilhelminischen Reich. Struktur, Ideologie und politische Wirksamkeit eines Interessenverbandes in der konstitutionellen Monarchie', in W. Rüegg and O. Neuloh eds, *Zur soziologischen Theorie und Analyse des 19. Jahrhunderts* (Göttingen 1971), pp. 145–62; and in *Politische Agrarbewegungen in kapitalistischen Industriegesellschaften* (Göttingen 1975), pp. 28–112; and in 'Conservatism in Modern German History', in *Journal of Contemporary History*, 13 (1978), pp. 701–7.

9 Gerschenkron and Puhle have both stressed this. They have been widely followed. For a classic contemporary statement of the case, see R. Drill, *Soll Deutschland seinen ganzen Getreidebedarf selbst produzieren?* (Stuttgart, 1895).

10 See J. C. Hunt, 'Peasants, Grain Tariffs and Meat Quotas', *Central European History*, 7 (1974), pp. 311–31; R. G. Moeller, 'Peasants and Tariffs in the *Kaiserreich*: How Backward were the Bauern?', *Agricultural History*, 55 (1981), pp. 370–84.

11 For details on this, see D. Blackbourn, *Class, Religion and Local Politics in Wilhelmine Germany* (London and New Haven, 1980), pp. 82–9.

12 U. Teichmann, *Die Politik der Agrarpreisstützung* (Cologne, 1955), pp. 543ff.

13 Details on co-operatives in: Teichmann, op. cit., pp. 546ff; Haushofer, op. cit., p. 218; J. Clapham, *The Economic Development of France and Germany* (Cambridge, 1936), pp. 224–7; J. Wernicke, *Kapitalismus und Mittelstandspolitik* (Jena, 1922), tables, pp. 931–2. It should be noted that, with the exception of dairy farmers, it was credit co-operatives which were most successful amongst the peasantry.

14 Cited in P. Mettenleiter, *Destruktion der Heimatdichtung* (Tübingen, 1974), p. 207.

15 E. Weber, *Peasants into Frenchmen. The Modernization of Rural France, 1870–1914* (London, 1977).

16 G. A. Ritter and J. Kocka, eds., *Deutsche Sozialgeschichte. Band 1: 1870–1914* (Munich 1974), pp. 209–10; Haushofer, op. cit., p. 198.

17 O. Muser, *Die Agrarfrage* (Karlsruhe, 1895), p. 30.

18 W. Brepohl, 'Bäuerliche Heilkunde in einem Dorf des Mindener Landes um die Jahrhundertwende', *Mindener Beiträge zur Geschichte, Landes- und Volkskunde, Neue Folge*, 2 (1950), pp. 9ff.

19 M. Koenig, *Die Bäuerliche Kulturlandschaft der hohen Schwabenalb* (Tübingen, 1958), p. 38.

20 4,500,000 Germans emigrated to the USA between 1820 and 1890. It has been calculated that one third of emigrants, a large number of whom came from rural areas, were able to emigrate only because of remittances from those who had preceded them. See M. Walker, *Germany and the Emigration, 1815–1914* (Cambridge, Mass., 1964).

21 The number of travelling salesmen in Germany increased from 45,000 to 70,000 between 1884 and 1898 (Wernicke, *Kapitalismus*, p. 213). By 1914 the Tietz concern had 100 delivery vans serving the area between Hamburg and Berlin alone. See G. Tietz, *Hermann Tietz: Geschichte einer Familie und ihrer Warenhäuser* (Stuttgart, 1965), p. 148.

22 See D. Blackbourn, 'The *Mittelstand* in German society and politics, 1871–1914', *Social History*, 4 (1977), pp. 426–8.

23 'When the young lady comes home she no longer wants to know about the piglet'. For details on this and the following, see Blackbourn, *Class, Religion and Local Politics*, pp. 138–40, 158–64. For an Austrian parallel, E. Bruckmüller, 'Bäuerlicher Konservatismus in Oberösterreich', *Zeitschrift für bayerische Landesgeschichte*, 37 (1974); and a further very thoughtful discussion of these problems, also based on Austria, G. Lewis, 'The Peasantry, Rural Change and Conservative Agrarianism: Lower Austria at the Turn of the Century', *Past & Present*, 81 (1978), pp. 119–43.

24 Quoted by Centre politician Hans Kiene in *Verhandlungen der Württembergischen Kammer der Abgeordneten, 36 Landtag, Protokoll-Bd. IV*, 2483, *100 Sitzung*, 14 June 1905.

25 I. Farr, 'Populism in the Countryside', in R. J. Evans ed., *Society and Politics in Wilhelmine Germany* (London, 1978), p. 137.

26 Centre back-bencher Theophil Egger, in *Verhandlungen der Württembergischen Kammer der Abgeordneten, 33 Landtag, Protokoll-Bd.1*, pp. 374–5, *21 Sitzung*, 7 May 1895.

27 T. Thyssen, *Bauer und Selbstverwaltung* (Neumünster, 1958), p. 147.

28 Ibid., p. 167.
29 Farr, op. cit., p. 156 no. 5. It should be noted that such organizations were principally interested in organizing the better-off peasantry, often defined as those who were *spannfähig*, i.e. possessed draught-animals.
30 On this, see Puhle, *Agrarische Interessenpolitik*.
31 H. G. Lehmann, *Die Agrarfrage in der Theorie und Praxis der deutschen und internationalen Sozialdemokratie* (Tübingen, 1970), p. 10. For a recent, detailed study of SPD and peasantry, see A. Hussain and K. Tribe, *Marxism and the Agrarian Question, Volume One: German Social Democracy and the Peasantry 1890–1907* (London, 1981).
32 Lehmann, op. cit., p. 11ff.
33 On the following, see generally P. W. Massing, *Rehearsal for Destruction* (New York, 1949), especially Chapters 5–7; R. S. Levy, *The Downfall of the Anti-Semitic Political Parties in Imperial Germany* (New Haven, 1975); J. A. Nichols, *Germany after Bismarck* (Cambridge, Mass., 1959); S. R. Tirrell, *German Agrarian Politics after Bismarck's Fall* (New York, 1951). On the Böckel movement, see D. S. White, *The Splintered Party. National Liberalism in Hessen and the Reich 1867–1918* (Cambridge, Mass., 1976), especially p. 136ff. On the BBB: Farr, op. cit.; H. Haushofer, 'Der Bayerische Bauernbund (1893–1933)', in H. Gollwitzer, ed., *Europäische Bauernparteien im 20. Jahrhundert* (Stuttgart, 1977), pp. 562–86; K. Möckl, *Die Prinzregentenzeit* (Munich, 1972), especially p. 451ff.
34 Lehmann, op. cit., pp. 28–9.
35 Levy, op. cit., pp. 55–60; White, op. cit., p. 136ff.
36 Jacobs, *Bauernführer*, p. 113; Haushofer, 'Bauernbund', p. 571.
37 A. Schnorbus, *Arbeit und Sozialordnung in Bayern vor dem Ersten Weltkrieg* (Munich, 1969), p. 76.
38 Hauptstaatsarchiv Stuttgart, E 41, Anhang II, Bü 44: 'Votum des Staatsministeriums', concerning Württemberg constitutional reform.
39 K. E. Demandt, 'Leopold von Sacher-Masoch und sein Oberhessischer Volksbildungsverein zwischen Schwarzen, Roten und Antisemiten', *Hessisches Jahrbuch für Landesgeschichte*, 18 (1968), p. 191; White, op. cit., pp. 145–6.
40 Haushofer, 'Bauernbund', p. 570.
41 Möckl, op. cit., pp. 451–3. Haushofer, 'Bauernbund', pp. 570–3; Farr, op. cit., pp. 138–9.
42 On early nineteenth-century bandits and their relationship to the peasant population, see C. Küther, *Räuber und Gauner in Deutschland* (Göttingen 1976), especially pp. 52ff., 103ff and 130ff, on Matthias Klostermayer, the 'bayerischer Hiesel'. For an example of one prominent 'peasant advocate', Andreas Wiest, see C. Bauer, *Politischer Katholizismus in Württemberg biz zum Jahre 1848* (Freiburg, 1929), p. 128.
43 On Sigl and Wieland, see Haushofer, 'Bauernbund', pp. 570–1; on Ahlwardt: Massing, op. cit., especially pp. 94–5.
44 Cited in Mettenleiter, op. cit., p. 325.
45 J. Becker, ed., *Heinrich Köhler: Lebenserinnerungen* (Stuttgart, 1964), p. 21.
46 Details of National Liberal decline in states like Baden, Württemberg, Hessen and Bavaria in H. Kalkhoff ed., *Nationalliberale Parlamentarier* (Berlin, 1917), tables, pp. 272, 303, 338, 371, 405. There are good tables also in J. J. Sheehan *German Liberalism in the Nineteenth Century* (Chicago, 1978).
47 G. Egelhaaf, *Lebenserinnerungen* (Stuttgart, 1960), pp. 40–2, 58, 125.
48 Sheehan, *Liberalism*, pp. 233–4.
49 Demandt, op. cit., pp. 180–83.
50 On Württemberg, for example, see the two books on the left-liberal *Volkspartei*: K. Simon, *Die württembergischen Demokraten* (Stuttgart, 1969); and J. C. Hunt, *The People's Party in Württemberg and Southern Germany, 1890–1914* (Stuttgart, 1975). In the case of Hessen, see the 1881 election slogan of the left liberals in the Hanau Reichstag constituency: 'Junker und Pfaffen im Bund/Richten Bürger und Bauer zu Grund!'. Cited in White, op. cit., pp. 100, 273 note 33.
51 On Baden, see L. Gall, 'Die Problematik des badischen Kulturkampfes', *Zeitschrift für die Geschichte des Oberrheins*, 113 (1965), pp. 151–96; and G. Zang, ed., *Provinzialisierung einer Region. Zur Entstehung der bürgerlichen Gesellschaft in der*

Provinz (Frankfurt/Main, 1978). The Bavarian *Patriotenpartei* is dealt with by G. C. Windell, *The Catholics and German Unity, 1866–71* (Minneapolis, 1954), and Möckl, op. cit., pp. 36–9.

52 Blackbourn, *Class, Religion and Local Politics*, pp. 74–99.

53 F. Payer, 'Mein Lebenslauf', typed MS, Stuttgart 1932, pp. 35–6.

54 Blackbourn, *Class, Religion and Local Politics*, p. 97.

55 Details of Centre abstentions and votes against the Austrian, Italian, Romanian and Russian treaties in Nichols, op. cit., p. 149; Tirrell, op. cit., pp. 120–3, 243–5, 294; K. Bachem, *Vorgeschichte, Geschichte und Politik der Deutschen Zentrumspartei* (Cologne, 1927–32), V, 253–4; M. Spahn, *Ernst Lieber als Parlamentarier* (Gotha, 1906), p. 37.

56 Blackbourn, *Class, Religion and Local Politics*, pp. 44–51.

57 White, op. cit., p. 142.

58 Pfälzische Landesbibliothek Speyer, Ernst Lieber Papers, L 32, Lieber to Schädler, 6 June 1894.

59 Cited in Massing, op. cit., p. 66.

60 Ibid., p. 64.

61 Lehmann, op. cit., especially pp. 191ff; R. Jansen, *Georg von Vollmar* (Düsseldorf, 1958), pp. 57–63.

62 See Hunt, 'Peasants, Grain Tariffs and Meat Quotas', pp. 311–31. Expenditure by the Prussian government on agriculture as a whole rose from 11,250,000 Marks in 1890 to 20,250,000 Marks in 1899 to 26,500,000 Marks in 1904.

63 Puhle, *Agrarische Interessenpolitik*, p. 278.

64 Ibid. See especially the final chapter on the changing style of agrarian Conservatism, and the comments on Diederich Hahn, pp. 296–7. The work of Hans Rosenberg should also be noted here.

65 Puhle, *Agrarische Interessenpolitik*, pp. 193–9; White, op. cit., p. 142ff. Hunt, 'Peasants, Grain Tariffs and Meat Quotas', p.329 and note 47.

66 *Verhandlungen der Württembergischen Kammer der Abgeordneten, 36 Landtag, Protokoll-Bd. I*, 226, *13 Sitzung*, 1 February 1901. Of the six who staged the revolt, four deputies had faced serious agrarian opposition in the state elections shortly before the vote. See *Deutsches Volksblatt*, 4 February 1901. For details of local left-liberal accommodation to agrarian realities, see *Deutsches Volksblatt*, 16 March, 6 April and 9 April 1901. See also Hunt, *People's Party*, pp. 102–3.

67 White, op. cit., p. 178.

68 *Der Beobachter*, 28 August 1908. ('If you are nothing and can do nothing/Go on the posts and railways').

69 Pfälzische Landesbibliothek Speyer, Ernst Lieber Papers, G 63, August Grunau to Lieber, 6 February 1896.

70 Among various observations of this kind by Hertling, see his *Erinnerungen*, Volume II (Munich, 1920), pp. 175–6, 249.

71 For a typical complaint about this, see Adolf Gröber's letter to Lieber, cited in H. Gottwald, 'Zentrum und Imperialismus', dissertation, Jena 1966, pp. 65–6 note 163; see also T. Nipperdey, *Die Organisation der deutschen Parteien vor 1918* (Düsseldorf 1961), p. 277.

72 See D. Blackbourn, 'Roman Catholics, the Centre Party and Anti-Semitism in Imperial Germany', in P. Kennedy and A. Nicholls, eds, *Nationalist and Racialist Movements in Britain and Germany before 1914* (London, 1981), pp. 106–29.

73 In the case of the Centre Party I have tried in various places to explore this process. See *Class, Religion and Local Politics*; 'Roman Catholics, the Centre Party and Anti-Semitism', and 'Die Zentrumspartei und die deutschen Katholiken während des Kulturkampfes und danach', in O. Pflanze, ed., *Innenpolitische Probleme des Bismarck-Reiches* (Munich, 1983).

74 Puhle, *Agrarische Interessenpolitik*, p. 275.

75 H. Bodewig, *Geistliche Wahlbeeinflussungen in ihrer Theorie und Praxis dargestellt* (Munich, 1909).

76 For examples, see Blackbourn, *Class, Religion and Local Politics*, p. 114.

77 *Anzeiger vom Oberland*, 25 November 1912.

78 H. Beyer, 'Landbevölkerung und Nationalsozialismus in Schleswig-Holstein', *Zeitschrift für Agrargeschichte und Agrarsoziologie*, 12 (1964), p. 69.

79 P. Molt, *Der Reichstag vor der improvisierten Revolution* (Cologne and Opladen, 1963), pp. 131, 136 note 36. The total membership of Christian Peasant Associations in 1909 was already 320,000. See Gottwald, op. cit., p. 7. It is noteworthy that those with the largest membership were in areas where aristocratic notables were least in evidence as a political force.

80 Farr, 'Populism in the Countryside', pp. 151, 158 note 62.

81 C. Severing, *Mein Lebensweg*, Volume I (Cologne, 1951), p. 146.

82 White, op. cit., p. 172.

83 See Moeller (note 10) and Lewis (note 23).

84 See M. Scharfe, 'Towards a cultural history: notes on contemporary *Volkskunde* (folklore) in German-speaking countries', *Social History*, 4, 2 (1979), pp. 333–43.

85 See L. Niethammer, 'Anmerkungen zur Alltagsgeschichte', *Geschichtsdidaktik*, 5 (1980), pp. 231–42.

86 Jürgen Kocka has been notable for his warnings about the dangers of sentimentality coupled with hostility to theory in *Alltagsgeschichte*. See, for example, his 'Theorien in der Geschichtswissenschaft', in P. Leidinger, ed., *Theoriedebatte und Geschichtsunterricht* (Paderborn, 1982), 7–27.

87 See especially H.-J. Puhle, *Von der Agrarkrise zum Präfaschismus. Thesen zum Stellenwert der agrarischen Interessenverbände in der Politik am Ende des 19. Jahrhunderts* (Wiesbaden, 1972).

PART III

Catholics and Politics

7

Progress and Piety: Liberals, Catholics and the State in Bismarck's Germany

In 1804 Schiller wrote to a friend that Berlin was destined to become 'the capital of Protestantism'. He may have been thinking of theological scholarship in particular, but the nineteenth century was to confirm his judgment in a broader sense. The universities, the bureaucracy, the army and of course the Hohenzollern dynasty of the expanding Prussian state all bore a powerful Protestant imprint. This was an important element in the Prussian historical mission celebrated by historians like Treitschke, and it was carried over into the unified German state of 1871. The architect of Imperial Germany was the Protestant Bismarck. 'Lesser Germany', with Austria excluded, had a two-thirds Protestant majority and was ruled by self-consciously Protestant emperors.

Catholics constituted a pariah community within the new Germany. They had long been discriminated against, in Prussia and elsewhere, across a wide range of public appointments. They now found themselves branded by Bismarck as 'enemies of the Reich', a kind of fifth column within a state that had been created following the defeat of two Catholic foreign powers on the battlefield. That provides part of the background to the anti-clerical *Kulturkampf* of the 1870s in Prussia. But there was also a *Kulturkampf* in very un-Prussian German states like Baden; and the anti-clerical cause was by no means supported only (or even mainly) by conservatives like Bismarck. The term *Kulturkampf* (meaning literally 'struggle of civilizations') was coined by a left liberal, and it reflected liberal hopes for 'progress' in the optimistic 1860s and 70s. For liberals, Catholics stood for 'backwardness' in all its forms: economic, social and intellectual. This belief was reinforced by the revival of Catholic piety in the decades after 1848, in Germany as elsewhere, along lines that seemed to be symbolized by Pope Pius IX and his rejection of 'modernity' in the Syllabus of Errors. The following article is concerned with the clash between liberals and Catholics in the *Kulturkampf*, and tries to show that this was something more than an episode in church–state relations or Bismarckian political calculation. At the same time, I have tried to examine the complex triangular relationship between Catholics, liberals and the state during the 1870s. I hope that the result casts some light on Bismarck's Germany from a less familiar angle.

The first research and writing I did was on Catholics in Imperial Germany. They provided the subject of my earliest articles and my first book. The subject remains a central interest, but the focus of that interest has shifted in the last few years, both chronologically and thematically. Whereas my research centred for many years on the period from about 1890 to 1914, I have been more concerned recently with the *Kulturkampf*, which remains remarkably under-researched. I have also become increasingly interested in the changing nature of Catholicism in nineteenth-century Germany – the relations between clergy and laity, changing devotional forms, the emergence of more 'organized' (and more commercialized) forms of piety. I am currently engaged in research on reported apparitions of the

Virgin Mary in Germany during the 1870s. These more recent interests are reflected, to some extent, in the present article, which also had a number of precursors. I first tried to address the problem of the *Kulturkampf* directly in a paper presented to a conference of the *Historisches Kolleg* in Munich in June 1981, and later published as 'Die Zentrumspartei und die deutschen Katholiken während des Kulturkampfes und danach', in O. Pflanze (ed.), *Innenpolitische Probleme des Bismarck-Reiches* (Munich and Vienna, 1983), pp. 73–94. Many of the points made below about liberalism were first formulated in a paper given at a conference organized in Oxford by the History Workshop Centre in June 1984, which remains unpublished. Finally, a German version of the present text was written during 1985 and presented to audiences at a number of universities and at the Institute for European History in Mainz. An extended version of the present article will appear in 1987, in a series published on behalf of the Institute for European History, under the title *Volksfrömmigkeit und Fortschrittsglaube im Kulturkampf*.

Historians often find themselves faced with the task of puncturing an overblown concept to let some of the air out. The *Kulturkampf* presents the opposite problem: to try and restore something to its full historical importance. For the *Kulturkampf* was neither so anodyne an affair, nor of such limited significance, as the textbooks often suggest. It was not just a little local difficulty between church and state; nor was it simply another example of Bismarck's manipulatory repertoire. It was both of these things in part, but it was also a conflict over the future shape of Germany, in which material, social, moral and intellectual interests were at stake. Moreover, this 'struggle of civilizations' helped to expose and define many of the underlying political realities of Bismarckian Germany. One way of summarizing this conflict is to describe it as a clash between progress and piety. To avoid misunderstanding I should add that this does not mean it was a clash between 'modernity' and 'tradition'. Indeed, one of the incidental virtues of the *Kulturkampf* as a subject is that it provides excellent material to show how misleading those overworked categories can be. The progress espoused by German liberals in the *Kulturkampf* did not represent some benign increment of 'modernity'. True, many of the institutions and values for which they fought were eventually to become self-evident; but that is not how they were viewed at the time, and the imposition of them was neither bland, nor achieved without a price. Equally, the piety of German Catholics during the *Kulturkampf* was not 'traditional'. Or, to put it another way, much of the tradition was of fairly recent provenance.

The following article tries to elaborate these points, and it has four parts. The first looks at developments in Catholic Germany in the first two-thirds of the nineteenth century, and examines how liberals opposed their belief in progress to the 'backwardness' of Catholics. The second sets liberal ambitions during the *Kulturkampf* within the context of a broader liberal programme, and considers Catholic resistance to it. The third suggests how and why lack of popular consent for the liberal

Kulturkampf required coercive state action to accomplish it. The final section looks at the legacy of antagonism between a weakened liberalism and a strengthened political Catholicism following the *Kulturkampf*, and tries to draw some general conclusions. European comparisons have been attempted where they seemed appropriate.

I

Catholics constituted a third of the population in the Prussian-based Lesser Germany established in 1871. They formed a reluctant periphery around the Protestant heartland of the Reich, a characteristic that was reinforced in the case of those Catholics – Alsatians, Poles – who were also non-German. They were concentrated geographically in the countryside and small towns, occupationally in agriculture and small business. Catholics became increasingly involved in industry and commerce as the century went on, but they were much more commonly found on the shop-floor and in the pit than they were among the owners of capital, managers or technical personnel.[1] When Max Weber later put forward his celebrated thesis on the Protestant ethic and the spirit of capitalism, he did so against the background of a long-running German debate about Catholic 'backwardness'.[2]

From the liberal point of view, material and cultural 'backwardness' went together: both were the product of a tightly disciplined, clerically controlled and 'medieval' Catholicism. It is therefore important to recognize the novel features in the German Catholicism that liberals were to confront during the *Kulturkampf*. Forty or fifty years earlier the position of the Catholic Church in Germany had been a miserable one. During the Napoleonic period it had lost its secular power as many tiny ecclesiastical states were abolished, and had also forfeited large amounts of property as a result of secularization.[3] In subsequent decades the church was severely restricted in its autonomy by prevailing ideas of the state church. When the post-Napoleonic German states reorganized their administrations to take account of territorial changes, for example, they reorganized diocesan boundaries at the same time. That was the situation both in the Prussian Rhine Province and in Württemberg, where the new Catholic subjects of the kingdom were arbitrarily assigned to a bishop in distant Rottenburg, chosen for the administrative convenience of the secular power because it was close to the state capital in Stuttgart and the state university in Tübingen.[4] The state intervened in many aspects of church life, including the appointment of clergy. In the Duchy of Nassau deacons were known as 'ducal deacons', while the concept of the 'royal priest' persisted in Bavaria well into the nineteenth century. In Württemberg the state even laid down the length of sermons and the times when confessions could be heard.[5]

If this presents a picture very different from the one we find later in the century, the same is true of the attitude generally taken by the ecclesiastical hierarchy towards popular forms of piety. In the spirit of the Catholic Enlightenment the hierarchy sought to extirpate embarrassing 'excesses', and zealous priests found themselves called to account by their bishops if they were suspected of breaching this austere doctrine.[6] That was the fate in the 1840s of the young Bensheim priest Christoph Moufang, later the celebrated regent of one of Germany's foremost seminaries in Mainz.[7] But enlightened or politically prudent bishops agreed with more conservative or ultramontane clergy on one point: that the religious feelings of German Catholics left much to be desired. Thus it was frequently complained that people arrived for services late and drunk, or that they arrived promptly for the mass, only to leave before the sermon. In one Rhenish town the sermons had to be given by the chaplain while the priest manned the door. There were similar complaints about behaviour in church. Members of the congregation talked and smoked during services, and it was reported from one parish that young people climbed into the rafters of the church and on to the organ, from where they jeered at the priest.[8] Pilgrimages, often undertaken without clerical accompaniment or even approval, were another source of complaint. Their attraction was considered to be the element of novelty or unfamiliarity, and the danger of pilgrims indulging in immorality, drunkenness or other forms of worldliness was frequently emphasized. The behaviour of Catholic youth was of particular concern here, and that is also true of the repeated misgivings expressed about the mingling of the sacred and profane during Catholic feast days.[9] Even taking into account the clerical tendency to exaggerate the dangers of immorality, the situation in earlier decades of the century seems to have been very different from what it later became. The Saarland village of Marpingen, for example, which later became a symbol of piety following a series of reported apparitions of the Virgin in the 1870s, was still described in the 1840s as a parish marked by gambling, drunkenness, disrespect and every kind of boorishness and immorality.[10]

The change began to take place in the 1830s and 1840s. The Catholic painter of the Nazarene school, Karl Müller – who could not recite the Lord's Prayer when he attended confirmation class as a fifteen-year-old in the mid-1830s – later pointed to the so-called Cologne events of 1837 as a turning-point.[11] Catholics on that occasion rallied strongly behind the Archbishop of Cologne, who had been imprisoned following a dispute with the state over mixed marriages, and the circumstances provided a foretaste of what was later to happen during the *Kulturkampf*. Historians have also drawn attention to the significance of the Trier pilgrimage of 1844 to the Holy Shroud, which can be seen as an important watershed in the revival of Catholic piety.[12] Certainly the second third of the century, and the period from the 1840s in particular, witnessed the patient and purposive construction of new forms of popular piety. These years saw the development in Catholic Germany, as elsewhere in Europe, of powerful, emotionally laden and highly external devotional forms like the cults of the Virgin and the Sacred Heart.[13] Serious efforts were made, at the same time, to integrate children and young people more closely into the life of the church, and the age of confirmation tended to fall. These were things that the Church at the end of the eighteenth century and the beginning of the nineteenth had tried to discourage; now it sought to foster and canalise them. The new forms of piety encouraged by the Church were an attempt to go with the grain of popular practices, but to impose order on spontaneity. The new religious brotherhoods and congregations established by parish priests were, for example, much more under clerical control than many of their predecessors had been. Pilgrimages changed in a similar way. New ones were established, often to replace earlier (especially local) pilgrimages that had fallen into disrepute with the Church. A number of large pilgrimages were effectively reinvented, such as the Aachen procession of relics, and on occasions such as this the clergy now sought to exercise its own authority more firmly. The increasing rationalization and centralization of pilgrimages was aided by new means of communication.[14]

The exertion of clerical control was a key feature in the revival of Catholic piety that gathered pace in the 1850s and 1860s. In this context it is important that the Church functioned in these years with less external interference in its affairs. The post-revolutionary circumstances of the 1850s had much to do with this. Although some priests had attracted the attention of the authorities in 1848 as 'troublemakers', the Church was generally seen in the reactionary 1850s as a partner of the state against revolutionary upheaval, and granted a greater autonomy to fulfil this role.[15] The greater freedom of the Church was reflected in the Prussian constitution of 1851 and in the concordats and conventions between church and state elsewhere in Germany. It was equally a sign of changed times that the Jesuits, Redemptorists and other orders were now allowed to hold their large-scale missions on German soil. That contributed to the revival of Catholic piety in the 1850s and 1860s; so did the effects of a new generation of more ultramontane and zealously spiritual clergy,[16] trained in reconstituted seminaries independent of state control like Eichstätt, Mainz, Münster and Würzburg.[17] The resurgence of popular piety in these years went hand in hand with the revival of clerical organization. A new attention was paid to pilgrimage transportation and the logistics of mounting processions and inaugurations; particular social groups were targeted for attention during the popular missions, and tokens were even handed out to control the queues for the confessional boxes.[18] In its methods and internal organization the Catholic Church in Germany adapted itself to the age of the railway and telegraph, even if it followed the Syllabus of Errors in decisively rejecting many aspects of 'modernity'.

This was the Catholic Germany that liberals in the 1860s and 1870s viewed with growing suspicion. To the extent that their own aspirations were inseparably linked to the cause of German unity, liberal aspirations necessarily overlapped with Bismarck's. There was a partial identity of interest over anti-clericalism, as there was over other issues. But the emphasis was differently placed. Bismarck's concern, when not purely tactical, was with the threat that the Catholic fifth column supposedly posed to the security of the German power-state (*Machtstaat*); liberals saw a threat to the German *Kulturstaat*.[19] The difference becomes clear when one looks, for example, at the respective attitudes towards the Polish–Catholic areas of the new Reich. We should be clear, in fact, why liberals of both right-wing and left-wing persuasion valued the German nation state so highly. It was not because they identified automatically with the blood-and-iron achievements of Bismarck and the Prussian army. Such views naturally existed, especially among self-consciously 'realist' National Liberals, and were well illustrated in that form of secular piety which led so many liberals to worship the anniversary of 'Saint Sedan'.[20] The real common denominator, however, was the liberal view of the nation state as the harbinger of progress, the provider of schools, universities and new means of communications, a guarantor of the free movement of men, goods and ideas. Hence the distrust of Catholics, whose loyalties were thought to be both trans-national (to the 'prisoner in the Vatican') and provincial or particularist.

That is why the phrase *Kulturkampf* deserves to be taken at face value. It was actually coined by a left liberal, the doctor, pathologist and scientific popularizer Rudolf Virchow. And for liberals generally this 'struggle of civilizations' was concerned with far more than church-state relations in the narrow and formal sense: it was a clash between their own 'modern' outlook embodied in a liberal nationalism, and the backwardness and stubborn parochialism imputed to German Catholics. Liberal attacks on papal infallibility, the Jesuits and the regular clergy were a broadly conceived assault on superstition and the institutions through which the Church supposedly laboured to perpetuate it: seminaries independent of the state, closed orders, Catholic schools, and an extensive array of charitable foundations. On this reading, the clergy 'stupified' the people and kept them 'in leading strings'.[21] Closed orders, on which there was a large and highly prurient *exposé* literature, were condemned as prisons of the mind and body.[22] Charitable foundations were attacked as institutions that forged the mental and material shackles of 'medievalism' (although very large numbers of them actually dated from the post-Napoleonic period). This liberal anti-clericalism clearly owed something to the Enlightenment vocabulary of the eighteenth century; but it also expressed the highly materialist liberalism of the mid-nineteenth century. Even the terms in which liberals cast their condemnations of Catholicism reveal the debt to a particular vision of economic and social progress. The Frankfurt liberal, the natural scientist Karl Vogt, had viewed the Church in the 1840s as a 'brake on civilization'.[23] A National Liberal academic argued in the 1870s that charitable foundations should be fought as one would fight against 'phylloxera, Colorado beetle and other enemies of the Reich'.[24]

This was a highly Manichaean view of the world. Liberal discourse on the subject of Catholics was organized around a set of metaphors (darkness/light, flood/canalization, stagnation/progress) that would repay close textual analysis.[25] Three general points about the way in which liberals linked their thinking on Catholics and on social change are worth drawing out. The first is its strongly elitist thrust. German liberals in the 1860s and 1870s were still able to claim considerable support among the (Protestant) petty bourgeoisie and even working class; but the dominant tone was set by those members of the propertied and educated middle class (*Besitz- und Bildungsbürgertum*) who provided left liberals and National Liberals alike with their national spokesmen, local leaders and intellectuals. Their view of Catholics was lofty. 'It is not exactly education and property that distinguish the Romans of the nineteenth century on Lake Constance', wrote one left-liberal paper in Baden.[26] This was the general chorus from the Progressive Party, the National Liberal Party, liberal academics and newspapers. The *National-Zeitung* summed up a general view when it argued in 1873 that Catholicism was to a large extent the religion of 'the uneducated'. At its head were 'the priests, a few princes and nobles, and behind them a retinue of talkers, sophists and miracle workers'; but 'the great mass of its supporters are workers and peasants'.[27] Liberals drew the conclusions they generally drew about workers and peasants. They were indicated by Rudolf Virchow as early as 1848, when he visited an area of Silesia where typhoid had broken out. He blamed the Catholic clergy for the fact that the local population was 'lazy, unclean, doglike in its devotion and inflexibly averse to any physical or mental exertion'. 'The people', continued Virchow, 'is physically and morally weak and needs some kind of tutelary guidance.'[28]

Lack of property or education meant, in the liberal view, that the bulk of German Catholics lacked a crucial attribute: independence.[29] That raises the second point, for the liberal version of independence was defined in gender as well as class terms. As the statutes of the Progressive Party in the Bavarian town of Rothenburg put it, a candidate for membership should be 'a man who has reached majority, is of blameless character, and independent'.[30] The laws of association required the gender restriction; but it is also true that the liberal view of Catholic dependence had women very firmly at its centre. Women in orders constituted for liberals the perfect symbol of backwardness, while the influence of priests over Catholic women (both inside and outside the confessional box) was a well-worked theme. The Bishop of Münster had, according to one liberal state prosecutor, incited hostility to the state by 'using the easily aroused feelings of women for his own ends'.[31] Countless observations of a similar kind can be found in the liberal press when the Marian apparitions of the 1870s were discussed.

There is no doubt that liberals had some grounds for this particular emphasis; but it should not be seen as a simple 'reflection' of realities in the Catholic world.[32] The centrality of the dependent-woman motif is a telling indication of liberal social views, even if its full meaning is far from straightforward. On the one hand there were certainly those, as in other European countries, who wished to emancipate women from clerical tutelage in the name of independence and civic maturity. This attitude was common among left liberals.[33] But the ideal of the publicly emancipated woman was by no means the only counterpart to the figure of the cloistered nun or the 'priest-dominated' wife and mother. Many German liberals were undoubtedly concerned about the 'easily aroused feelings of women' because those feelings were allegedly being abused by the clergy in ways which seemed to violate the rules of bourgeois family life. The girl who preferred the convent to motherhood, or the wife who 'betrayed' her husband with the priest, violated this canon in one way;[34] the mass appearance of women (and children) in popular Catholic demonstrations violated it in another. The presence of women and children in various kinds of Catholic public protest was certainly marked, and it was often seized upon by liberals as an argument with which to discredit the clerical opponent.[35] Indeed, certain types of Catholic mass agitation appear to have been branded by liberals as female, whether the individuals concerned were women or men – just as French crowd theorists like Gabriel Tarde and Gustave Le Bon were to characterize all crowds as 'female'.[36]

When liberals attacked Catholic 'beggar-women' (*Betweiber*), they therefore had a number of targets simultaneously in mind: clerical dominance, lack of material independence and moral fecklessness. That illustrates well the third general point about liberal thinking: that material and non-material elements can hardly be disentangled. The *Kulturkampf* was about the place of religion and the relations between church and state; it was also about shaping the economic and social future of Germany. At one level, gaining control over Catholic charitable foundations was a matter of removing 'medieval' remnants; at another level it was concerned with freeing both labour and capital from the 'dead hand' of the Church, thus releasing resources for investment and breaking the ties of dependence of paupers and marginal producers.[37] Similarly, closed orders were not only, as one liberal petition put it in 1869, 'hotbeds of fornication and superstition', but also – significantly – of 'sloth'.[38] Perhaps most important of all, liberal ambitions in the sphere of education were twofold: to break the power of the priest, and to create the conditions for a model labour force.[39] In all of these areas liberals opposed the doctrine of 'Freie Bahn dem Tüchtigen' (careers open to talent) to the Catholic charitable principle of 'Freigebigkeit für die Dürftigen' (generosity to the needy).[40] There are very clear parallels here with liberal hostility towards guilds, which were likewise seen as institutions that feather-bedded their members and sapped initiative.

In the optimistic decades of the 1860s and 1870s, liberals of different persuasions were the principal advocates of the view that material progress, civic emancipation and moral improvement went hand in hand. The various components of this belief in progress were expressed with a striking and often vulgar openness. Liberals sought to cast off material, social and mental shackles by creating a new *homo oeconomicus* in a free market, and a free citizen in a brave new world where the school inspector, the railway timetable and the model orphanage would replace the priest, the rosary and the charitable foundation. It was not only the much-derided Catholic 'workers and peasants' who stood to pay the social price, at least in the short term, for the success of this programme.

II

This emphasis on the materialist side of liberalism provides the necessary corrective to a familiar but potentially misleading historical stereotype: that of the overly abstract, academic and unworldly German liberal, at home in a comfortable pre-industrial world and anxious about 'modernity'. Not that the familiar picture is entirely false. The Frankfurt Parliament was noted for its liberal professors, and university-educated *Bildungsbürger* certainly played a larger part in German liberal parties, both nationally and locally, than factory owners or bankers. It is also true that a good number of liberals, at least from the 1840s, showed signs of pessimism about the social effects of industrialization, urbanization and social mobility, long before these sentiments became more general towards the end of the nineteenth century.[41] But these facts should be kept in proportion. The aspirations and interests served by a political party cannot be read off neatly from the occupations of its leaders; and Ludwig Beutin was probably right to argue that in the middle decades of the century a belief in progress was one of the things that actually united the propertied and educated middle class.[42] Among liberal politicians, paeans to progress certainly came at least as readily from professors, journalists and officials in this period as they did from busy industrialists themselves. The railway was the most obvious symbol of this optimistic belief in the future. The journalist Heinrich Brüggemann expressed a characteristic pleasure in the new mode of communication: 'Our joy is a liberal joy, a pleasure over new triumphs which will increase the power of liberal and humane principles'.[43] Friedrich Harkort believed that the railway engine would be the hearse that delivered the nobility to the graveyard, and self-consciously bourgeois and liberal writers like Spielhagen and Gutzkow included gloating references in their novels to outmoded aristocrats, wearing out their horses in fruitless, Quixotic attempts to outrace the iron steed.[44] The railway, like the steamship and the telegraph, was expected to bring social, political and moral improvement in its wake. A liberal verse writer during the *Kulturkampf* put the same idea the other way round. Rejecting a compromise with the Catholic Church, he argued that 'going to Canossa will bring us no railways'.[45]

Industrialization and social change in nineteenth-century Germany was not something unpleasant that happened to liberals; it was something liberals believed in and tried to further (even if they did not always like the social consequences). Indeed, the era of national unification and consolidation in the 1860s and 1870s saw the realization of many aspects of the liberals' broad economic and social programme. These included improved communications, freedom of movement for individuals, trade liberalization that confirmed the demise of guilds and made the setting up of limited companies easier, the creation of a single internal market, and a uniform currency, patent laws and weights and measures. These measures were achieved, first in many individual German states (including Prussia) and then in the Reich, in alliance with a state bureacracy that – after the 1850s – was often liberal-minded on issues of this kind, and which many liberal politicians themselves served as officials. The *Kulturkampf* formed only one part of this broad liberal programme, although an important part.[46]

That is the background against which we should place popular Catholic resistance to the *Kulturkampf*. The focus of this resistance was the defence of the faith and Catholic religious institutions, especially against the laws on the non-clerical supervision of schools, on church funds and charitable foundations, and on the training and appointment of the clergy. Sometimes the resistance took a violent form; more often physical force remained a latent threat. 'Passive resistance' was the phrase that was universally applied by Catholics, liberals and state officials to the most typical forms of Catholic defiance:[47] disguising and hiding priests on the run, accompanying convicted clergy to the gates of the gaol and garlanding them with flowers on their return, buying up ecclesiastical property at forced sales and returning it secretly to the church authorities, hiding church funds and charitable foundation deeds before the state commissioners could take possession of them, flying the forbidden papal flag.[48] This popular Catholic resistance has good claim to be considered a broad social movement. Just as liberals attacked religious institutions in the name of material, social and moral progress, so the Catholic defence of those institutions against liberal-backed administrative measures makes it difficult to draw a clear line between the 'religious' and the 'socio-economic'. What was clearly at stake on both sides was a way of life. Catholics defended charitable foundations and orders as vehicles of Christian charity – but also because, for many, they were the only imaginable means of subsistence. Educational reform was resisted because it signalled the arrival (or potential arrival) of the non-denominational school – but also because liberal designs for more strictly enforced school attendance and new syllabuses would threaten the availability of childrens' labour on the farm or in the workshop, and raise their expectations.[49] Catholics defended the parish priest as a spiritual leader – but also as the 'father of the community', the organizer of craftsmens' and peasant loan banks, journeyman associations and miners' brotherhoods.[50] It is worth noting here that in Germany (unlike most of France, but very like Belgium, Switzerland and elsewhere) the priest was seen, not as the representative of a privileged old order, to the overthrow of which the common man owed land and small property, but as a tribune against a privileged new order which was perceived as a threat to land and small property.[51]

Like other social movements, this one assumed different forms. It was, in some respects, highly spontaneous. This was true of the many occasions when state officials were met with dumb insolence, and of the more infrequent occasions when they were forcibly restrained from arresting a priest. It was perhaps most obviously true of some of the least familiar episodes in the *Kulturkampf*, when scores of thousands of Catholic pilgrims (to the surprise and alarm of the church authorities) streamed to villages in the Saarland, the Ermland and Bavaria where the Virgin Mary had supposedly appeared as a sign during the 1870s.[52] Even at their most spontaneous, however, the collective responses of German Catholics to the *Kulturkampf* had a pattern and an inner logic. When liberal nationalists celebrated Sedan Day, Catholics absented themselves ostentatiously. When it was proposed to erect a statue to the Prussian reformer Stein in Münster, local Catholics suggested alternative figures who might be honoured. When Catholic processions were banned, flowers were displayed ceremonially in the windows of Catholic homes, and when the papal flag was banned in the streets it was flown in the woods. When the site of one of the Marian apparitions was declared a no-go area, Catholics evaded the gendarmes to visit it. Such incidents suggest a sharp awareness of a struggle over public space. And the various symbols of Catholic resistance – the flags, garlands and ubiquitous white-clad girls – indicate that we are dealing with a popular movement that, like the emerging labour movement, possessed highly developed iconographical forms. The Catholic crowd in the *Kulturkampf* was a highly structured crowd.[53]

It was often a highly organized crowd as well, and the liberals had few doubts that it was priests who had done the organizing. On many occasions they were plainly wrong: the Marian apparitions revealed a Catholic laity that was prepared to cut across the lines of clerical authority, and there were other recorded incidents where priests restrained angry Catholic crowds. But it is true that many of the demonstrations, deputations, petitions and processions of the *Kulturkampf* years do bear unmistakable signs of clerical inspiration.[54] Popular resistance was generally embedded within the disciplines and rituals of the Church, fostered by the newly revived piety and the devotional forms that had developed in the 1850s and 1860s. At the same time, the deputations and petitions suggest a clearly 'modern' form of social action. They went well beyond the kind of natural deference Catholic priests might once have expected (but not always received) from their parishioners. This is an important reminder of how, at a time of rapidly changing communications and growing mobility, others were able to attack the liberals with weapons drawn from the liberals' own armoury. This is true, above all, of that most characteristic of all liberal institutions, the voluntary association. The cultural, educational, philanthropic or political association was the classic vehicle used by liberals to try to mobilize and shape public opinion. Indeed it was the means by which, during the first half of the nineteenth century, they tried to create a 'public sphere' (Öffentlichkeit) in the first place, as well as the symbol of a society of citizens able to deliberate independently of the state or corporate institutions like the Church and guild.[55] In the second half of the century, however, the voluntary association became a vehicle that enabled opinion to be mobilized against liberalism.[56] The way in which liberal workers' educational associations stimulated the formation of independent working-class associations in the 1860s is well known. The adoption of the associational form was also a major characteristic of Catholic social and political mobilization.

In the nineteenth century Germany became what Hubert Jedin has called the 'classic land' of Catholic associational life.[57] From the middle of the century a dense network of occupational, charitable, social and educational associations gave a distinctive stamp to Catholic society in Germany, by comparison with France or Italy. Voluntary associations supplemented the pastoral functions of the priest by giving him a series of additional roles in the Pius association or the journeymens' association. They also provided the means by which the laity organized itself. This was true even when the purpose of a particular association was closely tied to Church concerns, as in the case of the Boniface and Borromeo associations. But Catholic associational life was much broader than this (broad enough, in fact, that it sometimes worried the German Bishops' conference).[58] Westphalian and Rhenish aristocrats, for example, deprived of their former sinecures in the pre-Napoleonic ecclesiastical states, set up peasant associations.[59] The *Casinos*, or clubs, of middle-class Catholics became the centre of attempts to construct organizations that would attract Catholics from the urban lower classes.[60] By the 1870s the process was already well underway, whereby the liberal network of associations was faced with a Catholic rival.

The *Kulturkampf* gave a fillip to this development. It also did much to realize the political potential of the associations, for the Catholic Centre Party that emerged in the 1870s could support itself on this already existing substructure. There was nothing automatic about the emergence of political Catholicism in Germany. There were, after all, many social and political divisions among German Catholics that threatened (or promised) to outweigh the common religious bond. Catholic workers were attracted by the emerging labour movement, especially its Lassallean wing.[61] Catholic aristocrats shared many of the conservative political leanings of their Protestant peers.[62] A significant number of university-trained and professional Catholics, uneasy about the Syllabus of Errors and the doctrine of infallibility, were anxious that German Catholicism not retreat into a ghetto: they were prepared to take economic liberalization and civil marriage in their stride.[63] It is worth remembering that a Catholic party in Prussia during the 1850s proved a failure; and no Centre Party emerged in Württemberg in the 1870s, which was an 'oasis of peace' during the *Kulturkampf*.[64] The *Kulturkampf* made the differences between German Catholics weigh less heavily in the balance by branding all Catholics as pariahs. As the Catholic art historian August Reichensperger put it, 'we ultramontanes are all to some extent unclean'.[65] In social terms, men like this continued to have more in common with their liberal counterparts than with the mariolatrous Catholic peasant; in political terms they sided with the peasant. The resentments that fuelled Catholic resistance to the *Kulturkampf* and the growth of the Centre Party were not uniform; but on this point they converged. The *Kulturkampf* also exposed Catholics to a common enemy. That enemy was double-headed: the alliance of liberalism and the state. German states like Prussia, which had appeared sympathetic to the Church in the aftermath of 1848, now appeared to have gone into partnership with anti-clerical liberalism. And liberals, who had themselves been persecuted during the reactionary 1850s, now seemed willing to support the persecution of Catholics by states such as Prussia as the price for securing social progress.

III

Catholic resistance to the *Kulturkampf*, and the emergence of an organized social and political Catholicism, were defeats for German liberalism as well as for Bismarck. The nature of liberal failure directs our attention to the double flaw in the *Kulturkampf* programme as liberals conceived it: the coercion that was required to enforce that programme, because of the lack of consent on which it rested. The *Kulturkampf* was more than the hiccup in church–state relations depicted in some accounts; it was also more violent than often supposed.[66] Attempts to enforce its measures encompassed the closing of meetings, the sealing of churches, the searching of homes. Thousands of parishes were left without their priest, hundreds of clergy were imprisoned, and wanted notices were issued for bishops ('Dr theol. Paulus Melchers, formerly Archbishop of Cologne, born in Münster and last known to be living in Cologne, 64 years of age, 1.70 metres tall, with blond hair and eyebrows, open forehead, brown eyes, slightly bent nose, normal mouth, pointed chin, elongated face, pale complexion and slender build').[67] Heavy-handed interventions against Catholics by the police were common, as for example at Schweich near Trier, where eighteen gendarmes tried to prevent a festive reception for a chaplain just released from jail, and eleven girls were later sentenced to eight days' imprisonment and a three Taler fine each for being apprehended in possession of a garland.[68] On occasion even *agents provocateurs* and the Prussian army were employed.[69]

There were undoubtedly liberals who actually welcomed repression of this kind, particularly officials and academics of a National Liberal and governmentalist persuasion. Those who were strongly and self-consciously Protestant could be particularly brutal in the verbal support they gave to the *Kulturkampf*. But educated liberal rage against the 'dark' Catholics also produced fairly stark expressions of support for strong measures among established politicians. The National Liberal leader Rudolf von Bennigsen reported 'happily' to his wife in November 1871 that Bismarck would 'take up the struggle against Rome and the Romans with his characteristic energy'. Three and a half years later he indicated to his wife that a further piece of *Kulturkampf* legislation would 'go off like a bomb underneath the clericals'.[70] It was a liberal member of the St Wendel town council who, in his capacity as mayor of Alsweiler, called out the Prussian infantry against Catholic pilgrims in a Saarland village where the Virgin Mary had reportedly appeared.[71] These were the German liberals who viewed the state as a social and cultural steamroller, and clearly enjoyed the vicarious experience of watching its power being applied. They were the liberals who had few qualms about Bismarck.

It would be too simple, however, to argue that many or even most liberals actually relished the *Kulturkampf* in this way. Misgivings were expressed, for example, by the liberal press. Even in Münster, where the *Kulturkampf* was particularly bitter, the liberal press voiced its 'astonishment' when the local *Oberpräsident* tried to prevent officials and teachers from joining or visiting a Catholic social club.[72] The liberal *Frankfurter Zeitung*, which anxiously monitored the record of custodial sentences meted out to Catholics, remarked on one occasion that Germany resembled 'one great prison'.[73] Within the political parties, virtually all left liberals and many on the left wing of National Liberalism were concerned about the arbitrary use of state power. This was true not only in a southern state like Baden, but in Prussia too. Rudolf Virchow himself, who was generally critical of the harsh face of Borussianism and as hostile to many of Bismarck's policies as he was to 'ultramontanism', called for the tempering of the arbitrary administrative methods sometimes employed during the *Kulturkampf*.[74] He also described one of the laws on school supervision passed in the 1870s as dictatorial.

Virchow nevertheless voted for the measure in question. As Constantin Frantz cruelly observed, 'he accepted it with a heavy heart, but found himself eased by the thought that the dictatorship appeared indispensable for the progress of culture'.[75] Another prominent left liberal, the co-operative organizer Schulze-Delitzsch, accepted in similar fashion the implications of that 'ruthless struggle' against ultramontanism which he believed necessary. As a recent biographer of Schulze has noted, left liberals like him were prepared – in the name of progress – to take up Bismarck's offer to conduct 'proxy wars' (*Stellvertreterkriege*).[76] In this sphere, as in others, we are not dealing therefore with a straightforward capitulation of German liberalism to Bismarck and state power. Liberal complicity in the coercion used against Catholics in the *Kulturkampf* (like their complicity in the coercion of the later anti-socialist law) followed the logic of their wish to see a particular kind of economic and social order established, while lacking a broad base of consent or popular support for their programme.

The liberals' problems in this respect were twofold, and they did not apply only to relations with Catholics. Lack of liberal popular support was partly a result of social isolation and the Olympian detachment of liberal notable politics (*Honoratiorenpolitik*). In Catholic regions where the class and religious divisions ran along the same lines the problem was especially acute, but it had more general applicability. The liberal historian Sybel wrote to his fellow liberal historian Hermann Baumgarten in 1863 that he knew in great detail the wishes of the 'Krefeld notables', but had to report grave doubts in the Progressive Party about its ability to organize successful mass deputations.[77] This sense of isolation from a broader public was a regular liberal refrain in the 1860s and 1870s, and it was realistic. The cultural and philanthropic associations, the Harmony Clubs and Monday Clubs in which liberals characteristically gathered among their own kind were usually too exclusive to mould a larger opinion.[78] At the same time, restrictive or indirect franchise arrangements in many individual states (above all Prussia) served to reinforce popular political indifference. There were liberal attempts to broaden its social base. In the 1860s prominent Prussian liberals like Schulze-Delitzsch and Benedikt

Waldeck owed their position as leaders partly to the fact that they were thought to have links to the social strata of workers, craftsmen and *Mittelstand*.[79] Moreover in some west German towns, like Mainz and Saarbrücken, local social structure and historical links with France combined to create the potential for a popular left-liberal movement that resembled French radicalism.[80] Something similar was true in parts of the south-western states of Baden and Württemberg.

Here, however, the second aspect of the liberals' social problem arises. Liberal difficulties in winning a broadly based following was not always a result of popular indifference; it was sometimes a result of active popular hostility. When liberals talked of progress they claimed to represent a general interest in society. But their ideal of equality of access to the market by citizens equal before the law took little account of the substantive inequalities their own programme helped to create. Nor did liberals generally like to dwell on the short-term costs incurred by those who paid the price for this socially engineered progress (society as a laboratory being a favourite liberal metaphor of the period). Liberals like Schulze-Delitzsch, who supported co-operatives and educational associations, wanted to nurture a sturdily independent *Mittelstand* as the core of a classless society of citizens. The effect of many liberal economic and social policies was almost the exact opposite: class relations became sharper and more polarized, the *Mittelstand* began to fragment, and the distance that separated the emerging bourgeoisie proper from workers, petty bourgeoisie and peasantry grew.[81] The ensuing form of class politics in Germany, where the representation of sectional interests was to play such a major role, proved highly damaging to liberal fortunes and morale alike.

These general liberal problems have more relevance to the issues raised in the *Kulturkampf* than might appear at first sight. The *Kulturkampf* was, of course, a very specific conflict over the autonomy of the Church in areas such as education and the appointment of clergy; and it was the involuntary achievement of the liberals that they provoked a cross-class alliance of Catholics against the measures of the 1870s. As we have seen, however, the contentious issues of the *Kulturkampf* were inextricably connected to larger social questions. And just as the *Kulturkampf* formed part of a broader liberal programme, so the problems it raised should be seen in a wider context. This is true above all of the way in which the popular Catholic resistance to the *Kulturkampf* was symptomatic of the strains that arose in relations between German liberalism and subordinate social classes. The alienation of Catholic workers ran parallel to the alienation of Protestant workers in the 1860s and 70s; the hostility of the Catholic peasantry and petty bourgeoisie prefigured the hostility that liberals faced from their Protestant counterparts later in the century. Similarly, the scathing liberal attacks on 'dependent' Catholics who lacked property or education belong to a larger (and damaging) vocabulary of liberal disdain for 'the masses'. Liberal discussions of universal manhood suffrage bring this out very clearly. Hermann Baumgarten warned of 'the dominance of the raw instincts of the masses'; Karl Twesten expressed alarm about the 'dilettantism and charlatanry' that would result from direct appeals to the people; and Schulze-Delitzsch, who actually supported universal manhood suffrage, argued that it was all too easy to 'cross the dark borderline where the animal touches on the human', adding that the 'unbound beast' when once aroused would 'tear everything apart with its lion claws'.[82] Bestial metaphors of this kind (like the familiar language of 'darkness' and 'light') pervaded much liberal thinking on the problem of the masses in general, as well as their views on the Catholic masses in particular.

Both left liberals and National Liberals lacked the language of a common revolutionary tradition with which to appeal to the popular classes as their French counterparts did. They also lacked a plausible appeal to the shared 'respectability', of the kind that was so important in attaching petty bourgeoisie and skilled workers to Gladstonian liberalism – although some left liberals worked towards this end. These were general liberal weaknesses; they applied to lower-class Protestants as well as lower-class Catholics. In the case of Protestants, however, the political and electoral effects of these weaknesses became fully apparent only later. In the short term it may well be the case, in fact, that liberal anti-clericalism actually gained the liberals some support among the Protestant working class, petty bourgeoisie and peasantry. Evidence from the grassroots struggle of the *Kulturkampf* suggests a considerable reservoir of popular Protestant anti-clerical (and anti-Catholic) sentiment.[83] It would be interesting to investigate how far liberals chose to tap this sentiment. To what extent, for example, was the liberal rhetoric about independence ever aimed specifically at Protestant craftsmen and skilled workers, in an attempt to convince them that they were superior in this respect to their Catholic counterparts? At the moment, the subject of popular Protestantism in nineteenth-century Germany still awaits its historian. It does seem clear, however, that the anti-clerical issue could serve as a useful lightning-rod for liberals, deflecting attention from more troublesome economic and social issues.[84]

It is even more clear that German liberals were unable to convince more than a small minority of Catholics from any class that the Church and the clergy were exploiters and parasites. It was liberals who found themselves cast in that role. Nor did German liberalism, with rare exceptions, try to appeal to the localist resentments of peripheral Catholic communities, in the way that Gladstonian liberalism addressed the British Celtic fringe. Rather, liberals themselves were understandably identified by Catholics as centralizers who shared the dominant Protestant religion. As a result of these liberal weaknesses, both those which were general and those which affected its relations with Catholics in particular, the *Kulturkampf* had to be carried out from above because it could not be carried out from below. In Baden, for example, the southern Baden *Kulturkämpfer* tried hard in the 1860s to win popular Catholic support for their programme; but they failed, and found themselves stalemated as Catholic resistance made plain the lack of consent they enjoyed. The outcome was a much more *étatiste Kulturkampf* run by the Baden governmental bureaucracy in Karlsruhe.[85] In Prussia the same logic made liberals as much the tools of Bismarck as the reverse, however much the National Liberal leader von Bennigsen talked complacently of using 'all *our* legal measures' against officials who failed to implement *Kulturkampf* legislation to the letter.[86] Eugen Richter, one of the few liberals who opposed the *Kulturkampf* unequivocally, was nearer the mark when he suggested that liberals undermined their own position by supporting the use of weapons drawn 'from the armoury of reaction'.[87]

To return to that liberal verse writer of the 1870s: the liberals received their railways, even if Bismarck (eventually) went to Canossa. But it would probably be generally agreed that they paid a higher price for their victory than he did for his defeat. On this issue, as on others, Bismarck made genuine concessions to the economic and social demands of bourgeois liberalism, but retained the political initiative. The liberals obtained much of what they wanted in social and economic terms, but at some cost to their political position. German liberals were men in a hurry, engaged in an internal civilizing mission in a latecomer nation state. In the case of Catholics, but not only in that particular case, the logic of the liberal position entailed a resort to state power, to what one of them once referred to as 'the magic spear that heals as well as wounds'.[88]

IV

The *Kulturkampf* left a political legacy that was the opposite of what liberals wanted. It made them beholden to Bismarck; and it helped to consolidate political Catholicism in Germany. The Centre Party gained more than four-fifths of votes cast by Catholics in Reichstag elections during the *Kulturkampf*. In subsequent years the Centre continued to live off the moral capital it had accumulated by defending the Cinderella community of the faithful in the 1870s. When this capital began to run out and threatening splits started to appear within the Centre electorate, the party reinforced its position by continuing to play upon the dangers posed by liberalism. On the one hand, the Centre successfully branded liberals as dangerous innovators on issues such as education and sexual morality. On the other hand, the party addressed itself shrewdly to the grievances of Catholic peasants, craftsmen and (rather less successfully) workers, by equating liberalism with so-called Manchesterism and economic exploitation. What bound these elements together was the Centre's deft construction of a liberal bogeyman that went with the grain of its voters' own experience. Liberalism could thus be plausibly associated with a distant but threatening elite of speculators, officials, professors and journalists: in short, with parasites of one sort or another.[89]

A European comparison may be useful here. Political efforts of a similar kind failed in France because they were identified with a reactionary elite, and because the bishops nipped lay initiatives in the bud. Political Catholicism succeeded in Germany because the Centre was able to shape itself into a popular and populist party that claimed, among other things, to defend the common man (and woman) against a liberalism tainted with material exploitation and governmentalism. This process was furthered by the advent of a genuine mass politics in Germany and by the growing importance of interest-politics. Both harmed liberals and worked to the advantage of the Centre. Where liberals had achieved electoral success in the 1860s and 1870s, it had often been the rather deceptive product of restrictive franchises, indirect voting systems or (in the case of the Reichstag) low electoral turn-out; at local level it was sometimes even the result of gerrymandered boundaries. Local electoral reform and a rise in electoral participation at all levels swamped many political enclaves of liberal notables and gave the Centre Party a growing presence in town halls and state parliaments as well as in the Reichstag. At the same time, the much greater adeptness shown by the Centre in harnessing interest-group demands served to underline how difficult the liberals found it to step down from their rather lofty preoccupation with the 'general' social interest. The success of the Catholic Centre was, in fact, only one symptom of the narrowing and fracturing of the liberal base. The largest and best-organized political Catholicism in Europe stood, by the 1890s, alongside the largest and best-organized labour movement in the world, as well as a revitalized and populist conservatism whose political style in Protestant areas was often similar to that of the Centre in Catholic ones. Each of these movements challenged the liberal definition of social progress and dented the electoral strength of liberalism.

The final irony, perhaps, is that the populist Centre also to some extent replaced the National Liberals as a party of government. The Centre could not, of course, help to form governments: no Imperial German Party was able to do that. But it used its solid block of Reichstag seats to lend essential support to successive German chancellors. In the words of one perceptive left-liberal critic of the Centre, the party became 'the measure of all things' in German politics.[90] Bismarck's successors gained an ally in the passage of major pieces of legislation: the navy laws, the civil code, financial reform. The Centre, for its part, received policy concessions (on economic, social and cultural, as well as narrowly religious issues), in addition to gaining a bargaining counter in its demands for a greater 'parity' in the employment of Catholics in the public bureaucracy.

Both the means by which the Centre secured popularity with its own voters, and the way it used its strategic position in national political life, caused deep liberal anger. In this respect, at least, the 'new liberalism' at the turn of the century was very like the old. The new brooms within left liberalism and the Young Liberal wing of National Liberalism struck attitudes on Catholics that are strongly reminiscent of those struck by their predecessors during the *Kulturkampf*. Then German liberals had preached the virtues of material progress and social emancipation, and linked these to the achievement of a powerful nation state. Now they advocated technocracy and social reform, and linked these to the achievement of a successful imperialism. Catholics were a principal target of the new liberalism, as they had been of the old. In the 1870s Catholics were branded as stubbornly backward; forty years later one of Germany's foremost liberal academics argued that 'Catholic professors of history are and remain a monstrosity'.[91]

Just as liberals had viewed Catholic Germany as a block to German progress in the 1860s and 1870s, so their successors a generation later reacted with outrage to the fact that matters of national importance such as naval construction and financial reform depended on the goodwill of Catholic politicians in the Reichstag. Liberals viewed the Centre as doubly illegitimate: the party of raw demagogy in the streets and of horse-trading in parliament. Neither charge was without some truth (or levelled solely by liberals). The Centre was highly demagogic, although liberal insistence on the point was more than a little self-serving. The Centre was also adept at parliamentary wheeler-dealing, although liberals certainly exaggerated the extent to which the party was able to exploit its position to set up a patronage network of jobs for the Catholic boys. Cologne was not Chicago; it was not even Vienna. The ferocity of the liberal response to the Catholic Centre, often exceeding the hostility directed against the Social Democrats, was a symptom of their own vulnerability. The liberal revival after the turn of the century only slightly reversed the liberal political and electoral decline that reached its nadir in the 1890s. The advocacy by the new liberalism of imperialism and social reform bore strong resemblances to the liberal support for nationalism and progress during the *Kulturkampf*; and Catholics continued to be a central target of liberal hostility. The overall political context had changed, however. In the 1870s a buoyant liberalism enlisted Bismarck's aid to drive through its programme against allegedly backward and anti-national Catholics; less than forty years later an electorally weakened and politically neutered liberalism watched Centre Party leaders negotiate with Bismarck's successors about the shape of national legislation.

NOTES

1 Evidence and references in D. Blackbourn, *Class, Religion and Local Politics in Wilhelmine Germany* (London and New Haven, 1980), Chapter 1.
2 J. Rost, *Die wirtschaftliche und kulturelle Lage der deutschen Katholiken* (Cologne, 1911) provides an introduction to this debate.
3 See A. Langner (ed.), *Säkularisation and Säkularisierung im 19. Jahrhundert* (Munich, Paderborn and Vienna, 1978).
4 For a Prussian example, see W. Corsten, 'Zur Wiedereinführung der Dekanatsverfassung und Dekanatseinteilung in der Erzdiözese Köln (1827)', in W. Corsten, A. Frotz and P. Linden (eds), *Die Kirche und ihre Amter und Stände* (Cologne, 1960), pp. 538–54. On Württemberg, C. Bauer, *Politischer Katholizismus in Württemberg bis zum Jahre 1848* (Freiburg i.B, 1929), pp. 14–19; K. Bachem, *Vorgeschichte, Geschichte und Politik der Deutschen Zentrumspartei*, 9 volumes (Cologne, 1927–32), Vol. 1, pp. 230–35.
5 Corsten, 'Zur Wiedereinführung', p. 54, n. 18; H. Storz, *Staat und Kirche in Deutschland im Lichte der Würzburger Bischofsdenkschrift von 1848* (Bonn, 1934), p. 40 n. 71; Bauer, *Politischer Katholizismus*, p. 14.
6 E. Hegel, *Die Katholische Kirche Deutschlands unter dem Einfluss der Aufklärung des 18. Jahrhunderts* (Opladen, 1975); G. Korff, 'Zwischen Sinnlichkeit und Kirchlichkeit. Notizen zum Wandel populärer Frömmigkeit im 18. und 19. Jahrhundert', in J. Held (ed.), *Kultur zwischen Bürgertum und Volk* (Berlin, 1983), pp. 136–48.
7 J. Götten, *Christoph Moufang, Theologe und Politiker 1817–1890* (Mainz, 1969), p. 21.
8 J. Sperber, *Popular Catholicism in Nineteenth-Century Germany* (Princeton, NJ, 1984), pp. 14–16.
9 Ibid., p. 18 ff; E. Gatz, *Rheinische Volksmission im 19. Jahrhundert* (Düsseldorf, 1963), pp. 28–33, 43–5; W. R. Lee, *Population Growth, Economic Development and Social Change in Bavaria 1750–1850* (New York, 1977), pp. 298–306; H. Hörger, *Dorfreligion und bäuerliche Gesellschaft* (Munich, 1978), pp. 240–48. These sources also discuss another phenomenon that alarmed the clergy: rising rates of illegitimacy.
10 H. Derr, 'Geschichte der Pfarrei Marpingen' (Trier, 1935), typescript available in the Priesterseminar Trier, pp. 27–8.
11 L. Pastor, *Tagebücher, Briefe, Erinnerungen*, ed. W. Wühr (Heidelberg, 1950), p. 242.
12 W. Schieder, 'Kirche und Revolution. Sozialgeschichtliche Aspekte der Trierer Wallfahrt von 1844', *Archiv für Sozialgeschichte*, vol. 14 (1974), pp. 425–6.
13 H. Jedin (ed.), *Handbuch der Kirchengeschichte*, volume VI/1: *Die Kirche zwischen Revolution und Restauration* (Freiburg i.B., 1971), pp. 662–70; volume VI/2: *Die Kirche zwischen Anpassung und Widerstand* (Freiburg i. B., 1973), pp. 265–78.
14 G. Korff, 'Heiligenverehrung und soziale Frage. Zur Ideologisierung der populären Frömmigkeit im späten 19. Jahrhundert', in G. Wiegelmann (ed.), *Kultureller Wandel im 19. Jahrhundert* (Göttingen, 1978), pp. 102–11; W. K. Blessing, *Staat und Kirche in der Gesellschaft. Institutionelle Autorität und mentaler Wandel in Bayern während des 19. Jahrhunderts* (Göttingen, 1982), pp. 84–98; Sperber, *Popular Catholicism*, Chapter 2. On the Aachen pilgrimage, see H. Schiffers, *Kulturgeschichte der Aachener Heiligtumsfahrt* (Cologne, 1930); and for a detailed account of the revival of one particular saint, see L. Lenhart, 'Die Bonifatius-Renaissance des 19. Jahrhunderts', in *Sankt Bonifatius. Gedenkgabe zum zwölfhundertsten Todestag* (Fulda, 1954), pp. 533–85.
15 An excellent account of the mutual accommodation between church and state in one part of the Prussian Rhine Province is given in the early sections of C. Weber, *Kirchliche Politik zwischen Rom, Berlin und Trier 1876–1888* (Mainz, 1970). The political element in the new piety has been stressed in a number of articles by Gottfried Korff. See notes 6 and 14, and also 'Politischer "Heiligenkult" im 19. und 20. Jahrhundert', *Zeitschrift für Volkskunde*, vol. 71 (1975), pp. 202–20. There is an admirably balanced account of the position in the Rhineland in Sperber, *Popular Catholicism*, p. 99ff, while Blessing, *Staat und Kirche*, discusses thoughtfully the changing relations between church and state in Bavaria throughout the nineteenth century.
16 On 'ultramontanism', see H. Raab, 'Zur Geschichte und Bedeutung des Schlagwortes

"ultramontan" im 18. und frühen 19. Jahrhundert', *Historisches Jahrbuch*, no. 81 (1962), pp. 159–73.

17 Götten, *Christoph Moufang*, pp. 115–37.

18 On the pilgrimage as a 'modern mass spectacle' (Korff), see the works cited in note 15; on the choreographing of inaugurations, Weber, *Kirchenpolitik*, pp. 57–8; on the missions, Gatz, *Rheinische Volksmission*, pp. 119–24.

19 There are two useful introductory articles dealing with research on the *Kulturkampf* by Rudolf Morsey: 'Bismarck und der Kulturkampf. Ein Forschungs- und Literaturbericht 1945–1957', *Archiv für Kulturgeschichte*, vol. 39 (1957), pp. 232–70; and 'Probleme der Kulturkampf-Forschung', *Historisches Jahrbuch*, vol. 83 (1964), pp. 217–45. More recently, see W. Becker, 'Der Kulturkampf also europäisches und als deutsches Phänomen', *Historisches Jahrbuch*, vol. 101 (1981), pp. 422–46.

20 On 'Saint Sedan', the annual celebration of victory over the French in the battle of that name, see Blessing, *Staat und Kirche*, pp. 181, 190–1, 198, 236; W. Jestaedt, *Der Kulturkampf im Fudlaer Land* (Fulda, 1960), pp. 134–5; J. B. Kissling, *Geschichte des Kulturkampfes im Deutschen Reiche*, 3 volumes (Freiburg i. B., 1911–16), Vol. 2, p. 279.

21 The phrase 'in leading strings' from the *Westfälische Provinzialzeitung*, cited in L. Ficker, *Der Kulturkampf in Münster*, ed. O. Hellinghaus (Münster, 1923), p. 204. Along similar lines, see the verse beginning 'Ihr verdammten Volksverdummer', in A. Birke, *Bischof Ketteler und der deutsche Liberalismus* (Mainz, 1971), p. 45; and Birke, 'Zur Entwicklung und politischen Funktion des bürgerlichen Kulturkampfverständnisses in Preussen-Deutschland', in D. Kurze (ed.), *Aus Theorie und Praxis der Geschichtswissenschaft. Festschrift für Hans Herzfeld* (Berlin, 1972), pp. 257–79.

22 See, for example, *Pfaffenunwesen, Mönchsskandale und Nonnenspuk. Beitrag zur Naturgeschichte des Katholizismus und der Klöster von Luzifer Illuminator* (Leipzig, 1871); *Memoiren einer Nonne* (Munich, 1874).

23 Birke, *Bischof Ketteler*, p. 22.

24 Kissling, *Kulturkampf*, Vol. 3, p. 58.

25 Along the lines, perhaps, of the analysis of Freikorps members' autobiographies undertaken by Klaus Theweleit in *Männerphantasien*, 2 volumes (Frankfurt/M., 1977), and more recently by Roger Chickering on the language of the Pan-Germans in *We Men Who Feel Most German. A Cultural Study of the Pan-German League 1886–1914* (London, 1984), esp. pp. 74–101.

26 G. Zang (ed.), *Provinzialisierung einer Region. Zur Entstehung der bürgerlichen Gesellschaft in der Provinz* (Frankfurt/M., 1978), p. 315.

27 *National-Zeitung*, 16 February 1873, cited in Kissling, *Kulturkampf*, Vol. 2, p. 280.

28 E. Meyer, *Rudolf Virchow* (Wiesbaden, 1956), p. 41.

29 The importance of this in liberal thinking generally is well brought out in J. Sheehan, *German Liberalism in the Nineteenth Century* (Chicago, 1978).

30 G. Eisfeld, *Die Entstehung der liberalen Parteien in Deutschland 1858–1870* (Hannover, 1969), p. 132.

31 Ficker, *Kulturkampf in Münster*, p. 186. On the alleged massaging of female sensibilities by the Jesuits in particular, see B. Duhr, *Jesuitenfabeln* (Freiburg i.B., 1891), pp. 746–79.

32 These points will be considered at greater length in my forthcoming study of Marian apparitions in Germany during the 1870s.

33 On the strong historical affinities between left liberalism and the bourgeois feminist movement in Germany, see R. J. Evans, *The Feminist Movement in Germany 1894–1933* (London and Beverly Hills, 1976).

34 The stories serialized in National Liberal-inclined family journals such as the *Gartenlaube* often suggested betrayals without the inverted commas.

35 Examples in Zang (ed.), *Provinzialisierung*, pp. 206, 315, 328.

36 S. Barrows, *Distorting Mirrors. Visions of the Crowd in Late Nineteenth-Century France* (New Haven and London, 1981).

37 Zang (ed.), *Provinzialisierung*, pp. 315–6, 324–7; D. Blackbourn, 'Die Zentrumspartei während des Kulturkampfes und danach', in O. Pflanze (ed.), *Innenpolitische Probleme des Bismarck-Reiches* (Munich and Vienna, 1983), pp. 86–8. On the struggle in Münster over the Ferdinandeische Stiftung and the Seppelersche Stiftung, see Ficker, *Kulturkampf*

in Münster, p. 175 ff. A classic defence of precisely that aspect of the foundations which liberals attacked as the 'dead hand' was made by the Romantic intellectual Adam Müller. He wrote in 1816 about 'the capital which past centuries accumulated and rightly immobilized', and protested against those who wished to 'commercialize' it. See J. Droz, *Le romantisme politique en Allemagne* (Paris, 1963), pp. 98–9. In fact, many of the foundations were of much more modern vintage: the Seppelersche was set up in 1867.

38 M. L. Anderson, *Windthorst. A Political Biography* (Oxford, 1981), p. 124.

39 Zang (ed.), *Provinzialisierung*, pp. 413–4.

40 H. Reif, *Westfälischer Adel 1770–1860* (Göttingen, 1979), pp. 445–8. Reif is generally excellent on the endowing of new foundations in the 1850s and 1860s.

41 Sheehan, *German Liberalism*, pp. 29–34.

42 L. Beutin, 'Das Bürgertum als Gesellschaftsstand im 19. Jahrhundert', *Gesammelte Schriften zur Wirtschafts- und Sozialgeschichte*, ed. H. Kellenbenz (Cologne and Graz, 1963), p. 292 ff.

43 Sheehan, *German Liberalism*, p. 28.

44 See D. Blackbourn and G. Eley, *The Peculiarities of German History* (Oxford, 1984), pp. 185–8, and the works cited there – esp. those by Riedel, Schivelbusch and Sternberger. For an example of the specific place of the railway in liberal programmes, see Eisfeld, *Entstehung*, pp. 128–9.

45 Kissling, *Kulturkampf*, Vol. 2, p. 295.

46 The existence of a 'liberal era' in these respects is generally accepted by historians, including those whose overall emphasis is rather different from my own.

47 Pius IX had called on German Catholics to practise passive resistance in an encyclical of February 1875 in which he declared the May Laws of the *Kulturkampf* 'null and void'. See Bachem, *Zentrumspartei*, Vol. 3, p. 299 ff.

48 The material in the following paragraphs on Catholic resistance draws heavily on a number of detailed local accounts: Ficker, *Kulturkampf in Münster*; Jestaedt, *Kulturkampf im Fuldaer Land*; K. Kammer, *Trierer Kulturkampfpriester* (Trier, 1926); H. Schiffers, *Der Kulturkampf in Stadt und Regierungsbezirk Aachen* (Aachen, 1929); as well as the material gathered together in Kissling, *Kulturkampf*, and a number of other more general accounts.

49 J. Lukas, *Der Schulzwang, ein Stück moderner Tyrannei* (Landshut, 1865); Zang (ed.), *Provinzialisierung*, esp. the contributions by Bellmann (pp. 183–263) and Zang (pp. 307–73); L. Gall, 'Die partei- und sozialgeschichtliche Problematik des badischen Kulturkampfes', *Zeitschrift für die Geschichte des Oberrheins*, vol. 113 (1965), pp. 151–96; J. Becker, *Liberaler Staat und Kirche in der Ara von Reichsgründung und Kulturkampf* (Mainz, 1973), pp. 255–69. For an interesting Austrian parallel in the sphere of education, see E. Bruckmüller, 'Bäuerlicher Konservatismus in Oberösterreich', *Zeitschrift für Bayerische Landesgeschichte*, vol. 37 (1974), pp. 121–43.

50 The journeymen's associations initiated by Father Adolf Kolping and the Trier Peasant Association founded and run by Curate Georg Dasbach are two of the earliest and most familiar examples of this sort of activity. But hundreds of priests were engaged in less prominent undertakings of a similar kind.

51 For a broad comparative perspective, see Becker, 'Der Kulturkampf als europäisches und als deutsches Phänomen'. The concept of the 'common man' was applied by Peter Blickle to the period of the sixteenth-century peasant war, in *Die Revolution von 1525* (Munich, 1975). It has recently been plausibly used for the modern period by Werner Blessing, in *Staat und Kirche*, and by Hugo Lacher, in 'Liberalismus, Staat und Kirche in Baden 1860–1918', *Zeitschrift für Hohenzollerische Geschichte*, vol. 99 (1976), pp. 187–95.

52 The most important of these incidents took place in Marpingen, in the Saarland (part of the Prussian Rhine Province). It is mentioned briefly in a number of fairly well-known autobiographies, such as J. Bachem, *Erinnerungen eines alten Publizisten und Politikers* (Cologne, 1913), pp. 133–42, and K. Schorn, *Lebenserinnerungen*, 2 volumes (Bonn, 1898), Vol. 2, pp. 259–62. I have been able to trace eleven detailed accounts of the apparitions at Marpingen, one of which is available in the British Library: *Marpingen und seine Gnadenmonate* (Münster, 1878). There are also contemporary pamphlets on the other apparitions, such as B. Braunmüller, *Kurzer Bericht über die Erscheinungen U. L. Frau bei Mettenbuch* (Deggendorf, 1878). This literature is informative but largely

uncritical. The anxieties created in the Church by the apparitions is evident from the ecclesiastical archives, and I shall deal with this aspect of the subject at length in my forthcoming study.

53 On Marpingen, there is abundant evidence in the Bistumsarchiv Trier, B III 11, 14, Bde. 3–8. On the other incidents, see the works cited in note 48.

54 This is true of the *Kulturkampf* in Baden, as well as Prussia. Gall, 'Partei- und sozialgeschichtliche Problematik', gives a good account of this aspect.

55 See T. Nipperdey, 'Verein als soziale Struktur in Deutschland im späten 18. und frühen 19. Jahrhundert', in T. Nipperdey, *Gesellschaft, Kultur, Theorie* (Göttingen, 1976), pp. 174–205; Sheehan, *German Liberalism*, esp. pp. 32–3.

56 This phenomenon is discussed elsewhere in the present book, esp. in Chapters 4–6. I have also tried to address the question in Blackbourn and Eley, *Peculiarities*, pp. 195–8, 224–7.

57 Jedin, *Handbuch der Kirchengeschichte*, VI/2, p. 220.

58 See Chapter 9, pp. 198–9.

59 On the involvement of Westphalian aristocrats in associational life, see the excellent account in Reif, *Westfälischer Adel*, pp. 398–431.

60 Jestaedt, *Kulturkampf im Fuldaer Land*, pp. 120–5, describes this well for the town of Fulda, esp. in his account of the 'Männergesellschaft M.N.' (the 'Black Casino'). A description of the parallel Casino movement in Baden is given by F. Dor, *Jacob Lindau. Ein Badischer Politiker und Volksmann* (Freiburg i.B., 1909).

61 See H. Grote, *Sozialdemokratie und Religion* (Tübingen, 1968).

62 During the 1890s the hostility of Catholic aristocrats to the apparently more 'democratic' trend of the Centre Party emerged strongly, and was one of the major sources of party disunity in the period. See Blackbourn, *Class, Religion and Local Politics*, Chapter 1; and J. K. Zeender, *The German Center Party 1890–1906* (Philadelphia, Pa., 1976), pp. 19–34.

63 See Anderson, *Windthorst*, pp. 119–29, for a general outline. In a letter of 11 July 1870 the Catholic academic Franz Brentano wrote as follows to Georg Hertling, the later Centre leader, about the Vatican Council: 'The news from Rome no longer agitates me. The spectacle began as a tragedy but is becoming more and more a farce'. Bundesarchiv Koblenz, Hertling Papers, 45, 3–4. On civil marriage, note the position of the Reichenspergers, Peter and August, discussed in S. Buchholz, *Eherecht zwischen Staat und Kirche* (Frankfurt/M., 1981), pp. 93–4.

64 See Bachem, *Zentrumspartei*, Vol. 8, Chapter 8: 'Die Oase des Friedens'.

65 L. Pastor, *August Reichensperger*, 2 volumes (Freiburg i.B., 1899), Vol. 1, p. 424.

66 There is an extremely detailed account in M. Scholle, *Die Preussische Strafjustiz im Kulturkampf 1873–1880* (Marburg, 1974). See also R. J. Ross, 'Enforcing the Kulturkampf in the Bismarckian State and the Limits of Coercion in Imperial Germany', *Journal of Modern History*, vol. 56 (1984), pp. 456–82. Ross rightly notes the difficulties of enforcing the *Kulturkampf*. I would agree, on the basis of my own research, that it is also striking how the Prussian state tried to adhere to the letter of the law, although it remains important not to play down the coercive aspects of the *Kulturkampf*.

67 Ficker, *Kulturkampf in Münster*, pp. 250–1.

68 Kammer, *Trierer Kulturkampfpriester*, p. 94.

69 This is true, for example, of the Prussian response to the inhabitants of Marpingen, where apparitions of the Virgin were reported.

70 H. Oncken, *Rudolf von Bennigsen. Ein deutscher liberaler Politiker*, 2 vols (Stuttgart and Leipzig, 1910), Vol. 2, pp. 235–6, 280.

71 The role of mayor Woytt of Alsweiler in calling in the troops at Marpingen is clear both from Catholic accounts and from the administrative records of the Prussian Rhine Province, in the Landeshauptarchiv Koblenz, 403/16730. On Woytt as a liberal on the St Wendel council, see M. Müller, *Die Geschichte der Stadt St Wendel von ihren Anfängen bis zum Weltkriege* (St Wendel, 1927), p. 394.

72 Ficker, *Kulturkampf in Münster*, p. 207.

73 Kissling, *Kulturkampf*, Vol. 2, p. 292.

74 Meyer, *Virchow*, pp. 115–7; Kissling, *Kulturkampf*, Vol. 3, pp. 121–2.

75 C. Frantz, *Die Religion des Nationalliberalismus* (Leipzig, 1872), p. 105.

76 R. Aldenhoff, *Schulze-Delitzsch* (Baden-Baden, 1984), p. 233.

77 L. Krieger, *The German Idea of Freedom* (Chicago, 1957), p. 400.

78 Nipperdey, 'Verein als soziale Struktur', pp. 186–7. Zang (ed.), *Provinzialisierung*, has some excellent detail on the Konstanz Monday Club, and the National Liberal Gottlob Egelhaaf has a comparable description in his *Lebenserinnerungen*, ed. A. Rapp (Stuttgart, 1960), pp. 23, 29. Also similar are the accounts in Eugen Richter, *Jugenderinnerungen* (Berlin, 1892), pp. 24, 59. T. Nipperdey, *Die Organisation der deutschen Parteien vor 1918* (Düsseldorf, 1961) also has good material on liberal *Honoratiorenpolitik*.

79 Krieger, *German Idea of Freedom*, p. 401.

80 On Mainz, see S. Zucker, *Ludwig Bamberger* (Pittsburg, Pa, 1975); on Saarbrücken, J. Bellot, *Hundert Jahre politisches Leben an der Saar unter preussischer Herrschaft (1815–1918)* (Bonn, 1954).

81 On the *Mittelstand*, see Chapter 5. On liberalism and the idea of the *Mittelstand*, see L. Gall, 'Liberalismus und "Bürgerliche Gesellschaft": Zu Charakter und Entwicklung der Liberalen Bewegung in Deutschland', *Historische Zeitschrift*, no. 220 (1975), pp. 324–56; Sheehan, *German Liberalism*, pp. 88–90, 244–54.

82 W. J. Mommsen, *Max Weber und die deutsche Politik 1890–1920* (Tübingen, 1959), p. 6; M. Gugel, *Industrieller Aufstieg und bürgerliche Herrschaft* (Cologne, 1975), pp. 184–8.

83 I base this observation on the strong impressions received from both Prussian archival sources and contemporary pamphlet literature while working on my study of Marian apparitions and reactions to them. I hope in the future to look more closely at this neglected subject of popular Protestantism. Virtually all books on German liberalism note that liberals come to have a predominantly Protestant constituency; but Protestantism is treated largely as a residual category, i.e. Protestants were non-Catholics.

84 I looked briefly at this in my book, *Class, Religion and Local Politics*. See also J. C. Hunt, *The People's Party in Württemberg and Southern Germany*, 1890–1914 (Stuttgart, 1975), p. 80.

85 See, above all, the contributions to Zang (ed.), *Provinzialisierung*.

86 Emphasis added. See Oncken, *Bennigsen*, Vol. 2, p. 281. On the widespread removal of Catholic officials, and of other officials who were considered lukewarm on the *Kulturkampf*, see the important article by M. L. Anderson and K. Barkin, 'The Myth of the Puttkamer Purge and the Reality of the *Kulturkampf*: Some Reflections on the Historiography of Imperial Germany', *Journal of Modern History*, vol. 54 (1982), pp. 647–86.

87 I. S. Lorenz, *Eugen Richter* (Husum, 1980), p. 116, and pp. 111–25 generally.

88 Friedrich Dahlmann, cited in Sheehan, *German Liberalism*, p. 39.

89 Many of the points made in this final section are discussed in greater detail in Chapter 9, as well as in Blackbourn, *Class, Religion and Local Politics*.

90 F. Naumann, *Die politischen Parteien* (Berlin, 1910), p. 39.

91 Friedrich Meinecke, in a letter of 1901, cited in R. J. Ross, *Beleaguered Tower: The Dilemma of Political Catholicism in Wilhelmine Germany* (Notre Dame, Ind., 1976), p. 27. On the 'Spahn affair', which provides the immediate background to Meinecke's remark, see Ross, pp. 26–8, and C. Weber, *Der 'Fall Spahn' (1901). Ein Beitrag zur Wissenschafts- und Kulturdiskussion im ausgehenden 19. Jahrhundert* (Rome, 1980).

8

Catholics, the Centre Party and Anti-Semitism

In many European countries, popular anti-semitic movements in the modern period have drawn on a Catholic tradition of anti-Jewish sentiment. Austria, Poland and France provide familiar examples. In these countries Catholicism was the religion of the majority. In Germany the situation was different. There Protestants formed a two-thirds majority. It was also Protestants in areas such as Hessen and Saxony who provided the major support for the anti-semitic political parties of Imperial Germany, as Protestants generally did later for the Nazis. Catholics in Germany were conspicuous by their absence among supporters of these movements. They not only themselves constituted a minority; they were a minority which – like the Jews – faced both discrimination from a Protestant-dominated power structure, and popular resentment. Indeed, modern racial anti-semites were often as hostile to 'decadent' Catholics as they were to Jews.

Yet anti-semitism did have a place in German Catholic politics, even if it took a less virulent form than the anti-semitism espoused by Protestants in Germany and by Catholics elsewhere. The following article discusses the nature of that anti-semitism and suggests how the minority status of German Catholics simultaneously fostered anti-Jewish resentment and set limits to the political expression it assumed. One of my concerns is to illustrate how the pecking order among different minorities can generate and sustain its own forms of prejudice, a phenomenon that has perhaps been less explored in the German case than in some others. I have tried at the same time to make those necessary distinctions – morally distasteful though they are – between 'respectable' and 'gutter' anti-semitism, religious anti-Jewish sentiment and pseudo-scientific racial anti-semitism, anti-semitism as private prejudice and political anti-semitism. My intention, finally, was to examine – in the case of one particular political party in a given period – how a prejudice of this kind can be institutionalized into everyday political practice by the use of certain coded words and phrases. Political anti-semitism, like its equivalents, can exist in more subtle forms than we associate with the Nazis or the Agrarian League of Imperial Germany, as the experience of the Centre Party indicates.

This article was written earlier than any other in the present collection, for a colloquium at Oxford in April 1978. It was published, along with the other contributions, in P. Kennedy and A. Nicholls (eds), *Nationalist and Racialist Movements in Britain and Germany before 1914* (London, 1981), pp. 106–29. My thesis, mentioned in note 58 below, has since appeared in revised form as *Class, Religion and Local Politics in Wilhelmine Germany* (London and New Haven, Conn., 1980). Both there, and in the article printed below as Chapter 10, I have tried to extend the ideas about political demagogy tentatively outlined here in the specific context of Catholics, the Centre Party and anti-semitism. One excellent recent publication deserves particular mention for the light it throws on the respective positions of Catholics and Jews within Imperial Germany. It is Peter

Pulzer, 'Religion and Judicial Appointments in Germany, 1869–1918', *Year Book of the Leo Baeck Institute*, no. 28 (1983), pp. 185–204.

I

Catholic anti-semitism in Germany has received nothing like the attention given to its counterparts in France and Austria, and the reasons for this are not hard to find. France and Austria were predominantly Catholic countries, whose indigenous traditions of anti-semitism drew upon and reflected this background. This is true of the anti-semitism espoused by the *Croix de Feu* and Austrian 'clerical fascists' in the interwar years; it is also true of the anti-Dreyfusard movement and Karl Lueger's Christian Social Party in Vienna before 1914. The position in Germany was clearly very different. There Catholics themselves formed a minority, and were likely for that reason to be more circumspect about supporting political movements which preached anti-semitism. It is well known that Catholics provided the National Socialists with very little of their popular electoral support prior to the seizure of power in 1933, just as few of them supported the anti-semitic political parties of Stöcker, Liebermann von Sonnenberg and others before 1914. They voted instead for the Centre, the party of German Catholics and one in which the role played by anti-semitism has commonly been regarded by historians as slight.

In the period before the First World War, in fact, it is normally argued that anti-semitism among Catholics and in the Centre Party had reached its high point in the 1870s.[1] Certainly Catholic feelings were expressed very strongly at the time, and this was the result of two particular developments. First, Jews were singled out by Catholics for their alleged prominence in those liberal circles which supported Bismarck's *Kulturkampf* against the Church. Sourly resentful comparisons were made between the recent emancipation of the Jews and the new disabilities suffered by Catholics. Secondly, the financial crash of 1873 and the onset of the Great Depression led to a general discrediting of economic liberalism.[2] Among Catholics there was a marked tendency to blame Jewish 'swindlers' for the losses of Christian savings, and to view self-righteously the apparent collapse of a characteristically 'Jewish' liberal capitalism. Certainly the idea of anti-semitism as Nemesis, the retribution visited on the Jews for their alleged religious intolerance and material avarice, was a powerful impulse behind Catholic attitudes at this time. It can be seen, for example, in the anti-semitic articles run by the newspaper *Germania*, and in the sentiments mouthed by Centre politicians during the notorious Prussian Landtag debate of 1880 on the 'Jewish question'.[3] It is usually maintained, however, that Catholic anti-semitism declined after 1880, along with the sources of resentment which had helped to fuel it. The *Kulturkampf* was wound up. The National Liberal Party which had supported it declined in strength, to be replaced eventually by the Centre Party itself as a party of government. There was, finally, a marked move away from liberal economic policies on the part of the Imperial Government after 1879. This was clearly a source of satisfaction to many Catholics and to the Centre, and it has been suggested that it was – like the other developments – a change which reduced their propensity to anti-semitism.[4] Under Ludwig Windthorst and Ernst Lieber, moreover, the Centre was led for thirty years by men who firmly resisted the incorporation of anti-semitism as a formal element of party policy. Overall, therefore, Catholic attitudes in the 1870s appear to have been an ugly but short-lived outpouring of feeling.

This essay will argue that anti-semitism among German Catholics was actually of considerable importance. The essay does not attempt to identify a specifically religious form of Catholic anti-semitism, but is concerned rather with the forms of anti-semitism which developed within different parts of the Catholic community in pre-1914 Germany, and with the ways in which these sentiments found political expression. There were, of course, certain circumstances peculiar to Catholics as a whole, above all a common religious identity and a pervasive sense of being discriminated against. The resentment which followed from this, however, assumed widely differing forms; and so did the anti-semitism which made up a part of the resentment. This very diversity makes it possible to draw broader conclusions from Catholic experiences. The anti-semitism of Catholic peasants, for example, based on antipathy towards allegedly exploitative Jewish grain dealers and money lenders, had much in common with Protestant peasant anti-semitism. The anti-semitism of Catholic publicists and Centre Party politicians, on the other hand, was of the more muted, 'respectable' kind found in other, non-Catholic bourgeois circles. Moreover, the fact that anti-semitism among Catholics took on both these forms makes it necessary to consider the question of the relationship between the two. This problem is of considerable general importance to students of anti-semitism. It is also central to recent interpretations of the political system in Imperial Germany. For we now have a major body of work which stresses the manipulative intentions of Germany's ruling elite in these years – including their use of scapegoats like the Jews to achieve a form of 'negative integration' socially and politically.[5] We also have a growing body of work which is concerned with the political self-mobilization of groups like the peasantry and petty bourgeoisie.[6] What requires elucidation is the interaction between the two, and an analysis of anti-semitism among German Catholics provides an opportunity to look at this relationship in a particular case. This essay is therefore concerned both with the attitudes of Catholic public leaders, and with the rather different forms of popular Catholic anti-semitism. It is also concerned with the demagogic plank thrown down between the one and the other.

II

Catholics made up about one third of the population in Imperial Germany, a minority which generally felt itself to be under attack. This was most obviously the case during the *Kulturkampf*, which resulted in the imprisonment of bishops, priests and politicians, discrimination by the state over appointments to official posts, and social discrimination in the form of anti-Catholic trade boycotts.[7] As we shall see, however, the Catholic sense of vulnerability persisted well beyond the end of the *Kulturkampf*, and it is no accident that the political symbol of the Centre Party was a tower. One effect of this was certainly to equip Catholic political leaders at least with a special sensitivity where attacks on other minorities were concerned. Like Germany's Jews, they had had the experience of being labelled 'enemies of the Reich', and they were clearly right to see similarities between Bismarck's references to the liberal Lasker as a 'stupid Jewboy' and his unflattering epithets about themselves.[8] In concrete terms, Catholic political leaders were reluctant to support legislation – like that proposed by the anti-semitic political parties – to limit the civil equality of Jews. Measures of this kind would have constituted a potential threat to Catholics, and the *Kulturkampf* had provided a clear warning of what 'exceptional legislation' (*Ausnahmegesetzgebung*) could mean. To take one example of Centre caution in the legislative sphere, the party consistently resisted the introduction of formal exceptional legislation aimed at kosher slaughtering rights. Ernst Lieber, the leader of the Centre from 1893 to 1902, spelled out very clearly the thinking behind this restraint:

> We, as a minority in the Reich, have not forgotten what happened to us, and for that reason, even if more elevated considerations and more fundamental motives did not restrain us, we cannot offer to forge the weapon to be used against the Jews today, the Poles tomorrow and the Catholics the day after that.[9]

It was not only *vis-à-vis* government that Catholics shared with Jews a comparably vulnerable position. Prominent figures such as Treitschke attacked both minorities as alien to German *Kultur*, while one inventive anti-semitic pamphleteer actually warned the public of the threat from 'Juda-Jesuitismus'.[10] The gifted versifier and cartoonist, Wilhelm Busch, falls into a similar category: the anti-semitism contained in much of his earlier work found its parallel in the often crude anti-Catholicism of *Die fromme Helene* and *Pater Filuzius*. More virulent anti-semites frequently attacked Catholics with two particular charges normally levelled at Jews. In the first place Catholics, like Jews, were supposedly guilty of bringing about a degeneration of German culture and morals.[11] Secondly, Catholics were accused of internationalism and lack of attachment to German interests – of being, in other words, agents of the black international rather than the gold. Liebermann von Sonnenberg talked of the Catholic with 'his feet in Germany and his head in Rome'.[12] In a similar vein, Hermann Ahlwardt, at the end of his career as a professional anti-semite, approached Theodor Fritsch with the suggestion that they take up the fight against those other international conspirators, the Freemasons and the Jesuits.[13] It is hardly surprising, in fact, that so few Catholics should have been attracted to the racially-based views of the anti-semitic political parties, when the purveyors of that doctrine produced – as the German Social Party did – a genealogical handbook in which they attributed Jewishness not only to Theodore Roosevelt, Jack Johnson and Leopold von Ranke, but also to eight popes and numerous cardinals.[14]

Catholics, then, were frequently bracketed together with Jews as a cancerous element within German society. Yet one should be wary of assuming that the mutual relations between such minorities in Imperial Germany proceeded on the principle that my enemy's enemy is my friend. These relations were in fact extremely ambiguous. Catholic political leaders were certainly firm in resisting formal, legislative discrimination against Jews, just as – after 1890 at least – they refused to vote for openly repressive legislation against the Social Democratic Party and labour movement. In neither case, however, was this prudential restraint accompanied by any real sentiment of fellow-feeling. Rather the reverse. The very sense of vulnerability among Catholics could make them under certain circumstances less rather than more tolerant of other threatened groups, as they struck out against those whom they regarded as persecutors rather than as fellow victims. This was undoubtedly the case with Catholic and Centre Party outbursts against Jews during the later 1870s.[15] Indeed, one can see this phenomenon as early as 1872, in the comments made by the prominent Silesian Centre Party figure, von Ballestrem, on the election appeal of his principal election opponent:

> At the head of this poster I noticed the cross and our old Prussian electoral slogan, 'With God, for King and Fatherland'. I could not work out the connection between this heading and the content of the text. In terms of the latter, it would have been appropriate to have had anything but a cross, and most appropriate to have had an apron and trowel, along with the slogan, 'With the Jews, for the liberals and Freemasons'.[16]

This illustrates well the ambiguities and cross-currents which beset relations in Imperial Germany between one vulnerable group and another. If, as we have seen, the anti-semitic political parties bracketed together Catholics and Freemasons, it was common on the Catholic side to bracket together Freemasons and Jews. Nor did the 1870s remain an isolated instance of Catholic anti-semitism nurtured by fear. In 1907 the Centre faced an election campaign more fiercely anti-Catholic than anything since the *Kulturkampf*. It blamed this state of affairs, like that of the 1870s, on an unholy alliance of government and liberals; and once more there was a recrudescence of anti-semitic feeling in the party.[17] Again, after Centre defeats and sweeping SPD successes during the Reichstag elections of 1912, Martin Spahn, a young Centre politician who had himself been a prominent victim of anti-Catholic prejudice, wrote a strongly anti-semitic article in the periodical *Hochland*, making Jews a scapegoat for the turn to the left in Germany.[18]

Anti-semitism of this kind was sparked off, therefore, when Catholics felt under external attack. Such reactions were in themselves fitful; but they were the product of a deep-seated resentment of the Jew which derived from a Catholic sense of being discriminated against, not only as a religious minority, but economically and socially. It was the circumstances of what came to be known as 'Catholic backwardness' that provided the real cutting edge of Catholic anti-semitism. Measured against the population as a whole, Catholics in Imperial Germany were over-represented in the poorer countryside and small towns, under-represented in the better-off towns and cities. They were over-represented among those who gained a livelihood from agriculture and small business, under-represented in industry, commerce and the free professions. It was a measure of this situation that Catholics paid relatively low amounts of tax.[19] By contrast, as a result of the historically very different forms of discrimination to which they had been subject, Jews were over-represented in the towns and cities, over-represented in certain categories of business and the free professions, and paid relatively large amounts of tax. The education statistics mirrored this Catholic–Jewish disparity. In Prussian *Gymnasien* in 1896, 64.1 per cent of the pupils were Protestant, 27.5 per cent Catholic and 8.2 per cent Jewish. In the *Realgymnasien* the figures were 79 per cent, 12.6 per cent and 8.5 per cent respectively.[20] The contrast between the proportionately small number of Catholics and the proportionately large number of Jews was even more marked in the universities, especially among women students.

As the problem of 'backwardness' began to preoccupy a generation of Catholic public leaders in the last decade or so of the nineteenth century, statistics of this kind were regularly cited, often with anti-semitic undertones. The prominent publicist Hans Rost, for example, in the course of exhorting fellow Catholics to play a more prominent role in the Bavarian universities, used the highly pejorative phrase *verjudet* to describe a number of those universities.[21] Rost's comments on the world of business carried a similar emphasis. 'Who', he asked plaintively, 'has not had the experience that business contracts, Christmas purchases, orders of goods have been placed by Catholics, yes, even by Catholic associations and clerical persons, with Jews and those of other faiths'. It was, he continued, 'highly regrettable when so many purchases for the Christmas tree, when crucifixes and holy statues, prayer books and pictures are made from Jews (*bei Juden*)'. Indeed, according to Rost, the problem did not even end there: it was, he argued, 'a perhaps little known but undeniably regrettable truth that in Lourdes almost all the shops selling devotional materials, rosaries, prayer books and souvenirs are in the hands of the Jews'. He suggested that Bavarian pilgrims were the victims of similar circumstances.[22]

One of Rost's intentions, of course, was to urge Catholics to display more entrepreneurial energy, a sentiment shared by Catholic opponents of anti-semitism, like Ludwig Windthorst.[23] Rost's arguments, however, also carried a clear attack on the 'unfair' or outright 'dishonest' methods by which Jews had allegedly reached positions of economic prominence. He referred, for example, to the thousands of Catholic housewives who were bewitched by the 'Jewish department stores' into believing that they had actually made bargain purchases, particularly when they received 'copies of wicked Zola novels thrown in as a free gift'.[24] Arguments of this kind, shorn of their more fanciful embellishments, became common currency among prominent Centre politicians. Karl Bachem, the later historian of the party, referred to 'pushy Jewry' (*das vordrängende Judentum*),[25] while his cousin Julius corresponded with Centre leader Lieber in the 1890s on a bill to curb 'Jewish business excesses'.[26] In fact, the discussions which took place in the Reichstag on various Centre measures designed to outlaw 'unfair competition' often resembled debates on the 'Jewish question'.[27] Similar sentiments can be found in the speeches made by Matthias Erzberger during the 1912 Reichstag election campaign, when he referred disparagingly to the alleged machinations of those who owned 'mobile capital'.[28]

The experience of belonging to a self-consciously backward minority in Imperial Germany conditioned the form of anti-semitism espoused by Centre leaders and other middle-class Catholics in two important ways. It fostered resentments, while at the same time setting limits to their expression. The sense of outrage felt by Windthorst over anti-semitism, an issue on which he threatened resignation from the Centre,[29] was uncommon; but so, too, was the full-blooded anti-semitism enunciated by certain Catholic politicians, journalists and academics. Perhaps most widespread was a dislike of Jews bordering on hostility, which was restrained not only by a Catholic sense of vulnerability but also by a bourgeois distaste for rabble-rousing anti-semitism. Such attitudes constituted, in fact, a Catholic variant of 'respectable' bourgeois anti-semitism. The tone was well captured by Hermann Cardauns, editor of the influential *Kölnische Volkszeitung*, in his biography of a south German Centre leader. Adolf Gröber, said his biographer, was 'no friend of the Jews (*kein Judenfreund*), but opposed restrictions on [kosher] slaughtering'.[30]

III

While the kind of anti-semitism described above was usually expressed in a muted form, this was not the case throughout the Catholic community. It is the relationship between 'respectable' and popular anti-semitism which this essay will now consider. The latter, like the former, was a product of Catholic backwardness: Catholics were concentrated in the poorest, relatively outlying regions of Germany, and there was considerable resentment amongst the peasantry against the Jewish money lender and cattle dealer,[31] just as there was hostility amongst Catholic artisans towards the popularly-evoked figure of the hard-hearted Jewish businessman and banker. Popular antagonism towards the Jew formed part of a more general animus towards allegedly parasitical or dangerous outsiders, who at various points in the nineteenth century included also the landlord's agent, the tax official and the itinerant tradesman. Like the gipsy,[32] however, the Jew remained a consistent target of this kind of community disapproval, something which is illustrated by two sets of occasions, half a century apart in time, when hostility extended to threats of physical violence. In 1848, Catholic peasant radicalism (like Protestant peasant radicalism) was heavily tinged with anti-semitism directed against the Jew as a symbol of the alien outsider.[33] Similarly, in the Rhineland town of Xanten in 1891 and in the West Prussian town of Konitz in 1900, intensely hostile Catholic feelings were aroused when unsolved local crimes led to popular accusations that Jewish ritual murders had taken place.[34] In these cases, as in 1848, anti-semitism manifested itself as a form of violent parochialism.

It was a significant feature of this parochialism, however, that certain outsiders were able to gain acceptance for themselves by playing up to local anti-semitic feelings. This was true of the relationship between the bandit Schinderhannes and the Catholic peasantry of the Hunsrück,[35] and it was true in a rather different sense of the lawyers in Catholic south-west Germany who acquired popularity in the first half of the nineteenth century by acting as peasant advocates in usury cases.[36] By the second half of the century, however, this indemnity card had passed from bandits and lawyers to politicians. It was the Centre Party, together with its newspapers and auxiliary organizations, which now claimed to be protecting the interests of the Catholic peasant and artisan; and in assuming the mantle of protector, it also assumed some of the sentiments of popular anti-semitism. Anti-semitism started to become a significant feature of emergent political Catholicism in the 1860s. Jewish emancipation, finally achieved during that decade in most German states,[37] was unpopular in the poor Catholic countryside and small towns, particularly as it was enacted in states like Baden and Bavaria by liberal-bureaucratic regimes whose other reforms also aroused general Catholic hostility. Emancipation was therefore condemned, alongside state encroachment on clerical education, and measures which established greater freedom of trade and citizenship rights, as yet another piece of legislative meddling from 'outside', at odds with popular Catholic feelings and needs. Under these circumstances, anti-semitism readily formed part of the broader anti-liberal and anti-bureaucratic appeal which was made by the political forerunners of the Centre – Catholic parties such as the Bavarian *Patriotenpartei* and the *Katholische Volkspartei* in Baden.[38] In the process, the anti-semitism of the *Stammtisch* was brought on to the public stage.

The role played by anti-semitism in the process of Catholic political mobilization was evident in the newly founded Centre Party during the 1870s. Against a background of religious persecution, economic distress and liberal legislative dominance in the Reichstag, over 80 per cent of Catholics who went to the polls voted for the party.[39] This unity was reinforced by the identification of common external enemies, among whom the Jew – the alleged disturber of both the religious and economic peace – was prominently depicted. Leading Centre politicians like Julius Bachem and Peter Reichensperger, major newspapers like *Germania*, and organizations such as the Westphalian Peasant Association lent the weight of their respectability to popular anti-semitic views. With variations in tone, all helped to underline the idea of the Jew as anti-Christian and usurious; and all claimed a form of popular sanction for their expression of views by arguing that Jews had brought about their own unpopularity.[40] The Centre Party's willingness to play the anti-semitic card in the 1870s was striking because it involved prominent national figures and newspapers, and because it occurred at a time when there was a general outburst of anti-Jewish feeling. As we have seen, however, this was not a novel departure for German political Catholicism; and equally the 1870s did not mark the end of such a course.

It is certainly true that many of the national conditions which had encouraged the Centre in its anti-Semitism were unique to the 1870s: the *Kulturkampf*, the onset of the Great Depression, the liberal legislative dominance in the Reichstag and the short-term tactical need to find common political ground with the Conservatives (which was achieved in 1879).[41] It is also true that Windthorst and Lieber prevented the systematic adoption of anti-semitism by the Centre in national German politics. Anti-semitism remained, however, an important feature of Centre Party local politics well beyond the 1870s. This was so because the circumstances which had incubated it in states like Baden and Bavaria in the 1860s, and nationally in the 1870s, remained significantly unaltered at the local level. In the first place, Catholic economic backwardness continued, its amelioration proceeding more slowly than Catholic awareness of it grew. In fact, with the advent of the Great Depression, the Catholic peasantry and petty bourgeoisie faced serious new economic problems created by low price levels, rising costs and the increasing power of large industrial and commercial concentrations.[42] Furthermore, as the individual states within the Reich and the local authorities took on a larger role as employers and as the providers of public works and welfare, so the opportunities for discrimination and injured Catholic esteem (real or imagined) increased in proportion.[43] Catholic anti-governmental rancour therefore remained very great in the states and municipalities; and it was reinforced by another important element in local political life. Liberal influence in the Reichstag had declined notably after the 1870s, but this was by no means the pattern locally. In numerous town halls and some important state parliaments, liberal or 'liberal-governmental' groups remained powerful or even dominant until the end of the century, assisted usually by restrictive franchise arrangements and sometimes by outright gerrymandering, of which Catholics were frequently the victims.[44]

It is hardly surprising in these circumstances that the Centre successfully assumed the role of the 'outsider' party, addressing itself to the popular Catholic sense of exclusion, discrimination and neglect. In the years between 1880 and the turn of the century the Centre emerged as a powerful mass party at local level, partly by mobilizing previously non-voting Catholics, partly by winning over former liberal voters, and partly by using its growing strength to enforce favourable franchise reforms.[45] In this process of political mobilization, more thorough and more vigorous than earlier efforts, anti-semitism again formed part of the Centre's broader anti-governmental and anti-liberal appeal. The arrogant liberal lawyer, the distant manipulative capitalist and the Olympian state official – city-dwellers – were politically stigmatized as the enemies of the downtrodden Catholic peasant, artisan and small-town dweller; and the Jew was portrayed either as one of them, or at least as their agent in the immediate community.[46] Once again, the values of the *Stammtisch* were incorporated into a larger populist ideology.

It is not easy to reconstruct the ways in which the raw stuff of popular sentiment, 'the affects, the whisperings, the motions of the people', was transmuted into a political ideology – or demonology – of this kind. An attempt can be made, however, by looking at some of the principal agencies within the Centre Party through which anti-semitic assumptions were flattered and encouraged. Four of these are now considered, although the list is not exhaustive.

Firstly, there were the Catholic Peasant Associations. These existed in all the major German states by the end of the century: they embodied institutionally the party's powerful agrarian wing, and employed a political vocabulary heavily coloured by anti-semitism. This was not only true of the better-known Westphalian and Rhineland associations, which were led by aristocrats who stood on the conservative right of the party.[47] It applied also to the associations in areas like Bavaria, Baden, Württemberg and Trier, where the leadership was largely in the hands of the local clergy. These agrarian organizations paid great attention to the everyday problems of the Catholic primary producer – credit, marketing, the question of price rings formed by fertilizer manufacturers – and in fact took over much more systematically the role of the old peasant advocates, in taking peasant grievances to court. Between 1884 and 1918 the Trier association fought a total of 13,500 anti-usury cases against money lenders and dealers in hops, wine, wood, grain and tobacco.[48] In these capacities the associations put themselves forward as the protectors of the peasant; and the appeal to the peasant to organize and help himself was commonly coupled with the injunction to stay out of the clutches of the Jew.[49]

Secondly, there was the *Volksverein für das katholische Deutschland*. Established in 1890 on Windthorst's initiative, the People's Association of German Catholics had over 850,000 members by 1914 and constituted the mass organization of the Centre (which was not itself a membership party).[50] It was centrally administered from the Rhineland, the region in which German political Catholicism in general was organizationally most progressive, and it has a reputation for political modernity. It certainly provided an institutional counterweight to reactionary clerical influence within the Centre and produced an impressive volume of pamphlet literature on the social problem, geared to the needs of party speakers addressing social groups of all kinds, including the Catholic working class.[51] But in the small towns and rural areas where the bulk of the Centre electorate lived, *Volksverein* meetings betrayed little evidence of advanced social notions. They were usually addressed by the local priest, and the tone of reports suggests that Jews, like governmental officials, liberals and Freemasons, were the object of frequent and almost automatic condemnation. At one such meeting, for example, the speaker put the following gloss on local state proposals, warmly supported by the left liberals, to extend educational provision:

> The Democrats [i.e. the left liberals] want everyone who attends school to be brought to the stage that they can later secure themselves against any need, and no longer fall into the hands of the Jew. Against this it must be said that already highly-educated (*hochstudierte*) peasants have fallen victim to the usurious Jews (*Wucherjuden*).[52]

Thirdly, we may consider the local press. The number of Centre Party local newspapers increased enormously in the 1880s and 1890s, and they too commonly reinforced anti-semitic attitudes. The treatment of Austrian news provides an example: attacks on clerical education were taken as evidence of the 'Jewish and masonic brigade in Austria'; the German nationalist Wolf went 'hand in hand with the Jews' at elections; and Karl Lueger, the popular hero of Centre editors, was commended for his boldness in taking on 'Jewish' power in the Viennese stock exchange and press.[53] In a similar vein, the Dreyfus affair provided an opportunity for attacks on the 'Jews and Freemasons who sit at the rudder of the French ship of state'.[54] German news, national and local, was also reported in a clearly anti-semitic manner. The *Frankfurter Zeitung* was rendered as the *Judenblatt*, while in reports of bankruptcy proceedings concerning Jewish businesses, the names involved would be followed by exclamation marks or printed in bold type.[55] In articles which dealt with the stock exchange, agricultural prices or retail trade (especially that *bête noire*, the department store), malign Jewish influence was attributed almost as a matter of course. In addition to this, local Centre newspapers advertised other works which were themselves anti-semitic: church calendars,[56] for example, or the 30-*Pfennig* pamphlet warmly recommended by one newspaper, entitled 'Vampire, or usurious Jewry', a 'popular and grippingly written little work' which 'steers clear of any exaggeration'.[57]

Lastly, there were the local Centre politicians. Just as most Centre supporters would be more familiar with a local newspaper than with, say, the more sober *Kölnische Volkszeitung*, so they would naturally have more direct contact with local politicians than with Centre notables in the Reichstag and state parliaments (and many party leaders at state level also had political commitments in Berlin). The number, and probably the importance, of such local politicians increased with the intensification of Centre popular politics in the 1880s and 1890s; and as the Centre presence in state and municipal assemblies grew, an identifiable group of backbench deputies and councillors emerged as the direct spokesman for local, parish-pump interests. Often prominent figures within their own small communities – priests, primary school teachers or village mayors – their status as elected representatives who were nevertheless self-consciously 'of the people' lent a certain legitimacy to the attitudes which they struck, including sometimes violent expressions of anti-semitism. Many examples could be given, but one particular case will perhaps convey something of the texture of this populist politics. From 1895 until his death in 1902, Theophil Egger[58] represented the Württemberg Landtag constituency of Ravensburg. A retired primary school teacher and an octogenarian, Egger was an indefatigable contributor to parliamentary debates,[59] making regular attacks on 'Jewish' department stores, accusing legislators of paying too much heed to Jewish financial interests, requesting that the state military authorities purchase their horses direct from the peasant, not from 'the Jew', and even airing in parliament a legal action in his constituency involving a Jewish horse dealer. Egger was certainly a maverick: he also campaigned against the bicycle as a threat to the rural way of life; but he was characteristic of many in the directness with which he articulated commonplace views as political concerns. For many of his predominantly rural voters, Egger undoubtedly personified Centre politics at the turn of the century.

Agriculture and small business continued to predominate in the majority of Centre constituencies up to 1914;[60] but it was important for the party's claim to represent Catholics of all classes that the growing number of Catholic working-class voters not be lost to the Left. Here too anti-semitism had a place in the politics of the Centre. There was no systematic attempt by the party to emulate Adolf Stöcker's enterprise of the 1880s: to try to wean workers away from Social Democracy by offering them the 'socialism of fools' as an alternative.[61] The leaders of the *Volksverein*, for example, which had been established with the need to keep Catholic workers within the Centre fold very much in mind, steered clear of anti-semitic appeals. This was not, however, true of the Centre Party everywhere. Matthias Erzberger's references to the Free Trade Unions as *stark verjudet* is well known.[62] In Alsace-Lorraine a generation of young clerical activists in the Centre met the SPD challenge in the 1890s with a similarly anti-semitic counter-assault.[63] It was common for party newspapers and those addressing local Centre meetings to draw attention to those Jews who were prominent in German (and Austrian) Social Democracy. Paul Singer, chairman of the SPD group in the German Reichstag, appears to have been a particular target, as both a wealthy Jew and an SPD leader. Attacks on Singer and other Jews, in fact, followed a common pattern: honest Christian workers, it was alleged, were naturally loyal to the Church and the established social order, but were seduced by the blandishments of Jewish socialist agitators.

The Centre actually suffered a considerable loss of Catholic working-class support before 1914 in cities like Cologne, Dortmund, Strasbourg and Munich.[64] The attitude of most Centre leaders towards social issues continued to be paternalistic, and the party's economic policies, particularly its support for agricultural tariffs, were widely unpopular among Catholic workers. But it seems possible that the branding of Social Democracy as partly Jewish-inspired may have had some effect on other groups of Catholics to whom the SPD might have proved attractive – struggling small masters, agricultural labourers and small peasants, for example. It is certainly the case that in rural areas, newspapers, politicians and the parish clergy encouraged the Catholic peasantry and petty bourgeoisie to draw the most unfavourable conclusions about Jewish involvement in Social Democratic politics.

IV

Three conclusions are offered from this essay. Two concern its relevance to the continuing debate over the political system of Imperial Germany; the third looks ahead more generally to the problem of Catholic anti-semitism in relation to the Nazi seizure of power. Many recent works on Imperial Germany have developed the idea that a narrow ruling elite sought to stabilize the social and political *status quo* before 1914 by diverting potentially reformist energies into other channels. Illiberal and chauvinist values, it has been argued, were fostered from above by means of a foreign policy geared to domestic political consumption, and through agencies like the army, churches and schools. There can be no doubt about the valuable contribution which this work has made to our understanding of Imperial German politics, nor about the fillip it has given and continues to give to research on the subject. There can equally be no doubt, however, that as a result, phenomena such as anti-socialism, anti-English feeling and anti-semitism have been viewed largely in an instrumental light, as the product of an interested manipulation of popular uncertainties and anxieties by a narrow elite. I have argued elsewhere that this model, as it stands, generally fits neither the collective behaviour of German Catholics, nor the reasons for that behaviour.[65] A consideration of Catholic anti-semitism appears to reinforce this view.

Catholic anti-semitism was certainly more extensive than historians have usually suggested, but it was not the outcome of this kind of indoctrination or diversionary ploy. In most important respects it was generated by Catholics' own experience of backwardness, repression, discrimination and neglect. These dictated the forms which Catholic anti-semitism took. Among bourgeois Catholics resentment focused on the post-emancipatory success of Jews in certain branches of business and the professions, spheres in which Catholics themselves were notably under-represented. While among the Catholic peasantry and petty bourgeoisie, anti-semitism was a less muted expression of hostility towards the Jew as an allegedly parasitical outsider. The genesis of Catholic anti-semitism in Catholic experience also dictated the forms it did *not* take; and this was equally important. The rural and small-town base of German political Catholicism, together with Centre leaders' particular concern with this part of their support, helped to militate against the emergence of an urban Catholic, 'rabble-rousing' anti-semitism (*Raddau-Antisemitismus*) of the kind that developed in Berlin and Dresden. With respect to exceptional legislation as well, natural convictions among Centre leaders were reinforced by the prudent recognition that Catholics were also a vulnerable minority. More generally, the open espousal of anti-semitism by Catholic leaders was made more difficult by their own experience of being labelled as 'enemies of the Reich', just as their full-blooded espousal of militarism was made more difficult by the experience of anti-Catholic discrimination on the part of the Prussian army.

Anti-semitic feelings and similar sentiments were no doubt cynically manipulated in Imperial Germany; but not always by government, the ruling elite and their agencies. In the Catholic case, such conduct might well be attributed to the leadership of the Centre Party itself; for anti-semitism certainly had a place in Centre politics, as the result of a process whereby commonplace prejudice was cast in political form. It is the nature of this process which provides the second conclusion of this essay. In its mobilization of Catholic popular support, the leaders of the Centre were clearly not blind to the political usefulness of anti-semitic postures: to what extent, therefore, should one talk here of manipulation from above, to what extent of pressure from below? What was the relative importance of 'pull' and 'push'? This article has tried to show that a two-way process was in fact taking place. There seems to be little doubt, on the one hand, that anti-semitic views were widespread among Centre supporters. This was particularly the case among the Catholic peasantry and petty bourgeoisie, where anti-semitism constituted a form of soured emancipatory impulse: a truculent, sometimes violent set of reactions which expressed a very genuine sense of exploitation and neglect – economic, social and institutional. It resembled and paralleled, in fact, the anti-elitist distemper of the Protestant peasantry and petty bourgeoisie in Hesse, Thuringia and Saxony during the same period, which found expression through the anti-semitic political parties. Like the more general agrarian and petty bourgeois discontent of which it formed a part, this strain of popular Catholic anti-semitism could actually be a source of serious embarrassment and concern to Centre leaders. In political terms, it represented a threat as well as an opportunity. For as Lieber noted anxiously in 1894, if the Centre dissolved, its rural electorate would go to the anti-semitic political parties.[66]

Centre leaders at different levels helped to bring this problem on themselves, however, by their willingness to harness popular anti-semitic feelings. On this issue, as on others which affected their peasant and petty bourgeois supporters, like tariffs, department store taxation and the reintroduction of guilds, they bent with the wind, demagogically encouraging sentiments which could be used against the party's political enemies – governments, liberals, socialists. In Bavaria, for example, there was a powerful popular animus around the turn of the century against the often Jewish-owned department stores: alongside demands for special restrictions and taxes on the stores, embittered shopkeepers organized physical disruption of their business.[67] It was in these circumstances that one of the Centre's leaders in the state, Franz Xaver Schädler, told the department store owner Oscar Tietz that the party 'had to do something to counter the seething state of popular feelings; they want a department store tax; we know that is unjust and economically stupid, but the others are the majority'.[68] Turnover taxes on department stores predictably proved as irrelevant to the problems of small shopkeepers as physical disruption had been. The effect of Centre policy, in fact, was to feed appetites rather than to satisfy them, just as it tended to encourage anti-semitic feelings rather than discourage them.

A similar process was at work at all levels of the Centre. Figures like Theophil Egger, the Württemberg Landtag deputy, were able to secure their own local popularity by employing an anti-semitic vocabulary: indeed, Egger was not alone in using this popularity, in turn, to fend off efforts by the state leadership of the Centre to unseat him. At the level of state politics itself, the usefulness of this kind of politics was tacitly acknowledged. Centre leaders themselves were not above the occasional exercise in studied demagogy; and while they would usually try to dissociate themselves from the wilder demands of a man like Egger, this applied more to the form than the substance of what was demanded. Policies with popular anti-semitic overtones, like department store taxation, were officially adopted, divested only of the offensively robust terms in which they continued to be discussed in the small towns and villages. As far as anti-semitism was concerned, Centre leaders picked up the baggage without the labels. This was also true at national level. During the 1890s, for example, the Centre took up a number of proposals on grain futures trading and 'unfair competition' which were popularly regarded as attacks on 'Jewish capital'. They were not presented in the Reichstag as anti-semitic issues; but in private correspondence Julius Bachem referred to the need to curb 'Jewish business excesses', and there is no doubt that this is how such measures were treated in the constituencies. Once again, the anti-semitic labels were missing; but everyone knew what the baggage contained.

Anti-semitism, then, by no means disappeared from Centre Party politics after the 1870s. It did not appear as a set of formal demands and policies; but its assumptions had been tacitly incorporated into the party's politics. Anti-semitism, in fact, was institutionalized into Centre politics in the same way that it was institutionalized into the politics of the prewar Conservatives and *Bund der Landwirte*.[69] Over a longer period the process was actually more successful, and this allows a third and final conclusion to be drawn. In the 1920s the DNVP and the *Reichslandbund* found it more difficult than their Conservative predecessors in Imperial Germany to maintain their popular support by demagogic adjustments of this kind. Pressure from below was strong, as it had been in the 1880s and 1890s, and in the late 1920s the forces of the political right found themselves deserted by those whose discontents they had tried to harness. The political and electoral decline of the DNVP helped to swell Nazi popular support. The Centre Party, by contrast, held up its support against the Nazis. It did so at least partly because of its own more successful, if less strident, demagogy. With anti-semitism, as with other issues exploited by the Nazis, such as anti-communism, the plight of the *Mittelstand* and the position of women, the Centre already offered its supporters a more muted version of the same appeal. This had another effect, of course: the Centre also played its part, like the DNVP, in establishing a political atmosphere which helped to make the Nazis appear more respectable. As a result, the Centre was able to preserve itself electorally up until 1933; but it was unable to offer any serious moral or political resistance to the Nazi seizure of power.

NOTES

1 See, for example, P. W. Massing, *Rehearsal for Destruction: A Study of Political Anti-Semitism in Imperial Germany* (New York, 1949) and P. G. J. Pulzer, *The Rise of Political Anti-Semitism in Germany and Austria* (New York, 1964). While both of these writers consider the residual existence of Catholic anti-semitism in later years, even this is denied in R. S. Levy, *The Downfall of the Anti-Semitic Political Parties in Imperial Germany* (New Haven and London, 1975).

2 Central to interpretations of the Great Depression is H. Rosenberg, *Grosse Depression und Bismarckzeit. Wirtschaftsablauf, Gesellschaft und Politik in Mitelteuropa* (Berlin, 1967).

3 See, J. Lange, *Die Stellung der überregionalen katholischen deutschen Tagespresse zum Kulturkampf in Preussen (1871–1878)* (Frankfurt/M and Bern, 1974), pp. 124–5; R. Rürup, *Emanzipation und Antisemitismus* (Göttingen, 1975), p. 173, n. 40; E. Heinen, 'Antisemitische Strömungen im politischen Katholizismus während des Kulturkampfs', E. Heinen and H. J. Schoeps (eds.), *Geschichte in der Gegenwart. Festschrift für Kurt Kluxen zu seinem 60. Geburtstag* (Paderborn, 1972), pp. 286–91.

4 Massing's *Rehearsal for Destruction*, pp. 216–17, stresses the importance of Catholics' access to the government through the Centre Party, and also suggests that economic growth in areas like the Rhineland and Silesia took the edge off Catholic anti-semitism. As this essay will suggest, these are the right questions, but not perhaps the right answers.

5 The views which make up this interpretation are most conveniently brought together in H.-U. Wehler, *Das deutsche Kaiserreich 1871–1918* (Göttingen, 1973). An idea of the contribution which Wehler and similarly-minded scholars have made to historical debate on Imperial Germany can be gathered from the reviews and commentaries on this work: H.-G. Zmarzlik, 'Das Kaiserreich in neuer Sicht?', *Historische Zeitschrift*, 222 (1976), pp. 105–26; T. Nipperdey, 'Wehlers "Kaissereich". Eine kritische Auseinandersetzung', *Geschichte und Gesellschaft*, I (1975), pp. 539–60; V. R. Berghahn, 'Der Bericht der preussischen Oberrechnungskammer. "Wehlers" Kaiserreich und seine Kritiker', *Geschichte und Gesellschaft*, 2 (1976), pp. 125–36; R. J. Evans, 'Wilhelm II's Germany and the Historians', R. J. Evans (ed.), *Society and Politics in Wilhelmine Germany* (London, 1978), pp. 11–39.

6 For this process among shopkeepers and artisans, see respectively R. Gellately, *The Politics of Economic Despair: Shopkeepers and German Politics 1890–1914* (London, 1974) and S. Volkov, *The Rise of Popular Antimodernism in Germany: the Urban Master Artisans, 1873–1896* (Princeton, 1978). The concept of self-mobilization, however, is widely diffused in other works. It forms something of a *leitmotif* in the volume of essays edited by Richard J. Evans and cited in the previous note.

7 On the *Kulturkampf*, see E. Schmidt-Volkmar, *Der Kulturkampf in Deutschland, 1871–1890* (Göttingen, 1962).

8 Cited in Wehler, *Das deutsche Kaiserreich*, p. 112.

9 R. Lill, 'Die deutschen Katholiken und die Juden in der Zeit von 1850 bis zur Machtübernahme durch Hitler', K. H. Rengstorf and S. Kortzfleich (eds.), *Kirche und Synagoge*, vol. II (Stuttgart, 1970), p. 384.

10 O. Beta, *Darwin, Deutschland und die Juden Oder Der Juda-Jesuitismus* (Berlin, n.d.), cited in Rosenberg, *Grosse Depression*, p. 104, n. 103.

11 This charge was later to be levelled by Nazi writers against Christianity in general. See A. Miller, *Völkentartung unter dem Kreuz. Der abendländische Geisterpolyp als Fluch der Welt* (Leipzig, 1933).
12 Levy, *Downfall of the Anti-Semitic Political Parties*, p. 185.
13 Massing, *Rehearsal for Destruction*, p. 114.
14 Levy, *Downfall of the Anti-Semitic Political Parties*, p. 248.
15 *Germania*, the most anti-semitic of major Centre newspapers, had five of its editorial staff serving gaol sentences at one stage in the *Kulturkampf*, including the particularly virulent anti-semite Paul Majunke, a Reichstag deputy who was controversially arrested during a Reichstag session. See Lange, *Die Stellung der überregionalen katholischen deutschen Tagespresse*, p. 86, and M. Stürmer, *Regierung und Reichstag im Bismarckstaat 1871–1880* (Düsseldorf, 1974), p. 130. It is a measure of the way in which anti-semitism was part of a 'closing of ranks' under external attack, that the *Schlesische Volkszeitung*, having initially attacked *Germania* for its anti-semitic articles, should have fallen in with the press campaign after charges that it lacked solidarity. See Heinen, 'Antisemitische Strömungen', p. 272.
16 Election address at Oppeln, 11 March 1872, Ballestrem Papers, folder IV, in private family possession. I am grateful to the Ballestrem family for allowing me access to these papers.
17 During the Reichstag election campaign, for example, *Germania* attacked the 'National Catholic', i.e. anti-Centre, mayor of Wilms in Posen, commenting acidly that 'the Jews have expressly made him a present of their goodwill'. Cited in H. Bodewig, *Geistliche Wahlbeeinflussungen in ihrer Theorie und Praxis dargestellt* (Munich, 1909), p. 5.
18 Spahn had been appointed in 1901, at the age of twenty-six, to a chair in history at the newly-created University of Strassburg. The appointment was certainly motivated by political considerations, but the outcry which followed was also characterized by marked anti-Catholic feeling. Meinecke wrote that 'Catholic history professors are and remain a monstrosity.' For accounts of the 'Spahn Affair', see *Schulthess' Europäischer Geschichtskalender, 1901* (Munich, 1902), pp. 145–7, and R. J. Ross, *Beleaguered Tower. The Dilemma of Political Catholicism in Wilhelmine Germany* (Notre Dame, 1976), pp. 26–8.
19 On the question of 'Catholic backwardness', see J. Rost, *Die wirtschaftliche und kulturelle Lage der deutschen Katholiken* (Cologne, 1911); A. Neher, *Die wirtschaftliche und soziale Lage der Katholiken im westlichen Deutschland* (Rottweil, 1927); C. Bauer, *Deutscher Katholizismus. Entwicklungslinien und Profile* (Frankfurt/M, 1964).
20 Rost, *Die wirtschaftliche und kulturelle Lage*, p. 100. There were a number of reasons for this long-standing Catholic *Bildungsdefizit*. They included the often lukewarm or even hostile attitudes towards education (particularly women's education) in many Catholic communities, and the tendency for gifted young Catholics to be 'creamed off' for the priesthood.
21 Ibid., p. 205. Rost suggested that it would require a man with the 'frankness of a Lueger' to rectify such a state of affairs.
22 Ibid., pp. 202–3.
23 Even in the case of Windthorst, however, the subject of Catholic entrepreneurial sloth seems irresistibly to have brought the Jewish contrast to mind: 'The Jews make their nests happily in Catholic areas because the Catholics are lazy. Our priests preach too much about the birds and flowers of the field, which neither sow nor reap, yet receive enough to live.' H. Cardauns, *Adolf Gröber* (M.-Gladbach, 1921), p. 43.
24 Rost, *Die wirtschaftliche und kulturelle Lage*, p. 202.
25 In a note of 1880, cited in Heinen, 'Antisemitische Strömungen', p. 282, n. 99a.
26 Pfälzische Landesbibliothek Speyer, Ernst Lieber Papers, B. 216, Julius Bachem to Lieber, 11 January 1893. This is also cited in J. K. Zeender, *The German Center Party 1890–1906* (Philadelphia, 1976), p. 46.
27 S. Zucker, *Ludwig Bamberger: German Liberal Politician and Social Critic, 1823–1899* (Pittsburgh, 1975), p. 250.
28 See, for example, his speech at Wolfegg on 9 December 1911, reported in *Waldse'er Wochenblatt*, 12 December 1911.
29 Zeender, *The German Center Party*, p. 14.
30 Cardauns, *Adolf Gröber*, p. 152.

31 There is an interesting account, in the autobiography of the butcher Bernhard Gottron, of the relationship between peasant and Jew in the area around Mainz just after the middle of the century: 'As there were still no loan banks and the like, the Jews in rural areas were asked for credit, particularly for buying cattle. In this capacity the Jews were generally one-sidedly and unfairly judged. If, for example, the money lender had a peasant's goods auctioned, because despite waiting he had been unable to obtain either his interest or his capital, then it was generally said: "The wicked Jew has ruined the poor man". Or if more than five per cent was asked of someone without security, then the Jew was publicly branded as a usurer.' B. Gottron, *Erlebtes und Erlauschtes aus dem Mainzer Metzgergewerbe im 19. Jahrhundert* (Mainz, 1928), p. 33.

32 For a detailed account of a violent clash between the inhabitants of a small Catholic village and a group of gipsies, see *Der Oberländer*, 10 November 1896, report headed 'Zigeunerschlacht'.

33 See V. Valentin, *Geschichte der deutschen Revolution von 1848–9*, 2 vols (Berlin, 1930–1).

34 Massing, *Rehearsal for Destruction*, p. 108.

35 C. Küther, *Räuber und Gauner in Deutschland. Das organisierte Bandenwesen im 18. und frühen 19. Jahrhundert* (Göttingen, 1976), pp. 27, 46, 111, 114, 115 n. 63.

36 See the case of Andreas Wiest, for example: C. Bauer, *Politischer Katholizismus in Württemberg bis zum Jahr 1848* (Freiburg, 1929), p. 128.

37 It was achieved in Bavaria in 1861, Württemberg in 1861–4, Baden in 1862, and Prussia and the North German Confederation in 1869.

38 For Baden, see L. Gall, 'Die Problematik des badischen Kulturkampfes', *Zeitschrift für die Geschichte des Oberrheins*, 113 (1965), pp. 151–96; and Rürup, *Emanzipation und Antisemitismus*, pp. 37–73, especially pp. 71–3. For Bavaria, the *Patriotenpartei* in the 1860s is dealt with in G. C. Windell, *The Catholics and German Unity, 1866–71* (Minneapolis, 1954). See also K. Möckl, *Die Prinzregentenzeit. Gesellschaft und Politik während der Ara des Prinzregenten Luitpold in Bayern* (Munich and Vienna, 1972), pp. 36–9.

39 R. Morsey, 'Die deutschen Katholiken und der Nationalstaat zwischen Kulturkampf und dem ersten Weltkrieg', *Historisches Jahrbuch* (1970), p. 35.

40 See, for example, Reichensperger's speech, cited in Heinen, 'Antisemitische Strömungen', pp. 286–8, and the *Germania* article of 15 November 1880, cited ibid., p. 283.

41 The years 1878–9 saw the passing of the anti-socialist law and protective tariffs, the beginnings of a reactionary purge of the Prussian bureaucracy, the embarrassment of political liberalism, and the related movement of the Centre Party closer to both government and Conservatives. The significance of these interconnected events as a turning-point has been strongly stressed, perhaps even over-stressed, by recent works. See especially, Rosenberg, *Grosse Depression*; H. Böhme, *Deutschlands Weg zur Grossmacht. Studien zum Verhältnis von Wirtschaft und Staat während der Reichsgründungszeit 1848–1881* (Cologne, 1966); Wehler, *Das deutsche Kaiserreich*; Stürmer, *Regierung und Reichstag*.

42 I have written about this elsewhere on a number of occasions. See, for example, 'The Political Alignment of the Centre Party in Wilhelmine Germany: A Study of the Party's Emergence in Nineteenth-Century Württemberg', *Historical Journal*, XVIII, 4 (1975), pp. 821–50.

43 Injured *amour-propre* might be either personal or communal. It was the reaction of the Catholic who failed to obtain employment with the public library or abattoir as a result of discrimination; and it was the reaction also of the many Catholic communities which felt themselves neglected when it came to the provision of agricultural officials, railway branch lines and so on.

44 On gerrymandering in Baden, see J. Schofer, *Erinnerungen an Theodor Wacker* (Karlsruhe, 1921), pp. 15, 84–5; and on the Rhineland, Pfälzische Landesbibliothek Speyer, Ernst Lieber Papers, T. 20, Karl Trimborn to Lieber, 1 August 1898, and H. Cardauns, *Karl Trimborn* (M.-Gladbach, 1922), pp. 83–7.

45 On Centre pressure for the electoral reform of 1906 in Bavaria, and its favourable effects, see Möckl, *Die Prinzregentenzeit*, pp. 491–532. For the similar effects of the 1904 reform in Baden, Schofer, *Erinnerungen*, pp. 86–8.

46 For the broader background of this kind of political appeal by the Centre, see my article 'The Problem of Democratisation: German Catholics and the Role of the Centre Party', Evans, *Society and Politics*, pp. 160–85.

47 The leader of the Westphalian association, Schorlemer, had been a prominent Centre Party anti-semite in 1880. For his conservative-agrarian stance in the 1880s and especially the 1890s, see the long retrospective article in the *Kölnische Volkszeiting*, 28 May 1912; K. Bachem, *Vorgeschichte, Geschichte und Politik der Deutschen Zentrumspartei*, 9 vols (Cologne, 1927–32), V, pp. 23–4, 291–2; T. Nipperdey, *Die Organisation der deutschen Partein vor 1918* (Düsseldorf, 1961), pp. 277–80. On Felix von Loë and the Rhineland association, see K. Müller, 'Zentrumspartei und agrarische Bewegung im Rheinland, 1882–1903', K. Repgen and S. Skalweit (eds.), *Spiegel der Geschichte: Festgabe für M. Braubach zum 10. April 1964* (Münster, 1964), pp. 828–57.

48 F. Jacobs, *Deutsche Bauernführer* (Düsseldorf, 1958), p. 76.

49 Zeender, *German Center Party*, p. 13.

50 D. Fricke (ed.), *Die bürgerlichen Parteien in Deutschland 1830–1945*, 2 vols (Leipzig, 1968–70), II, p. 810.

51 On the 'modern', non-clerical complexion of the *Volksverein* leadership, see Historisches Archiv der Stadt Köln, Karl Bachem Papers, 1006/59, memorandum of Bachem on founding of the association; Cardauns, *Karl Trimborn*, p. 73; Nipperdey, *Die Organisation*, p. 281.

52 Report on *Volksverein* meeting in Schussenried, in *Waldse'er Wochenblatt*, 13 May 1897. At a meeting earlier in the year in the same village, a different clerical speaker referred to liberal educational reformers as 'Wolves in sheeps' clothing, who bleed the common people white in the manner of Jewish vampires, robbing them not only of their earthly, but of their heavenly goods'. *Waldse'er Wochenblatt*, 11 February 1898.

53 *Waldse'er Wochenblatt*, 15 January 1895, 4 December 1897, 6 February 1898.

54 Ibid., 14 March 1897.

55 See, for example, the *Ipf-Zeitung* (Bopfingen), 3 January 1899.

56 Such as the *Kalender für Zeit und Ewigkeit*. See Lill, 'Die deutschen Katholiken', p. 376.

57 *Waldse'er Wochenblatt*, 23 April 1895.

58 On Egger, see my Ph.D. thesis, 'The Centre Party in Wilhelmine Germany: the example of Württemberg' (Cambridge, 1976), pp. 150–1, 310–11.

59 He claimed in 1900 to have spoken more than 300 times in the Landtag during the preceding five years. *Schwäbischer Merkur*, 3 December 1900.

60 It has been calculated that this was the case in 78 of the 113 Reichstag constituencies won by the Centre and its allies in 1907. H. Gabler, 'Die Entwicklung der Parteien auf landwirtschaftlicher Grundlage von 1871–1912', (dissertation, Berlin, 1934), p. 16.

61 Stöcker, nevertheless, had some unlikely admirers in the Centre Party, like Karl Trimborn. See Cardauns, *Karl Trimborn*, p. 106.

62 K. Epstein, *Matthias Erzberger and the Dilemma of German Democracy* (Princeton, 1959), p. 42; G. Lewy, *The Catholic Church and Nazi Germany* (London, 1964), p. 270.

63 D. P. Silverman, 'Political Catholicism and Social Democracy in Alsace-Lorraine, 1871–1914', *Catholic Historical Review*, 52 (1966), p. 59. Silverman, however, is principally concerned with Centre attacks on big business as *Judenindustrie*, rather than with attempts to brand Social Democracy itself as Jewish-influenced.

64 Between 1874 and 1912, the Centre share of the votes cast by Catholics at Reichstag elections fell from 83 per cent to 54.6 per cent. The evidence suggests that the losses were heaviest in working-class constituencies. On the Centre's problems with the Catholic working class, see Ross, *Beleaguered Tower*, pp. 79 ff. For a contemporary view, O. Hue, 'Die Katholischen Arbeiter und das Zentrum', *Neue Zeit*, II (1903), pp. 473–6.

65 See 'The Problem of Democratisation', Evans, *Society and Politics*, pp. 160–85.

66 Zeender, *German Center Party*, p. 46.

67 On the background to anti-department store feeling in Bavaria and other states, J. Wernicke, *Kapitalismus und Mittelstandspolitik* (Jena, 1907), pp. 546–738.

68 G. Tietz, *Hermann Tietz: Geschichte einer Familie und ihrer Warenhäuser* (Stuttgart, 1955), p. 46.

69 See, especially, the work by H.-J. Puhle, *Agrarische Interessenpolitik und preussischer Konservatismus im wilhelminischen Reich, 1893–1914* (Hanover, 1966).

9

Catholics and Politics in Imperial Germany: the Centre Party and its Constituency

The following chapter is more general in scope than either of the last two, but in many respects it complements Chapter 7. It looks at the legacy of the *Kulturkampf* in the decades after the 1870s; and it focuses more sharply on the place of the Centre Party within the political landscape of Imperial Germany. The status and treatment of the Catholic minority continued, even after the end of the *Kulturkampf*, to provide a barometer that enables us to gauge what was happening in German society and politics more generally. But the various ways in which German Catholics responded to their circumstances – to economic 'backwardness', discrimination over public appointments, the existence of widespread anti-Catholic sentiment – also gave them a more active and positive importance. This was most obviously the case in the sphere of politics. There are parallels here with that other great pariah group of Imperial Germany, the organized working class. For if, by 1914, the SPD was the largest and best organized working-class movement in the world, the Centre Party and its auxiliary organizations represented the largest and best organized exponent of political Catholicism.

In the twenty-five years before the First World War the Centre Party gained or consolidated an influential position in state parliaments and town halls across many parts of Germany. In the national parliament, the Reichstag, it disposed of a regular block of around a hundred seats, a quarter of the total. This gave the party of the minority a pivotal position in Imperial German politics. Many things combined to bring this situation about, including the concentration of the Catholic vote, the nature of the political system bequeathed by Bismarck, and the division of the non-Catholic vote. But we should also consider the means by which the Centre Party translated its potential Catholic constituency into actual electoral strength and political influence. This was by no means as straightforward as the party's opponents often claimed. The position of the Centre within Catholic Germany rested on complex foundations. The party spoke for Catholic interests on matters like education, public morality and the status of the Church, even if it always kept the German bishops (and Rome) at arm's length. It also carried the hopes of those who wanted an end to anti-Catholic discrimination over public appointments, those who wished to establish the national *bona fides* of German Catholics by supporting measures like the construction of a battle fleet, and those who simply wanted to break out of the ghetto and achieve Catholic 'respectability'. At the same time, however, the Centre maintained its support at the grassroots by cultivating a well-judged anti-governmentalism: it harnessed the votes of Catholic peasants and workers who were largely indifferent or hostile to causes like the navy, and it organized these and other groups into powerful interest organizations. The following chapter therefore looks at the crucial role played by the Centre in Imperial German politics; it also examines how the party reflected and tried to harmonize the very contradictory aspirations of German Catholics.

The chapter was written in its present form during the early summer of 1982 for an essay collection that, at time of writing, is still in the press (John C. Fout, ed., *Politics, Parties, and the Authoritarian State: Imperial Germany 1871–1918*, New York, 1987). The material and the arguments it contains build on my long-standing interest in the subject, but there is a more detailed consideration of the part played by religion in Centre politics than in much of my previous work. For that reason, this article seemed a stronger candidate for inclusion in the present collection than an earlier attempt to take stock: 'The Problem of Democratisation: German Catholics and the Role of the Centre Party', in Richard J. Evans (ed.), *Society and Politics in Wilhelmine Germany* (London, 1978), pp. 160–85.

I

Imperial Germany had a population which was two-thirds Protestant, and a Protestant Church which is rightly regarded by historians as a pillar of the authoritarian state. Yet, paradoxically, it was the Centre Party, the political representative of the Catholic minority, which Friedrich Naumann described as 'the measure of all things' in German politics.[1] How had this position come about? The Centre Party was formed at the very end of 1870, simultaneously with the defeat of France which finally established the new German state. The party quickly became a focus for the various political aspirations of German Catholics. But it was during the *Kulturkampf*, the struggle between church and state in the 1870s, that the Centre really consolidated its political position. At that time, as the Catholic Church and its adherents came under fierce attack, the Centre gained the support of more than four-fifths of voting Catholics. As most of these voters were in geographically concentrated areas, the party was able to secure a powerful block of seats in the new Reichstag, as well as in many of the state parliaments, including the Prussian Chamber of Deputies. This strength was largely retained after the *Kulturkampf*; and with the rapid electoral growth of the SPD after 1890, the strategic value of the Centre's parliamentary seats was enhanced still further. The way the party chose to vote, in the Reichstag especially, became a matter of crucial importance. It held the balance between left and right, between anti-governmental and governmental forces, and it showed itself to be very aware of this pivotal position.[2] From 1890 up to the First World War, political commentators of all persuasions expended considerable energy dilating on this apparent Catholic wedge in the Protestant state.

Most of this commentary was hostile. Indeed, many liberals and radical nationalists attacked the Centre as vigorously as they did the Social Democrats. This hostility to the Centre Party is less obviously explicable to later generations than contemporary anti-socialism, and perhaps less acknowledged. But it was a political fact of prime importance, and it can be explained by three alleged features of the Centre: its influence, its irresponsibility, and its Catholic aims. The decisive political position of the Centre was widely disliked by many government ministers, not least because they usually had to cultivate the party's leaders in order to achieve anything. Kaiser Wilhelm II's intermittent ravings stand as an extreme example of the frustration with which official Protestant Germany viewed the Centre's awkward presence. Resentment was often even greater among the other political parties. It was shared to some degree by all of them, although it was undoubtedly strongest in liberal and nationalist circles and weakest among Social Democrats (who believed that the political future was theirs anyway, and viewed the discomfiture of their non-Catholic bourgeois rivals with a certain *Schadenfreude*). If the key position of the Centre was in itself a source of hostility, the irresponsibility with which the Centre was alleged to exploit this position only compounded the offence. The Centre was widely regarded as *bündnisunfähig*: incapable of any serious political alliance. It was thought to be a party lacking in fixed principle, consistent only in its inconsistency. The party's parliamentary behaviour was taken to demonstrate this. For the Centre's habitual approach to legislative measures was to reserve its position on the first reading of a new bill, to try and bend the legislation into a different shape in committee, and to make its support at the third reading conditional on achieving the concessions it sought. This, together with the backstairs accommodations between Centre leaders and ministers, lay behind Max Weber's acid comment that the Centre strove solely and irresponsibly for 'bonbons'.[3]

In many ways this sort of conduct was hardly surprising in a multi-party system where party leaders were not themselves able to assume ministerial responsibility. The Centre provided only the most obvious example of that 'horse-trading' (*Kuhhandel*) which contemporary critics on the right saw as a product of parliamentarism and critics on the left as a product of pseudo-parliamentarism. But both sets of critics singled out the Centre for special obloquy, and not only because the party's leaders played the game so deftly. Hostility was sharpened by the purposes which were believed to underlay Centre horse-trading. It was here that the denominational element was important. Both the pivotal position of the Centre and the irresponsibility with which the party was said to wield it were made more unbearable because the Centre was a party of Catholics. And it was Catholic interests which were allegedly advanced by the party's political intriguing. It was, so commentators endlessly argued, in the interests of Rome or the German bishops, of the Jesuits or Catholic schools, of Catholic missionaries or job-hunters, that the Centre behaved as it did. From Bismarck's argument that the Centre was the party of the Jesuits,[4] to the radical-nationalist critique of sinister, non-German interests behind 'the oppressive weight of the Centre's unrelenting fist',[5] it was the Catholic nature of the party which brought criticism of the Centre into focus. The party was not just overmighty and untrustworthy; it was seen as an undesirable survivor of the *Kulturkampf* era, a political oddity whose very existence was politically illegitimate.

Subsequent historians have continued to see the Centre as an oddity. In many ways it remains the awkward party, as difficult for historians to fit into the normal political spectrum as it was for contemporaries to accept as a normal political party. At times, indeed, it almost seems as if historians do not think that the Centre 'ought' to have existed at all. Such a view is expressed by Erich Foerster, the biographer of the *Kulturkampf* Minister of Public Worship, Adalbert Falk. Here we read of the Centre disrupting the 'normal balance between the right and left' and preventing a proper dialogue between the 'two great valid basic political standpoints'.[6] If this is predictable, the unspoken assumptions are nevertheless revealing. A more recent writer strikes a similar note when he refers to 'the emergence of a Catholic political mass movement, which can only with some difficulty be fitted into the picture of an emerging modern "national state"'.[7] The view that the Centre was something of a historical mistake is encountered fairly often, if only implicitly. And it has an important corollary: that this mistake must be marked down especially to liberalism, because of its capitulation to Bismarck and its self-betrayal. Approached in this way, the complicated triangular relationship between state, liberalism and the Catholic Centre Party has often formed part of a broader account of Imperial Germany's political misdevelopment. On this reading, liberalism was the original culprit for endorsing the illiberalism of the *Kulturkampf*, thus consolidating the power of the Centre. The Centre, in turn, is seen to have revenged itself on German politics by its subsequent political opportunism. The Centre is therefore viewed as one important part of Germany's political misdevelopment. The irresponsibility with which the party is said to have exercised its key role appears to be both symptom and part-cause of Germany's failure to achieve mature constitutional and political arrangements prior to 1914. Here we have the contribution of the Centre Party to the persistence of the authoritarian state. This view of the Centre and its significance has remained largely undisturbed by the new wave of historians who, in the wake of Fritz Fischer, have offered such a fruitful re-examination of Imperial Germany. Their analysis of liberal weakness has certainly deepened our understanding of the role played in this process, not just by the *Kulturkampf*, but also by economic compromises (the 'marriage of iron and rye') and political calculation from above (Bismarck's 'Caesarism'). But the Centre itself has been mostly untouched by such revisionism. It is seen as a party which emerged strengthened out of the interaction between Bismarckian calculation and liberal frailty; but it is still seen as a creature apart. It appears to be subject to a political dynamic of its own. If we turn to Eckart Kehr, for example, from whose pioneering questions so much recent work has proceeded, we find this quite clearly. In Kehr's classic analysis of *Sammlungspolitik* at the end of the 1890s, the reconciling of the National Liberals and the Conservatives is interpreted as part of a complex trade-off between different economic and social interests: bourgeoisie and Junker landowners, iron and rye, the navy and agricultural tariffs. But the Centre, Kehr tells us, was won for the Tirpitz plan by the promise of *political* hegemony alone.[8] Here, again, we have the idea of the Centre as a denominationally based and politically opportunist party: a special case.

Our view of the Centre as a party which does not fit into the political landscape of Imperial Germany has, ironically, been reinforced by writing from within the Catholic camp. Sometimes this writing has been hagiographical, tracing back a pedigree of social and political Catholicism which leads inexorably to the present. Other writers have criticized such cosy ancestor worship, preferring to stress the stifling conformity of 'milieu-Catholicism'.[9] In both cases, though, the long-term persistence of such a Catholic milieu has been central to the account; and this also makes it difficult to avoid seeing the Centre Party as a special case. For if the party was the 'action committee of political Catholicism',[10] embedded within the Catholic milieu or subculture, then it is hard to see how it might be judged like other parties. The view of the Centre as a special case is therefore also, in part, a legacy of the historical and cultural special identity of German Catholicism, dating back in its modern form at least to the middle of the last century and powerfully reinforced by the *Kulturkampf*. In a famous article in 1906, Julius Bachem urged his co-religionists to leave the 'Centre tower'.[11] The defence works of this tower, originally designed to protect the party, continue to obscure it.

To refer to the continuing relevance of the Centre tower is, of course, in itself to acknowledge how much truth there is in the notion of a distinctively Catholic milieu in Germany, of which the Centre Party was one component. The present article does not seek to deny the existence of such a milieu, but to explore some of its divisions and its limitations as an explanatory tool. These divisions deserve more emphasis, nowhere more than in the case of the Centre. And in investigating some of them, it may be possible that the Centre will seem a little less odd. As I have argued elsewhere, the Centre was indeed in some respects a special case.[12] The question is: how special? This essay attempts to present the Centre in a way which allows parallels to be drawn with other political parties. For only if we recognize the existence of such parallels is it possible to see what was truly distinctive about the Centre Party and its relationship to German Catholics. The essay accordingly has three parts. The first takes up a major concern of current historiography and looks at the Centre in its role as a vehicle for economic and social interests. Here, both the successes and the failures of the Centre parallel the experience of other parties. The second section turns to the central question of religion, and considers the importance for Centre politics both of the church and of Catholic faith and piety more broadly. The argument here lays stress on the divisions as well as the elements of unity in 'Catholic Germany'. Both had great importance for Centre politics. In the last section of this essay I try to bring these themes together, looking at the community of sentiment and interest which held the Centre and its constituency together, but also suggesting the rifts which were readily apparent by 1914.

II

One way of putting the Centre and its relationship to German Catholics into fresh perspective is to look, as historians of other parties have done, at the play of economic interests and antagonisms within the party. This enterprise has been relatively neglected, and understandably so. If we consider Centre Party programmes between 1871 and 1914 they seem astonishingly bland and unchanging when they address economic and social issues. They talked of an 'even-handed justice', offering something to all social classes but not too much to any one. The Centre projected itself as a 'true people's party, embracing all classes and estates.'[13] Historians, in turn, have regularly drawn attention to this even-handedness of approach, noting that the Centre included among its supporters every social group, from Westphalian miners to Silesian aristocrats, from Bavarian peasants to the Rhenish bourgeoisie. Historians within the tradition of political Catholicism have given this point a particular emphasis, underlining the all-embracing nature of the social Catholicism espoused by the Centre. They have constructed a family tree which depicts the development of a Catholic social policy going beyond simple charity, and its adoption by the Centre Party in response to the social needs of its constituency. The milestones on this road are usually marked out on the one side by the writings and activities of key individuals like Franz von Buss and Bishop Ketteler, and on the other side by the gradual creation of a dense and comprehensive Catholic associational life (*Vereinswesen*).[14] The crucial point has always been that within this social Catholic network was something for everyone: workers' associations, businessmen's associations, associations for female domestic servants and male apprentices, associations for peasants and for state steamship employees. In the light of this it is difficult to see the social and economic interests gathered under the aegis of the Centre as having anything in common with the more narrowly class-based interest groups of the other parties: the trade unions and consumer co-operatives of the SPD, the light and heavy industrial interests associated with left-wing and National Liberals respectively, or the much-cited *Bund der Landwirte* whose 'agrarian radicalism overran Conservatism'.[15]

In fact, however, there was a large element of rhetoric in play when the Centre claimed to stand above the vulgar traffic in sectional interests. Its boast of standing above and harmonizing the interests of German Catholics was as misleading in its way as the similar claims of the other parties – all of whom, after all, made some sort of 'universal' claim. The basic pattern of Centre social and economic policy, in fact if not in theory, owed much to the geographical and occupational structure of the German Catholic population. This was not a simple cross section of the overall population of Imperial Germany. Geographically, Centre support constituted a kind of German 'Celtic Fringe' to the west, east and south of the Protestant heartland of the Empire. Sociologically, something between two-thirds and three-quarters of the Reichstag seats habitually won by the Centre were in constituencies where agriculture and small business predominated.[16] This remained the case up to 1914, perpetuated in part by the unchanging constituency boundaries which led to the over-representation of such constituencies. A similar pattern of electoral geography was evident at the state level too. It is possible to show, as I have tried to do elsewhere in detail, that the formation of a vigorous agrarian policy and a commitment to *Mittelstandspolitik*, in line with the importance of peasants, shopkeepers and small businessmen as voters, was basic to Centre economic and social policy. It is, in fact, one of the keys to the party's politics overall. It is difficult to get the Centre into perspective without taking account of its support for agricultural tariffs, meat import quotas and anti-margarine legislation, its advocacy of laws against itinerant trade, department stores and 'unfair competition', its call for the re-introduction of a modified guild system and other measures to preserve the 'honest craftsman'.[17]

The most detailed elaboration of such policies came after the end of the *Kulturkampf*. It was in the 1890s that the Centre supported the removal of vending machines from railway stations in the interests of shopkeepers.[18] It was in the same decade that a Rhenish agent of the party complained in the following terms to party leader, Ernst Lieber:

> The Centre has conceded too much to the partially justified complaints of peasants and aristocratic disturbers of the peace, that too little has been done in recent years for agriculture; and the impression has been created that certain gentlemen in the Centre, of whom Herr Deputy Bachem is one, believe they can win back the peasantry through unheard of concessions over the margarine question.[19]

It was the same period which provoked Georg von Hertling's complaint that the Bavarian Centre had turned itself into the party of 'grain tariffs and compulsory guilds'.[20] The orientation of the Centre towards these groups was, however, already evident during the *Kulturkampf*. The basic line of support for pro-craftsman legislation and agricultural protectionism emerged in the 1870s. The rhetoric which accompanied it comes over very clearly, for example, in the anti-semitic articles carried by *Germania* and other Centre papers in that decade.[21] In the years after 1890, as earlier, the principal loser as far as interest politics was concerned was the Catholic working class. It was their material interests which were particularly damaged by Centre economic and fiscal policy, their organizations which came off worst in the party, their individual representatives who found it most difficult to become adopted as official Centre election candidates.[22]

If we look at the Centre from this angle, the one from which other parties have been viewed, we can see that it had features in common with other parties. In the first place, the Centre was, like other parties, a vehicle for particular economic interests; and the nature of those interests helps us to explain the political alignment of the party, at least from the end of the 1870s. For alongside the short-term inconsistency of Centre policy was an underlying tendency to align itself with the right and against the left. And this can be related, in turn, to the way in which agrarian-protectionist and pro-*Mittelstand* policies gave the Centre much in common with the Conservatives, while dividing it from the anti-protectionist, pro-consumer position of the left. The importance of this factor can scarcely be exaggerated.[23]

Secondly, and no less important, the role of interest politics can also throw light upon the inconsistency of the Centre on a day-to-day basis. For the Centre was, like other parties, not simply a vehicle for material interests; it was also subject to the pressure of, and conflict between, the interests it claimed to serve. Internal divisions were a cause of great tension within the party. Its leaders believed at various points in the 1890s that the very existence of the Centre was at stake because of sectional strife of this kind.[24] In this respect, then, the Centre shared the problems of the other parties, perhaps particularly – and ironically – those of the liberal parties. The very fact that the Centre claimed to be a people's party, appealing across class lines, made it exceptionally vulnerable to the gap between rhetoric and performance. The Centre's boast that it was a universal party only gave it universal problems. And it was the attempt to reconcile one set of conflicting interests with another which accounts for much of the tactical trimming – between first, second and third readings of parliamentary bills, for example – and the seeming unscrupulousness of the Centre. Conflicts of this kind occurred most obviously where the party had to appear to be representing Catholic working-class aspirations. They occurred more generally when Centre leaders tried to reconcile the demands of town and country, agriculture and industry, producer and consumer. Even within the legislative field dignified with the single label *Mittelstandspolitik*, there were irreconcilable conflicts of interest over which party policy makers tripped.[25]

The evenhanded justice to which the Centre's spokesmen paid lip service was often then, in reality, a dangerous tightrope dance. Nor were these difficulties confined to balancing above particular interests. In a sense the course preferred by most party leaders created problems with rank and file supporters of all classes. When it came to economic and social policy, an increasingly bourgeois leadership felt itself to be potentially isolated from popular (and often aristocratic) aspirations, a feeling which the ending of the *Kulturkampf* reinforced. The leadership, as we have seen, was prepared to enunciate a selectively anti-industrialist and anti-capitalist rhetoric for the benefit of agrarian, petty-bourgeois and working-class supporters. The aristocratic wing of the party also, for the most part, expected gestures in this direction. But the leadership's own position, even in the 1870s and 1880s, was generally more affirmative, privately less critical of economic developments in the Reich. Ludwig Windthorst and his colleagues made sure that the Centre kept its distance from the stridently anti-capitalist and corporatist ideas being urged from some quarters. They headed off extreme corporatist demands from Catholic master craftsmen, just as they scotched initiatives like the reactionary 'Haid Theses' of Karl Löwenstein and his aristocratic circle.[26] Windthorst's successors, spitefully dubbed the 'Bachem-Lieber family' by their enemies in the party, were still more committed to a German future under industrial and commercial capitalism.[27] Their scornful hostility towards the neo-feudal corporatism of the Oberdörffer programme in the 1890s was characteristic.[28] This stance readily became a source of tension which threatened to isolate the leadership over practical economic and fiscal measures. Taken together with the particular conflicts of interest already noted, this latent antagonism left powerful traces on the Centre. It explains some of the leadership's parliamentary slipperiness. And, along with other divisions which I want to consider below, where the political fault lines ran in the same direction, this also accounts for a good deal of the extra-parliamentary demagogy in which party leaders indulged during the Wilhelmine period.

III

Approaching the Centre through the role played by economic interests can expose some of the springs of action within the party. It also allows us to see the features of the Centre which it had in common with other parties. But such an approach also raises problems. Recent writing on

Imperial Germany has sometimes seemed to present an overly mechanical account of politics dominated by leagues and pressure groups. In the rejection of a narrowly political kind of historical account there is clearly the danger of reducing the politics simply to the play and interplay of interests.

This general caveat has particular application in the case of the Centre. If we look at the Centre as a 'normal' party, stressing the role of the interests, an obvious question arises: do we not, of necessity, undervalue the importance of the Catholic Church and of religious faith more generally? It is to this point that I now want to turn. There undoubtedly is the risk that, in reading Centre politics against the grain, one reduces its Catholic quality to a merely contingent element. This clearly needs to be avoided. It is, nevertheless, equally important to try to break down the imposing monolith of 'Catholic Germany' and the place of the Centre Party within it. Looking at the clamour of economic interests is an indirect way of doing this. But we can also question directly the role of religion in the party. There is no reason why this should necessarily diminish rather than increase the importance we attach to the religious impulse and its political resonance. At least we can aim not to take it for granted. In pursuing this issue in the present section, I want to deal in turn with the significance for the Centre of the Church itself and of Catholic faith and piety in a broader sense.

Research has established quite clearly that the Centre was not a clerical party. It was not the political arm of the German hierarchy, still less of Rome. On this issue at least we can take Centre politicians at face value when they stressed with wearying regularity that the Centre was a *political* party. The driving force in the Centre was lay, not clerical, and it is worth noting here the contrast with Italy and France. In Italy the Church demanded a Catholic boycott of politics in the newly unified state, and no political party on the lines of the German Centre emerged until 1919. The situation was similar in France, where the bishops first prevented *Ralliement* by obstructing the political organization of Catholics, then damned the movement with their support. In Germany by contrast, as in Switzerland and Belgium, the Centre was inspired and brought into existence by laymen, and relations with the ecclesiastical establishment were frequently strained. The very naming of the party was a deliberate political act, designed to bury the memory of the unsuccessful Catholic Fraction in the Prussian Chamber of Deputies in the previous decades, and to signify that narrowly clerical politics would be eschewed.[29] Tension between Church and party was, like so many other disagreements, naturally muted during the *Kulturkampf*. But even in the 1870s and 1880s there was friction when Centre leaders believed that some members of the hierarchy were too cynical and too pliant in dealing at the diplomatic, non-political level with state authorities. On the other side, Rome and a number of German bishops were suspicious of the 'hotspurs' in the Centre, whose overtly political approach cut across the lines of clerical authority.[30]

These differences underlay the poor relations between Centre leaders and Rome over the winding up of the *Kulturkampf*, when Pope Leo XIII, his advisers and German episcopal supporters (above all Bishop Kopp) negotiated with Bismarck over the heads of the party leadership. The mutual bitterness caused by the conflict between a 'Windthorst solution' and a 'Kopp solution' to the *Kulturkampf* has been well documented. The crucial point, perhaps, is the determination of the Centre's lay leaders not to become politically subordinate to Rome and its German episcopal allies. Windthorst refused in 1887 to trim the party's line over Bismarck's *Septennat* in order to smooth the way for a diplomatic solution of the *Kulturkampf*, and resistance to honeyed clerical tones became a matter of principle in the Centre. Windthorst's successors shared his desire to 'make German, not Roman politics' and Ernst Lieber was as angry as his predecessor in 1887 when Rome made similar approaches at the time of Chancellor Caprivi's military bill in 1893.[31] These overtures, like the earlier ones, were rejected. Of course there were many issues on which Centre policy mirrored that of the Church; this was generally true of matters which concerned the family and education, as well as the freedom of the Church. The party was also happy on occasion to receive concessions to the Church as a reward for its support of government policy. This was the case with the return of previously impounded Church property, and with permission for the banned Redemptorist order to return to Germany. Yet the Centre jealously guarded its right to strike out independently as a political party. It is characteristic that in the 1890s Lieber and the Centre leadership in Prussia decided to seek reform of the Rhineland electoral law, rather than repeal of the anti-Jesuit law, in exchange for its support of the proposed Mittelland canal.[32]

A similar desire to resist clerical tutelage informed many of those vital auxiliaries of the Centre, the Catholic associations (*Vereine*). Germany was 'the classic land of the Catholic associational movement',[33] and there was a close connection between the Centre and organizations like the Pius Association,[34] the Boniface Association and the various occupational aasociations for peasants, craftsmen and workers. But this evidence speaks against the Centre as a political arm of the Church, not for it. The associations, like the Centre itself, reflected the intensely laicized nature of German Catholicism, compared with Italy or France. The associations were essentially lay creations; the Bonifice Association, significantly enough, owed much to Ignaz von Döllinger.[35] They were voluntary in form, and thus formed a part of that generally burgeoning *Vereinswesen* of the nineteenth century.[36] This was true even when individual priests were actively involved. It was precisely this 'modern' principle of voluntary association which, as with the case of the Centre itself, antagonized the more conservative episcopal mind.[37] And the more general the scope of such organizations, the greater the suspicion which was likely to be aroused. Occupational organizations, and other associations with a clearly prescribed purpose, might be acceptable – even though Lorenz Werthmann's *Deutscher Caritas-Verband* had to wait eighteen years before it was grudgingly approved by the German Bishops' Conference.[38] But the conflict over the founding of the *Volksverein für das katholische Deutschland* in 1890 provides the most telling example of the gap which separated both the Centre Party and self-consciously lay Catholic associations from clerical conceptions of organization. The Centre's leaders fought energetically to prevent this mass organization of German Catholics from becoming an instrument of the hierarchy. Bishop Korum of Trier and Bishop Hartmann of Cologne were especially anxious to see the *Volksverein* become a pliable instrument of the church authorities, aimed against the newly-formed Evangelical League. But Windthorst and his colleagues successfully fought off these attempts, and later efforts to clericalize the *Volksverein* were just as firmly resisted by Franz Brandts and Karl Trimborn, the association's organizers.[39]

The Centre was not a clerical party, therefore, in the sense that it acted as the political arm of the Church. Much more complex is the question of how far the party nevertheless embodied a specifically Catholic faith and piety in its politics. The centre prided itself on the Protestants in its parliamentary fractions, and on the fact that it received electoral support from the Protestant Guelphs, the Hanoverians who rejected Hanover's incorporation into Prussia in 1866. Beyond that, the influential Bachemite wing of the party advocated a Christian, non-denominational course for the Centre with some vigour. But this was not, of course, to be achieved until the 1940s. Prior to 1914 the Protestant element in the Centre was as much a token as the Protestant presence in the Christian trade unions. With the tiny exception of the Guelphs, being Catholic was a necessary if not sufficient condition of voting for the Centre. Not all Catholics voted Centre; but virtually all Centre voters were Catholics. It would be perverse to deny that common faith – and the belief that this common faith should have public as well as private resonance – formed a common denominator within the party. It was this question of the public and political expression of faith which formally divided adherents of the Centre from the many Catholics who supported and were even deputies of other political parties. It was this which also divided leaders of the Centre from prominent Catholic figures in public life like the Bavarian Prime Minister Lutz and the Imperial Chancellor Hohenlohe, who looked on 'Ultramontanism' with some disdain.[40]

This common faith informed the everyday reality of Centre politics in countless ways, large and small. For party leaders and for ordinary voters, faith and politics were closely interwoven. The annual assemblies of German Catholics served in place of party conferences. Centre leaders endowed churches and timed rallies to coincide with major religious festivals like Whitsuntide. The party press carried articles on the German Bishops' Conference, on Catholic missionary activities and on the latest insult mounted against the faith by pro-cremationists or the advocates of non-denominational schools. In the countryside and small towns especially, it was common for religious observance to be closely combined with Centre meetings (and collections), and it was not unknown for a Catholic burial ceremony to serve as a rallying of the faithful for electoral purposes.[41] The pulpit was commonly used for political exhortations,[42] while defence-of-the-Church slogans were an obvious weapon in the Centre's armoury. Moreover, the Centre was not above trying to influence male voting intentions by awakening the apprehensions of female members of the household about threats to the Church.[43] This, of course, underlines the importance of the local clergy for the party. For although the Centre was not a clerical party, in the sense that it took orders from Rome or the German hierarchy, the parish clergy – far more than the bishops – helped to set the tone of the Centre, as well as providing a vital cadre of unpaid party functionaries at the local level.

Even the political language of the Centre betrayed the party's religious roots. While liberals addressed their supporters as citizens and the SPD its adherents as comrades, the Centre tended to see its supporters as 'the Catholic people', or even as the Catholic 'flock'. The most commonplace ideas found expression in a religious idiom. We encounter references to the practice of reading a pro-Centre newspaper as the 'baptismal certificate' of the modern Catholic.[44] Again, we find capitalism, socialism and militarism described, along with unbelief and self-indulgence, as the 'five wounds' of Europe.[45] Similarly, Windthorst remarked at one particularly fraught political moment that going to Berlin was '*ein wahrer Kreuzgang*'.[46]

All of this shows how necessary it is to see the Centre as firmly located within a distinctively Catholic milieu. But it is nevertheless misleading to think of this German-Catholic milieu or the Centre Party as a seamless web. The capacity of a common faith to provide the Centre with a special cohesion almost certainly appeared greater and more complete than it actually was, just as Catholics tended to exaggerate the monolithic strength of, say, Freemasonry. Adherence to the Church and its collective life provided the Centre and its followers with a common ambience; it did not necessarily provide them with a common purpose. In this case the medium was not the message. The shared religious idiom of the party was, in the end, just a shared idiom; it did not transcend substantive political differences such as those described above. It is important to recognize, in fact, that the rhetoric of shared faith was often very consciously wielded by Centre leaders as a weapon to try and achieve unity where little existed. In the troubled 1890s especially, the Catholic card was played to distract attention from other differences. Ernst Lieber was notable for this, but the pattern was more general.[47] Appeals by the Centre leadership for Catholic unity thus had a purpose similar to appeals in other political parties for agrarian or national unity. And in the one case, as in the others, such appeals could fail. When Windthorst referred to the *Kreuzgang* involved in going to Berlin, he was after all alluding to rifts in the Centre which the common religious bond was unable to bridge. His successors were often to complain that since the *Kulturkampf* the appeal to Catholic unity fell on deaf ears.

Appeals of this kind could, in fact, backfire. This has to be borne in mind when evaluating the role of the clergy in the Centre. Their pastoral zeal was undoubtedly utilized by the party for very worldly political purposes. But a price had to be paid for this. The use of priests by party leaders, especially at the local level, not only antagonized the more conservative bishops; it also antagonized dissident groups within the Centre who resented the mobilization of the clergy behind heavy-handed drives for unity by the party leadership. Priests who acted as troubleshooters in this way ran the risk of being indicted as 'heaven's dragoons'.[48] In the last resort, the vital role played by the clergy in the party press, in local party organizations, in the *Volksverein* and at elections meant that they were themselves drawn into political disputes on different sides. The frequent arguments over the selection of parliamentary candidates show clearly how local priests came to be divided on political lines. In this respect the political fault lines within the Centre also ran through the clergy.

Common religious sentiment, then, did not always paper over the cracks within Catholic Germany and the Centre Party; it could even make them wider. But there is a further point here. The nature of that common religious sentiment could sometimes *itself* be a source of disunity. This becomes clear if we turn to another telling use by Windthorst of religious idiom. Talking in the 1880s to a group of Centre confidants, he noted waspishly that 'the Jews nest happily in Catholic areas because the Catholics are lazy; our clergy preach too much about the birds and flowers of the field, which neither sow nor reap, yet receive the means to live'.[49] This was by no means a random observation. It falls into a consistent pattern of criticism among the increasingly bourgeois leadership of the Centre: that the much-remarked phenomenon of 'Catholic backwardness' was partly the fault of Catholics themselves and their religiosity. It was, for example, commonly argued that too many intelligent young Catholics entered the priesthood rather than business or the professions.[50] This sentiment had a cutting edge directed not so much against clerical influence in the party, but against an excess of piety in general.

On this very basic point Catholic Germany showed signs of division, and these were certainly evident in the Centre. To understand this we need to recall some important changes in the tenor of German Catholicism from the middle of the nineteenth century. This period witnessed the emergence of a powerful current of emotionally laden, often very sentimental popular piety. This was marked by new and more external forms of devotion, of which the most obvious were the veneration of the Sacred Heart and the cult of the Virgin.[51] New saints were adopted, established ones venerated with a new intensity, and pilgrimages like those to Aachen, Altötting and Kevelaer underwent a considerable revival.[52] The new piety was reinforced by the popular missions of the 1850s and 1860s, often Jesuit-led, and it was warmly encouraged by Pope Pius IX.[53]

The founders of the Centre were less than enthusiastic about these developments. Doubt on Infallibility was accompanied by suspicion of the Jesuits and coolness towards popular devotional extravagance.[54] But the *Kulturkampf*, which expelled the Jesuits and heightened popular piety, also had the immediate effect of closing the latent gap between the values of Centre politicians and popular Catholic religiosity. Partly, the *Kulturkampf* brought a significant number of Catholic aristocrats into Centre politics, and in matters of faith they were far less troubled by the austere scruples of some of the party's bourgeois founding fathers. This was certainly true of Karl von Löwenstein, Burghard von Schorlemer-Alst and Felix von Loë, and other members of the Bavarian, Westphalian and Rhenish aristocracy.[55] In addition, the Centre's national and local leaders – the merchants and lawyers who provided the backbone of the Catholic club or *Kasino* movement of the 1860s and 1870s – rallied instinctively to the cause in the face of overt state repression which included the seizing of the consecrated host and the widespread imprisoning of bishops and priests.[56] Disquiet about popular piety was muted when the state forbade 'political' pilgrimages and torch-light processions, or prevented religious pictures from being displayed in windows. Doubts about the Marian cult were overridden when military force was used to disperse Catholic crowds gathered at Marpingen in 1876, one of a number of places where the Virgin was popularly believed to have appeared.[57] Windthorst attacked the expulsion of the Jesuits, despite his lack of sympathy for the order. Julius Bachem, later to be accused by some of his co-religionists of disloyalty to the Catholic cause, had an experience which was typical of those years. He found himself plunged by the *Kulturkampf* into the less rarified air of religious sentiment outside cosmopolitan Cologne. He served as chairman of the parish council in St Ursula, a markedly pious community of peasants and craftsmen just outside the walls of the Rhineland's principal city. He also found himself (successfully) defending those who were charged with breach of the peace and deception after the events in Marpingen.[58]

With the ending of the *Kulturkampf*, unity of sentiment at this most basic level was strained, as it was at others. On the one hand, popular piety did not diminish, rather the contrary. Pilgrimages were held on an even larger scale,[59] and new places of local pilgrimage emerged at the end of the nineteenth century, like the grave of Elisabetha Bona ('Good Beth') in the Württemberg hamlet of Reute. Saints like the Tyrolean St Notburga and other 'patrons of the peasantry' became the objects of a new veneration.[60] At the same time the cults of Mary and the Sacred Heart spread and encouraged popular belief in divine intercessions in the profane world. The *Messenger of the Sacred Heart* informed its readers of miracles which included cases of cattle disease prevented by a novena, a skull broken by a horse's kick which was healed by a prayer to Mary, and a meditation in honour of the sacred hearts of Jesus, Mary and Joseph which secured exemption from military service.[61]

Such forms of religiosity provoked a backlash within parts of Catholic Germany, above all among the Catholic bourgeoisie. The reaction came particularly from an impatience among university-educated Catholics with what was seen as popular credulity, as well as with the growing volume of kitsch which accompanied it: the gingerbread Virgins, the mass-produced flasks of holy water, the sentimental and superstition-laden popular novels of writers like Joseph Spillmann.[62] Karl Muth's well-known criticism of Spillmann's writings in the *Veremundus* pamphlets was paralleled by Julius Bachem's objection to devotional kitsch like that purveyed after 'the miracle of Marpingen'.[63] In both cases the criticism was based on more than dislike simply of vulgarity and sentimentality. The extravagance of popular religiosity was seen by key sections of the Catholic bourgeoisie as desperately embarrassing, as a poor advertisement for *their* kind of thoroughly modern Catholicism. In some ways, in fact, the 1890s and the early years of the new century saw a renewal of the debates which had taken place in the 1860s, centered above all on Döllinger. In the later period it was Reform Catholics like Hermann Schell and Albert Ehrlich whose role is best known. But this debate was located within a broader set of arguments about Catholic 'backwardness' and how this might be overcome. Prominent Centre politicians played a major part in this debate. Partly, of course, in the name of Catholic parity, they attacked the state for discrimination in areas such as the employment of Catholics in the bureaucracy. But they also turned their attacks against certain features of Catholic Germany itself. Hertling, for example, used the platform of the Görres Society to call for a less cloying and inward-looking form of Catholicism.[64] The Bachem cousins, Julius and Karl, represented a similar viewpoint on a wide range of issues, from devotionalia to papal jubilees. In a telling intervention, Julius Bachem was closely involved in trying to distance German Catholics from the Taxil hoax of the 1890s,[65] when the willingness of the pious to embrace the most extravagant 'revelations' about Freemasonry caused acute embarrassment among all those who saw Catholicism – in Hermann Schell's words – as 'A Principle of Progress'.[66] It is noteworthy that the Augustinus Press Association, in which the Bachems were prominent, attempted to keep potentially embarrassing material like this out of the Centre press.

On these and similar questions the rifts within Catholic Germany extended to the faith itself. To many prominent figures in the Centre, leaving the tower did not just mean keeping Rome and the bishops at arm's length from the party; it also meant presenting a more appetizingly 'modern' form of faith to the outside world. It is therefore appropriate that the debates over Reform Catholicism and Modernism in Germany should have overlapped so closely with the debate over the nature of the Centre Party – the so-called *Zentrumsstreit*.[67] It is also significant that this debate, in turn, overlapped with the conflict in the Centre over class and sectional interests. For these different debates had a common origin in the Catholic experience of being treated as second-class citizens in the new German Empire. It is to this common experience in the broadest sense, and to the reaction which followed from it, that I want finally to turn.

IV

The Centre was a vehicle for the material interests of German Catholics; it also spoke for Catholic religious sentiment in the political arena. To look at both of these roles is to take two different cross sections through the same world. In the final section of the essay I want to consider this world as a whole. The material and the religious were closely interwoven in the politics of the Centre because the Catholic experience had made them so. Feelings both of religious outrage and of material grievance were products of a common pattern of discrimination and repression which Catholics met with at the hands of state power and its liberal enthusiasts. During the *Kulturkampf*, for example, the attack on Catholic orders and charitable foundations was certainly intended as an assault on religious institutions which the state and liberal *Kulturkämpfer* viewed as medieval remnants. But it was also a broader attack on the 'dead hand' of the Church, seen by state and liberals alike as an obstacle to the emancipation of social and civic energies in the new Reich.[68] The *Kulturkampf*, in fact, deserved its rather grandiose label as a 'struggle of civilizations'. It was an offensive, not just on the forms of a particular faith or even on the power of the Catholic Church as such, but on a whole way of life which was seen from outside as disgracefully backward. In the eyes of an Adalbert Falk or a liberal newspaper like the *National-Zeitung*, the religious and the material were two sides of the same coin: 'going to Canossa will bring us no railways', as one writer revealingly put it.[69] Excluding religious orders from teaching and nursing, expropriating the charitable foundations and recasting the schools would not only free Catholics from their mental shackles; these measures were also, so it was believed, a prerequisite for the development of a superior social and moral order.

The Catholic, in short, was under attack as believer, as citizen and as *homo oeconomicus*. He – and she – responded in kind.[70] Where state and liberals saw a mesh of values and institutions to be attacked, Catholics saw a mesh of values and institutions to be defended. They hid the renegade priest as a spiritual leader, but also as the man who defended the community through the craftsmens' or peasants' association.[71] They defended the orders and foundations as agencies of Christian charity; but they also viewed their demise as the prelude to a harsher regime for those who were marginal to the brave new economic world. Educational reform was resisted because it signalled the eventual arrival of the non-denominational school; but it also meant more rigorously enforced school attendance, threatening the loss of labour from farm or workshop and raising expectations among children. Like other measures of liberal governmental reform, it was feared as a threat to the piety of the Catholic family. But it was also thought to presage the overturning of the family as a finely balanced unit of work or production.[72] It is noteworthy that the very forms of popular piety noted earlier betrayed the material context which lent them meaning. Cattle disease and kicks from horses were the disasters against which protection was sought from the Virgin or the Sacred Heart. The saints who enjoyed local popularity were the patrons of the peasant, the craftsman or the worker. The spiritual and the material are therefore difficult to separate cleanly. What is clear is that the state, especially but not only in the period of the *Kulturkampf*, was a focus of Catholic fears and resentments. It shared this role with liberalism, as a moral and material creed personified in the figure of the distant banker, lawyer or academic. The socialist journalist or functionary later joined the demonology. All of these, like the gendarme or the arrogant railway, postal or agricultural official, were seen as olympian outsiders who had as little feeling for the everyday needs of Catholic communities as they had for the Catholic faith.

It was apprehensions of this kind which the Centre Party was able to harness. It addressed itself directly to a Catholic *grande peur*, which it heightened by painting a vivid picture of the threat posed to stable and pious communities from 'outside'.[73] During the *Kulturkampf* in Baden, a liberal newspaper depicted the party's approach in the following terms:

> There are two ways of being popular. Either one represents the interests of the people with perseverance and selflessness, while trying to move the people itself towards better insight and greater cultivation; this is one way, but it presupposes the possession of certain qualities of

> character. The second way consists in going to the people in public houses, flattering them, abusing others and, depending on the audience, inflaming their passions with rough pleasantries and vulgarity. If they are really common then you have to outbid them, until they say: He's a good fellow, he's the sort of person we like! This second approach is a perfect likeness of the method which the ultramontane party has adopted as its own.[74]

The source here is naturally suspect, and reveals a good deal about the fateful arrogance of German liberals. But even making allowances for this, the description of the Centre's political style identifies a truth with relevance beyond Baden. The Centre's vigorous and highly coloured populism was all the more natural during the *Kulturkampf*, when German Catholics of different classes shared a real sense of being both oppressed and derided. Even those Catholics who were themselves lawyers, academics or well-established businessmen had their language sharpened by the experience of discrimination. Catholic officials were subject to discriminatory action. Businessmen found themselves boycotted. A would-be academic like Hermann Cardauns, later editor of the *Kölnische Volkszeitung*, was thwarted in his original choice of career.[75] Even police measures and the experience of incarceration were felt by Catholics of all classes, as a flourishing genre of prison memoirs showed.[76] The 'fit' between the experience of leaders and led, of Centre politicians and their broader constituency, was very close during the *Kulturkampf*. All, in one way or another, were touched by anti-Catholic repression and, perhaps even more, derision. Beneficiaries of charitable foundations were labelled 'beggar-women' and lower-class Catholics were generally assumed to be exceptionally ill-educated and feckless.[77] Bourgeois Catholics could only smart at observations like that made by one academic commentator, to the effect that Catholicism was able to sustain itself only in wine-drinking areas where rational thought was at a premium.[78] All Catholics were, to some degree, outsiders in a hostile world.

During the *Kulturkampf*, then, the Centre was the political voice of a pariah community. It was this which helped to give the party its support among four-fifths of voting Catholics and accounted for the relatively high degree of party unity in the 1870s and into the 1880s. Between the 1880s and 1914, however, the situation threatened to change. The explanation for this does not lie in some easily-plotted change in what the party stood for; it was not a 'religious' party during the *Kulturkampf* and a party of material interests thereafter. The two were as difficult to separate in later years as they were during the *Kulturkampf* itself. As I have tried to suggest, it is much more plausible to see the divisions within the Centre as running through both the material and the spiritual strands of the party. Differences over forms of religious piety, like sectional conflicts of interest, existed during the *Kulturkampf*; but both were held in check by the presence of an external threat and the common sense of belonging to a pariah community. The ending of the *Kulturkampf* in its overt form weakened the external threat, thus highlighting the differences within the Catholic population and bringing them more into the open.

Here we return to those divisions within Catholic Germany which are so important for an understanding of the Centre Party. After the ending of the open *Kulturkampf*, the sense of forming a pariah community continued to provide a common denominator for Catholics. But the reactions to this varied sharply. For large sections of the Catholic peasantry, *Mittelstand* and working class – despite their other differences – the sense of alienation from the social and political order not only remained powerful; it also continued to be worn almost as a badge of identity. Beyond the end of the formal *Kulturkampf*, this feeling continued to manifest itself in a widespread, if often inchoate, anti-capitalism and anti-industrialism. This was accompanied by a profound distrust of the professional middle classes who were seen as central to this alien order, and in which Protestants and Jews were clearly over-represented. Nor did Catholics willingly identify with the power and civilizing mission of the German nation and state.[79] They were as little inclined to support the moral and mechanical symbols of German Culture in the Wilhelmine period as they had been to embrace its equivalents during the *Kulturkampf*. In the 1870s they had boycotted Sedan Day; in the 1900s they turned their backs on the navy.[80] Instead they inhabited a world at once larger and smaller than that of the Wilhelmine nation-state. It was larger in that it drew moral strength from 'the prisoner in the Vatican' and shared the devotional forms of co-religionists in Italy and France. It was smaller in its orientation towards the local and parochial – socially to the village or working-class 'black quarter',[81] spiritually to the Bavarian shrine or the miners' or peasants' saint. The material, the religious and the political thus continued to work together in sustaining a self-conscious distance from the established order in the Kaiser's Germany.

Among the leadership of the Centre Party the reaction to Catholic pariah status was rather different. In this they echoed a shift of sentiment within broad sections of the Catholic bourgeoisie. They did not wish Catholic Germany to persist as a Cinderella community. They wanted Catholics to become insiders rather than remain outsiders, to 'come into their own' as the phrase went. If this aspiration was clear in the writings of Reform Catholics, it can be discerned much more generally in the less ghetto-ridden and more affirmative tone of Catholic academics, writers and publicists. Karl Muth's *Hochland*, the *Görres Staatslexikon* and the *Kölnische Volkszeitung* are representative. A comparable, if less powerful trend was evident among Catholic businessmen. In all of these circles, from which Centre leaders themselves were increasingly drawn, there was a marked concern, from about the late 1880s, with Catholic 'backwardness' and how to overcome it. This was perceived partly as a matter of encouraging more Catholics to become entrepreneurs and professionals. But it also found expression in the Centre Party campaign to achieve 'parity' for Catholics in the state bureaucracy. This was what Max Weber meant by 'bonbons'. At the same time, this more positive stance had its counterpart in the Centre's highly deliberate and considered support for national legislation like the civil code and the navy programme. Support of this kind was to serve as a reminder of the Centre's pivotal political position; it was also intended as an earnest of good intentions.[82]

Here we can see the size of the gap which, potentially and sometimes in practice, separated popular Catholic sentiment from the mental world of Centre leaders and their circles. The expressions of discontent from below with party notables were one sign of this. The leadership itself recognized the gap. They also acknowledged – at least in private – their impatience with many aspects of popular sentiment. If we look at the reasons for this impatience, we can see how, once again, the economic, the religious and the political went together. Craftsmen who were thought to give up their sons too readily to the priesthood were also criticized for their obsession with compulsory guilds. The peasantry whose veneration of local saints occasioned unease were also castigated for the 'idiocy' of their agrarian demands.[83] When Karl Bachem complained about the weight of these agrarian or master-artisan special interests within the party, he linked his criticism with the frustration he felt about the political 'nonentities' that interest-politics spawned.[84] For these nonentities were at best useless, at worst openly obstructive, when the Centre sought to demonstrate, through 'constructive' legislative activity, that Catholics were worthy of a domestic place in the sun. Centre leaders and their allies looked forward to the parity of esteem which, they believed, could and should be enjoyed by German Catholics within the German nation-state. Popular Catholic truculence, whether stubborn adherence to the benediction of cows or equally stubborn hostility to the navy, let down the cause.

In the light of all this, it is worth returning to a central question of this essay: how did the Centre actually manage to retain its constituency? Part of the answer is that it did not. Unchanged constituency boundaries and the geographical concentration of Catholics helped to disguise the drift of Catholics away from the Centre between the 1870s and 1914. Indeed, only female suffrage arrested this long-term decline.[85] Before 1914 there were several occasions, as we have already seen, when it was genuinely feared that the Centre would disintegrate. That this did not occur was not due to any innate cohesion within the Catholic milieu; rather, it can be attributed in large measure to the political plasticity and opportunism of the Centre leadership. At one level, the appeal to Catholic unity was calculatedly produced at moments of serious internal conflict. If this entailed the encouragement of sentiments about which Centre leaders were themselves uneasy, then private scruple had to take second place to public necessity. Similarly, party leaders frequently went against their own inclinations in accommodating a range of (often contradictory) material demands. Bachem's 'unheard-of concessions over the margarine question' formed only one part of a large pattern of flexible interest-broking. On tariffs and commodity exchange reform, on guilds and department store taxation, the leadership combined private reservations with public enthusiasm in a striking manner. Above all, and integrating these related elements of its appeal, the Centre continued to project itself as the voice of the pariah community. And it did so with populist pathos. Even while Centre leaders embodied bourgeois Catholic aspirations to 'come into their own' in the national community, they also encouraged and underwrote a larger Catholic feeling of remaining in the ghetto. Prominent Centre politicians continued to pick off the easy targets of the *Kulturkampf* era, winning popularity by attacking outsiders like the 'unfeeling' official, the 'impious' professor, the representative of 'mobile' capital. The substance of this was difficult to square with their private views; but just for this reason, the populist style of rhetoric was valuable in shifting attention away from divisions within the Catholic camp. The demagogy of the Centre had been an almost natural and instinctive characteristic of the party during its heroic period. In later years the style became more conscious as it became more central to the unity of the party.[86]

V

Contemporary critics saw the Centre as a special case. They portrayed it as a uniquely irresponsible party which used its key position to further clerical and Catholic interests. I have tried to argue that they were only partly right. The party certainly deserved its reputation for political unreliability. But the horse-trading and opportunism which were so characteristic of the Centre did not occur because the party danced to the tune of Rome, the Jesuits or the German bishops. The Centre was not a clerical party in that sense. Even as the political voice of Catholic Germany it was not the mouthpiece of a monolithic interest. It is true that the daily life of the Church and its institutions provided a common ambience within Centre politics; and the lower clergy played a major role as unpaid party workers. This gave the Centre and its constituency a shared idiom. But the Centre was also divided, just as Catholic Germany itself was. Sometimes conflicts could be resolved by wielding the weapon of Catholic unity but this was not always assured of success, and could even backfire; and sometimes religion itself was a source of discord. The important point is that within the Centre and its constituency it was disharmony as much as harmony which explains the consistent inconsistency of the party.

Here is a starting point, perhaps, for keeping the peculiarity of the Centre in perspective. I have tried to show that when we start to break down Centre relations with 'Catholic Germany', we find many features which are familiar from other parts of the political spectrum. Interest groups, for example, played an important role in the party, as they did elsewhere. But this was not the whole story. The material grievances of Catholics were embedded in a sense of discrimination and exclusion which embraced the religious, the social and the political. The Centre harnessed the widespread sense of resentment among Catholics that they were oppressed and held in contempt by distant authority. In the *Kulturkampf* and beyond, the Centre forged this complex mesh of feelings into a potentially powerful political weapon. But this was not a painless process. At the level of material demands, for example, the interests the Centre claimed to represent were often mutually exclusive. Ironically, the party had much in common here with German liberalism. As with the liberals, it was the very universality of the Centre's rhetoric which gave it universal problems with economic interests. In the case of the Centre the degree of success in dealing with these problems was greater than it was with the liberals, but there was a price to be paid. Reconciling the irreconcilable contributed much to those parliamentary gymnastics for which the Centre became notorious.

Nor was it easy, in broader terms, to translate the pariah mentality of Catholic Germany into a consistent party policy. The leadership hoped to use its pivotal position in the parliamentary arena to assure successive governments about the national *bona fides* of German Catholics. In this it faithfully reflected feeling among broad sections of the Catholic bourgeoisie. In this way, Catholics might achieve parity of esteem in the Reich, becoming insiders rather than staying outsiders. But this ambition cut across the popular Catholic sense of alienation from the established order, which was both widespread and persistent. This basic difference in mentality was the most general expression of the distance between the Centre and its constituency. These differences existed even during the *Kulturkampf*; later years brought them more into the open. This, too, made the Centre appear inconsistent and opportunist when it came to major pieces of legislation. Party leaders often found themselves facing two ways at once; as a result they hedged their parliamentary bets, which only reinforced the party's reputation for unreliability.

It is problems of this kind which also make explicable the persistent strain of populist rhetoric which became so characteristic of the Centre. Demagogy of the kind described in this essay was the plank thrown down by party leaders to bridge the gap between leaders and led. Thus the Centre acquired still more of a reputation for political inconsistency. Opportunism did not derive from the Centre's clerical horse-trading. It was the product of a highly worldly attempt to represent the conflicting demands and sentiments of Catholic Germany, in a political system which combined the opportunities and challenges of universal suffrage with the absence of ministerial responsibility. The Centre was not a strange interloper on the political stage of Imperial Germany; it was a quintessential product of that system. It is perhaps not too much to say that the Centre represents, in microcosm, many of the problems which beset Imperial Germany as a whole. That is the final irony of the place occupied by the Catholic minority and its political party within the Protestant German state.

NOTES

This article was completed in May 1982, and no account could therefore be taken of works published since that date.

1 Friedrich Naumann, *Die politischen Parteien* (Berlin, 1910), p. 39.
2 David Blackbourn, *Class, Religion and Local Politics in Wilhelmine Germany* (London and New Haven, 1980), pp. 23–26.
3 Letter to Naumann, 14 December 1906: Marianne Weber, *Max Weber: A Biography* (New York, 1975), p. 399.
4 Otto von Bismarck, *Gedanken und Erinnerungen*, 2 vols (Stuttgart, 1898), vol. 2, pp. 126–7.
5 Geoff Eley, *Reshaping the German Right* (London and New Haven, 1980), p. 261.
6 Erich Foerster, *Adalbert Falk* (Gotha, 1927), p. 141.
7 Adolf M. Birke, 'Zur Entwicklung und politischen Funktion des bürgerlichen Kulturkampfverständnisses in Preussen-Deutschland', in Dietrich Kurze, ed., *Aus Theorie und Praxis. Festschrift für Hans Herzfeld* (Berlin, 1972), pp. 260–1.
8 Eckart Kehr, *Schlachtflottenbau und Parteipolitik* (Berlin, 1930), p. 205.
9 Thoughtful criticism in Carl Amery, *Die Kapitulation oder deutscher Katholizismus heute* (Reinbek, 1963).
10 M. Rainer Lepsius, 'Parteiensystem und Sozialstruktur: Zum Problem der Demokratisierung der deutschen Gesellschaft', in Wilhelm Abel *et al.*, eds, *Wirtschaft, Geschichte und Wirtschaftsgeschichte. Festschrift zum 65. Geburtstag von Friederich Lütge* (Stuttgart, 1966), p. 391.
11 Julius Bachem, 'Wir müssen aus dem Turm heraus', *Historisch-Politische Blätter*, 1 (1906), pp. 376–86.
12 See note 2 above.
13 This characteristic phrase is taken from the 1903 Reichstag election programme of the Centre. Ludwig Bergsträsser, *Der politische Katholizismus. Dokumente seiner Entwicklung*, 2 vols (Munich, 1921–23), Vol. 2, p. 330.
14 Representative writing of this kind in the contributions by Ernst Heinen and Michael Klöcker in Lothar Koch and Josef G. Stanzel, eds, *Christliches Engagement in Gesellschaft und Politik* (Frankfurt/M., 1979).
15 Hans-Jürgen Puhle, *Agrarische Interessenpolitik und preussischer Konservatismus* (Hanover, 1966), p. 278.
16 Hans Gabler, *Die Entwicklung der Parteien auf landwirtschaftlicher Grundlage von 1871–1912*, dissertation (Berlin, 1934), p. 16.
17 Details in Blackbourn, *Class, Religion and Local Politics*, especially Chapters 1, 5 and 7.
18 Ibid., p. 151.
19 Pfälzische Landesbibliothek Speyer, Ernst Lieber Papers, G. 63, August Grunau to Lieber, 6 February 1886. Anti-margarine legislation was an important demand of the dairy wing of the agrarian lobby.

20 Georg von Hertling, *Erinnerungen aus meinem Leben* 2 vols. (Munich, 1919–20), Vol. 2., p. 54. Cf. Hertling's complaint to Lieber that the Centre was becoming too much a 'Handwerkerpartei': Pfälzische Landesbibliothek Speyer, Lieber Papers, H. 168, Hertling to Lieber, 5 November 1896.

21 Ernst Heinen, 'Antisemitische Strömungen im politischen Katholizismus während des Kulturkampfes', in Ernst Heinen and Hans-Julius Schoeps, eds, *Geschichte in der Gegenwart. Festschrift für Kurt Kluxen* (Paderborn, 1972), pp. 259–99. See also the preceding chapter.

22 See, for example, the chapter on the Centre in Thomas Nipperdey, *Die Organisation der deutschen Parteien vor 1918* (Düsseldorf, 1961).

23 Blackbourn, *Class, Religion and Local Politics*, pp. 23–60.

24 Ibid., pp. 47–50.

25 Ibid., pp. 172–88.

26 Shulamit Volkov, *The Rise of Popular Antimodernism in Germany* (Princeton, 1976), pp. 205–6, 227–28; Karl Buchheim, *Ultramontanismus und Demokratie* (Munich, 1963), pp. 329–31.

27 Frh. v. Fechenbach-Laudenbach, 'Die Familie Bachem-Lieber', *Die Zunkunft*, no. 14 (1896), pp. 155–57. See also Herbert Gottwald, *Zentrum und Imperialismus*, dissertation (Jena, 1966), especially pp. 24–31; and Rudolf Morsey, 'Die deutschen Katholiken und der Nationalstaat zwischen Kulturkampf und Erstem Weltkrieg', Historisches Jahrbuch, no. 90, (1970), pp. 48–59.

28 Stadtarchiv Cologne, Karl Bachem Papers, 14: 'Oberdörffer'sches Programm'; Klaus Müller, 'Zentrumspartei und agrarische Bewegung im Rheinland, 1882–1903', in Konrad Repgen and Stephan Skalweit, eds, *Spiegel der Geschichte. Festgabe für Max Braubach* (Münster, 1964), pp. 807–9.

29 Eduard Hüsgen, *Ludwig Windthorst* (Cologne, 1911), pp. 94–99; Martin Spahn, *Das deutsche Zentrum* (Mainz, 1907), pp. 33–47.

30 Winfried Jestaedt, *Der Kulturkampf im Fuldaer Land* (Fulda, 1960), p. 94.

31 Rudolf Morsey, 'Die deutschen Katholiken,' especially pp. 43–48; and Rudolf Morsey, 'Probleme der Kulturkampf-Forschung', *Historisches Jahrbuch*, no. 83, (1963), pp. 217–45.

32 Hermann Cardauns, *Karl Trimborn* (Mönchen-Gladbach, 1922), pp. 83–84.

33 Hubert Jedin, ed., *Handbuch der Kirchengeschichte*, vol. 6, no. 2: *Die Kirche zwischen Anpassung und Widerstand (1876 bis 1914)* (Freiburg/B., 1973), p. 220.

34 There were places where the Centre campaigned in local elections under the name of the Pius Association: Blackbourn, *Class, Religion and Local Politics*, p. 109.

35 Jedin, *Handbuch der Kirchengeschichte*, vol. 6, no. 1: *Die Kirche zwischen Revolution und Restauration* (Freiburg/B., 1971), pp. 543–46.

36 See Thomas Nipperdey, 'Verein als soziale Struktur in Deutschland im späten 18. und frühen 19. Jahrhundert', in Hartmut Boockmann, *et al.*, eds, *Geschichtswissenschaft und Vereinswesen im 19. Jahrhundert* (Göttingen, 1972), pp. 1–44. For an excellent discussion of *Vereinswesen* in the context of German Catholics, Heinz Reif, *Westfälischer Adel 1770–1860* (Göttingen, 1979), pp. 398 ff. ('Vereinsaktivitäten').

37 See, for example, the criticism by the Bishop of Passau of even the conservative *Verein deutscher Katholiken*, Johannes B. Kissling, *Geschichte des Kulturkampfes im deutschen Reiche*, 5 vols (Freiburg/B., 1911–16), 2, pp. 315–16.

38 Jedin, *Handbuch der Kirchengeschichte*, vol. 6, no. 2, p. 268.

39 Stadtarchiv Cologne, Karl Bachem Papers, 59: Bachem memoranda on the founding of the *Volksverein*; Buchheim, pp. 343–50; Margaret Lavinia Anderson, *Windthorst, A Political Biography* (Oxford, 1981), pp. 391–93.

40 Hugo Lacher, 'Liberalismus, Staat und Kirche in Baden 1860–1918', *Zeitschrift für Hohenzollerische Geschichte*, no. 99 (1976), especially pp. 190, 193.

41 Julius Bachem, *Erinnerungen eines alten Publizisten und Politikers* (Cologne, 1913), p. 60.

42 Hartmann Bodewig, *Geistliche Wahlbeeinflussungen in ihrer Theorie und Praxis dargestellt* (Munich, 1909).

43 Hauptstaatsarchiv Stuttgart, Conrad Haussmann Papers Q 1/2, 104: Centre Party election pamphlet, Schramberg, 22 July 1908, 'Ein ernstes Wort an unsere christlichen Frauen'.

44 Gottwald, *Zentrum*, p. 55.
45 See the speeches by curate Kappler to a series of *Volksverein* meetings in Upper Swabia, reported in *Waldse'er Wochenblatt*, 16 June and 3 August 1895.
46 Hermann Cardauns, *Aus dem Leben eines deutschen Redakteurs* (Cologne, 1912), p. 153.
47 On Lieber's use of agitation against the Jesuit law, see Martin Spahn, *Ernst Lieber als Parlamentarier* (Gotha, 1906), p. 57. For a local example, Blackbourn, *Class, Religion and Local Politics*, p. 205. On Windthorst's use of the same strategy, John K. Zeender, *The German Center Party 1890–1906* (Philadelphia, 1976), p. 16.
48 The phrase comes from Theophil Egger, a Centre deputy in the Württemberg Landtag: *Schwäbischer Merkur*, 3 December 1900. Rhineland agrarian dissidents complained with equal bitterness about this 'Pfaffenwirtschaft': Müller, p. 849.
49 Hermann Cardauns, *Adolf Gröber* (Mönchen-Gladbach, 1921), p. 43. On this point, see also Zeender, p. 15, n 62.
50 Johannes Rost, *Die wirtschaftliche und kulturelle Lage der deutschen Katholiken* (Cologne, 1911), pp. 181, 201.
51 Jedin, *Handbuch der Kirchengeschichte*, vol. 6, no. 1, pp. 662–70; vol. 6, no. 2, pp. 265–78.
52 On the seven-yearly Procession of Relics at Aachen, see Heinrich Schiffers, *Kulturgeschichte der Aachener Heiligtumsfahrt* (Cologne, 1930). For a good picture of popular piety in Lower Bavaria, see the first volume of Hans Carossa's memoirs, *Eine Kindheit* (Leipzig, 1922), especially pp. 26ff.
53 Erwin Gatz, *Rheinische Volksmission im 19. Jahrhundert* (Düsseldorf, 1969).
54 See Anderson, *Windthorst*, pp. 121–29.
55 On Löwenstein, see Buchheim, *Ultramontanismus und Demokratie*, which is heavily based on his papers; and on the piety of the Westphalian aristocracy, see the latter parts of Reif's exemplary study of the *Westfälischer Adel*.
56 On the *Kasino* movement, Franz Dor, *Jakob Lindau* (Freiburg/B., 1909), on Baden; and Jestaedt, *Kulturkampf*, pp. 74–75, 121–24, 140–43, which has an account of the Fulda 'Männergesellschaft M. N.' or 'Schwarzes Casino'.
57 On Marpingen, Julius Bachem, *Erinnerungen*, pp. 133–42; Kissling, 3, pp. 118–21; Karl Schorn, *Lebenserinnerungen* (2 vols; Bonn, 1898), Vol. 2, pp. 259–62. The Virgin was also believed to have appeared in Mettenbuch (Bavaria) and Dittrichswalde (Ermland). See also Chapter 7.
58 Julius Bachem, *Erinnerungen*, pp. 58–63, 133–42.
59 Newly extended means of communications helped, of course. For a description of the 1891 Trier pilgrimage, see Ludwig Pastor, *August Reichensperger*, 2 vols (Freiburg/B., 1899), 1, p. 189. Over three-quarters of a million were officially estimated to have attended the Aachen Procession of Relics in 1909; Schiffers, pp. 14–15.
60 Gottfried Korff, *Heiligenverehrung in der Gegenwart* (Tübingen, 1970), pp. 17–31.
61 Paul von Hoensbroech, *Fourteen Years a Jesuit*, 2 vols (London, 1911), 2, pp. 306–8. Gottfried Korff, 'Heiligenverehrung und soziale Frage', in Günter Wiegelmann, ed., *Kultureller Wandel im 19. Jahrhundert* (Göttingen, 1973), pp. 102–11, has systematically used the *Sendbote des Göttlichen Herzens Jesu* as a source.
62 Jedin, *Handbuch der Kirchengeschichte*, vol. 6, no. 1, p. 664, and vol. 6, no. 2, pp. 260–68; Schiffers, especially pp. 217–20. For the 1874 pilgrimage, no less than 6 tons of rosaries, holy pictures and the like were imported from France and Switzerland. Novels like Spillmann's *Die Wunderblume von Woxindon* (Freiburg i.B., 1893) enjoyed enormous success.
63 On Muth, see *Der Katholizismus in Deutschland und der Verlag Herder 1801–1951* (Freiburg i.B., 1951) pp. 176–77; and Markus Ettinger *et al.*, eds., *Wiederbegegnung von Kirche und Kultur in Deutschland. Eine Gabe für Karl Muth* (Munich, 1927). On Bachem, Julius Bachem, *Erinnerungen*, p. 142.
64 Jedin, *Handbuch der Kirchengeschichte*, vol. 6, no. 2, p. 259.
65 On the 'Taxiliade', Stadtarchiv Cologne, Karl Bachem Papers, 17: Bachem memoranda on the Landshut *Katholikenversammlung* of 1897; Buchheim, pp. 470–93; Julius Bachem, *Erinnerungen*, pp. 161–75.
66 Hermann Schell, *Der Katholizismus als Prinzip des Fortschritts* (Würzburg, 1897).

67 See particularly Ronald J. Ross, *Beleaguered Tower: The Dilemma of Political Catholicism in Wilhelmine Germany* (Notre Dame, 1976).
68 See Gert Zang ed., *Provinzialisierung einer Region. Zur Entstehung der bürgerlichen Gesellschaft in der Provinz* (Frankfurt/M., 1978).
69 Kissling, *Geschichte*, Vol. 2, p. 295.
70 The importance of women in the popular Catholic resistance to the *Kulturkampf* deserves greater attention. They were the particular objects of contempt for *Kulturkämpfer*, whether as members of female orders, or merely as the supposed priest-ridden founts of popular credulity.
71 On renegade priests, Kissling, *Geschichte*, Vol. 3, pp. 108ff; Jestaedt, *Kulturkampf*, pp. 71–80. On the priests' activities in peasants', craftsmens' and other associations, Blackbourn, *Class, Religion and Local Politics*, pp. 50, 110; in Silesia, Helmut Neubach, 'Schlesische Geistliche als Reichstagsabgeordnete 1867–1918', *Archiv für schlesische Kirchengeschichte*, vol. 26 (1968), pp. 251–78.
72 See Zang, especially articles by Dieter Bellmann, pp. 183–263 and Gert Zang, pp. 307–73; Lothar Gall, 'Die partei- und sozialgeschichtliche Problematik des badischen Kulturkampfes', *Zeitschrift für die Geschichte des Oberrheins*, no. 113 (1965), pp. 151–96. For a telling Austrian parallel, Ernst Bruckmüller, 'Bäuerlicher Konservatismus in Oberösterreich', *Zeitschrift für bayerische Landesgeschichte*, 37 (1974).
73 I have tried to show the ways in which the Centre addressed itself to such apprehensions in Chapter 8.
74 *Konstanzer Zeitung*, 16 June 1867, cited in Zang, *Provinzialisierung*, p. 206.
75 Cardauns, *Aus dem Leben eines deutschen Redakteurs*, pp. 72–4.
76 See Heinrich Hansjakob, *Im Gefängnisse. Erinnerungen eines badischen Staatsgefangenen* (Mainz, 1873); Philipp Wasserburg, *Zwei Monate auf der Festung Darmstadt* (Mainz, 1874).
77 See, for example, Zang, *Provinzialisierung*, pp. 206, 244, 315, 328.
78 Kissling, *Geschichte*, Vol. 3, p. 173. Cf. August Reichensperger's remark that 'as ultramontanes we are all, to a certain extent, "unclean"': Pastor, *August Reichensperger*, Vol. 1, p. 424.
79 On Catholic workers in the Ruhr, see for example, Karl Rohe, 'Vom alten Ruhr zum heutigen Ruhrgebiet', in Karl Rohe and Herbert Kühr, eds, *Politik und Gesellschaft im Ruhrgebiet* (Hain, 1979), pp. 44–5. Numerous studies make this point about the peasantry.
80 On Sedan Day: Kissling, *Geschichte*, Vol. 2, p. 279; Jestaedt, pp. 134–5. On the navy, Blackbourn, *Class, Religion and Local Politics*, pp. 48, 59, 258.
81 On the urban Catholic *Negerdorf*, see Stephen Hickey, 'The Shaping of the German Labour Movement: Miners in the Ruhr', in Richard J. Evans, ed., *Society and Politics in Wilhelmine Germany* (London, 1978), p. 218.
82 Blackbourn, *Class, Religion and Local Politics*, pp. 32–41.
83 Dieter Fricke, ed., *Die bürgerlichen Parteien in Deutschland 1830–1945*, 2 vols. (Leipzig, 1968–70), Vol. 2, p. 896.
84 Stadtarchiv Cologne, Karl Bachem Papers, 21: copy of *Augustinus-Blatt*, containing a speech by Bachem to Augustinus Press Association on 2 September 1900. For a similar lament by Hertling on the non-constructive qualities of his fellow Bavarians, Pfälzische Landesbibliothek Speyer, Lieber Papers, H. 142, Hertling to Lieber, 26 March 1891.
85 See Johannes Schauff, *Die deutschen Katholiken und die Zentrumspartei* (Cologne, 1928). Between 1874 and 1912 the Centre's share of Catholic votes cast at Reichstag elections is estimated to have fallen from 83 per cent to 54.6 per cent (Schauff, p. 75).
86 I have written about the Centre's particular form of demagogy in *Class, Religion and Local Politics*.

IV

Populists and Patricians

10

The Politics of Demagogy in Imperial Germany

Allegations of demagogy were often heard in the overheated politics of Imperial Germany, and have often been repeated by later writers. German historians writing since the great historiographical watershed of the 1960s have established what is perhaps the most widely influential use of the term. For them, demagogy was one of the weapons wielded by the traditional ruling elite to stave off social and political reform. Junker Conservatives won political support from the peasantry and *Mittelstand* partly because of the demagogy with which they branded liberals, socialists and Jews as the common enemy. More generally, so the argument runs, German 'World Policy' as a whole and naval construction in particular were 'an enterprise of national demagogy' (Imanuel Geiss), designed to rally popular support behind an unreconstructed domestic order. These lines of argument echo the critique of some contemporary liberals and radicals, who also accused the German ruling elite of agrarian demagogy at home and demagogic sabre-rattling abroad. For the historians in question this approach to the politics of demagogy is also consistent with, in fact forms one part of, a larger view of Imperial Germany that rests on two important assumptions. The first is that the striking degree of political mobilization on the right in Imperial Germany took place from the top down. The second holds that the continuity between Imperial and Weimar Germany is the continuity of a persistent old elite engaged in manipulation and sleight of hand.

This chapter offers an alternative reading of the politics of demagogy, with different implications for our view of continuity. It is, however, an attempt to go beyond the arguments outlined above, not to turn the clock back: no apologia is intended here for the Imperial German elite. Heinz Haushofer insisted too much when he insisted that the Junkers were 'no demagogues'; and those historians who have presented Bismarck's successors in the Imperial Chancellery as well-meaning men hampered by noisy extremists in the Pan-German League are hardly more convincing. For all that, it remains the case that the shrill and demagogic form of politics observable in Germany in the two decades before 1914 owed much to new political forces that arose on the right, parallel to the SPD and outside elite circles. I argue below that it was the popular agrarian, anti-semitic, *Mittelstand* and radical-nationalist movements, and the new kinds of leader they produced, which first injected a new demagogic element into German political life. Established elites found themselves faced with both a threat and an opportunity. And our attention should be focused, not on some effortless political legerdemain by the elite, but on their cynical but not always successful efforts to tame and harness these dangerous new forces – to deploy what one Conservative supporter called 'demagogy in the good sense'. It is the potentially explosive interplay between new right and old, between populists and patricians, that provides an important part of the background to German politics both on the eve of the First World War and on the eve of the Nazi seizure of power.

This chapter was first given as a paper at a number of universities in California during April 1981. It has been extended and refined at several points over the years, not least as a result of the comments and questions it elicited from those original audiences, and from later ones in both the USA and Britain. A period of sabbatical leave in 1984–5 gave me the opportunity for further reading and reflection. That is also when I wrote the present text, which was published under the same title in *Past and Present*, no. 113 (1986), pp. 152–84.

I

Hitler, the *terrible simplificateur*, is everyone's idea of the perfect demagogue. The dramatized rhetoric, the charismatic yet common touch, the talk of hidden enemies: these demagogue's arts have a central place in our view of Hitler as the great snake-charmer. But it is not the Führer alone who is thought to have seduced the German people in this way. Nazi use of the big lie is seldom absent from accounts of the seizure of power. Together with the staging of Nazi politics – the marches, lights, banners – it is often seen as a major reason why the National Socialists were able to win mass support. There is indeed no doubt that the Nazis availed themselves successfully of a demagogic political style. They adopted a self-consciously populist idiom, presenting a conspiratorial picture of betrayal in high places and offering themselves as the simple, virtuous alternative. The demagogic language and self-presentation of the Nazis deserve attention, provided we recognize that there are limits to what can be explained in terms of this siren-song. For it remains a stubborn fact that the Nazi appeal proved much more potent to some than others. It was more successful in the countryside and small towns than in the cities, more effective with the peasantry, petty bourgeoisie and middle class than with workers.[1] As many writers have pointed out, the National Socialists addressed themselves effectively to the prosaic, everyday anxieties and aspirations of these groups. Demagogy worked where it went with the grain of particular experiences and interests.

That is no less true of German politics before the First World War. The present article is concerned with the emergence of a demagogic mode of politics on the German right before 1914. It is an attempt to look at political style without losing sight of political content, and it deals particularly with the movements that embodied the new politics of the Wilhelmine period: the anti-semitic political parties, agrarian populism, the so-called *Mittelstand* movement of the petty bourgeoisie, and radical nationalism. The article is concerned explicitly with one important question and implicitly with another. The first is the nature of popular political mobilization in the Kaiser's Germany, a subject of considerable debate in recent years. Did this mobilization occur 'from above', as a form of manipulation by a stubborn old elite, or should one speak rather of a form of self-mobilization 'from below'?[2] The argument here is that the febrile form of politics that developed in Germany before 1914 can best be understood if we look at the interaction of the two. The concept of a demagogic politics is particularly useful here. The term was widely used by contemporaries, and the different meanings they attached to it give a good idea of the different interests at stake. This ambiguity alerts us especially to the dangers that attended efforts to tap popular sentiment as a means of bolstering up the old regime. For demagogy was a double-edged sword. A figure like Chancellor Bülow or a Conservative grandee might view the radical nationalists or anti-semites as demagogues, rudely disturbing the deliberations of the political class. But when chancellors and old right tried to appropriate the new politics for their own purposes, they in turn were branded as demagogues by those whose political clothes they had stolen. This article tries to show how, and with what unintended consequences, this interplay between old right and new proceeded.

That raises the second important question: the continuity between Imperial Germany and the Weimar Republic. There are undoubtedly affinities of both form and substance between the organizations considered below and the later Nazi movement. The activities of the pre-1914 anti-semites were a 'rehearsal for destruction', the Agrarian League was 'proto-fascist', the Pan-German League offered 'a chilling anticipation' of the Nazi programme.[3] The social groups to whom these organizations appealed, their programmes, and the demagogic political style they shared constantly seem to prefigure Nazism. In this respect, as in others, the success of National Socialism was no short-term product of crisis, an 'accident' or *Betriebsunfall*. The question about continuity is not whether it existed, but what particular form it took. Here, once again, the notion of a dangerously demagogic politics is useful. The demagogy of the old elite, in Wilhelmine as in Weimar Germany, was perilous precisely because it was not an act of manipulation, repeatable at will, but an attempt to harness forces that could not be fully controlled. The logic of their political efforts was the logic of the sorcerer's apprentice. Thus the continuity between pre- and postwar Germany was not a simple, linear affair: it was a cumulative, convulsive continuity, in which the room for manoeuvre of the old political class became progressively narrower as their own demagogic efforts back-fired. It is the onset of that process in the years before 1914 that I hope to illustrate below.

II

For much of the nineteenth century, 'demagogy' was a term used largely by government and elite against those who allegedly stirred up the lower orders. The demagogues of pre-1848 Germany were the Jacobins and republicans, the students of Young Germany and the radical ballad singers. The censorship measures of 1836 were known, for example, as the *Demagogenverfolgung*. If the term was sometimes worn as a badge of honour on the left, conservatives used it to indicate their regret that after 1789 the 'masses' were the object of political attention at all, and their belief that it was unscrupulous agitators who set those masses in motion. This is the sense in which Bismarck was using the term around the middle of the century, attacking the 'demagogues' who encouraged resentment and illegitimate aspirations among the poor, criticizing urban populations which let themselves 'be led by ambitious and lying demagogues'. His rejection of daily allowances for deputies of the North German Confederation followed similar reasoning: salaries would encourage 'demagogy as a professional enterprise'.[4]

Arguments of this kind were also common currency in the ranks of bourgeois liberalism. Liberals suspected the poor and uneducated of lacking true independence and thus of becoming the potential 'political tools of unscrupulous demagogues'.[5] Liberal debates over manhood suffrage revealed these fears very clearly. Even in the generally optimistic 1860s, for example, liberal anxieties were reflected in the lurid terms in which they warned about the dangers of arousing mass emotions. Karl Twesten was concerned about the 'charlatanry' that would result from truckling to the people. Even a supporter of universal manhood suffrage like Schulze-Delitzsch warned of stimulating popular 'passions'. It was, he argued, all too easy 'to cross the dark frontier where the animal and human meet'; and then the 'unbound beast', once aroused, would 'tear everything apart with its lion claws'.[6] References to demagogues were as common as bestial metaphors in this liberal discourse. Here the liberals differed from a figure like Bismarck chiefly in that their fears extended also to the rural population, while he stressed the innate good sense of those bound to the soil.

There was, however, another important difference. If Bismarck and like-minded conservatives saw the threat of demagogy on the left, liberals saw it on the right as well. The landowner or priest with the common touch was, in liberal eyes, no less dangerous than the socialist agitator. All appealed to the people over the heads of liberal notables, playing on the supposed credulity of the unenlightened. From the middle of the century this became a familiar charge. The liberal critique of right-wing rabble-rousing was addressed to Bismarck himself, the 'white revolutionary'. Hermann Baumgarten accused him of 'caesarist demagogy', by which he meant encouraging 'the dominance of the raw instincts of the masses'.[7] By the last decades before 1914, this liberal charge directed itself against an increasingly wide range of individuals and movements on the political right. Max Weber, the most trenchant liberal commentator of the prewar years, made particularly free with the label of demagogue. He attached it over a period of thirty years to practically every movement and individual on the right, from the anti-semites to the Agrarian League, from the Pan-Germans to Admiral Tirpitz.[8] In this respect, as in others, he was representative of liberal thinking. Alongside this liberal critique ran a parallel radical-democratic rejection of conservative demagogy. A striking early example is Heinrich Heine's phrase about 'Gothic madness and the modern lie'.[9]

Both of these lines of argument were muted in the Weimar Republic and uprooted in the Third Reich: both have re-emerged strongly in the work of German historians writing since the 1960s. This critique has become a familiar version of German history from Bismarck to Hitler, an ambitious attempt to pin down the malign continuity that connects the reckless Right of Imperial Germany with the manipulators who 'helped Hitler into the saddle'. The detailed work of these historians has concentrated on the period before 1914, and the charge of a right-wing demagogy in the period comes in a smaller and larger version. The smaller version concentrates on the Junkers, those all-purpose villains of modern German history. This is an approach associated particularly with the pioneering work of Hans Rosenberg, although it has found much wider acceptance. According to this account, the Junkers underwent a process of 'pseudo-democratization', staving off a serious threat of political isolation during the Great Depression by persuading the peasantry and petty bourgeoisie that they shared a common interest against the urban, liberal, socialist and Jewish enemy. The prime vehicle in this enterprise was the Junker-dominated Agrarian League, founded in 1893.[10] Just as a liberal critic had referred in 1911 to 'agrarian demagogy in Germany', so Rosenberg talked of the Junkers 'gradually becoming demagogues', and of agrarian demagogy 'with its appeal to irrationality and dark urges'.[11]

The second version of right-wing demagogy is a broader variant of the first. It suggests that the ruling elite of Prussia-Germany as a whole, the Old Gang of government, administration and army, faced with demands for political reform and social emancipation at home, sought to deflect these threats by means of an aggressive foreign policy. The origins of this demagogic departure have been seen in Bismarck's 'social imperialism'.[12] Subsequently, navy building and *Weltpolitik* were intended to rally popular support behind an unreconstructed elite, through a major propaganda effort and the massaging of public opinion via nationalist pressure groups. This programme has therefore been viewed as a means by which an anachronistic elite tried to guarantee itself a further lease of life. Like the parallel efforts of the Junkers in the Agrarian League, demagogy has been viewed as a manipulative tool. One historian has talked of *Weltpolitik* as 'a red herring of the ruling classes ... an enterprise of national demagogy'.[13]

This work of historical revision has major achievements to its credit.

It is difficult for historians to maintain any longer that the Junkers were 'in no way demagogues',[14] or that navy building and German imperialism before 1914 were products principally of the diplomatic balance and the 'primacy of foreign policy'.[15] Our attention has been directed instead to the domestic problems faced by elite groups, and to the emergence at the end of the nineteenth century of what Hans Rosenberg called a political mass market. The problem is that the masses in this political market place have been painted very much as passive consumers. To vary the metaphor, the puppet masters pulled the strings and the puppets danced.[16] Thus, in one account, the petty bourgeoisie was 'waiting to be organized. And organized they became'.[17] Against this, there is plenty of evidence to suggest an alternative reading. In the last twenty-five years before the First World War, the 'consumer' was rather more potent in the German political market place than in the real market. These years saw a genuine political ferment at the base of German society; and it was this leavening of political life that first injected a qualitatively new demagogic element into public life.

III

Between the 1880s and the beginning of the new century the face of German politics changed. The content and tempo of politics in the age of the typewriter and slide-show was transformed by comparison with the polite, rather distant ritual it had been in earlier decades. Electoral participation gives one indication of the change. Reichstag election turn-out grew from little above the 50 per cent mark in Bismarck's hey-day to 84 per cent in 1907 and 1912, while the increase at state and municipal level was often greater still. There were by-elections where the turn-out was as high as 94 per cent.[18] The lively sale of black market tickets to the Reichstag gallery provides a sign of the way in which politics had become a popular drama. During the debate over the Moroccan-Congo treaty in 1911 people were reportedly willing to pay prices comparable to an appearance by Caruso.[19] But we are dealing here with political actors as well as spectators. As early as 1880 one prescient Conservative noted that 'the masses are coming more into play',[20] and this was to become an insistent theme as new political organizations and pressure groups mushroomed.

The crucial watershed was the decade from the end of the 1880s to the end of the 1890s. The most familiar element in this political mobilization is the growth of the Social Democratic Party (SPD), newly legalized after the lifting of the anti-socialist law in 1890 and advancing rapidly in both membership and electoral success. But the ferment of the 1890s was considerably broader than this. The same period saw the formation of the

German Peace Society and the German feminist movement, the Evangelical League and the People's Association of German Catholics, as well as numerous smaller single-issue movements that insisted with a new stridency that politics should be defined more broadly than had hitherto been the case. One south German minister indicated the range of these organizations when he referred sourly to 'the homeopaths, the anti-inoculationists, the pro-cremationists, the agrarians and the publicans'.[21] Above all, the ten years from the late 1880s saw the arrival on the political stage of those groups with whom we are principally concerned. The peasantry assumed organized political form in the Bavarian Peasant League and the Central German peasant movement of Otto Böckel.[22] Alongside these arose numerous organizations of craftsmen, shopkeepers, house owners and white-collar workers, together with umbrella organizations that claimed to speak for this *Mittelstand* as a whole. There was a considerable degree of overlap between many of the agrarian and *Mittelstand* groups, and the anti-semitic parties that emerged during the same period in both town and country.[23] And alongside these *völkisch* formations in turn came the radical nationalist organizations such as the Pan-German League (1891) and Navy League (1898).[24] Between the Germany of court, elite, bureaucracy and bourgeois notables on the one hand, and proletarian Germany on the other, it is possible to talk of a political stirring among peasants, petty bourgeoisie and the middle classes which paralleled that of the labour movement.

This political mobilization had a number of causes. For the peasantry, long-term problems with rising costs, indebtedness and overseas competition were joined in the early 1890s by a number of major short-term grievances.[25] Peasant volatility found its counterpart among craftsmen and shopkeepers, who experienced the same period as one of particular crisis and anxiety.[26] A stimulus to political organization was also given by growing state regulation, which animated many individual occupational groups. Similarly, the great expansion of further education and rapid changes in employment patterns and prospects produced tensions that left their mark on officials in public service and on members of many free professions – between the humanistically and technically trained, for example, or between those from established backgrounds and petty bourgeois newcomers.[27] It was not narrow material preoccupations alone that prompted the political leavening in Germany in this period. Nor was it simply status-anxiety among those, peasants, craftsmen or professionals, who faced the prospect of 'modernity' with apprehension. Advances in education, transport and communications allowed new demands to be formulated, both material and non-material, as well as providing an opportunity for those demands to be expressed in new ways. If the 1850s and 1860s were the decades in which the German inter-city railway network was built, the 1880s and 1890s were the years in which branch lines and municipal transport networks effectively joined the countryside, the small towns and the suburbs to the political nation. The growth of the press was exactly parallel to this development.[28]

For the peasantry and petty bourgeoisie, what tied these developments together to produce political ferment was a simple equation: material and social demands were more likely to be realized in Germany through political mobilization than they were in the spheres of economy and society themselves. It is well known that the strength of the SPD in Germany was in many ways the counterpart to workers' weakness on the shop floor – an inversion of the situation in Britain. In the dynamic, heavily concentrated capitalism of Wilhelmine Germany this was true of other groups, from barley growers to butchers, from grocers to pharmacists. In comparative European perspective, such groups found it difficult to organize themselves successfully at the point of production or distribution – in craftsmens' producer co-ops, shopkeepers' raw materials co-ops or peasants' sales co-ops. By contrast, the political organizations of peasantry and *Mittelstand* were comparatively strong. Relative failure in the market place, in other words, led to a displacement of material demands into the political market place. In similar fashion, myriad resentments of everyday life were discharged at the political level. The slights that craftsmen or white-collar workers received at the hands of their 'betters' in the trade or philanthropic association, the unbending formalism with which the German courts were perceived to treat the problems of the small man, the Olympian detachment of high officials and local notables: for all of these grievances the sphere of politics offered at least the prospect of an outlet. At the same time, political organization presented a means of resisting the labour movement by imitating its methods: opposing SPD claims about the imminent proletarianization of the small man, and seeking legislation to counter organized labour where it seemed to harm the peasant or petty bourgeois – consumer co-operative competition and trade union incursions into the workshop, for instance.

In one sense, radical nationalism was at odds with this new politics. Interest-politics was deemed to be 'horse-trading', detracting from the national political task. Radical nationalists strove for a new form of politics that would stand above politics in this divisive sense.[29] Yet it is also of great significance that they saw a positive message in these novel forms of popular mobilization. As one of them rather tremulously put it, 'the masses have come of age (through elementary schooling, mass conscription, universal suffrage and the cheap oil lamp)'.[30] In many respects radical nationalism was itself a product of this political leavening. It recruited heavily among the new *couches sociales* of post-unification Germany, among the educated and half-educated who shared a marked impatience with complacent officialdom and the stuffiness of local notable establishments. It is telling that Pan-German activists had a social profile subtly but significantly less elevated than the cream of notable society. These awkward new men were Oberlehrer rather than professors, civil servants in less fashionable departments rather than judges, men in professions such as engineering and pharmacy that still had something to prove.[31] The notably large number of radical nationalists from the generation that had come of age with the Reich reinforced the restiveness with which they elbowed their way on to the political stage.[32]

Neither the agrarian and *Mittelstand* movements nor the new radical-nationalist public was 'waiting to be organized'. Both, certainly, were illiberal, hostile to socialism and often anti-semitic. Peasants and craftsmen attacked 'Manchesterism' for favouring the Jew, harming the Christian producer and opening the road to socialism. Pan-Germans and naval enthusiasts attacked soggy internationalism and fulminated against the enemy within, whether ethnic, socialist or Catholic. But the animus, in each case, was broader and more ambiguous. The peasant movement, above all, was volatile and disrespectful of authority. From Bavaria to Schleswig-Holstein there was hostility to semi-official agricultural associations that were identified with distant government and large landowners.[33] In party-political terms the agrarians challenged the deference expected by National Liberal notables; but they also spurned Conservative grandees. Otto Böckel won the Marburg seat from a Conservative in 1887, while that maverick peasant tribune Hermann Ahlwardt began his anti-semitic career in similar fashion at a by-election in 1892. Eight of the eleven seats won by agrarian anti-semites in 1893 were at Conservative expense.[34] The Böckel movement adopted the slogan 'against the Junkers and Jews', and its programme called for a progressive income tax and the abolition of the three-class franchise in Prussia. Similarly, the Bavarian Peasant League fought on the slogan 'no aristocrats, no priests, no doctors and no professors, only peasants for the representation of peasant interests'. It also called for a democratic local franchise and full freedom of speech, press and assembly.[35] The volatile *Mittelstand* movement also testified to a belief that the small man had been let down by government, bureaucracy and established parties. In rejecting the old ways of seeking influence and demanding legislation against 'unfair competition' the organized *Mittelstand* betrayed anger and frustration that it was not being taken seriously in high places. The plethora of new organizations and the criticisms they made of governments and officials were an earnest of the petty bourgeois intention to demand a domestic place in the sun.[36]

The political upthrust of peasantry and petty bourgeoisie in the 1890s resembled a re-run of 1848 under new conditions. The same awkward, inchoate small-man radicalism was there, the same verbal shot-gun scatter of resentment. The Böckel movement actually adopted the red-black-gold colours of 1848 in its torch-lit processions.[37] Radical nationalism was also a soured parody of 1848. This is not only true of the movement's composition – educated bourgeois generals, professional and petty-bourgeois NCOs and footsoldiers. It applies also, and crucially, to the radical nationalists' impatience with established political forms. Heinrich Claß, later leader of the Pan-Germans, described how he had learned from an old forty-eighter friend of his father's how one could be 'an enthusiastic son of one's people and yet a determined opponent of one's rulers'. Others boasted a similar pedigree.[38] Radical nationalists were correspondingly critical of what they called the 'Byzantinism' of German rulers and officials,[39] demanding instead the active participation of 'citizens not subjects'.[40] They scorned the purely formal, decorative aspects of nation-statehood, symbolized by monuments and postage stamps. Claß argued that 'stage pageants and celebrations, parades and the unveiling of statues' merely disguised the lack of true national will at the top.[41] The journalist Victor Schweinburg remarked similarly of the Navy League that 'it was not founded in order to make a big noise once a year, to send a telegram to the Kaiser, and at the end of the great feast to sing *Lieb Vaterland, magst ruhig sein* through a drunken haze'.[42] Activists sought to appropriate the tired official symbols of the Reich and rejuvenate them by an injection of popular energy. In tone as well as content this constituted a challenge to the official custodians of the national idea.

IV

In the case of both of those grouped along the agrarian-Mittelstand axis, and of radical-nationalist organizations, we are dealing with independent movements of some vigour. One measure of this was the capacity of both kinds of organization to produce their own leaders. It was this novel leadership stratum, often different in background and always different in style from the old clubbable notables, which did most to imprint a new demagogic idiom on German public life. Two broad types of new leader can, in fact, be distinguished. The first might be called the popular tribune: the parish-pump politicians writ large who were so common in the agrarian movement especially. These were the men who claimed the sanction of the local community because they were self-consciously of that community. A classic example is Philipp Köhler, Böckel's deputy and later successor in the Central German Peasants Association. Köhler was *Dorfkönig*, king of the village, in his native Langsdorf: mayor, jury foreman, civil registrar, postmaster and founder of the savings and loan bank. He was also a man who played on the fact that he was himself an agriculturalist.[43] Many leaders of the Bavarian Peasant League boasted a similar pedigree.[44] Indeed the better-off peasant and village mayor who made a point of stressing that he remained a tiller of the soil was a familiar figure in the agrarian movement. Leaders of this kind were novel in the sense that their role indicated the growing importance of the way in which local and parochial concerns – as such – were coming to be articulated within the Imperial political system. Their counterparts were those craftsmen-politicians who came to the fore in the *Handwerkerbewegung* while continuing to emphasize their attachment to the ideals of honourable labour that informed the small workshop.

The second type of leader generated by these movements was rather different. He might be called the maverick or political freebooter, who made a living (or tried to)[45] from political and publicistic activity. In the case of the agrarian and anti-semitic movements these were men who worked hard to persuade audiences that their popular credentials counted for more than their non-native roots. Ahlwardt, the headmaster sacked for embezzlement turned professional anti-semite, was such a figure: so was Otto Böckel, the archivist and folklorist turned 'peasant king of Hessen'. A number of Bavarian Peasant League leaders came out of the same mould: the ex-priest Ratzinger, the newspaper editors Sigl and Schwab.[46] As mavericks with the common touch, such men belonged properly neither to classes nor masses. They enjoyed something of the position occupied by those earlier anti-establishment outsiders, the 'peasant advocates', who gained acceptance by cultivating a rural following.[47]

The Mittelstand movement produced many similar individuals, as increasingly institutionalized organizations felt the need for speakers, pamphleteers and functionaries. The German craftsmens' movement housed many 'political speculators' and 'adventurers',[48] as did shopkeeper leagues and organizations of the white-collar 'new *Mittelstand*'. Friedrich Raab,[49] for example, was a founder of the radical-right German National League of Commerical Employees (1893). He was also a leading officer in the Hamburg Anti-Semitic Electoral League, and of the anti-semitic German Reform Party both locally and regionally, before becoming a Hamburg councillor and later a member of the Reichstag. Like so many other new men, Raab also had publishing interests.[50] Still more ubiquitous was the Saxon-based Theodor Fritsch, *Mittelstand* organizer and anti-semite at large. Fritsch also exemplifies the links between these movements and radical nationalism: his anti-semitic (and anti-Catholic) interests brought him into frequent contact with nationalist groups, and he became particularly close to leading figures in the Pan-German League.[51] Within the heavily interlocked radical-nationalist organizations themselves, there were many full-time organizers and publicists who moved easily between different groups. Albert Bovenschen, publicist and executive secretary in turn of the Eastern Marches Association (the 'Hakatisten') and of the Imperial League against Social Democracy, provides a good example.[52] These political freebooters, whether operating in the agrarian and *Mittelstand* milieu or in radical-nationalist circles – or, like Fritsch, with a foot in both – were an important new breed of *de facto* professional politicians. They were men who, in Max Weber's well-known formulation, lived 'from' rather than 'for' politics.[53]

The popular tribune and the freebooter had in common their demagogic political idiom. Central to this was a self-conscious cult of 'authenticity'.[54] Whether speaking at meetings or writing 20-Pfennig pamphlets, they portrayed themselves as beacons, men who were honest and straight-speaking in a political world that was allegedly mealy-mouthed and corrupt. In making a public issue of their personal virtue they also traded on a widespread belief that government, officials and established politicians were at best complacent, at worst venal or treacherous. Agrarian and anti-semitic leaders had much to say about 'Jewish' commodity exchange swindles, unregulated by official action, while Ahlwardt regaled his rural voters in Brandenburg with stories about the defective rifles supposedly sold by Jewish businessmen to the War Ministry.[55] *Mittelstand* spokesmen complained about the iniquities of the 'Jewish' department stores that allegedly strangled honest Christian businesses, and wondered aloud why the authorities did nothing to save the small man from 'unfair competition'. In each case, the demagogue's art consisted in flattering the audience that the speaker's honesty was a reflection of their own, by contrast with the duplicity to be found in high places. There was a comparable rhetoric among radical nationalists, in which 'disclosures' and 'unveiling' had a conspicuous part. The editor of the *Tägliche Rundschau*, Heinrich Rippler, talked darkly of 'obstacles . . . from above'.[56] The Hakatisten constantly 'exposed' officials who were soft on the Poles, attacking high office-holders – including generals, Oberpräsidenten and a Prussian Minister of Agriculture – with charges that ranged from 'indecision' and 'cowardice' to 'sabotage' and 'national betrayal'.[57] When Bethmann-Hollweg announced his liberal policy of greater autonomy for Alsace in 1911, it was, commented the Pan-Germans' official historian tellingly, as if 'he had let the mask slip'.[58] Pan-German audiences were correspondingly told that they were 'independent men from the people', constituting 'islands', 'rocks' and 'fortresses' that stood alone against the socialist flood, the ethnic threat and the machinations of the Jesuits.[59]

Because this demagogic mode of political address drew heavily on the idea of betrayal in high places, brushes with the law were inevitable. They, in turn, merely reinforced the authority of what was being claimed. Ahlwardt made much political capital out of the libel action and imprisonment that followed his allegations about defective rifles. Böckel and his newspapers were fighting a total of 52 law suits in 1892. In Bavaria, Sigl and Wieland similarly wore their legal reverses as badges of honour.[60]

In the *Mittelstand* movement there were also many cases of brushes with the law. A good example is that of the intemperate Amandus Werbeck, leader of the Hamburg *Verein gegen Unwesen im Handel und Gewerbe* and active in other *Mittelstand* causes.[61] Among radical nationalists the emphasis on betrayal in high places was less often couched in actionable terms, but there were certainly others like the Hanover journalist Bruno Wagener, a violently nationalist anti-semite who faced problems because of his fierce attacks on civil servants and even on the Kaiser.[62]

The demagogy of popular tribunes and political speculators shared one final common feature. Both helped to shift the border between the private and the public by lending a new public legitimacy to sentiments which, even two decades earlier, would have remained the stuff of private grumbles. When Böckel or Fritsch berated Jews or officials they were hardly saying something new: the fact that they were saying it openly, in the formal public arena, was the novelty. In making their 'disclosures', the new demagogues broke with the habits of public reticence that had generally characterized conservative notables and patricians. They brought the prejudices of the *Stammtisch* into the public meeting and parliamentary debate, amplifying them and lending them a new legitimacy. Similarly, the radical-nationalist idiom took complaints regularly aired in the *Ratskeller* and gave them political currency. It was the leaders generated by the organizations that emerged in the 1890s who did much to re-cast German public debate in a new, more demagogic mould. They contributed materially to the arrival in Wilhelmine Germany of what, borrowing a phrase from Carl Schorske, may be called 'politics in a new key'.[63]

V

'Wild agrarian demagogy' and 'national demagogy' were not the clever creations of conservatives and ruling elite. Indeed, the initial reaction of the latter to the new politics was more often a mixture of disdain and unease. The agrarians and anti-semites were viewed with horror by men like the Kaiser and Philipp Eulenburg. The Saxon Conservative von Friesen attacked their 'noise and scandal', their appeal to 'popular passions'. His fellow grandee, von Helldorff, spoke of a 'frightful brutalization of public opinion'.[64] Even Court Chaplain Adolf Stöcker, who had attempted in the 1880s – with no great success – to win the workers of Berlin for a social Kaiserdom laced with anti-semitism, found it possible to express his contempt for the 'foul demagogy' of the vulgarian interlopers. The expression *Raddauantisemitismus* – gutter anti-semitism – captured a widespread conservative view, and one that extended to agrarian and *Mittelstand* 'excesses' in general. Leaders of the Catholic

Centre Party offered similar observations on the Bavarian Peasant League.[65] Radical nationalism was also the object of fierce attacks from highly placed official figures. In a celebrated Reichstag philippic, Chancellor Bülow accused the Pan-Germans of 'beer-bench' politics.[66] Prince Würtzburg, a Bavarian patron of the Navy League, was to attack radical elements in that organization for their 'demagogic chauvinism'.[67]

Whether we are talking of conservative elites or the governmental elite, there is little doubt that the new movements excited alarm. Their tone was considered disturbingly disloyal, and the programme of the anti-semites and agrarians in particular was widely thought to lead in the direction of Social Democracy. In the early 1890s, at a time when plans for a *coup d'état* (*Staatsstreich*) were being aired in right-wing circles, there was much talk of the hostage to fortune that universal manhood suffrage had turned out to be.[68] Stöcker remarked of the Conservatives' 1892 conference at the Tivoli hall in Berlin, packed with restless agrarians and anti-semites, that it was 'not a party conference in black tails and white gloves, but in street clothes. This was the Conservative Party in the era of universal and equal suffrage.' As his astute party colleague Manteuffel noted of Tivoli and its unwelcome guests: 'We could not avoid the Jewish question unless we wanted to leave the demagogic anti-semites the full wind of a movement with which they would just have sailed right past us.'[69]

And that, of course, was the point. Conservatives like Manteuffel saw the threat, but they also saw the opportunity. They sought, with considerable success, to harness and domesticate the forces that had emerged from the countryside and the urban *Mittelstand*. As another of them put it, 'the great energy which lives in them must be steered into the correct channels'.[70] In electoral terms, this meant co-operating with the newcomers where necessary. Baron von Friesen may have found the anti-semitic German Reform Party 'nauseating and loathsome', but he concluded an electoral alliance with it that helped the Conservatives to retain a majority on the Dresden city council for nearly 20 years.[71] German Conservatism also assimilated many of the policies being demanded in the name of the people by peasant tribunes, *Mittelstand* organizers and anti-semitic freebooters. The Tivoli conference wrote an anti-semitic plank into the Conservative programme, and the party subsequently found many opportunities to demonstrate its hostility to the Jewish 'enemies' of peasant, craftsman and shopkeeper, whether speculators on the Berlin exchanges, manufacturers and department store owners using 'un-German' methods, or liberal and socialist *literati* who traduced the 'productive estates'. In the twenty years after Tivoli the Conservatives appropriated an impressive number of themes raised out of doors. These included various forms of agricultural protectionism for the peasant, and the policy of 'saving' the craftsman and shopkeeper through a so-called

Mittelstandspolitik.[72] The Agrarian League, founded in the wake of Tivoli and numbering a third of a million members by 1914, played a major role here. It institutionalized the new demagogic leadership type in the person of League speakers and functionaries like Hahn, Oertel and Kaufhold, while adopting much of the conspiratorial rhetoric of men like Böckel.[73] One of the Conservative speakers at Tivoli, a haberdasher from Chemnitz, had complained about the party's aloofness from popular sentiment:

> It is common practice today among the leading circles of the Conservative Party, that everything which comes from the heart, which comes from the heart with clear words on to the tongue, everything which moves the people, is very easily dismissed with the stock phrase 'demagogic' (Quite right!). I must ask our honourable deputies to become a little more 'demagogic' – but not in the bad sense, rather in the good sense (Bravo!).[74]

Twenty years later the Conservatives and the Agrarian League had gone a long way towards meeting this point.

It was not the Junkers alone, however, who appropriated the populist idiom of the 1890s and thereby lent it respectability. National Liberalism also survived in some rural areas by coming to terms electorally with agrarian anti-semitism, as well as with the Agrarian League: in the Palatinate, Hessen and Thuringia, for instance, part of that central belt of Germany in which so much of the *rapprochement* between the old politics and the new worked itself out.[75] Rather more successfully, the Centre Party followed the Conservatives in accommodating itself to the new populist forces, which party leaders had viewed in the first half of the 1890s as a threat to the Centre's existence.[76] The pro-agrarian and *Mittelstand* inflection of the party's economic and social policy became very marked: the disgruntled Bavarian notable Georg von Hertling complained that the Centre was turning itself into a party of 'grain tariffs and compulsory guilds'.[77] As in the case of the Conservatives, moreover, the Centre's genuflection to agrarian and petty bourgeois aspirations was accompanied by a sharply populist rhetoric. This was particularly marked in Bavaria, where local Centre politicians were often difficult to distinguish from those of the Peasant League.[78] But the same idiom can be found in other areas, where local Centre men assumed a recklessly anti-governmental, anti-elitist and (often) anti-semitic stance that differed only in degree from that of a Ratzinger or a Böckel. It is true that official party policy and the statements of Centre leaders in Berlin made no overt concessions to anti-semitism, in the way that Conservatives did. Both principled and prudential considerations (Catholics themselves being a vulnerable minority) set limits to what party notables were prepared to say. But the growing local machinery of the party – the small-town press, peasant associations, branches of the million-strong People's Association of German Catholics – used anti-semitism as a regular part of their appeal. This was tacitly sanctioned by leaders whose own measured public speeches used coded language such as 'unfair competition'. The anti-semitic labels were missing, but everyone knew what the baggage contained.[79] Like the Conservatives, the Centre Party legitimized the new demagogic rhetoric and institutionalized the parish-pump and maverick types of leader within its own organization. In this context, men like the 'peasant doctor' Georg Heim in Bavaria and the party's *Mittelstand* experts deserve as much attention as their equivalents in the Agrarian League. The Centre had long been criticized, by liberals in particular, for its demagogy: for stirring up 'evil passions' and 'flattery of the masses'.[80] In the two decades before 1914 it increasingly earned its reputation.

If the Conservatives and others on the right tried to absorb the demagogic currents of the 1890s, the governmental elite approached the challenge of radical nationalism in a similar spirit. For all Bülow's reservations about the Pan-Germans' tone, he saw a use for them in 'beating the national drum'.[81] During the passage of the first navy bill at the end of the 1890s the League was virtually 'co-opted' and liberally supplied with funds, pamphlets and information by the Information Bureau set up at the Navy Office by Tirpitz. Reserve officers were sent to speak at meetings held by the League and other patriotic organizations, slides were made available, rallies were subsidized.[82] In all of this we can see a clear governmental intention to exploit the energies of radical nationalists, however awkward these might be, in order to mobilize a broader public opinion. The journalist Bruno Wagener might be considered an 'unscrupulous politician' by the Prussian Ministry of the Interior, but he was used by the Navy Office who thought him a 'keen propagandist'.[83] When it came to journalists, in fact, the later Foreign Secretary, Kiderlen-Wächter, was to say that he could 'work best with dubious characters'.[84]

The so-called Hottentot elections of 1907 reveal a similar pattern. Bülow, having broken with the Centre Party as the radical nationalists had always demanded, called an election against the 'enemies of the Reich' in which the efforts of the popular nationalist organizations were harnessed in an unprecedented way. The government's election manifesto was issued in the form of an open letter from Bülow to von Liebert, the head of the Imperial League against Social Democracy, who was also a Pan-German activist and a Navy League radical. Although the Navy League was at the time the focus of nationalist discontent with government policy, it was nevertheless the beneficiary of large-scale funding solicited from leading businessmen and passed on by the government to the patriotic organizations. August Keim, leader of the Navy League radicals and a great uncoverer of government 'inadequacy' in military preparedness, became

Bülow's chief campaign advisor. The Pan-Germans reasonably assumed that the government had at last fallen into line with their wishes. After the election, Liebert claimed with some justification that 'all Pan-German demands in questions of the army, navy, colonies and world policy made up, so to speak, the electoral slogans'.[85]

In subsequent years, beating the national drum continued to mean recourse to the radical nationalists as the occasion required. As one foreign office official noted, 'if the Pan-German League did not exist, we would have to invent it'.[86] The clearest and most cynical attempt to harness radical-nationalist activism came in 1911, at the time of the second Moroccan crisis, when Foreign Secretary Kiderlen suggested to Heinrich Claß, the Pan-German leader and a consistently ferocious critic of official foreign policy, that they engage in a 'division of labour'. The Pan-Germans would make fiery demands in their meetings and in the press: Kiderlen would then be able to say to other governments, 'I am certainly conciliatory, but I have to take public opinion into account.'[87]

Kiderlen's reckless gambit – he called it 'letting all the dogs bark' – was an attempt to domesticate independent forces that invites comparison with the efforts of the political right faced with the awkward agrarian and *Mittelstand* challenge. In neither case was the elite in question innocent. Both in the policies and rhetoric they appropriated, and in the act of appropriating them, they proved themselves to be strikingly demagogic – what Kiderlen, like the haberdasher from Chemnitz, would no doubt have called 'demagogy in the good sense'. Yet it was precisely this partial appropriation that made them extremely vulnerable. For neither the party-political Conservatives and conservatives, nor Bülow and his successors in Berlin, had conjured up these dubious allies *ex nihilo*. They had not brought them into being and they could certainly not keep them under perfect control. As they were to find, riding the tiger could be a dangerous occupation.

VI

The movements that had seen their demands taken up and their language echoed usually viewed this, at least initially, as a victory. Leaders who had invested heavily in their own authenticity were able to imagine that virtue had finally prevailed. This led readily enough to disillusion, as the subsequent history of both agrarian-*Mittelstand* and radical-nationalist movements was to show.

The reactions of the former were by no means paranoid. The commitment made by the established parties of the right to the brash new politics was hedged and partial. Many Conservatives continued to believe that the 'acceptance of demagogy' into the party signified 'the mixing of fire and water'.[88] Even those Conservatives who studiously affected populist leanings had to balance this against the political calculation of retaining favour with a governmental apparatus to which they owed so much.[89] Among National Liberals, those who tied their fortunes most closely to the agrarian and anti-semitic movements were a source of embarrassment within a party that liked to see itself as both moderate and pro-governmental. This was particularly true of the so-called Wormser Ecke, whose support for an anti-semite in a Giessen by-election of 1911 precipitated a party crisis.[90] In the Centre Party there was a general resurgence of anti-populist conservatives after the turn of the century, and especially after 1907, which helped to marginalize men like Heim who were closest to agrarian and *Mittelstand* sentiment.[91] The Centre leadership, moreover, was determined to prove the national *bona fides* of German Catholics by an overt commitment to 'German' causes like the navy, which were highly unpopular with the peasantry in particular.[92] Thus the party's ostensible solicitude for the small man was undercut by policies that appeared to point in the opposite direction.

The Wilhelmine political system, coupling together universal manhood suffrage with a lack of parliamentary government or ministerial responsibility, encouraged political leaders to promise anything.[93] It also made it more difficult to redeem the promises. The economic and social policies placed on the agenda by Böckel and the *Mittelstand* were treated with elaborate public respect by many established politicians. There are nevertheless good grounds for questioning how much was actually achieved.[94] Thus the range of measures that Conservatives and their allies supported on behalf of craftsmen and shopkeepers looked impressive on paper, but their actual effect is open to doubt. Taxes on department stores, for example, were either passed on to deliverers or overcome by increased turnover – as critics had always warned. Indeed, politicians who liked to be known as supporters of department store taxation admitted privately that they were 'unjust and economically stupid'.[95] Legislation against consumer co-operatives also had markedly less effect than shokeepers hoped for. The same was true of the formal changes in the tender system that were supposed to benefit the small craft producer. Watered down in practice, they were completely disregarded by major government departments like the War Ministry. Above all, the great centre-piece of pro-*Mittelstand* policy, the legislation of 1897, proved disappointing: the guilds established under the new provisions of that year lacked muscle, and the legislation went considerably less far in establishing masters' control over apprentices than artisan spokesmen wished.

There were ultimately too many interests ranged against the small man for *Mittelstandspolitik* to be much more than cosmetic. The peasantry fared somewhat better: tariffs, meat import quotas, anti-margarine legislation and other measures offered some genuine protection,[96] although improvements in world price levels may have done more. But it remains the case that large estate owners, Junker Conservatives prominent among them, did even better out of the complex Imperial system of agricultural protection and fiscal privilege.[97] Moreover, Conservatives and their political allies were never remotely likely to take up demands, like those emanating from the Böckel movement, for the break-up of large estates and the introduction of a graduated income tax. The established parties stripped the programmes that had originally been demanded from below of their inchoate but radical core, while retaining the rhetorical attacks on symbolic targets: 'Jewish' capital, or the fat urban consumer.

This conservative species of demagogy produced a back-lash among those who felt they had been duped. By attempting to harness peasant and petty-bourgeois resentment against selected kinds of 'outsider', whether Manchester liberal, socialist, bureaucrat or Jew, conservatives only encouraged a politics of disrespect that could rebound on themselves. In 1898, for example, Friedrich Raab was a joint candidate of the anti-semites and the Agrarian League in Flensburg: he won the seat, and in the same year ran for the Hamburg city parliament on a platform that included the confiscation of large estates, land distribution and a progressive income tax.[98] In Hessen, Böckel's old organization was effectively absorbed into the Agrarian League by about 1904, but according to Köhler it had degenerated into serving the 'interests of the leaseholders and gentlemen farmers'. Renewed and partially successful agrarian anti-semitic protest in 1907 was the result.[99] This pattern persisted up to the war. In 1907, Carl Böhme had been elected in Marburg as a joint candidate of the anti-semitic German Social Party and the Agrarian League. By 1909 he was to be found on the governing body of the liberal Peasant Alliance, and in 1911 he was advocating Prussian electoral reform and anti-Junker economic policies.[100] Hostility to the 'demagogic' Junkers was widespread among agrarian radicals, and the history of rebel election candidates in Centre Party rural constituencies testifies to a similar distrust and political volatility.

There were many respects in which *Mittelstand* appetites were also fed rather than satisfied by the cosmetic policies of the Right. The issue of masters' control over apprentices offers an example: even before the so-called 'little certificate' of mastership was on the statute book, disgruntled agitation began for the 'large' certificate and continued down to 1914. Here is a classic case of the perils of demagogy in raising expectations that could not be satisfied.[101] It also became apparent that some policies pursued by Conservatives and their allies did positive damage even to the more substantial *Mittelstand*: the harm done to butchers by tariffs and meat import quotas is a specific example, the regressive fiscal system a general one.[102] There was an open breach with the Right over the issue of tax reform in 1909, when a section of the *Mittelstand* movement defected to the liberal Hansabund.[103] There remained a latent suspicion among organized artisans and retailers that they were the political pawns of the Right: that the latter's espousal of the cause was inauthentic. This was one of the major causes of disunity and fractional splintering within the *Mittelstand* movement, as new leaders emerged who could claim to be untainted by co-optation.

By 1911 there was a re-grouping of the majority of *Mittelstand* organizations in the Conservative-fostered Imperial German Mittelstand League, which in turn was to form part of the far-right Cartel of Productive Estates two years later.[104] By the same date it was clear that the German peasantry was also more integrated within the established parties of the Right than it had been twenty years earlier.[105] The two decades before the war had nevertheless shown that the demagogic game could be perilous. The true dangers became fully apparent only in the following two decades, as war, inflation and depression in turn threatened the links that tied peasantry and *Mittelstand* to the old Right. For these links now owed little to natural deference. If the revamped Conservative and right-liberal parties of Weimar, the DNVP and DVP, temporarily won back their following among these groups, the middle years of the republic already witnessed a further twist in the demagogic spiral. New agrarian and *Mittelstand* organizations, once again with a strongly localist inflection, emerged to voice the disillusion of peasants, craftsmen and shopkeepers.[106] On this occasion, however, a demagogic appropriation of this protest by the established Right proved less successful. It was the Nazis who were to harness the vote of the small man. Those who had tried to counter one sort of demagogy with a self-serving species of their own found themselves finally outbid by a party wielding the same weapon with much greater skill, and able to benefit from a cumulative sense of betrayal by the 'system' that extended back to Imperial Germany. It is difficult not to feel that this *dénouement* had a powerful inner logic.

The pattern of relations between radical nationalism and those who attempted to use it has some strikingly similar features. Here, also, was a demagogic spiral: radical demands, attempted domestication, followed by further demands bred of frustrated hopes.[107] Thus, at the end of the 1890s, the Pan-Germans and other organizations initially saw in Bülow and Tirpitz men of their own persuasion. But the Imperial government wanted to be able to turn the tap off as well as on. It saw that the Pan-German demands would have destroyed Bülow's carefully constructed co-operation with the Centre Party, which he believed essential for the achievement of national legislation such as the naval programme, as well as damaging seriously German relations with Britain and, probably, the Habsburg Monarchy as well. Yet, of course, radical nationalist ambitions were fostered, not appeased, by the experience of finding themselves called upon by government. After apparent success over the navy the Pan-Germans called for a more active policy on a number of fronts, from the 'defence of Germans' in the Habsburg Monarchy, through Samoa to the Boer war.[108] In these campaigns, the radical nationalist critique was sustained by a strong sense that, once again, a healthy policy had been abandoned because of obstruction in high places. Even on the navy, the issue over which co-operation with the government had taken place, there were conflicts of both content and style. After the passage of the first navy bill the Pan-Germans called for a second; and when the second was announced they found it wanting. It was, indeed, partly in order to try and obtain a more pliable extra-parliamentary pacemaker that the Imperial government took a hand in the formation of the Navy League.[109]

But the Navy League in turn proved a tap that was easier to turn on than off. By 1904, at the latest, the radical wing of the League under Keim was openly criticizing the pace of naval construction and the parliamentary reliance on the Centre Party which helped to determine it. The hostility towards official policy echoed the long-standing rhetoric of radical nationalism. What was missing, for men like Keim, was 'energy, purpose and gravity' at the top: in the Navy Office, the Imperial Chancellery and even in 'the All-Highest Himself'.[110] This was little different from the attacks of the 'beer-bench' Pan-Germans. It is hardly surprising, therefore, that Keim and his followers should have scented victory when Bülow turned once again to the awkward forces of radical nationalism in 1907. In a letter from Keim to Bülow during the election campaign there is more than a hint of the demand for political payment due for services rendered: 'It would be a great mistake to snub the Navy League ... now that it has placed itself with manliness at the head of the national movement. One must now show the courage to own up publicly to one's friends.'[111] Again, however, Bülow had raised expectations he was quite unable to fulfil. Instead he created great bitterness by allowing Keim and his supporters to be driven out of the Navy League (and into the arms of the Pan-Germans), and involuntarily strengthened the belief in these circles that the government was an unworthy custodian of the German national idea.[112]

There was a further twist to the spiral of radical-nationalist expectations in 1911. After Kiderlen's overtures to Heinrich Claß, the Pan-Germans found the subsequent back-tracking of the Foreign Office over Morocco 'an intolerable humiliation of our Fatherland'.[113] The opinion was echoed less extravagantly, but fed by the same sense of betrayal, in the Navy League, the Colonial Society and among the nationalist public generally. The disillusion that followed the second Moroccan crisis proved, in fact, to be the catalyst that fused a 'national oppostion' on the right before 1914. It brought together the different nationalist organizations and it prompted the establishment of the Defence League, whose self-proclaimed task was 'in the final analysis to compel even the parties and the government to do their duty'.[114] The tone of the new organization, and the identity of its major founders, showed just how little it felt itself dependent on official goodwill. As in the years around the turn of the century, and again in 1907, official efforts to harness radical nationalism for limited purposes had back-fired. The domestic room for manoeuvre enjoyed by Chancellor Bethmann in the last years before the war was correspondingly narrower.

The demagogy of different kinds present on both sides in dealings between radical nationalists and Imperial governments has considerable relevance for the debate over 'war guilt'. If Imperial Germany was indeed in a 'blind alley' by the summer of 1914,[115] then successive governments had helped to bring this state of affairs on themselves. The immediate intentions of Bethmann in the period 1912–14 by no means exhaust the question of German 'responsibility'; for if Bethmann eschewed extravagant rhetoric,[116] the pressure of nationalist opinion on the govenment can hardly be seen as just a nasty accident. Bülow, Tirpitz and Kiderlen had whetted nationalist appetites often enough: that the latter expected at last to feast on a substantial success was hardly surprising. This provides part of the background to the fatalism of the civilian as well as military elite in 1914. If it found itself in a domestic corner during the July crisis, then it was a corner into which it had painted itself.

Like the agrarian, *Mittelstand* and anti-semitic organizations, radical nationalism lit a long fuse. The repeated cycle of raised hopes and disillusionment sharpened a consciousness that governments, and ultimately even the Kaiser, were inadequate guardians of German national virtue. The way in which radical nationalists celebrated the centenary of the battle of Leipzig in 1913 as a popular struggle gave an indication of how 'the people', not parties or governments or even the 'All-Highest', had begun to take a central place in the nationalist mystique. The war, once again, intensified these developments. The Fatherland party in particular, founded in September 1917 with a major radical-nationalist contribution, marked the powerful consolidation of a 'national opposition' with large-scale popular support. Within a year it had 800,000 members.[117] Defeat and the departure of 'Guillaume le Timide' in 1918 served further to radicalize the 'anti-political' nationalist public of Weimar in a direction already indicated before 1914. This was the significance of the legacy bequeathed by a prewar radicalism that had been thwarted, yet also rendered respectable, by successive Imperial governments. When Weimar parties and governments tried to wrap themselves in the mantle of national virtue, they did so from a starting point that already owed much to the agenda of the radicals. As in the case of cynically demagogic appeals to the peasant or craftsman by the old Right, such attempts to play the nationalist card selectively became even more dangerous than they had been before 1914.

VII

It is hardly possible to write about demagogy in Imperial Germany without being aware of the shadow cast by 1933. For that reason we need to be particularly aware of the dangers that can arise when demagogy and 'mass politics' are under discussion. It is easy, but misleading, to view Nazi popular support as the product of an irrational herd instinct, in which demagogy becomes synonymous with political seduction. Much is thereby lost from view. The real failures of the Weimar system can come off unduly lightly, while the functions and interests served by German fascism receive insufficient attention. But even as an approach to Nazism as a popular phenomenon, undue emphasis on Hitler the bewitching orator leaves too much out of account. We need to recognize that Nazi demagogy was interwoven with specific interests and addressed to specific casts of mind: the myriad resentments of the peasant, the anxieties of the petty bourgeois and white-collar worker, 'trapped' between capital and labour, the provincialism of the *Mittelstand* as a whole, the impatient apolitical vision of many free professionals and civil servants. The parallels with Wilhelmine Germany are clear enough. For here too we are not – as an older historiography would have it – dealing with a dangerous, but undifferentiated 'revolt of the masses'. As I have tried to show, the demagogic politics that emerged in the Kaiser's Germany went hand in hand with very particular interests, at the level both of peasant, *Mittelstand* and middle-class perceptions, and of elite calculation.

The novelty of the mass politics that emerged in Wilhelmine Germany nevertheless deserves to be stressed. For all Bismarck's 'Bonapartist' introduction of universal manhood suffrage and manipulation of the press, it seems clear that the late 1880s and 1890s saw a qualitative shift: in political mobilization and participation, in interest demands and political idiom. And the new politics of this period was stamped initially less by elite legerdemain than by popular sentiment that had affinities with the movements of 1848. This is true whether we look at peasant volatility or petty-bourgeois rancour, at the measureless dissatisfaction of the new *couches sociales* or the strident 'people's' nationalism of the Pan-Germans. We are dealing here with movements that were difficult to contain within the Bismarckian polity, or within the deferential politics of notables that was its local expression. The new political formations were an unstable amalgam of soured emancipatory impulse and illiberalism, rejecting deference to conservatism while harshly hostile to socialism, Jews and other alleged enemies. It was out of these milieus, I have tried to suggest, that an important new breed of demagogue emerged.

Initially disdainful and sometimes alarmed, elite groups – including Junker Conservatives and the policy-makers in the Wilhelmstrasse – sought to harness and domesticate these awkward forces. Their intentions were undeniably demagogic: on that there can be little disagreement with the work of important recent historians. The irony is that the latter, by presenting the picture of a starkly manipulative elite, have actually underestimated the potential explosiveness of the situation. For elite efforts did more to make populist and chauvinist demagogy respectable than to defuse them. The attempts to meet one form of demagogy with another ('demagogy in the good sense') established a reciprocal relationship that was highly unstable and was to persist into the final years of Weimar. If we recognize this interplay between old Right and new, then one dangerous element of continuity between Wilhelmine and Weimar Germany is underlined. Far from being an accident, Hitler was the final revenge of those demagogues 'in the bad sense' whose appetites had grown rather than diminished through the years of attempted co-optation.

NOTES

I should like to thank Roger Chickering, Geoff Eley and Ray Stokes for their critical comments on a draft of this article.

1 See, most recently, T. Childers, *The Nazi Voter. The Social Foundations of Fascism in Germany 1919–1933* (Chapel Hill, NC and London, 1983).

2 On this debate, see R. J. Evans, 'Introduction: Wilhelm II's Germany and the Historians', in Evans (ed.), *Society and Politics in Wilhelmine Germany* (London, 1978), pp. 11–39; V. R. Berghahn, 'Politik und Gesellschaft im Wilhelminischen Deutschland', *Neue Politische Literatur*, 24 (1979), pp. 164–95; W. Mock, '"Manipulation von oben" oder Selbstorganisation an der Basis? Einige neuere Ansätze in der englischen Historiographie zur Geschichte des deutschen Kaiserreichs', *Historische Zeitschrift*, no. 232 (1981), pp. 358–75; R. G. Moeller, 'The Kaiserreich Recast? Continuity and Change in Modern German History', *Journal of Social History*, vol. 17 (1984), pp. 655–83. The two most recent contributions are by James Retallack and Roger Fletcher in *German Studies Review*, vol. 7, no. 2 (1984).

3 P. W. Massing, *Rehearsal for Destruction* (New York, 1949); H.-J. Puhle, *Von der Agrarkrise zum Präfaschismus* (Wiesbaden, 1972); R. Chickering, *We Men Who Feel Most German. A Cultural Study of the Pan-German League, 1886–1914* (London, 1984), p. 1.

4 L. Gall, *Bismarck. Der Weiße Revolutionär* (Frankfurt, Berlin, Vienna, 1980), pp. 104, 148, 388–9; *Bismarck*, 2 vols, trans. J. A. Underwood (London, 1987).

5 J. J. Sheehan, *German Liberalism in the Nineteenth Century* (Chicago, 1978), p. 32.

6 M. Gugel, *Industrieller Aufstieg und bürgerliche Herrschaft* (Cologne, 1975), pp. 184–8.

7 W. J. Mommsen, *Max Weber und die deutsche Politik 1890–1920* (Tübingen, 1959), p. 6.

8 Ibid., pp. 16, 241f, for examples.

9 His description of Germany's rulers in *Deutschland, ein Wintermärchen*. Compare Heine's acid comment from mid-century: 'A handful of Junkers, who have learned nothing but a bit of horse-trading, card sharping, dice-throwing, or other stupid rascally tricks with which at best peasants at fairs can be duped, think that they can befool an entire people.' Cited A. Gerschenkron, *Bread and Democracy in Germany* (Berkeley, 1943), p. 26.

10 H. Rosenberg, *Grosse Depression und Bismarckzeit* (Berlin, 1967), *Probleme der deutschen Sozialgeschichte* (Frankfurt, 1969), and *Machteliten und Wirtschaftskonjunkturen* (Göttingen, 1978); H.-J. Puhle, *Agrarische Interessenpolitik*

und Preußischer Konservatismus (Hanover, 1966).

11 C. Bürger, *Die Agrardemagogie in Deutschland* (Berlin, 1911); Rosenberg, *Probleme*, pp. 20, 79. See also p. 39, where Rosenberg refers to the 'wild agrarian demagogy of the 1890s'.

12 H.-U. Wehler, *Bismarck und der Imperialismus* (Cologne and Berlin, 1969).

13 I. Geiss, *German Foreign Policy, 1871–1914* (Boston, Mass., 1976), p. 78. Cf. Hans-Ulrich Wehler's description of German Weltpolitik as a piece of 'national demagogy': *Das Deutsche Kaiserreich 1871–1918* (Göttingen, 1973), p. 169.

14 H. Haushofer, *Die deutsche Landwirtschaft im technischen Zeitalter* (Stuttgart, 1963), p. 213.

15 It should be added, however, that, since the late 1970s, there has been a much-remarked revival of a methodologically conservative insistence on the 'primacy of foreign policy'. This has been paralleled by a growing inclination to take geopolitics seriously as a determinant of German relations with other powers. These trends seem to me to mark a retreat from the explanatory possibilities opened up by historians such as Wehler.

16 The metaphor was used by H.-G. Zmarzlik in his review of Wehler's *Das Deutsche Kaisereich*: 'Das Kaiserreich in neuer Sicht?', *Historische Zeitschrift*, no. 222 (1976), pp. 105–26. It was taken up by R. J. Evans in 'Wilhelm II's Germany and the Historians'.

17 V. R. Berghahn, *Germany and the Approach of War in 1914* (London, 1973), p. 151.

18 D. Blackbourn and G. Eley, *The Peculiarities of German History* (Oxford and New York, 1984), pp. 275–6.

19 *Vossische Zeitung*, 9 November 1911, cited in K. Wernecke, *Der Wille zur Weltgeltung* (Düsseldorf, 1970), p. 115.

20 The Bavarian aristocrat Fechenbach: J. Retallack, 'Reformist Conservatism and Political Mobilization: A Study of Factionalism and Movements for Reform within the German Conservative Party, 1876–1914', D.Phil., Oxford (1983), p. 71.

21 Hauptstaatsarchiv Stuttgart, E 41, Anhang II, Bü 4, 'Votum des Staatsministeriums'.

22 On the Bavarian Peasant League, I. Farr, 'Populism in the Countryside', in Evans (ed.), *Society and Politics*, pp. 136–59; H. Haushofer, 'Der Bayerische Bauernbund (1893–1933)', in H. Gollwitzer (ed.), *Europäische Bauernparteien im 20. Jahrhundert* (Stuttgart, 1977), pp. 562–86; K. Möckl, *Die Prinzregentenzeit* (Munich, 1972), esp. pp. 451ff. On the Böckel movement, D. S. White, *The Splintered Party. National Liberalism in Hessen and the Reich 1867–1918* (Cambridge, Mass., 1976), esp. pp. 136ff. See also above, Chapter 6.

23 S. Volkov, *The Rise of Popular Antimodernism: the Urban Master Artisans, 1873–1896* (Princeton, NJ, 1976); R. Gellately, *The Politics of Economic Despair: Shopkeepers and German Politics, 1890–1914* (Beverly Hills, Calif., 1974); D. Blackbourn, 'The *Mittelstand* in German Society and Politics, 1871–1914', *Social History*, no. 4 (1977), pp.409–33; P. G. J. Pulzer, *The Rise of Political Anti-Semitism in Germany and Austria* (London and New York, 1964); Massing, *Rehearsal*.

24 Chickering, *We Men*; G. Eley, *Reshaping the German Right. Radical Nationalism and Political Change after Bismarck* (London and New Haven, 1980).

25 These included a drop in prices and the spectre of tariff reductions, foot-and-mouth outbreaks and a severe feedstuff shortage in the south (both of which raised the problem of obtaining cheap credit to re-stock), and preparations for a large military bill that threatened to raise taxes.

26 See the works cited in note 22 above.

27 These tensions are sensitively explored in K. Jarausch, *Students, Society, and Politics in Imperial Germany* (Princeton, NJ, 1982).

28 On these developments, and evidence for the arguments in the following paragraph, see Blackbourn and Eley, *Peculiarities*, pp. 265–76.

29 This is a point on which the two most recent studies (Eley, *Reshaping*, and Chickering, *We Men*) are in full agreement.

30 Eley, *Reshaping*, p. 194.

31 Chickering, *We Men*, pp. 102–18. It is true that, sociologically speaking, Navy League activists enjoyed a higher status. The size of the organization and the emphasis placed on 'the people' nevertheless signalled a new departure. The tone is captured in the plea of a Navy League activist, the jurist Otto Stern, that the organization not 'degenerate

into a coterie of careerists and honour-chasers'. Eley, *Reshaping*, p. 201.

32 Heinrich Claß typifies the double sense of national mission felt by so many of his generation: to 'redeem' the work of the previous generation, but also not to allow the 'national achievement' to become a hollow source of complacency. See, for example, his repeated references to 'we young men' in *Wider den Strom* (Leipzig, 1932), pp. 61, 67, 88, 91.

33 Farr, 'Populism in the Countryside', p. 137; T. Thyssen, *Bauer und Selbstverwaltung* (Neumünster, 1958), pp. 147, 167. See also above, Chapter 6.

34 Pulzer, *Political Anti-Semitism*, p. 122.

35 R. S. Levy, *The Downfall of the Anti-Semitic Political Parties in Imperial Germany* (New Haven, Conn., 1975), pp. 55–60; White, *Splintered Party*, pp. 136ff; F. Jacobs, *Deutsche Bauernführer* (Düsseldorf, 1958), p. 113; Haushofer, 'Bauernbund', p. 571; A. Schnorbus, *Arbeit und Sozialordnung in Bayern vor dem Ersten Weltkrieg* (Munich, 1969), p. 76.

36 See above, Chapter 5, and for more detail, Blackbourn, 'La petite bourgeoisie et l'Etat dans l'Allemagne impériale, 1871–1914', *le Mouvement Social*, no. 127 (1984), pp. 3–28.

37 Levy, *Downfall*, pp. 55–60.

38 Claß, *Wider den Strom*, p. 19. J. F. Lehmann, the radical-nationalist publisher, co-founder of the Pan-Germans' Munich branch and a member of the Natinal Executive Committee from 1898, was also the son of an exiled forty-eighter, and a left liberal in his youth. See G. Stark, *Entrepreneurs of Ideology* (Chapel Hill, NC, 1981), pp. 19–22. Another Pan-German Executive Committee member, Adolf Fick, was a staunch republican – what Claß would have called a 'national democrat'. *Wider den Strom*, p. 50.

39 Cf. Ernst Hasse, cited in A. Kruck, *Geschichte des Alldeutschen Verbandes 1890–1939* (Wiesbaden, 1954), p. 45.

40 Claß, *Wider den Strom*, p. 96. Cf. Hermann Heydweiller's comment at the extraordinary congress of the Navy League in Kassel (June 1908): 'We are not vassals, but free citizens who are come of age'. Eley, *Reshaping*, p. 201.

41 In his 'Bilanz des Neuen Kurses' speech. See Claß, *Führergedanken. Aus Reden und Schriften von Justizrat Claß 1903–1913. Zuzammengestellt und eingeleitet von Dr Alexander Graf Brockdorff* (Berlin, n.d.), p. 6.

42 Eley, *Reshaping*, p. 192. Schweinburg was writing in 1907, at a time when radicals in the League were arguing that it had, indeed, degenerated into a cosy *Vereinsmeierei*. Ironically, Schweinburg had himself been the butt of similar populist hostility at the end of the 1890s.

43 K. E. Demandt, 'Leopold von Sacher-Masoch und sein Oberhessischer Volksbildungsverein zwischen Schwarzen, Roten und Antisemiten', *Hessisches Jahrbuch für Landesgeschichte*, no. 18 (1968), p. 191; White, *Splintered Party*, pp. 145–6.

44 Haushofer, 'Bauernbund', p. 570.

45 The frequency with which political freebooters of this kind had financial difficulties that brought them before the courts should not be read simply as a sign of their unsavoury lives. It also reflected the problem of trying to sustain a 'professional' political career without the independent means of the typical notable politician. Ahlwardt's difficulties are suggested by the fact that he was convicted of both embezzlement and blackmail (as well, of course, as libel). This combination of a general ferment in public life, coupled with the material opportunities it offered, may also be observed in the various movements and fads in which anti-semitic and other freebooters involved themselves: sun worship, theosophy, necromancy, wholemeal bread. Pulzer, *Political Anti-Semitism*, has some valuable asides on this subject.

46 Pulzer, *Political Anti-Semitism*, pp. 108–17; Möckl, *Prinzregentenzeit*, pp. 451–3; Haushofer, 'Bauernbund', pp. 570–3; Farr, 'Populism in the Countryside', pp. 138–9.

47 For an example of one prominent 'peasant advocate', Andreas Wiest, see C. Bauer, *Politischer Katholizismus in Württemberg bis zum Jahre 1848* (Freiburg, i. B., 1929), p. 128.

48 Rosenberg, *Grosse Depression*, p. 80.

49 On Raab, see I. Hamel, *Völkischer Verband und nationale Gewerkschaft. Der Deutschnationale Handlungsgehilfen-Verband 1893–1933* (Frankfurt, 1967), with biographical note on p. 45.
50 In the Hanseatische Druck- und Verlagsanstalt. Half of the sixteen anti-semites in the Reichstag in 1894 were either the owners or editors of newspapers (Levy, *Downfall*, p. 116). The Bavarian Peasant League had many similar figures. Prominent radical nationalists with the same pedigree included Friedrich Lange, Heinrich Rippler, Theodor Reismann-Grone and J. F. Lehmann.
51 Chickering, *We Men*, pp. 241–2; Pulzer, *Political Anti-Semitism*, pp. 104–7, 197, 231–3, 238. A study of Fritsch remains a desideratum.
52 On Bovenschen, see A. Galos, F.-H. Gentzen, W. Jakóbczyk, *Die Hakatisten. Der Deutsche Ostmarkenverein (1894–1934)* (Berlin, 1966), p. 50; Eley, *Reshaping*, p. 111, and pp. 107–14 for an excellent general discussion of these new kinds of politician.
53 M. Weber, 'Politics as a Vocation', in H. H. Gerth and C. Wright Mills (eds), *From Max Weber* (London, 1948), pp. 84–5.
54 My analysis owes a good deal to the general stimulus of Richard Sennett, *The Fall of Public Man* (Cambridge, 1972).
55 Pulzer, *Political Anti-Semitism*, pp. 112–13. Ahlwardt also claimed that Bismarck's banker, Bleichröder, had dealt corruptly with the police in an alimony case.
56 Eley, *Reshaping*, p. 97.
57 Galos, Gentzen, Jakóbczyk, *Die Hakatisten*, pp. 95–100, 187, 220ff.
58 O. Bonhard, *Geschichte des Alldeutschen Verbandes* (Leipzig and Berlin, 1920), p. 87.
59 Claß, *Wider den Strom*, p. 62; Chickering, *We Men*, pp. 81–6.
60 Massing, *Rehearsal*, pp. 94–5; Levy, *Downfall*, p. 140; Haushofer, 'Bauernbund', pp. 570–1.
61 Gellately, *Politics of Economic Despair*, pp. 88–93. The Hamburg anti-semites sarcastically thanked the local police for helping their cause in 1892 by closing down a meeting. They claimed to have recruited 100 members within 24 hours. Hamel, *Völkischer Verband*, p. 48.
62 Eley, *Reshaping*, p. 112 and footnote 35.
63 C. E. Schorske, *Fin-de-Siècle Vienna* (New York, 1981), pp. 116–80.
64 Retallack, 'Reformist Conservatism', pp. 168, 173.
65 See the criticism of the Peasant League leader Sigl, 'with his demagogue's instincts': J. Bachem, *Erinnerungen eines alten Publizisten und Politikers* (Cologne, 1913), p. 191.
66 Chickering, *We Men*, pp. 67–8.
67 Eley, *Reshaping*, p. 281.
68 E. Zechlin, *Staatsstreichpläne Bismarcks und Wilhelms II 1890 bis 1894* (Stuttgart, 1929).
69 Massing, *Rehearsal*, pp. 64, 66.
70 Retallack, 'Reformist Conservatism', p. 156.
71 Levy, *Downfall*, p. 282.
72 See Puhle, *Agrarische Interessenpolitik*. While Puhle's work tends to magnify the role of the Junkers and play down the degree of autonomous peasant rebelliousness, it nevertheless shows how Conservatives sought to harness rural protest.
73 Ibid., esp. the final chapter on the changing style of agrarian Conservatism, and the comments on Diederich Hahn, pp. 296–7. The work of Hans Rosenberg (note 10) is also important here.
74 Retallack, 'Reformist Conservatism', p. 156.
75 White, *Splintered Party*, pp. 142ff; Puhle, *Agrarische Interessenpolitik*, pp. 193–9; J. C. Hunt, 'Peasants, Grain Tariffs and Meat Quotas', *Central European History*, vol. 7 (1974), p. 219 and n. 47; Levy, *Downfall*, p. 183.
76 See Chapter 6, pp. 131–3.
77 G. von Hertling, *Erinnerungen aus meinem Leben*, 2 vols (Munich, 1919–20), Vol. 2, p. 54. Cf. Pfälzische Landesbibliothek Speyer, Ernst Lieber Papers, H.168, Hertling to Lieber, 5.11.1896.
78 For a typical complaint about this, see Adolf Gröber's letter to Ernst Lieber, cited in H. Gottwald, *Zentrum und Imperialismus*, Diss. Jena (1966), pp. 65–6 n. 163. Also

T. Nipperdey, *Die Organisation der deutschen Parteien vor 1918* (Düsseldorf, 1961), p. 277.

79 For further details, see Chapter 8.

80 M. Stürmer, *Regierung und Reichstag im Bismarckstaat 1871–1880* (Düsseldorf, 1974), pp. 77–8, 129; G. Zang, *Provinzialisierung einer Region* (Frankfurt, 1978), p. 241.

81 Chickering, *We Men*, p. 63.

82 Eley, *Reshaping*, p. 244; Chickering, *We Men*, pp. 58–9; Claß, *Wider den Strom*, p. 33.

83 Eley, *Reshaping*, p. 112, n. 35.

84 O. Hammann, *Der neue Kurs* (Berlin, 1918), p. 129.

85 Quotation from Chickering, *We Men*, p. 259. See, more generally, D. Fricke, 'Der deutsche Imperialismus und die Reichstagswahlen von 1907', *Zeitschrift für Geschichtswissenschaft*, vol. 9 (1961), pp. 538–76.

86 Bonhard, *Geschichte*, p. 223.

87 Claß, *Wider den Strom*, pp. 177–8; Wernecke, *Weltgeltung*, pp. 29ff; F. Fischer, *War of Illusions* (London, 1975), pp. 71ff.

88 The comment of the Berlin correspondent of the Conservative *Kreuz-Zeitung* on the Tivoli conference: Retallack, 'Reformist Conservatism', p. 173.

89 Particular mention should be made of the role played by the Junker Conservatives in the Prussian local administration, and the many economic and fiscal privileges the Junkers enjoyed. On the former, see L. W. Muncy, *The Junker in the Prussian Administration under Wilhelm II, 1888–1914* (New York, 1970); on the latter, the works of Hans Rosenberg (note 10 above), and P.-C. Witt, *Die Finanzpolitik des Deutschen Reiches von 1903 bis 1913* (Lübeck and Hamburg, 1970). It is worth noting that for Prussian Conservatives like Limburg-Stirum and Mirbach, the 'modern' Agrarian League was 'alien and unaristocratic': Puhle, *Agrarische Interessenpolitik*, p. 275.

90 Levy, *Downfall*, p. 183.

91 On Heim and the Bavarian situation, see Möckl, *Prinzregentenzeit*, pp. 535–47; at national level, W. Loth, *Katholiken im Kaiserreich. Der politische Katholizismus in der Krise des Wilhelminischen Deutschlands* (Düsseldorf, 1984), Chapters 3–5.

92 Blackbourn, *Class, Religion and Local Politics*.

93 Cf. Volkov, *Popular Antimodernism*, p. 275: 'the sham parliamentary system enabled the various political parties to make impractical demands without having to shoulder the responsibility for their implementation. It allowed them to carry on a political campaign and attract political support on the basis of half thought-out proposals and irresponsible plans.'

94 I have tried to deal with these questions in greater detail elsewhere (see Chapter 5 and notes 23 and 36 above), where detailed references can be found. A systematic study of *Mittelstandspolitik* and its effectiveness would be very welcome.

95 G. Tietz, *Hermann Tietz* (Stuttgart, 1955), p. 46.

96 Hunt, 'Peasants, Grain Tariffs and Meat Quotas'; R. G. Moeller, 'Peasants and Tariffs in the *Kaiserreich*: How Backward were the Bauern?', *Agricultural History*, vol. 55 (1981), pp. 370–84; U. Teichmann, *Die Politik der Agrarpreisstützung* (Cologne, 1955).

97 See, esp., the works of Rosenberg (note 10 above), and Gerschenkron, *Bread and Democracy*, who nevertheless exaggerates the extent to which protectionism was a Junker ramp.

98 Levy, *Downfall*, pp. 204–5.

99 White, *Splintered Party*, p. 172. Böckel had already denounced the Liebermann von Sonnenberg anti-semitic grouping as 'an appendage of the Conservative Party': Pulzer, *Political Anti-Semitism*, p. 191.

100 Levy, *Downfall*, p. 248.

101 On the cynicism with which craftsmen reacted to the 1897 legislation, see Blackbourn, 'The *Mittelstand*', pp. 418–19. Volkov (*Popular Antimodernism*, pp. 241, 278, 332–33) also suggests a pattern whereby craftsmens' hopes were alternately raised and dashed by legislative measures. There is, of course, a sense in which master artisans (like

peasants) could never be satisfied: they put up a maximum programme and complained when it was not fulfilled to the letter. See F. Blaich, *Staat und Verbände in Deutschland zwischen 1871 und 1945* (Wiesbaden, 1979), pp. 26–7. Nevertheless, the genuine anger in the *Mittelstand* should not be underestimated.

102 On the harm done to butchers, millers and bakers by tariffs, see J. Wernicke, *Kapitalismus und Mittelstandspolitik* (Jena, 1907), p. 162, and Blackbourn, 'The *Mittelstand*', p. 414. More generally, H. A. Winkler, 'Der rückversicherte Mittelstand. Die Interessenverbände von Handwerk und Kleinhandel im deutschen Kaiserreich', in W. Rüegg and O. Neuloh (eds), *Zur soziologischen Theorie und Analyse des 19. Jahrhunderts* (Göttingen, 1971), p. 175; Gellately, *Politics of Economic Despair*, pp. 158–61, 165 ff.

103 Winkler, 'Rückversicherte Mittelstand', p. 169; S. Mielke, *Der Hansa-Bund für Gewerbe, Handel und Industrie* (Göttingen, 1976), pp. 30 ff, 45–51.

104 Details in D. Stegmann, *Die Erben Bismarcks* (Cologne, 1970), pp. 342 ff.

105 See Chapter 6, pp. 129–35.

106 R. Heberle, *From Democracy to Nazism: A Regional Case Study of Political Parties in Germany* (New York, 1970); M. Schumacher, *Mittelstandsfront und Republik. Die Wirtschaftspartei – Reichspartei des deutschen Mittelstandes 1919–1933* (Düsseldorf, 1972); H. A. Winkler, *Mittelstand, Demokratie und Nationalsozialismus* (Cologne, 1972); L. E. Jones, '"The Dying Middle": Weimar Germany and the Fragmentation of Bourgeois Politics', *Central European History*, vol. 5 (1972), pp. 23–54.

107 Cf. Isabel Hull, *The Entourage of Kaiser Wilhelm II 1888–1918* (Cambridge, 1982), p. 128: 'As Varnbüler put it, bold strokes of *Weltpolitik* could "compensate for many grievances in the internal, socio-political sphere". But when these strokes were everywhere frustrated, the disillusionment was all the greater.'

108 Chickering, *We Men*, pp. 62–9.

109 Ibid., pp. 60–1; W. Deist, *Flottenpolitik und Flottenpropaganda* (Stuttgart, 1976), pp. 147–63.

110 Eley, *Reshaping*, p. 181.

111 Ibid., p. 260.

112 Ibid., pp. 271–9. Bülow tried to resist the pressure of Tirpitz and Boy-Ed at the Navy Office, and of prestigious Navy League moderates like Prince Rupprecht of Bavaria; but he ultimately disavowed the awkward Keim. In general, Bülow fully deserved his reputation as 'the eel'. One of the kinder expressions used to describe him by War Minister von Einem was 'the juggler'. K. von Einem, *Erinnerungen eines Soldaten* (Leipzig, 1933), p. 117. But see also pp. 119–20.

113 Chickering, *We Men*, p. 265. The most detailed account of German reactions to the 1911 treaty is Wernecke, *Weltgeltung*, pp. 102 ff.

114 Eley, *Reshaping*, pp. 322–30; Fischer, *War of Illusions*, pp. 105–9.

115 V. R. Berghahn, 'Das Kaiserreich in der Sackgasse', *Neue Politische Literatur*, vol. 16 (1971), pp. 494–506, and the writings more generally of Berghahn, Fritz Fischer and Hans-Ulrich Wehler. A contrary view is well argued by Gustav Schmidt in 'Innenpolitische Blockbildungen am Vorabend des Ersten Weltkrieges', *Aus Politik und Zeitgeschichte* (Beilage zur Wochenzeitung das Parlament), 20/1972, pp. 3–32, and 'Parlamentarisierung oder "Präventive Konterrevolution"? Die deutsche Innenpolitik im Spannungsfeld konservativer Sammlungsbewegungen und latenter Reformbestrebungen 1907–1914', in Gerhard A. Ritter (ed.), *Gesellschaft, Parlament und Regierung* (Düsseldorf, 1974), pp. 249–74.

116 See esp. the important article of Wolfgang J. Mommsen, 'Domestic Factors in German Foreign Policy before 1914', *Central European History*, 6 (1973), pp. 3–43. In his reply to the notorious Gebsattel memorandum of 1913, Bethmann talked scathingly of the way in which the electoral system placed a premium on 'currying favour with the voters'. See H. Pogge-von Strandmann, 'Staatsstreichpläne, Alldeutsche und Bethmann Hollweg', in Pogge-von Strandmann and I. Geiss, *Die Erforderlichkeit des Unmöglichen. Deutschland am Vorabend des ersten Weltkrieges* (Frankfurt/M., 1965), p. 20.

117 Stegmann, *Die Erben Bismarcks*, pp. 497 ff.

11

Politics as Theatre: Metaphors of the Stage in German History, 1848–1933

All the world's a stage, as we know, and the concept of a *theatrum mundi* is a venerable one. So too is the specific idea of politics as theatre, which can be found in classical antiquity. As an idea it may not seem very remarkable. Politics lives off metaphor, after all; and theatrical metaphor might appear especially appropriate to describe political activity. Do we not refer naturally to the political stage, to politicians assuming roles, to dramatic political scenes? This very naturalness derived from repeated usage presents both a problem and a challenge. For one of the tasks of the historian is to show how what has come to seem natural came to seem so: to restore the novelty of artefacts and institutions we take for granted, and to recover the impact of ideas worn smooth by repetition. I try to argue below that metaphors of politics as theatre can be more than just a figure of speech: that they had particular and revealing historical meanings in the period under consideration.

A number of interests converged in the writing of this essay. In recent years the fruitful influence of an anthropological perspective has helped to stimulate a greater concern among historians with rituals and symbolic forms. This has manifested itself in many different areas of historical research, one of which is the growing attention given to political ceremonial. This intellectual debt will be readily apparent below. In addition to that, I have been interested for a long time in the arguments of literary critics about 'modern' forms of consciousness in which role-playing, mask-wearing and other forms of dissimulation play a central part. Here I should like to acknowledge the extraordinarily fertile book by Lionel Trilling, *Sincerity and Authenticity* (London, 1972), whose arguments have influenced my own thinking both below and in the preceding chapter. This essay was also prompted, however, by more specific historical questions about modern German history. In the first place, I wanted to examine how and why politics became (as so many contemporaries reported) a form of dramatic public spectacle in Imperial Germany. Why did a black market develop for tickets to the visitors gallery of the *Reichstag*, and why were General von Einem and Max Weber agreed that the Kaiser's foreign policy was essentially theatrical? This line of enquiry derived partly from an interest in the nature of mass political mobilization in Germany at the end of the nineteenth century, partly from a desire to get to grips with the long-standing debate about Bismarck as a 'Bonapartist' exponent of bread and circuses. These arguments, in turn, pointed both backwards and forwards. They pointed backwards to 1848, when Marx and Engels were in agreement with more conservative observers that the revolutions were characterized by a meretricious theatricality. More obviously, this standpoint and the vocabulary that accompanied it was taken up by many writers (on both left and right, once again) who saw the highly choreographed spectacle of National Socialism in similar terms. Like many other essays in the present collection, this one is also therefore concerned with the threads of continuity in modern German history, although these are not always the lines of continuity with which other historians have concerned themselves.

This essay is the most speculative in the volume, and I hope it will be read as an attempt to map out some thoughts and stimulate more systematic investigation of a subject that deserves greater attention. The essay took shape in my mind over a number of years before it was first written up in the spring of 1985 and thoroughly reworked a year later into its present form. It was previously unpublished at time of writing, although I shall present a paper on the same subject to the Royal Historical Society in December 1986 which will appear later in the *Transactions* of the Society for 1986 (1987).

The idea of politics as theatre first appears as an important motif in modern European history in 1848. Few who have written on the events of that year have failed to note in passing the self-consciousness of the revolutionary actors, their verbal, gestural and sartorial theatricality. We know that Alphonse de Lamartine rehearsed his speeches – as he rehearsed much of his life – in front of a mirror, and that his public appearances as a political orator owed a debt to the virtuoso performances of his good friend Franz Liszt. We know that Ledru-Rollin had paid equally close attention to the impact made on his audiences by the celebrated actor Frédéric Lemaître.[1] And of course those two sharp-eyed observers, de Tocqueville and Marx, have helped to fix 1848 in our minds as a time when politics was a matter of performance. De Tocqueville described events in France on the 24th February in the following terms: 'I was never able to take the actors very seriously and the whole seemed to me like a bad tragedy performed by provincial actors.'[2] Marx's contemporary writing is littered with metaphors depicting political developments as theatre: on and off the stage, upstage and downstage, role playing and dramatic effect, chorus and solo performance, tragedy and farce. In a characteristic passage from *The Class Struggles in France*, Marx wrote: 'The official scene was transformed in a trice: scenery, costumes, language, actors, dummies, prompters, the themes of the play, the content of the conflict, the whole situation.'[3]

These are all French examples, and France might be thought of as the classic modern case of a national politics conceived as theatre. Was it not the revolutionary tradition that condemned French politicians to restage the same scenes and repeat the old lines? Many of the same themes can nevertheless be discerned in the German events of 1848–49. The would-be poet-revolutionary Georg Herwegh, for example, modelled himself very much on Lamartine.[4] And the critique of French events by the patrician de Tocqueville and the revolutionary Marx found echoes in the German case. Friedrich Wilhelm IV of Prussia attacked 'the sinful burlesques and the hateful play-acting of modern constitutions',[5] while Friedrich Engels's writings on Germany offer many parallels to those of Marx on France.

When the Prussian Constituent Assembly was threatened by General Wrangel's troops it began, for Engels, its 'grand comedy' of passive and legal resistance. The Frankfurt Assembly was likewise 'nothing but a stage where old and worn-out political characters exhibited their involuntary ludicrousness and their impotence of thought, as well as action'. These parliamentary puppets, he went on, served only to amuse and divert the shopkeepers and petty tradesmen, before the parliament came to its 'tragi-comical' end. And when renewed insurrection broke out in south-west Germany during the summer of 1849, the National Assembly simply 'disappeared from the political theatre without any notice being taken of its exit'.[6]

Patricians and revolutionaries therefore found much to agree about in 1848. Both used metaphors of the theatre to imply criticism and scorn, because they believed the political actors were not serious. They reached this conclusion for opposite reasons. Patricians assumed that the people was conservative and had been misled by men playing the role of demagogue. Marx and Engels assumed the people was revolutionary and had been misled by men who merely assumed the role of revolutionaries. Right and left agreed once again in associating the theatricality of 1848 with the existence of popular politics – with the presence of a 'public'. But here they drew opposite conclusions from the same premise. For a critic such as Friedrich Wilhelm IV the very entry of the people into public affairs created a dangerously theatrical politics; for Engels it was the diversion of the people that made the politics theatrical. This fundamental difference has persisted in attitudes towards the course of modern German history. The patrician view has been echoed by conservative historians, down to the connection they have drawn between the advent of Hitler and the revolt of the masses. For them, the roots of National Socialism are to be found in the dangerous political mobilization of the nineteenth century, typified by 1848, in which prudence and statesmanship came to be replaced by the meretricious appeal of the political actor or showman.[7] For historians of a more liberal or radical persuasion, it is not the revolt of the masses but their diversion which provides the link in the period from 1848 to the advent of fascism. On this reading, statesmen did not yield the political stage to showmen; they became showmen themselves.[8]

This provides a suggestive background against which to take a fresh look at some of the changes and continuities in German history between 1848 and the rise of Hitler. This essay is an attempt to explore a series of themes and arguments that arise out of the idea that politics was a form of theatre. Partly I want to examine the way in which contemporaries themselves used such terms; partly I want to see how metaphors of this kind have come to assume a place in accounts of modern German history, although this has received little notice or comment. In the first three sections of the essay I shall be concerned with Germany before the First World War. The fourth and final section tries to bring together the themes that have been raised in considering the advent of that most theatrical of political movements, National Socialism.

POLITICAL DRAMA AS DISTRACTION

The idea that politics, and especially foreign policy, can serve as a drama to distract public attention, is a fairly familiar one. It is also at least as old as the Roman emperors' provision of 'bread and circuses'. In our period the key concept is indeed Caesarism, or Bonapartism as it is more usually called. The modern idea of Caesarism or Bonapartism owes much to Marx, who developed it as a way of describing the regime of Napoleon III that followed the revolution of 1848 in France.[9] Of the many features of Bonapartist rule about which historians continue to argue, two are especially relevant here. One is the use of foreign policy success to divert opinion at home, the other the use of plebiscitary techniques to appeal direct to the people over the heads of political opponents. In recent years many German historians have looked at Bismarck's form of rule in this way. They have argued that his foreign policy can be interpreted as an attempt to deflect attention from pressing economic, social and political problems at home, whether the liberal-constitutionalist challenge of the 1860s, or the crises and uncertainties generated by the Great Depression. The stage-managing of the 1864 war against Denmark for domestic consumption, the playing up of the war-in-sight crisis of 1875, and the political uses to which colonial issues were put in the 1880s have all been cited as examples.[10] Bismarck's encouragement of Sedan Day as a new celebratory ritual could be viewed in the same light.[11] But this argument does not apply to foreign policy alone. Michael Stürmer has argued that Bismarck used domestic incidents during the 1870s in similar Caesarist fashion. He exploited the 'dramatic effects' of the attempt on his life by a Catholic journeyman in 1874, just as he 'dramatized the branding of a pistol into a murder attempt' when a similar experience befell the Kaiser in 1878. The first incident served to strengthen support for Bismarck's anti-Catholic *Kulturkampf* measures; the second provided the pretext for introducing the anti-socialist law. Similarly, when the Reichstag complained in 1874 about the arrest on press charges of the Catholic deputy Majunke during a parliamentary session, Bismarck 'staged a crisis' and 'dramatized the situation' by threatening to resign and warning of turmoil.[12]

It is possible to argue that historians such as Stürmer and Hans-Ulrich Wehler have exaggerated Bismarck's Caesarist intentions, that the Bonapartist technique of rule weighs less heavily in the balance than a more straightforwardly opportunist (but also fatalistic) conservatism.[13] But the more far-sighted and flexible German conservatives of the period, among whom Bismarck was certainly the most prominent, undoubtedly paid close attention to the form of regime developed by Napoleon III in France. Constantin Frantz in the 1850s, and Bismarck's close political ally Hermann Wagener in the 1860s, wrote appreciatively of Bonapartism.[14] And Bismarck himself argued against that dyed-in-the-wool Prussian conservative Ludwig von Gerlach that Bonapartism as practised in France, far from being revolutionary, put revolutionary principles at the service of social order.[15] There was at the very least a Bonapartist strain in Bismarck's policies, and the motif of a deliberately dramatized politics is certainly not just a construct of later historians. Nothing illustrates this better than the well-known incident when the new German Reichstag had read out to it a letter from Ludwig II of Bavaria, inviting Wilhelm I of Prussia to assume the German imperial crown. The scene was carefully prepared, and after a planted question Bismarck's deputy Delbrück rose to announce that he happened to have Ludwig's letter with him. He then had unfortunate difficulty finding it, causing widespread laughter as he fumbled about his person. When he finally read the letter out his dry diction further undermined the occasion. Bismarck's reaction was telling. The event, he remarked, 'needed a more skilful stage-manager, there should have been an effective *mise en scène*'.[16]

There can be little doubt that under Kaiser Wilhelm II and his ministers, and particularly under Bülow, the dramatization of politics in this sense assumed a new dimension. At the end of the 1890s, commenting on the passage of the first navy bill through the Reichstag, the Social Democrat Bruno Schoenlank observed sardonically that all that was missing was a navy theatre and a navy opera.[17] Many would argue that these were still to come: that the public launching of ships and the official encouragement of sailor suits, together with the rallies and slide shows funded by the Information Bureau of Tirpitz's Navy Office and mounted by the Navy League, marked a conscious effort to rally support behind an old governing elite by tapping popular enthusiasm for spectacle.[18] In this way the objects of public policy – in this case, above all, the navy – took on the aura of a public drama. Indeed General von Einem and Friedrich von Holstein both talked of the Kaiser's operetta politics.

This approach has undeniable appeal. It forms part of a more general rediscovery by historians of the part played in popular consciousness by ceremonial, monuments, national symbols and other 'invented traditions'.[19] The way in which such arguments have often been advanced in the German case has not, however, lacked its critics. One of them has argued with a good deal of plausibility that the picture of Imperial Germany thus painted resembles too closely a 'puppet-theatre': the puppet masters pulled the strings and the people danced.[20] The criticism here applies not so much to the intentions of the would-be puppet masters, more to the effects of their actions. In following up this point I want to suggest two respects at least in which the idea of a theatrical politics of this sort is for historians (as it was for contemporaries) considerably richer and more ambiguous than this straightforwardly 'diversionary' reading would allow.

First, there were many who remained singularly unimpressed by the spectacle being presented. They were unimpressed, not least, because an extravaganza carries with it the idea of extravagance. The more elaborate the spectacle, the broader the flank left open to charges of this kind. This was important in a country where indirect taxes on consumption formed such a major part of government revenue. In other words: where bread was particularly expensive, as a result of tariffs, the cost of the circuses was likely to have opponents.[21] This point applies with particular force to the Social Democrats, and the organized labour movement more generally, for whom opposition to dear food and hostility to military parades and naval razzmatazz went hand-in-hand. But it is also relevant to a group such as the peasantry, as the history of opposition to naval construction in rural areas demonstrates. The point applies even to a social group like the petty bourgeoisie, whose susceptibility to the mass emotion of nationalist issues is often, but wrongly, taken as axiomatic. Many craftsmen and shopkeepers seem to have begrudged the costs of the 'navy theatre' as much as they begrudged the financing of any other kinds of theatre.[22]

Secondly, there were those who were critical of the theatricality that surrounded the government's foreign policy from the 1890s for a different, although not entirely unrelated, reason: not because of its cost, but because they thought it – and this is their own language – *merely* theatrical, in the pejorative sense. Sometimes this criticism came from within the elite itself. One thinks of the Younger Moltke's exasperation that the Kaiser's mania for colourful uniforms had reduced military drill to 'nothing but a theatrical entertainment'.[23] It also came from critics outside. Many intelligent imperialists, of whom Max Weber may be taken as an exemplar, perceived a gap between rhetoric and deeds. Hence Weber's scorn for the 'noisy intermezzi' and 'theatrical methods' of German foreign policy, and his dismissal of the government's 'theatrical Moroccan policy' in 1911.[24] Doubts of this kind were by no means confined to liberal imperialists like Weber. They were expressed outspokenly on the radical right, by the nationalists of the Pan-German and Navy Leagues. Thus the Pan-German leader Heinrich Claß criticized 'stage pageants and celebrations, parades and the unveiling of statues',[25] for he argued that they merely concealed the failure of true national will at the top. Paradoxically, therefore, attempts by Imperial governments to stage-manage politics could provoke criticism precisely because of their 'theatricality', in the sense that they were frivolous and disguised the true state of affairs. The charge was levelled with particular frequency and venom against that soft-shoe shuffler, Bülow. Bülow may not, like his French contemporary Viviani, have taken lessons at the *Comédie Française*; but it often sounded as if he had.[26]

It was a favourite rhetorical device of the radical nationalists that the onstage presentation did not accord with the offstage reality. This was not, however, a figure that was unique to this section of opinion on this particular issue. To understand why this was so, we must turn to another important and widespread usage of theatrical metaphor in German political debate. That was the preoccupation with what went on 'behind the scenes'.

BEHIND THE SCENES

Radical nationalists talked a lot about hidden enemies. As one of the Pan-German leaders put it in 1908, 'a broadly based conspiracy has developed with the aim of harming Germandom'.[27] The League's publications argued that the covert enemies were more dangerous than the overt ones: those who posed 'behind the mask of harmlessness', those who remained 'behind the scenes'.[28] They included, among these, three familiar conspirators: the Red International of Socialism, the Gold International of Jewish finance capital and the Black International of ultramontanism. They also included those officials in high places whom Pan-Germans, like other radical nationalists, believed to be sacrificing true national interests. Yet this was a game that more than one could play. If those great anti-Polish Germanizers, the Hakatisten, talked darkly of 'sabotage' in high places, the writer Fritz Krysiak in turn offered a revelatory glimpse 'behind the scenes of the *Ostmarkenverein*, from the secret documents of the Prussian parallel government for the extermination of the Poles'.[29]

It is easy to be lofty about the conspiracy view of history, and to forget (as the original Caesar knew) that there are conspiracies in history, just as paranoiacs do have enemies – even, and perhaps especially, unpleasant paranoiacs. My concern is therefore to take the talk of men behind the scenes seriously, and to ask why it should have been so common in Imperial Germany. The preoccupation with hidden wire-pullers was not, of course, a peculiarity of German politics. The most cursory of glances at contemporary France shows similar concerns on both left and right. The latter saw Freemasons and Jews as the hidden influences; the former tended to focus on the 'two hundred families'. Each put its own gloss on the scandals that ran from Wilson and Panama through to Dreyfus. Parallel examples could doubtless be found elsewhere in Europe. It is nevertheless probably true that suspicions of this kind were more extensive in Imperial Germany, not least because the political system itself offered so many grounds for them.

Take, at the most obvious level, the way in which the Reichstag and other German parliaments worked. The third quarter of the nineteenth century had been the great age of the parliamentary orators: Lasker, Bennigsen, Windthorst and Bismarck himself. But the last years of the century saw a change. The great formal debaters departed and the balance shifted to committee men, especially lawyers. In the Reichstag, as in the state parliaments, considerably longer hours were worked; but the additional work now went on outside plenary sessions and set-piece debates, in committee.[30] Journalists and pamphlet writers who offered a glance behind the scenes reflected public recognition that a significant part of politics had disappeared from open view. This phenomenon had its counterparts elsewhere; but it was compounded in Germany by the general working of the complex constitutional and political system established by Bismarck. The open-ended, plastic constitution of the Reich required a high level of activity in the interstices of the formal system. The legacy of constitutional dualism, which strictly separated ministers from party leaders, also encouraged intense, behind-the-scenes consultations and short-term agreements, in which politics often became a matter of brokering. Parliamentary arithmetic intensified this tendency from the 1880s onwards, as Bismarck and his successors lived an increasingly hand-to-mouth existence in trying to keep government business running. All of this naturally excited suspicion of shabby deals and horse-trading behind the scenes – *Kuhhandel*, as it was generally called. Nowhere was this more true than in the case of the Catholic Centre Party, the spokesman of a minority, whose pivotal position in German politics united much of the rest of the nation in the belief that German government policy was being determined by whispered arrangements between Centre leaders and ministers.[31] Centre relations with successive governments after 1890 undoubtedly lent some credence to this view, and the leaders of the party appear sometimes to have played the part with a certain conspiratorial relish. Ernst Lieber, for example, discussing the logistics of a series of meetings with state secretary Posadowsky in 1894, used highly cloak-and-dagger language. On one occasion he suggested a visit to the Wilhelmstrasse late at night, and – in order to throw the 'pack of snoopers' off the scent – minus top hat.[32]

But chancellors and ministers did not just have to deal in this way with party leaders and experts. They also had to mediate between interests in the Reich, Prussia and the other individual states represented in the Bundesrat, as well as with the Kaiser. The Kaiser's particular form of attempted personal rule served to multiply the number of individuals from certain groups – the army, the bureaucracy, particular businessmen, the courtiers of the entourage – who had personal access to the All-Highest.[33] Contemporaries asked the question: 'Who rules in Berlin?' Historians have answered, accurately if inelegantly, that the system was a polycratic but unco-ordinated authoritarianism, a pseudo-constitutional semi-absolutism.[34] This system positively invited the emergence of what Hans-Ulrich Wehler has called 'secretive key figures, like Admiral von Tirpitz', and of courtiers like Philipp Eulenburg, of whom Fritz Hartung remarked that 'he preferred to remain behind the scenes in semi-darkness and from here exerted his influence'.[35] This system naturally also encouraged suspicion and rumour about the role played behind the scenes by these men, and by others such as Friedrich von Holstein, General Waldersee and the so-called Camarilla. It was not only Social Democrats and left liberals who talked in this context of backstairs intrigues and cover-ups: the growing radical right also habitually attacked the 'Byzantine' politics of the Kaiser's Germany, and increasingly did not exempt the All-Highest himself from their strictures.[36]

One of the most obvious objects of suspicion was the role supposedly played behind the scenes by economic interests. State and economy were interlocked to an exceptional degree in Imperial Germany, and these links were becoming closer in the years before the First World War. This much, at least, is generally agreed by historians who differ on whether to describe the result as state monopoly capitalism, organized capitalism or state corporatism.[37] The political parties were also notable for the way in which they served as the vehicles of major economic interests.[38] The political system devised by Bismarck encouraged them to become the brokers of particular interests by depriving the parties of positive responsibility in parliament. The rising costs of political organization and campaigning further increased the dependence of the parties on their various paymasters. Hence the growing political role exercized in the background, especially from the 1890s, by a wide spectrum of interest groups: the Agrarian League and the CVDI, representing perhaps the most influential interests of large-scale agriculture and heavy industry respectively, the BdI of smaller manufacturing industry, the Hansabund of bankers, shippers, insurers and exporters, the myriad organizations of craftsmen, shopkeepers and white-collar workers, and the trade unions and co-operatives of the working class. Hence, too, the mounting importance assumed by economic affairs in German political life. It has been calculated that they accounted, directly or indirectly, for 90 per cent of Reichstag business by 1914.[39]

Much of this business was dealt with in committee. In the legislative period 1890–3 alone, Reichstag committees considered the following: trade treaties, patents, the telegraph, railway freight, the protection of goods and trade-marks, working hours, the hire-purchase system, limited company law, the accountancy system, the taxation of distilled spirits, internal trade regulations, the bankruptcy code, trade descriptions, and labour statistics.[40] As the language of business entered political life – political speculator, broker, political nicknames based on popular advertisements[41] – so economic interests themselves retreated into the committee room, or outside parliament altogether. The number of businessmen in German parliaments dropped sharply towards the end of the century.[42] Increasingly it was not industrialists, bankers and landowners themselves who represented their interests in the political forum, but pressure-group spokesmen and other intermediaries. Gustav Stresemann, whose first political experience was to organize the Saxon chocolate manufacturers against the sugar cartel, provides only one of many instances.[43]

There is plenty to be said against a certain kind of muck-raking history *à la* Charles Beard, which reduces politics to the crude elaboration of material interests. But the interests were real enough, indeed ubiquitous, in the Imperial German political system; and they prompted frequent comment on the discrepancy between the public face of politics and the reality of what went on behind the scenes. This criticism came quite literally from left, right and centre. As early as the 1860s the National Liberal von Twesten noted gloomily that 'the landed interest calls itself conservative, the money interest liberal, the labour interest democratic'.[44] That continued to be the lament from a party that liked to see itself as universal rather than sectional, and tended to blame the rise of interest-politics for its own decline. Socialists and left liberals pointed, with some reason, to the hidden influence of the large Junker landowners, the heavy industrialists and the armaments manufacturers. Fritz Krupp was a classic target of such charges: a member of the Kaiser's entourage and his frequent host at Villa Hügel, a man who carefully cultivated key officials and officers and employed many ex-officers on his own payroll, Krupp enjoyed a reputation as a malevolent influence on government policy. It was, for example, widely rumoured – plausibly, although probably wrongly – that the Kaiser owned a substantial block of shares in the Krupp business.[45] With less warrant the political right claimed to detect the hidden power of Jewish capital operating behind the scenes. Bismarck's banker Bleichröder was one target, but the charge was more general. The *Kulturkampf* had been widely viewed on the right as a cloak behind which the 'swindlers' of laissez-faire capitalism in general, and Jewish interests in particular, prospered. During the stock exchange and commodity exchange scandals of the 1890s the charge of hidden Jewish political influence surfaced again on the agrarian, anti-semitic and Catholic right.

PARLIAMENT AS THEATRE

The presence, real or imagined, of powerful offstage interests did much to discredit the Imperial political 'system'. At the same time, there is also an undeniable sense in which politics in Germany became a form of popular spectacle in a way that had not been true earlier. In the third quarter of the nineteenth century political indifference was still widespread, election turn-out was low and results often followed the lines of deference. Even in the 1870s, when universal manhood suffrage existed for Reichstag elections, electoral participation remained around 55 per cent and there was little campaigning. The National Liberal leader Rudolf von Bennigsen wrote in December 1873 to a clergyman in his Reichstag constituency, explaining why he would be unable to visit the constituency at all before the election in the new year – and expressing the hope that he would be able to visit his Prussian Landtag constituency by the following summer.[46] His attitude was typical. Public life remained largely the preserve of a handful of notables (*Honoratioren*), who constituted the true political nation. In these circumstances, the Reichstag and state parliaments did indeed – as Rudolf Dill has noted – resemble theatres.[47] But they were theatres in which the narrow political class itself formed the public. When parliamentarians referred to themselves as 'actors' on the 'parliamentary stage', when deputies acted out entire scenes from Shakespeare in the course of their speeches, or when Bismarck reminded Lasker that 'the masks we wear are temporary', it is this lack of a broader audience that we should remember.[48] In fact those who spoke for 'out of doors', who 'played to the gallery', were often censured – especially Social Democrats, as the incidence of calls to order shows. A large number of parliamentarians in the 1870s would have echoed the National Liberal Jungermann when he stated: 'I have not come here for the sake of my constituents.'[49]

This genteel mode of politics crumbled towards the end of the century. Popular economic and social aspirations found a new level of political expression, a process helped by the spread of education, improved communications and a greatly expanded press. A much enlarged political nation emerged, signalled by the mobilization of new social strata, a markedly increased level of electoral participation and more intensive forms of campaigning. Turn-out reached 85 per cent in Reichstag elections and even higher in some keenly fought local contests. Patrician politicians like Georg von Hertling, who had been a member of the Reichstag in more leisurely times and rejoined it in the turbulent 1890s after a gap of some years, remarked on the great differences.[50] The changes all pointed to a new form of popular identification with politics. In rural areas such as Brandenburg or Upper Swabia politicians were now seen frequently in the flesh, and voters could read parliamentary speeches reported at length in the burgeoning local newspapers, alongside barley prices and advertisements for corsets. A thriving black market developed for tickets to the visitors gallery of the Reichstag.[51] In short, in the age of the ubiquitous local paper and politicians on the stump, politics assumed a new dimension as popular drama.

There is no contradiction between this political leavening, and the importance of behind-the-scenes decision-making. The two were mutually reinforcing. Bureaucrats and business leaders were more inclined to retreat from public view as the everyday surface of politics became more brash and noisy. As Krupp wrote to his managing director Jencke, on the subject of the navy: 'I should like to urge you strongly to confine your activity to that of an advisor – *as much as possible behind the scenes*.'[52] Newly mobilized political forces, in turn, saw in the drama of public life an opportunity to 'unmask' the powerful and influential. The new popular politics at the end of the nineteenth century contained a powerful rhetoric dedicated to the idea of disclosing and unmasking. Alex Hall has reminded us of the preoccupation in the SPD press with 'scandal and sensation'; the new organizations of the peasantry and lower middle class, like the anti-semitic political parties and the radical nationalists, employed similar terms.[53] The identity of those unmasked varied, from the Junkers to the Jesuits to the Jews, and the credence that we can give to the disclosures varies too; but the common metaphor of unmasking testifies to the explosive gap that existed in Germany between oligarchic, bureaucratic and corporate power wielded behind the scenes, and a vigorous (and often vindictive) popular politics that drew its energy from a thwarted, suspicious public.

Once again there are naturally analogues elsewhere, from American muckraking to the French concern with scandal. There are also, of course, non-German examples of politicians using the whistle-stop tour as a means of encouraging popular identification with the political drama. Gladstone's Midlothian campaign and Gambetta's great Republican sweep through France in 1871–2 come to mind. The difference lay in the overall political context. The German political system, combining constitutional but not parliamentary government on the one hand, with the possibilities offered by universal manhood suffrage on the other, invited a meretriciously theatrical politics. The non-responsibility of parliamentary politicians nurtured an irresponsible politics of posture. It was not only parliamentary mavericks who indulged in this game, such as the anti-semite Hermann Ahlwardt, who used the floor of the Reichstag to accuse the government of buying defective rifles from the Jews.[54] Party leaders could play to the gallery without running the danger of having to take responsibility for their words. Politicians came to the fore who were adept at presenting artfully edited accounts of their own party's parliamentary activities for outside consumption. Erzberger, the rising star of the Centre, is a prime example. The tabling of hopeless bills and filibustering speeches served the same purpose.

In the 1860s von Twesten, true to form, had warned that universal manhood suffrage would lead to political 'charlatanry'.[55] His doubts were echoed in the years before the war by many conservatives, concerned by what Bethmann Hollweg called 'currying favour with the voters'.[56] We should remember here that it was often other conservatives who were the worst offenders. The crucial point, however, is that it was not universal suffrage coupled with parliamentarism, but universal suffrage coupled with sham-parliamentarism, that explains why German politicians played to the gallery so brazenly in the years before 1914. The Reichstag became a 'theatre of opinions' – in Hermann Baumgarten's dismissive phrase[57] – for the same reason that it became a clearing-house for economic interests: because it could not become the seat of political power and responsibility. Popular and parliamentary politics thus became a form of 'acting out' of aspirations and resentments. In this it only paralleled the conduct of those at the top. We are already familiar with the Kaiser's 'operetta politics', and we have often been told that he sought a political stage on which to act out his dreams. Ekkehard-Teja Wilke is only one of many historians whose language conveys a sense that Wilhelmine high politics was, as he puts it, 'second-rate tragi-comedy'. But his conclusion about the many crises, scandals and affairs in the highest circles could reasonably be applied to German politics more generally in the years before 1914: they were 'symptomatic and an expression of political decadence – when politics disintegrates into mere role-playing and mere theatrical performance'.[58]

THE WEIMAR REPUBLIC: FASCISM AS THEATRE, HITLER AS PUPPET

Both decadence and theatricality have an obvious place in our understanding of Weimar Germany. Here, for example, is Peter Sloterdijk, talking about the idea we gain of Weimar when we approach it through the memoir literature and the oral recollections of contemporaries: these, argues Sloterdijk, suggest 'a time when politics and culture proceeded in a dramatic, vital and tumultuous way, full of upswings and downswings – as if theatricality had been the common denominator of all social expressions of life – from Expressionism to Marlene Dietrich's spectacular legs in the *Blue Angel*, from the bloody comedy of the 1923 Hitler putsch to the *Threepenny Opera*, from the imposing burial of Rathenau in 1923 to the *Schurkenstück* of the Reichstag fire in 1933. The permanent crisis, of which everyone spoke, proved itself a good director, able to produce impressive effects.'[59] This is a thoughtful and recognizable account of a certain Weimar atmosphere; but – like much similar writing – it remains very impressionistic. I think we can go further in following through the central theme of this essay by isolating two specific metaphors of the theatre that run through the literature on Weimar and the rise of Hitler. One is the idea of Nazism as a theatrical kind of political movement, the other the idea of Hitler himself as the puppet of hidden manipulators. Neither on its own convinces. When combined, however, the two approaches tell us a good deal about National Socialism. They also suggest links with what has already been discussed and thus underline some of the continuities between nineteenth- and twentieth-century German history.

The idea of National Socialist theatricality, indeed of fascist theatricality generally, is commonly encountered. A recent writer on the subject actually has a chapter headed 'fascism as theatrical politics',[60] and this has been a standard theme among those concerned with the outward political forms and the projected image of the Nazis. We are familiar with the concept of National Socialism as spectacle, the carefully lit rallies and the crowd scenes contributing to a very conscious *mise en scène*. Beno von Arent, who staged the Nuremberg rallies and received the title of *Reichsbühnenbildner* – Designer of Reich Stage Sets – had actually been a theatre director.[61] The idea of German fascism as theatre finds plenty of support in contemporary accounts, including fictional works like Thomas Mann's *Mario the Magician*, and there are certainly individuals who testified to the spellbinding quality of the Nazi performance.[62] George Mosse and others have reminded us that this strand of Nazism had nineteenth-century antecedents, from the choral societies to Wagner.[63]

Hard-headed historians are often sceptical about the large claims made by those who view National Socialism in this way, particularly because of what is omitted. Certainly, the glittering Nazi self-presentation tells us little about many important reasons for Nazi success, even their success specifically as a mass movement. If one focuses on the seductive drama it is, for example, easy to underestimate the real failures of the Weimar Republic, both as a structurally flawed democracy in the 1920s, and as an authoritarian political system lubricated by intrigue after autumn 1930. Nor do we generally learn from those who favour this approach why the drama proved so much more popular among some parts of the public than others, or whether the enthusiasm for National Socialism even among its supporters might not have had causes that were more prosaic than dramatic: the appeal, for example, to the material resentments of the small man, to the thwarted careerism of ambitious professionals, to provincial philistinism. We must therefore recognize limits to what can be explained in terms of Nazi success with a theatrical political style. Party rallies and Hitler's rhetoric hardly seduced the German people into rejecting a going political concern; and the Nazi spectacle commonly worked to reinforce the allegiance of those who had adequate reason to support the party anyway.

These qualifications made, we should not be too hard-headed to acknowledge the value of this approach. In many respects the Nazis only carried further a development that began before 1914, whereby politics became the acting out of aspirations and resentments. Just as Weimar's

Communists continued this SPD tradition on the left, so the Nazis continued it for that mass public of peasants, petty bourgeoisie and middle class that had been attracted before the war by agrarian populism, political anti-semitism and radical nationalism. As we have seen, Nazi criticism of the Weimar 'system' and its offstage machinations, like the rhetorical Nazi promise to unmask the guilty men, had clear precedents in prewar politics. And these were genuinely important aspects of the Nazi appeal. Playing to the gallery in this way succeeded because it spoke to the concerns of those same social groups, heightened as they had been by revolution, inflation and depression. It was all the more effective because the efforts of the established centre-right parties to use the same methods (as they had done before 1914) were undermined by the degree of political responsibility they now had to accept for their policies, however reluctantly, under Weimar's formal political democracy. In this respect, as in others, National Socialism enjoyed the best of both worlds. It promised a dramatic resolution of Germany's problems by transcending the parliamentary 'farce' for which it was itself partly responsible, just as it promised law and order in response to a lawlessness to which it had itself made a major contribution.

In this sense National Socialism did indeed 'aestheticize politics', as one of its victims, Walter Benjamin, remarked of fascism generally.[64] This undoubtedly contributes to our understanding of Nazism as a mass movement. But what of that other central question, the function performed by the Nazi mass movement? What of the silent beneficiaries? Here we must turn to another motif that recurs in accounts of the period: that of the puppet. The figure of the puppet seems to be a common one in discourse on German politics.[65] Thomas Mann's Adrian Leverkühn avails himself of a familiar idea when he suggests at one point in *Doctor Faustus* that German revolutions 'are the puppet-shows of world history': a point that both revolutionary left and reactionary right made about the 1918 revolution, just as their predecessors had about 1848. The metaphor clearly reflects both scorn, and a broad comment on the inability of the 'land of poets and thinkers' to produce a serious politics. But the puppet also carries the more specific connotation of a creature manipulated by unseen hands. That is the implication of Engels's 'parliamentary puppets' in 1848; and that is how his followers in the early 1930s depicted Hitler. 'Millions are behind me' reads the ironic text of John Heartfield's famous photomontage, as Hitler's hand, stretched back in the 'German greeting', receives millions of Reichsmarks. Here we have Hitler as the puppet of German capital. The relationship between the Nazi seizure of power and German capitalism is an important one, but it is by no means exhausted as a theme by narrowing the range of enquiry to active Nazi supporters and paymasters in big business. That is precisely the problem with the view of Hitler as capitalist puppet.[66] It is, arguably, the least plausible way of presenting the part played by capitalist interests in Nazi success, especially when support for Hitler is identified (as in Dimitrov's notorious Third International definition) with one exceptionally narrow section of capital. On this reading it is also difficult to make much sense of how (or why) the puppet sometimes turned on his puppet-master.

If the metaphor is ultimately unsatisfactory, it is nevertheless easy to see why it enjoyed such wide currency. And some comparable idea of Hitler as the player of a role is still needed, to balance and complement the way the Nazis presented themselves. For it remains true that what the Nazis alleged of their political opponents was even more true of themselves: appearances were deceptive, unseen hands were at work behind the scenes. The Nazis had the popular non-socialist votes. And Hitler found support from important parts of the ruling elite because he did what they themselves were neither able nor willing to do: to take the centre of the political stage. For businessmen, generals, Junkers and high officials, the Nazi movement was attractive because it promised to square the circle: to maintain their own interests in dangerous, potentially revolutionary times, without requiring them to appear themselves to be playing an overt political role.[67] Just as their Wilhelmine predecessors had shunned the political spotlight, so the Reichswehr generals and the industrialists left Hitler to get on with the politics while this in turn left them free to get on with their own interests. The fact that Hitler came to demand a larger role than the one for which he had been cast does not invalidate this fact. That is one of the reasons why the application of Bonapartist theories to National Socialism has proved so fruitful.[68]

Hitler was not a puppet. But he was, in this sense, an actor playing a role. In 1848, as we have seen, de Tocqueville had talked disdainfully of 'a bad tragedy performed by provincial actors'. The sentiment was echoed by Marx and Engels. Almost a century later, as the period of European fascism approached its end in 1944, Theodor Adorno and Max Horkheimer took up the same theme. Intellectually indebted to Marx, but sharing more than a little of de Tocqueville's patrician *hauteur*, they also talked of the modern *Führer* figures who resembled 'provincial actors'. They continued: 'The "leaders" have become what they already were in a less developed form throughout the bourgeois era: actors playing the part of leaders.'[69]

NOTES

1 R. Sennett, *The Fall of Public Man* (Cambridge, 1974), pp. 227–31, 236–7. W. Fortescue, *Alphonse de Lamartine* (London, 1983) has details on Lamartine's friendship with Liszt.

2 A. de Tocqueville, *Recollections* (New York, 1970), p. 53.

3 There is an outstanding discussion of this theme in S. S. Prawer, *Karl Marx and World Literature* (Oxford, 1976), where the passage from *The Class Struggles in France* is

also quoted (p. 167). *The Eighteenth Brumaire of Louis Napoleon* (1852) is the other contemporary work of Marx where theatrical metaphors are widely used.

4 W. J. Brazill, 'Georg Herwegh and the Aesthetics of German Unification', *Central European History*, vol. 5 (1972), pp. 99–126.

5 E. Kaeber, *Berlin 1848* (Berlin, 1948), p. 28.

6 F. Engels, *Germany: Revolution and Counter-revolution*, in *The German Revolutions*, ed. L. Krieger (Chicago, 1967), pp. 169, 205–14, 235.

7 This approach is well represented by the 'dean of German historians', Gerhard Ritter, who died in 1967. It can also be seen in the influential American historian, Carlton J. Hayes. For a recent example, see Noël O'Sullivan's *Fascism* (London, 1983).

8 See the quotation from Adorno and Horkheimer that concludes this essay, and more generally the writers on Bonapartism mentioned below. There are interesting pointers in the same direction in Sir Lewis Namier's essay on Napoleon III, 'The First Mountebank Dictator', in *Vanished Supremacies* (London, 1958).

9 In *The Eighteenth Brumaire of Louis Napoleon*.

10 See, especially, the works of Hans-Ulrich Wehler: *Bismarck und der Imperialismus* (Cologne and Berlin, 1969), and *The German Empire 1871–1918* (Leamington Spa, 1985).

11 On the new cult of *Sedanstag* and its operation in Bavaria, see W. Blessing, *Staat und Kirche in der Gesellschaft* (Göttingen, 1982), pp. 181, 190–1, 198, 236.

12 M. Stürmer, *Regiering und Reichstag im Bismarckstaat 1871–1880: Cäsarismus oder Parlamentarismus* (Düsseldorf, 1974), pp. 128–33.

13 Critics of the Bonapartist concept as applied to Bismarck make a wide range of points that cannot be dealt with here. The critics include Lothar Gall, 'Bismarck und der Bonapartismus', *Historische Zeitschrift*, no. 223 (1976), pp. 618–37, and A. Mitchell, 'Bonapartism as a Model of Bismarckian Politics', *Journal of Modern History*, vol. 49 (1977). This issue of the JMH also includes comments by O. Pflanze, C. Fohlen and M. Stürmer. See, most recently, O. Pflanze, 'Bismarcks Herrschaftstechnik als Problem der gegenwärtigen Historiographie', *Historische Zeitschrift*, no. 234 (1982), pp. 562–99.

14 G. Grünthal, *Parlamentarismus in Preußen 1848/49–1857/58* (Düsseldorf, 1982), pp. 261–95; Stürmer, *Regierung und Reichstag*, pp. 89, 96 ff; H. Gollwitzer, 'Der Cäsarismus Napoleons III. im Widerhall der öffentlichen Meinung Deutschlands', *Historische Zeitschrift*, no. 173 (1952), pp. 23–75.

15 On the major exchange of letters between the two men in 1857, see the works cited in footnote 14, and L. Gall, Bismarck: *Der weiße Revolutionär* (Frankfurt/M, Berlin and Vienna, 1980), pp. 173–84 (English edn, 2 vols, trans. J. A. Underwood, London, 1987).

16 R. W. Dill, *Der Parlamentarier Eduard Lasker und die parlamentarische Stilentwicklung der Jahre 1867–1884*, Dissertation (Erlangen, 1958), pp. 64–5.

17 J. Steinberg, *Yesterday's Deterrent. Tirpitz and the Birth of the German Battle Fleet* (London, 1965), pp. 167–8.

18 V. R. Berghahn, *Der Tirpitz-Plan. Genesis und Verfall einer innenpolitischen Krisenstrategie unter Wilhelm II* (Düsseldorf, 1971); Berghahn, *Germany and the Approach of War in 1914* (London, 1973); W. Deist, *Flottenpolitik und Flottenpropaganda. Das Nachrichtenbureau des Reichsmarineamtes 1897–1914* (Stuttgart, 1976).

19 On this subject generally, see E. Hobsbawm and T. Ranger (eds), *The Invention of Tradition* (Cambridge, 1983), esp. Chs 1 and 7 by Hobsbawm. On Germany specifically, there are very valuable pointers in T. Nipperdey, 'Nationalidee und Nationaldenkmal in Deutschland im 19. Jahrhundert', in Nipperdey, *Gesellschaft, Kultur, Theorie* (Göttingen, 1976), pp. 133–73, and E. Fehrenbach, *Wandlungen des Kaisergedankens 1871–1918* (Munich and Vienna, 1969).

20 H.-G. Zmarzlik, in his review of the German edition of Hans-Ulrich Wehler's *The German Empire*, 'Das Kaiserreich in neuer Sicht?', *Historische Zeitschrift*, no. 222 (1976), pp. 105–26.

21 It is worth noting in passing, that the high price of bread in Imperial Germany also points to a divergence from the classic Bonapartist model. Hitler, to whose regime the model has also been applied (see footnote 68), was – by contrast – always very concerned to

try and keep down the cost of living for reasons of social stability.

22 For details, see Chs 5 and 6 and the references given there.

23 E. Ludwig, *Kaiser Wilhelm II* (London, 1926), p. 277.

24 W. J. Mommsen, *Max Weber and German Politics* (Chicago, 1985), pp. 144, 154.

25 H. Claß, *Führergedanken. Aus Reden und Schriften von Justizrat Claß 1903–1913* (Berlin, n.d.), p. 6. See also Chapter 10.

26 On Viviani, see T. Zeldin, *France 1848–1945*, Vol. 1: *Ambition, Love and Politics* (Oxford, 1973), p. 760.

27 A writer in the *Alldeutsche Blätter*, cited in Roger Chickering, *We Men Who Feel Most German. A Cultural Study of the Pan-German League 1886–1914* (London, 1984), p. 123.

28 Ibid.

29 F. Krysiak, *Hinter den Kulissen des Ostmarkenvereins: Aus den Geheimakten der preussischen Nebenregierung für die Polenausrottung* (Posen, 1919). On the Hakatisten themselves, see A. Galos, F.-H. Gentzen, W. Jacóbczyk, *Die Hakatisten. Der Deutsche Ostmarkenverein (1894–1934)* (Berlin, 1966).

30 This change in the balance of parliamentary work in the Reichstag is noted in memoirs of the period. Some information can also be found in P. Molt, *Der Reichstag vor der improvisierten Revolution* (Cologne and Opladen, 1963), and in the work of Manfred Rauh: *Föderalismus und Parlamentarismus im Wilhelminischen Reich* (Düsseldorf, 1972), and *Die Parlamentarisierung des Deutschen Reiches* (Düsseldorf, 1977).

31 See Chapter 9, and D. Blackbourn, *Class, Religion and Local Politics in Wilhelmine Germany* (London and New Haven, 1980), esp. Ch. 1.

32 Pfälzische Landesbibliothek Speyer, Ernst Lieber Papers, L. 39, Lieber to Posadowsky, 10 July 1894. For similar conspiratorial communications, see ibid., L. 36–8, Lieber to Posadowsky, 24 June, 29 June and 3 July 1894.

33 See, now, the contributions to J. C. G. Röhl and N. Sombart (eds), *Kaiser Wilhelm II: New Interpretations* (Cambridge, 1982), esp. those by Röhl himself, Paul Kennedy, Wilhelm Deist, Isabel Hull, Kathy Lerman and Terence Cole.

34 See Wehler, *The German Empire*, esp. pp. 52–71.

35 Ibid., p. 63; Fritz Hartung quoted in E.-T. P. W. Wilke, *Political Decadence in Imperial Germany. Personnel-Political Aspects of the German Government Crisis 1894–97* (Urbana/Ill., 1976), p. 288.

36 See Chapter 10.

37 See the contributions to H. A. Winkler (ed.), *Organisierter Kapitalismus* (Göttingen, 1974), and for general discussion of these debates: G. Eley, 'Capitalism and the Wilhelmine State: Industrial Growth and Political Backwardness in German Historiography, 1890–1918', *Historical Journal*, vol. 21 (1978), pp. 737–50; and U. Nocken, 'Corporatism and Pluralism in Modern German History', in D. Stegmann, B.-J. Wendt, P.-C. Witt (eds.), *Industrielle Gesellschaft und Politisches System* (Bonn, 1978), pp. 37–56.

38 For an overview of the very large literature on this subject, see H.-J. Puhle, 'Parlament, Parteien und Interessenverbände 1890–1914', in M. Stürmer (ed.), *Das kaiserliche Deutschland. Politik und Gesellschaft 1870–1918* (Düsseldorf, 1970), pp. 340–77. The German literature is extensively drawn on in M. Kitchen, *The Political Economy of Germany 1815–1914* (London, 1978).

39 H. Jaeger, *Unternehmer in der deutschen Politik (1890–1913)* (Bonn, 1967), p. 95.

40 Ibid., p. 97.

41 The left liberal Georg Gothein, an extremely dull speaker, was referred to by the political wags as 'Gothë-in', after a popular sleeping draft. See Karl von Einem, *Erinnerungen eines Soldaten* (Leipzig, 1933), p. 69.

42 The decline of businessmen in parliaments, both local and national, is detailed by Jaeger, *Unternehmer*, pp. 25–106. For a good analysis of a particular group and region, which comes to the same conclusion, see T. Pierenkemper, *Die westfälischen Schwerindustriellen 1852–1913* (Göttingen, 1979), pp. 61–70.

43 G. Eley, *Reshaping the German Right* (London and New Haven, 1980), p. 311, and for further details on Stresemann, D. Warren, *The Red Kingdom of Saxony. Lobbying Grounds for Gustav Stresemann 1901–1909* (The Hague, 1964).

44 Cited in M. Gugel, *Industrieller Aufstieg und bürgerliche Herrschaft* (Cologne, 1975), p. 171.
45 R. Owen, 'Military-Industrial Relations: Krupp and the Imperial Navy Office', in R. J. Evans (ed.), *Society and Politics in Wilhelmine Germany* (London, 1978), pp. 71–89. On Krupp's role in the Kaiser's entourage, see I. V. Hull, *The entourage of Kaiser Wilhelm II 1888–1918* (Cambridge, 1982), pp. 146–74; and on the movement of government officials into large private concerns, J. Kocka, *Die Angestellten in der deutschen Geschichte 1850–1980* (Göttingen, 1981), pp. 80–81. This was something that engaged the interest of the Reichstag in 1912.
46 Bennigsen to Pastor Pfaff, 30 December 1873, cited in H. Oncken, *Rudolf von Bennigsen*, 2 vols (Stuttgart and Leipzig, 1910), Vol. 2, pp. 242–3.
47 Dill, *Parlamentarische Stilentwicklung*.
48 Ibid., pp. 45–6; L. Pastor, *August Reichensperger*, 2 vols (Freiburg i.B., 1899), Vol. 1, pp. 424–6, Vol. 2, pp. 179, 201.
49 Dill, *Parlamentarische Stilentwicklung*, p. 14.
50 G. von Hertling, *Erinnerungen aus meinem Leben*, 2 vols (Munich, 1919–20), Vol. 2, pp. 175–6.
51 R. S. Levy, *The Downfall of the Anti-Semitic Political Parties in Imperial Germany* (New Haven, Conn., 1975), p. 39; K. Wernecke, *Der Wille zur Weltgeltung* (Düsseldorf, 1970), p. 115. See also Chapter 10.
52 Owen, 'Military-Industrial Relations', p. 74 (emphasis in the original).
53 On the SPD, see A. Hall, *Scandal, Sensation and Social Democracy. The SPD Press in Wilhelmine Germany 1890–1914* (Cambridge, 1977). On the other movements, see Chapter 10.
54 On Ahlwardt, see above, pp. 124–6, 225–8.
55 Gugel, *Industrieller Aufstieg*, pp. 184–8.
56 H. Pogge-v. Strandmann and I. Geiss, *Die Erforderlichkeit des Unmöglichen* (Frankfurt/M, 1965), p. 20.
57 S. Zucker, *Ludwig Bamberger* (Pittsburg, Pa., 1975), p. 86.
58 Wilke, *Political Decadence*, p. 20.
59 P. Sloterdijk, *Kritik der zynischen Vernunft*, 2 vols (Frankfurt/M, 1983), Vol. 2, p. 705.
60 O'Sullivan, *Fascism*, Ch. 3.
61 Z. A. B. Zeman, *Nazi Propaganda* (Oxford, 1964), pp. 8–9.
62 Thus, as one convert put it: 'On April 20 1932, in Kassel, for the first time I heard the Führer Adolf Hitler speak in person. After this, there was only one thing for me, either to win with Adolf Hitler or to die for him. The personality of the Führer had me totally in its spell.' Cited in I. Kershaw, 'Ideology, Propaganda, and the Rise of the Nazi Party', in P. D. Stachura (ed.), *The Nazi Machtergreifung* (London, 1983), p. 176. Kershaw provides an exemplary introduction to the subject.
63 G. L. Mosse, *The Nationalization of the Masses. Political Symbolism and Mass Movements in Germany from the Napoleonic Wars through the Third Reich* (New York, 1975).
64 Walter Benjamin, *Das Kunstwerk im Zeitalter seiner technischen Reproduzierbarkeit* (Frankfurt/M, 1963), pp. 48, 51.
65 See also Chapter 3.
66 A good guide to the large literature on this subject is Dick Geary, 'The Industrial Elite and the Nazis in the Weimar Republic', in Stachura (ed.), *Nazi Machtergreifung*, pp. 85–100.
67 Michael Geyer provides a very convincing case for this reading of the Reichswehr, in 'Etudes in Political History: *Reichswehr*, NSDAP, and the Seizure of Power', in Stachura (ed.), *Nazi Machtergreifung*, pp. 101–23.
68 For a discussion of works that have applied the theory of Bonapartism to National Socialism, see J. Dülffer, 'Bonapartism, Fascism and National Socialism', *Journal of Contemporary History*, Vol. 11 (1976), pp. 109–28.
69 T. Adorno and M. Horkheimer, *Dialectic of Enlightenment* (London, 1979), pp. 236–7 (first published in 1944).

Index